The New Urban Atlantic

Series editor
Elizabeth Fay
University of Massachusetts Boston
Cambridge, Massachusetts, USA

The early modern period was witness to an incipient process of transculturation through exploration, mercantilism, colonization, and migration that set into motion a process of globalization that continues today. The purpose of this series is to bring together a cultural studies approach—which freely and unapologetically crosses disciplinary, theoretical, and political boundaries—with early modern texts and artefacts that bear the traces of transculturalization and globalization in order to deepen our understanding of sites of exchange between and within early modern culture(s). This process can be studied on a large as well as on a small scale, and this new series is dedicated to both. Possible topics of interest include, but are not limited to: texts dealing with mercantilism, travel, exploration, immigration, foreigners, enabling technologies (such as shipbuilding and navigational instrumentation), mathematics, science, rhetoric, art, architecture, intellectual history, religion, race, sexuality, and gender.

More information about this series at
http://www.springer.com/series/14425

Marlene L. Daut

Baron de Vastey and the Origins of Black Atlantic Humanism

palgrave
macmillan

Marlene L. Daut
Carter G. Woodson Institute
University of Virginia
Charlottesville, VA, USA

The New Urban Atlantic
ISBN 978-1-349-69376-4   ISBN 978-1-137-47067-6   (eBook)
DOI 10.1057/978-1-137-47067-6

Library of Congress Control Number: 2017944610

Cover illustration: © Nina Dietzel

Printed on acid-free paper

This Palgrave Macmillan imprint is published by the registered company Nature America,
Inc. part of Springer Nature
The registered company address is: 1 New York Plaza, New York, NY 10004, U.S.A.

Merci, les enfants

Acknowledgements

This book on the life and works of Baron de Vastey represents the culmination of nearly nine years of research. I have a very patient family. My partner (Sam) and our two children (Samy and Sébastien) probably know more about Vastey than they do about me ... but perhaps that is the point of academic scholarship when it turns around a single historical figure: to live and breathe one individual's life as much as it is possible to do so nearly 200 years after his death. I can only hope that my enthusiasm for bringing Vastey's writing to a larger audience will incite infectious interest outside of my family, whose members are hardly the only people who have had to listen to me discuss the painstaking details of Vastey's life. Indeed, there has rarely been an academic talk I have given in the last decade when I didn't sneak in some reference to Vastey.

There are so many people I have to thank, starting with Deborah Jenson who, in 2011, organized a Baron de Vastey colloquium as a part of Duke University's Haiti Lab. The comments of my fellow participants in that two-day experience, including Nick Nesbitt, Jean Casimir, Chris Bongie, and Cary Hector, were extremely helpful. Bongie deserves special mention since he may be the only person on earth who cares about Vastey as much as I do. I'd like also to thank Vastey's biographer, Laurent Quevilly, for his spirited dialogue about the ongoing controversies of the baron's life. I also want to thank Laurent Dubois for invaluable friendship and for helping me to perform emergency surgery at the 11th hour. Julia Gaffield, Lesley Curtis, Chelsea Stieber, Sara Johnson, Nathan Dize, and Grégory Pierrot have been enthusiastic friends (and patient listeners). The entire Duke Haiti crew deserves recognition, including, Mary-Caton Lingold, Laurent Dubois (again), Laura Wagner, Claire Payton, and Jonathan Katz, who all managed to keep me sane during a year's sabbatical alone with two children at the National Humanities Center in Research Triangle Park, NC.

At the Humanities Center, I also had the pleasure of making new friends, including Tsitsi Jaji and Adriane Lentz-Smith, and re-connecting with old ones like Harry Karahalios. Fellow humanists at the Center including Benjamin Kahan, Kim Hall, Richard Turits, James Mulholland, and Hannah Rosen also provided much needed laughs. My former advisors Glenn Hendler, Ivy Wilson, Julia Douthwaite, and Karen Richman have championed my work from the beginning.

Several colleagues at the Claremont Colleges lent an ear when it was most needed: Eve Oishi, April Mayes, Myriam Chancy, Marie-Denise Shelton, Terri Geis, Sheila Walker, and David Luis-Brown. New colleagues at the University of Virginia: Deborah McDowell, Anna Brickhouse, Cindy Hoelhler-Fatton, Robert Fatton, Jr., Njelle Hamilton, Tom Klubock, and Christina Mobley. Elizabeth Maddock Dillon and Michael Drexler gave me the opportunity to bring Vastey to early American studies circles. I must also thank Nazera Wright, Doris Garraway, Flora Cassen, Barbara Pelet, Maxine Reger, Gina Rho, Misty Schieberle, Christoper Freeburg, Gina Ulysse, Nadège Clitandre, Matthew Smith, and Daniel Desormeaux.

This work has been supported with funds from the University of Miami, the Claremont Graduate University, and the University of Virginia. My large family supported this work in non-monetary ways too. Sincere thanks to Rodney Daut I and Martha Flores, Leydy and Donald Kemper; Rodney Daut II and Anna Caples Daut; Tatiana and Deshano Kelly; Austin and Veronica Daut; Erika and Daniels Stewart; David Kemper; Jennifer and Matt Grubaugh; Samy Zaka, Sr. and Chantal Temple; and Roselinde and Dean Otto. I should also mention that my work was completed in Dakar, Senegal in the summer of 2016, and the many people I met, dined with, and who cared for me all enriched this book.

Sustenance comes in many forms. My partner loved me. My children and their hugs saved me.

CONTENTS

Prologue: On the Origins of Black Atlantic Humanism   xv

1 Introduction: Baron de Vastey in Haitian (Revolutionary)
  Context   1

2 What's *in* a Name? Unfolding the Consequences
  of a *Mistaken* Identity   27

3 The Uses of Vastey: Reading Black Sovereignty
  in the Atlantic Public Sphere   63

4 Baron de Vastey's *Testimonio* and the Politics of Black
  Memory   111

5 Baron de Vastey and the Twentieth-Century Theater
  of Haitian Independence   135

Epilogue: Colonialism After Sovereignty:
The Colonial Relation in René Philoctète's
Monsieur de Vastey (1975)   183

Bibliography   201

Author Index   231

Subject Index   237

Names of Publications (NEWSPAPERS, JOURNALS, MAGAZINES)   241

Places   243

LIST OF FIGURES

Fig. 2.1   Acte de Mariage de Jean Vastey and Élisabeth
"Mimi" Dumas, 1777   30

Fig. 2.2   Acte de Baptême, Jean Louis Vastey, 29 March 1788   33

Fig. 2.3   Baron de Vastey, *Notes à M. le Baron de V.P. Malouet*
(1814). Reprinted courtesy of the John Carter Brown
Library   34

Fig. 2.4   Baron de Vastey, *Essai sur les causes de la révolution et des
guerres civiles d'Hayti* (1819)   36

Fig. 2.5   1850 edition of Édouard Marie Oettinger's *Bibliographie
Biographique, ou, Dictionnaire de 26.000 Ouvrages*   42

Fig. 2.6   1851 *Catalogus Librorum Impressorum Bibliothecae
Bodleianae in Academia* Volume 4   43

Fig. 2.7   *Alphabetical Catalog of the Library of Congress* from 1864   44

Fig. 4.1   *Le Roi Henri 1er, Le Baron de Vastey* (1953) by Evans
Pierre Augustin. Courtesy of Figge Museum   133

PROLOGUE: ON THE ORIGINS OF BLACK ATLANTIC HUMANISM

Baron de Vastey, pronounced Vâtay (Romain 67), is best remembered as the most prolific secretary of early nineteenth-century Haiti's King Henry Christophe I and as the author of a scathing indictment of colonial slavery entitled, *Le Système colonial dévoilé* (1814). Although he is largely unknown outside of academic circles today, in the early nineteenth century Vastey was an international public figure, well known for his anti-colonial and black positivist writing. Vastey's damning exposé of the inhumanity of the "colonial system" circulated all across the nineteenth-century Atlantic World and was reviewed in French, US, German, and British journals and newspapers (Daut "The 'Alpha'" 60, Fanning 70, Schuller 40). By the time of his execution in 1820, Vastey's works had become so well-regarded that his two most widely referenced and reviewed books almost immediately appeared in English translation as *Reflections on the Blacks and Whites* (1817) and *Political Remarks on Some French Works and Newspapers* (1818); while a third British translation of Vastey's writing, *An Essay on the Causes of the Revolution and Civil Wars of Hayti*, would appear posthumously in 1823.

Translations of Vastey's writings helped his words travel far and wide in transatlantic abolitionist networks. In 1821, Vastey's *Essai sur les causes de la révolution et des guerres civiles d'Hayti* (1819), the first full-length history of Haiti written by a Haitian, appeared in Dutch translation.[1] In 1817, the Swiss anti-slavery historian Jean Charles Léonard (Sismonde) de Sismondi produced an important review, with large sections translated into Italian, of Vastey's *Réflexions politiques sur quelques ouvrages et journaux francais concernant Hayti* (1817), demonstrating that Vastey's reach had extended into the Mediterranean.[2] Reprints of the English translation of Vastey's *Réflexions sur une lettre de Mazères* (1816), probably one of the first examples of what is now known as critical race theory, appeared in 1828 and 1829 in the first African American newspaper *Freedom's Journal*.[3]

Many other anti-slavery writers from the Atlantic world incorporated the Haitian baron's publications into their analyses of slavery in smaller but no less significant ways.[4] Referred to by one nineteenth-century reviewer as "the most able Haytian of the present era" ("Review of New Books," 1818), Vastey's writings were often quoted in U.S. newspapers to produce compelling arguments for the humanity of black people or to

---

[1] The first of Vastey's works to be translated into English was his much less well-known *Communication officielle de trois lettres de Catineau Laroche, ex-Colon, Agent de Pétion* (1816), which was published for the British historian Marcus Rainsford in 1816. Although *Le Système colonial dévoilé* was not fully translated into English until 2014 when Chris Bongie produced *The Colonial System Unveiled* for Liverpool University Press, in November of 1816 *The Scots Magazine, and Edinburgh Literary Miscellany* did publish a lengthy of summary of the text along with a brief excerpt in English translation (Bongie, *The Colonial System*, 74 ftn19). The Dutch translation was called, *De Negerstaat van Hayti of Sint Domingo, geschetst in zijne geschiedenis en in zijnen tegenwoordigen toestand*.

[2] The Italian review of *Riflessioni Politiche sovra alcune Opere e Giorgnali francesi riguardanti Hayti* was apparently prevented from being published due to Austrian censorship (Pagliai, *Sismondiana*, 85). Sismondi's review was eventually published much later, however, in the *Museo del Risorgimento Nazionale's Pagine inedite del "Conciliatore" Publicate per Cura Del Comune di Milano* (1930), edited by Marcello Visconte di Modrone. See Cordié.

[3] For the excerpts in *Freedom's Journal*, see, "Extracts from the Baron De Vastey's work in answer to the ex-colonist Mazeres and others." *Freedom's Journal*. December 12, 1828; "AFRICA. Extract from Baron De Vastey," *Freedom's Journal*. February 7, 1829; "AFRICA. Extracts from Baron De Vastey." *Freedom's Journal*. February 14, 1829.

[4] For abolitionist works that refer to Vastey see, for example, John Wright's *A Refutation of the Sophisms, Gross Misrepresentations, and Erroneous Quotations Contained in 'An American's 'Letter to the Edinburgh Reviewers'* (1820, 33), William Newnham Blane's *Travels through the United States and Canada* (1824, 219), and Jeremy Bentham's *Canada: Emancipate Your Colonies!* (1838, iv).

demonstrate "African" literary abilities (see, Daut "Alpha and Omega"). Perhaps, most notably, the U.S. abolitionist James McCune Smith referred to Vastey's life and works as evidence of the inherent degradations of slavery in his famous *Lecture on the Haytian Revolutions* (1841, 4–5).

Although Vastey's popularity appears to have briefly waned in the later nineteenth-century, by the early 1900s, his writings began to once again distinctly enter U.S. African-American discourse. W.E.B. Du Bois (1905, 45), Alain Locke (1925, 425), Arthur Schomburg (1925, 671), and Mercer Cook (1948, 12) all reference Vastey's contributions to the cause of promoting racial justice. And his life was intriguing enough for several twentieth-century playwrights to promote him as the subject for dramatic performance.

Vastey was first immortalized in the theatrical work of May Miller in *Christophe's Daughters* (1935), and he would once again appear as a principal character in Selden Rodman's three-act play, *The Revolutionists* in 1942. In 1945, Dan Hammerman produced his own historical drama featuring Vastey called *Henri Christophe*. In 1963 Aimé Césaire placed Vastey center stage in his famous dramatization of the northern kingdom of Haiti, *La Tragédie du roi Christophe* (1963). The Haitian poet and playwright René Philoctète, one of the founders of the postmodern technique of "spiralism," would go even further by staging an important homage to the baron with the eponymous *Monsieur de Vastey* (1975). Perhaps most famously, Nobel prize winner Derek Walcott published a complicated vision of Vastey in two of the plays that make up his *Haitian Trilogy* (2002): *Henri Christophe* (1949) and *The Haitian Earth* (1984).[5]

The object of this exploration into the legacy of Vastey's writing is two-fold: to bring attention to a thinker who produced at least eleven different anti-slavery and anti-colonialist book-length publications in a span of only five years (1814–1819),[6] and to document how these

---

[5] Vastey does not appear in Walcott's *Drums and Colours* (1958).

[6] *Le Système colonial dévoilé* (1814); *Notes à M. le Baron V.P. de Malouet* (1814); *Le Cri de la patrie* (1815); *Le Cri de la conscience* (1815); *À mes concitoyens, Haytiens!* (1815); *Réflexions adressées aux Haytiens de partie de l'ouest et du sud, sur l'horrible assassinat du Général Delvare, commis au Port-au-Prince, dans la nuit du 25 décembre, 1815, par les ordres de Pétion* (1816); *Communication officielle de trois lettres de Catineau Laroche, ex-colon, agent de Pétion* (1816); *Relation de la fête de la Reine S. M. D'Hayti* (1816); *Réflexions sur une lettre de Mazères, ex-colon français, [...] sur les noirs et les blancs, la civilization de l'Afrique, le Royaume d'Hayti, etc.* (1816); *Réflexions politiques sur quelques ouvrages et journaux français concernant Hayti* (1817); and *Essai sur les causes de la Révolution et des guerres civiles d'Hayti* (1819).

writings were read from Vastey's era up until the present day. In so doing, I hope to capture the various rhetorical and ideological functions that his often *avant la lettre* arguments have been made to perform. For, I suggest that the significant *use* of Vastey's writings by both nineteenth-century abolitionists and twentieth-century anti-colonialists makes Vastey a foundational figure in a philosophical movement of Black Atlantic humanism whose goal was to disrupt the Enlightenment philosophies that undergirded colonial slavery and colonial racism.

The definition of what we might call Black Atlantic humanism and its parameters are intentionally broad. The term describes an intellectual endeavor begun in the eighteenth century on both sides of the Atlantic with the principal aim to prove that black people were equal to the white people who were enslaving them. The most well-known of early Black Atlantic writers, including Olaudah Equiano (1745–1797), John Marrant (1755–1791), Ottobah Cugoano (1757–1791), Ukawsaw Gronniosaw (1705–1775), Ignatius Sancho (1729–1780), and Phillis Wheatley (1753–1784) made the case that the people called negroes by enslavers deserved equality with whites. By chronicling in various forms the depredations of color prejudice that they had personally experienced, including in autobiographies, slave narratives, sermons, and lyric poetry, these writers argued for the recognition of black humanity in a world of chattel slavery.

Afro-diasporans in the public sphere pursued the mission of proving that their dark skin did not make them uncivilizable savages, destined for enslavement, because from the ancient to the early modern world reams of paper had been devoted to characterizing Africans as somehow less than human. "The roots of European and American prejudices against Africans are ancient," Bruce Dain reminds us, "preceding the introduction of slavery to the New World and much before then too. Rationalized languages of race are something else again. They are the product of eighteenth-century 'natural history', which was the first systematic modern attempt to describe and understand living nature on the basis of observation and reason operating upon sense experience" (6). The irony is that in much of the writing that has come to be described as "natural history" blackness was seen as anything other than natural.

Although he was a believer in monogenism, the generally anti-slavery Comte de Buffon wrote that the whiteness of European skin, because it was the "hue of heaven," was preferable to the putatively degenerate dark skin to be found among the blacks of Africa (6: 330). While blackness signified a form of human degradation to a natural scientist like Buffon, it was used by many other European *philosophes* in the eighteenth century to more directly justify the enslavement of Africans on American shores.[7] The collaboratively written, *Histoire philosophique et politique des établissements et du commerce des Européens dans les deux Indes* (1770–1780), a work signed by the Abbé Raynal, argues that the supposedly inherent ugliness and lack of intelligence of "Africans" could justify their enslavement:

> The passions, therefore, of fear and love, are carried to excess among these people; and this is the reason they are more effeminate, more indolent, weaker, and unhappily more fit for slavery. Besides, their intellectual faculties being nearly exhausted, by the excesses of sensual pleasures, they have neither memory nor understanding to supply by art the deficiency of their strength. (1776, 1: 101)[8]

---

[7] In the writings of many Enlightenment era thinkers, blackness was variously figured as ugly, inhuman, unintelligent, and uncivilizable, all of which could therefore be used as a justification for slavery. The famous philosopher David Hume claimed, for example, in a now infamous footnote in his *Essays on Treatises and Several Subjects* (1753–54),

> "I am apt to suspect the Negroes, and in general all the other species of men (for there are four or five different kinds) to be naturally inferior to the whites. There never was a civilized nation of any other complexion than white, nor even any individual eminent either in action or speculation. No ingenious manufacturers amongst them, no arts, no sciences ... Such a uniform and constant difference could not happen, in so many countries and ages, if nature had not made an original distinction betwixt these breeds of men." (337)

Immanuel Kant, too, contributed to such white supremacy when he wrote in his *Observations on the Feeling of the Beautiful and the Sublime* (1764), "[t]he Negroes of Africa have, by nature, no feeling that rises above the trifling ... So fundamental is the difference between these two races of man, and it appears to be as great in regard to mental capacities as in color ... [if a] man [is] black from head to foot, [it is] a clear proof that what he said was stupid" (110–111). Thomas Jefferson's white supremacist theories about *negroes* are by now also well-known: "Comparing them by their faculties of memory, reason, and imagination," Jefferson writes, "it appears to me that in memory they are equal to whites, in reason much inferior, as I think one could scarcely be found capable of tracing and comprehending the investigations of Euclid; and that in imagination they are dull, tasteless, and anomalous" (139).

[8] The Abbé Raynal is often cited as an abolitionist, even though he contested this label himself, and if he was anti-slavery at all, he believed in a policy of gradual emancipation (Reinhardt 51). Srinivas Aravamudan tells us, in fact, that even though the Jacobins adopted Raynal as a revolutionist, Raynal "was not prepared to assume this identity ... [it] was constructed as such a posteriori through the mechanisms of authorship" (295).

Attempts to justify slavery on the basis of blackness compelled one of the most famous Black Atlantic poets, Phillis Wheatley, to oppose the time-worn association of dark skin with evil in her famous poem, "On Being Brought from Africa to America:"

> Some view our sable race with scornful eye,
> "Their colour is a diabolic die."
> Remember, Christians, Negro's, black as Cain,
> May be refin'd, and join th' angelic train. (18)

Yet even in a world that had seen the publication of the first book of poetry produced by a writer of color when Wheatley's *Poems on Various Subjects* was published in 1773, it had been comparatively difficult for the voices of people of color to be heard. Baron de Vastey recognized as much when he lamented: "The small number of our unfortunate class have had a difficult time to throw even some small retorts against their numerous calumnies, having been compromised by the confluence of all the circumstances that smothered their voices" (*Système* 95). In citing a host of European writers, including Bernardin de Saint-Pierre and the Abbé Grégoire, however, Vastey acknowledged that resistance to discourses of black dehumanization could effectively come from many different corners. "If I were required to cite and recount here the whole of the testimony of every virtuous European who has resisted and braved all the insults of the ex-colonists in order to prove our equality with whites," Vastey wrote, "I would be prolific" (*RM* 12).

Indeed, the writings and speeches of many white eighteenth-century abolitionists and anti-slavery activists such as Anthony Benezet, Thomas Paine, and Granville Sharp, as well as those of their early nineteenth-century counterparts including Thomas Clarkson, the Abbé Grégoire, Zachary Macaulay, and William Wilberforce, contain elements of Black Atlantic humanism. These allies of the Black Atlantic helped to counter the voluminous narratives seeking to justify the enslavement and torture of black people produced in the European public sphere. They did so by using the privileges of whiteness (in the sense that their voices could be *heard*) to expose the iniquities of the slave trade and the inherent depredations of slavery. Baron de Vastey remarked, thus, that it was with "sentiments of appreciation and gratitude" toward those Europeans who had bravely taken on the subject before him that he had gained the courage and inspiration to himself "tackle the Gordian knot" of "proving to the ex-colonists, with the sword and the pen, that morally and physically [blacks] are not inferior to their type" (*RM* 13).

We might think of Vastey's comments as a reflection of the kind of "interdependency of black and white thinkers" that led to Paul Gilroy's development of the term "Black Atlantic" (31). Gilroy argued that framing the history of black thought within an Atlantic context (comprising the Americas, Africa, and Europe) could result in "a single, complex unit of analysis [...] of the modern world" whereby writings by people of African descent could be considered a crucial part of "the intellectual heritage of the West since the Enlightenment" (2). Studying Afro-diasporic thought as a central rather than marginal development in western history, Gilroy said, could "produce an explicitly transnational and intercultural perspective" (15). This is because, as Lisa A. Lindsay and John Wood Sweet have recently put it, "the Black Atlantic is both a space and an argument" (1), one that props up rather than sublimates the voices of people of color.

Black Atlantic humanism, then, as the most immediate space from which we can glimpse the weight of the contribution of black voices to anti-racist and anti-colonial thought, is not about the perceived race or skin color of the author. Rather, it names the discursive mode of challenging color prejudice and the strategies of argumentation deployed to contest the theories and material practices that have supported myriad forms of colonial violence against black people across the Atlantic World. The discourse of Black Atlantic humanism can, therefore, be entered into by anyone devoted to deconstructing the twin axes of colonial racism and colonial slavery.

The collaboration of anti-slavery activists with the post-independence Haitian state that produced Vastey is central to my examination of the wave of Black Atlantic humanistic thought that surfaced in the wake of the Haitian Revolution. The writings of early Haitian authors, including Vastey, can help us trace how attempts to argue for the end of slavery by abolitionists and other anti-slavery writers in the eighteenth-century led directly to the efforts of nineteenth-century activists to defend black sovereignty. It was one thing to make the case for the abolition of slavery, but it was quite another to assert that black people could become independent rulers of their own sovereign state.

In fact, Baron de Vastey's writing stands at the origins of a crucial shift in early Black Atlantic thought from being almost solely focused on the abolition of black slavery to arguing for the creation of black political institutions. Many earlier eighteenth-century formerly enslaved writers used their biographies to argue primarily for their own humanity. The racial politics discernible in these writings suggests to a large extent that slavery was a personal issue to be overcome either through religion or dogged individual resistance. Wheatley's famous poem, "On Being Brought from Africa to America" and many of Marrant's sermons imply that Christian conversion was the path to encouraging the recognition of black people as human beings, in effect arguing that Africans deserved equality in spite of their blackness rather than because of it (for Marrant, see Saillant, "Wipe Away all Tears from their Eyes"). Moreover, Equiano's role in enslaving others after his own emancipation, which is detailed in his 1789 autobiography (101–105), complicates his strongly worded arguments for the abolition of the slave trade; and Gronniosaw, in his *Narrative of the Most Remarkable Particulars in the Life of James Albert Ukawsaw Gronniosaw, an African Prince, as Related by Himself* (1772), does not denounce slavery at all. Only Sancho and Cugoano unequivocally condemn both slavery and the slave trade, but like most European and American abolitionists, they could not envision black sovereignty (see, Sancho, "Letter to Jack Wingrave;" Cugoano, *Thoughts and Sentiments on the Evil and Wicked Traffic of the Human Species*).[9]

In contrast, Vastey identified the U.S. American and French revolutions as incomplete because neither ended slavery nor promoted black freedom, comparing their outcomes to what he called the "fatal truth" of Haitian independence (*RM* 90). Vastey's comparison of the conflicting consequences of the Age of Revolutions focused not only on denouncing the oppression of all black people but on promoting black sovereignty as the necessary outcome of abolition. In his most important work, *Le Système colonial dévoilé*, he describes slavery and colonialism as an entire network of legal, social, and textual practices aimed at reproducing institutional rather than individual inequalities. Vastey recognized that color prejudice had been institutionalized to prevent black liberty when he discussed the difficulty of contesting black dehumanization in a white discursive space: "The friends of slavery, those eternal enemies of the human race have written thousands of volumes freely...they have made all the presses of Europe groan

---

[9] Most eighteenth-century abolitionists were proponents of policies of gradual emancipation. The nineteenth-century Haitian historian Thomas Madiou acknowledged as much in the specific context of French Saint-Domingue when he wrote, "you would have to be completely misled by passion or be completely ignorant of the facts to submit that in 1789, 1790, and 1792 ideas of general liberty had been completely formed [...], be it of the blacks, be it of the *hommes de couleur*" (565). For more on the various positions held by eighteenth and early nineteenth-century aboltionists, see Daut, *Tropics of Haiti* (565–567).

for centuries in order to reduce the black man below the brute" (*Système* 95). As a member of the only sovereign state of the Americas where slavery had been abolished, he viewed opposition to anti-black writing as both a necessary obligation and a logical consequence of Haiti's sovereignty, writing, "now that we have Haytian printing presses, we can reveal the crimes of the colonists and respond to even the most absurd calumnies invented by the prejudice and greed of our oppressors" (95). Vastey's identification here of the press as Haitian was more than just rhetorical. The press to which he refers was actually created by the state, meaning that in many ways, the defense of blackness was for the first time derived from the state itself.

One of these "oppressors" whom Vastey exposed through this state-sanctioned printing press was the former French colonist, Baron de Malouet.[10] In his *Collection de mémoires sur les colonies* (1802) Malouet made the argument that France needed to institute a "new" and improved form of colonization that could rectify what he called "this secret full of horror: the liberty of the blacks means their domination! It means the massacre or the enslavement of the whites, the burning of our fields and our cities." (quoted in Vastey, *Notes* 14; see also, Malouet, 4: 46) Vastey challenged Malouet's claim by using the strategy of what might today be referred to as a "postcolonial reversal" in exhorting: "*Now this secret full of horror can be known*: Le Système Colonial, means domination by Whites and the massacre and enslavement of Blacks." In the pages that follow, Vastey focuses on narrating dozens of specific atrocities committed against individual enslaved people and free people of color as the inevitable effect of a system that could only occasion black death and prevent black freedom, rather than as isolated examples of personal injury under slavery. What Vastey's analysis of blackness as a collective condition of oppression shared by Africans and their descendants all over the world (whether enslaved or free) shows us is that the idea of Afro-diasporic solidarity surfaces more apparently in the nineteenth-century era of Haitian independence than it did in the eighteenth-century world of European slavery.

Examination of the political theories and material practices developed in Haiti in the wake of independence, alongside that of transatlantic abolitionist writing, provides a clear illustration of how our understanding of the genesis, continuities, and contours of Black Atlantic thought remain incomplete without the inclusion of nineteenth-century Haitian

---

[10] For more on the state-run press of Christophe's kingdom, see, Patrick Tardieu (2004).

writers like Baron de Vastey. Although studies of first-person narratives composed and published by black authors from the pre-twentieth-century Caribbean are notoriously sparse, Haitian independence in 1804 ushered in a vibrant and diverse print culture that included poetry, plays, newspapers, and historical writing. From the pages of *La Gazette royale d'Hayti* (1811–1820)[11] to the poems of Jean-Baptiste Romane (1807–1858) to the historical writings of Louis-Félix Boisrond-Tonnerre (1776–1806) to the operas of Juste Chanlatte (1766–1828), there arose a distinct nineteenth-century literary culture in Haiti that was explicitly anti-slavery and decidedly pro-black sovereignty. Few of these writers, however, are ordinarily included in examinations of early African American or early Caribbean print culture,[12] largely because the transatlantic, transnational, and multi-racial abolitionist movement often theorized in scholarship as the "Black Atlantic" has traditionally excluded nineteenth-century Haitian authors through various kinds of epistemological silencing.[13]

---

[11] *La Gazette royale* was a continuation of *La Gazette officielle d'Hayti* (1807–1811), which dates from the time that Christophe first assumed control over the north of Haiti.

[12] For example, *Caribbeana* (1999), an anthology edited by Thomas Krise, contains only English-language writings. Scholarship by Haitians living in Haiti, in contrast, has long been devoted to remembering and recognizing early Haitian authorship, but only recently have Anglophone scholars joined them. What we are lacking remain volumes that place early Haitian writing in comparative, diasporic context. Deborah Jenson and Doris Kadish's recent volume, *The Poetry of Haitian Independence* (2015), for instance, brings the poetry of early Haitian poets like Antoine Dupré, Juste Chanlatte, Jules Solime Milscent, and Jean-Baptiste Romane to a wider audience through translation; Catherine A. Reinhardt, in *Claims to Memory* (2006), has examined some of the memoirs of free people of color along with plays, letters, and pamphlets from French Saint-Domingue; and Chris Bongie has recently provided some groundbreaking information about Juste Chanlatte's role in the construction of the Haitian Declaration of Independence in his article, "The Cry of History: Juste Chanlatte and the Unsettling (Presence) of Race in Early Haitian Literature" (2015).

[13] Trouillot characterized pro-slavery European apologists's reactions to the Haitian Revolution as a form of epistemological silencing: "It did not *really* happen; it was not that bad, or that important" (*Silencing* 96). A similar "formula of erasure" and "formula of banalization" has been used against early Haitian authors: either they did not really write these narratives (a charge often made against Toussaint Louverture [for examples, see Desormeaux 135]) or even if they did, their narratives are not really that important. For a description of ways in which nineteenth-century Haitian writing has been "dismissed as a time blind imitation," see Dash "Nineteenth-Century Haiti and the Archipelago of the Americas" (46).

The omission of early Haitian writers from Afro-diasporic intellectual and literary history is unfortunate since nineteenth-century Haitian intellectuals and political leaders were some of the first people of color to systematically deconstruct the racist perspectives of Western philosophers, and Haiti was the first postcolonial state in the Americas to insist upon freedom and equality for all of its citizens.[14] The transformation of French colonial Saint-Domingue into sovereign Haiti contributed not only to the making of the modern world system but to contemporary ideas about the meanings of freedom and liberation. Rewriting early Haitian authors, alongside the Haitian revolutionaries themselves, back into the intellectual history of modern humanism is crucial to this project of tracing how Black Atlantic ideas have contributed to our modern sense of what it means to be free.

Although the idea of the absolute logic of freedom is typically attributed to European philosophers like Georg Wilhem Friedrich Hegel or Baruch Spinoza (Buck-Morss 60; Nesbitt, *Universal* 22–23), Toussaint Louverture, who probably never read either of them, also espoused the concept when he wrote, "It is not a circumstantial liberty conceded to us that we wish, but the unequivocal adoption of the principle that no man, whether he be born red, black or white, can become the property of his fellow men" (qtd. in Hutton 54). The founder of independent Haiti, Jean-Jacques Dessalines' 1805 constitution not only forever abolished slavery (Article 2), but declared all Haitians, regardless of skin color, class, or social status, to be "equal before the law" (Article 3), making Haiti the first state to explicitly outlaw prejudice (Article 14). Henry Christophe's 1807 constitution similarly forbade slavery in perpetuity (Article 2), and proscribed that "Any person, resident in the territory of Haiti, is free with all rights" (Article 1). Christophe's constitution was also explicitly anti-imperial. While Article 36 suggested that Haiti would not interfere in the affairs of neighboring colonies, Article 37 proclaimed, "The people of Haiti will never pursue any conquests outside of this island, and limits itself to conserving its own territory." Vastey, too, explicitly noted that Haitians did not desire to create a Caribbean empire when he wrote: "The revolution did not transfer from the whites to the blacks the question of control over the West Indies …

---

[14] Michael Drexler and Ed White's article, "The Constitution of Toussaint: Another Origin of African American Literature" (2010), is a step in the right direction towards recognizing these contributions.

Haiti is one of the islands of this archipelago and is not itself the Caribbean" (*Notes* 7).[15]

What needs to be emphasized here is Haiti's role in creating the circumstances for anti-slavery and anti-racism positionalities to be considered normative elements of American democracy, pushing back against ideas of inevitable historical progress that begin with Europe. Before Haitian independence in 1804, there was little to suggest that the wholesale abolition of transatlantic slavery was forthcoming or that the other islands in the Caribbean would eventually become decolonized. Similarly, Haiti's connection to the anti-colonial/anti-conquest stance of postcolonial studies should not be taken for granted either, since in a very real sense the argument that empire was bad was derived from the first states of Haiti.

Despite increasing recognition of the centrality of the Haitian Revolution to political, philosophical, and intellectual histories of the modern world, scholars have had a difficult time incorporating discussions of early nineteenth-century Haitian political ideas into world-systems analyses. Immanuel Wallerstein, probably the most well-known of world-systems analysts, writes only of Haiti, "[t]he key element to remember is that there was a slave rebellion that succeeded, establishing the first Black state in the modern world-system, but that this state was marginalized and excluded by the world and other states in the Americas" (15). While the abstract state of Haiti has been painted as exceptionally isolated from the ideas of democracy governing the modern political world, Haitian leaders have been portrayed as autocratic rulers isolated from and by their own people. "Authoritarianism on the part of the government and political irresponsibility or apathy on the part of the mass of the population," David Nicholls writes, "have gone together in independent Haiti" (*From Dessalines* 246). Perpetuating the twin mythologies of the Haitian state's essential disconnectedness from world politics and the Haitian people's putative disregard for political participation

---

[15] Here, Vastey specifically refutes the writing of the former French colonist Malouet, who had written that "the [Haitian] revolution has transferred from the whites to the blacks the question of control over the Caribbean, and our unfortunate rivalries must give way in the face of the great interest in the region that is obviously developing" (*Collection de mémoires*, 4: 2). Christophe's Code had followed in the stead of Dessalines's constitution, which had mandated, "The Emperor will never form any enterprise with the view of conquest or of troubling the peace or domestic regimes of foreign colonies" (Art. 36).

and domestic governance,[16] contributes toward erasing the role of early Haitian political leaders in developing anti-slavery and anti-color prejudice policies more immediately associated with post-1848 France and the post-Civil War U.S. Moreover, the silencing of what Deborah Jenson has called the "radical anti-colonial" discourse of early Haiti obscures the "provocative recontextualization of the Enlightenment as an ideology both illuminated and refashioned" not only by "slaves or former slaves," (Jenson, "Malcom" 331) but also by the very real, as opposed to "apparent states" (Glick-Schiller and Fouron, *Georges Woke Up Laughing*, 27; Braziel, "Haiti, Guantánamo" 12) of early nineteenth-century Haiti.

It is important to affirm how the early state(s) of Haiti challenged the concept of (white) Enlightenment humanism with unequivocal proclamations of (black) liberty, and to emphasize Haiti's role in the implementation of universal equality as a democratic sine qua non. Haitian independence marks not only a signal transformation in the history of modern democracy, but the theories undergirding it contributed to contemporary philosophical ideas about what it means to be free and to live a good life: the Haitian state was the first to proclaim that no human beings could ever be enslaved by, for, or in the state. Acknowledging Vastey's own contributions to the intellectual fields we now call postcolonial studies and critical race theory allows us to emphasize the impact of the Haitian state on the decolonization of the Americas, as well as the involvement of the Haitian people in promoting the very ideas of racial equality that have shaped the trajectory of modern political theory.

Bringing early Haitian writing to the fore of Atlantic intellectual history also illuminates the contributions of nineteenth-century Haitian historians like Vastey to a discourse of historicizing slavery that has been much more closely associated with either U.S. or European abolitionists and/or later nineteenth- and early twentieth-century Anglophone African American and Caribbean writers. Vastey was one of the most prolific and widely read historians of color in the nineteenth century on both sides of the Atlantic, leading one early nineteenth-century U.S. newspaper editor to refer to him as "the Alpha and Omega of Haytian intellect and literature" (see, Daut, "The 'Alpha and Omega'"). Even though the 1971 Annual Report of the Library Company of Philadelphia

---

[16] For a recent counter to the idea of Haiti's disconnectedness from world politics and general isolation from the world powers in the nineteenth century, see Julia Gaffield's meticulous, *Haitian Connections in the Atlantic World: Recognition After Revolution* (2015).

wrote that Vastey was not only "a pioneer [...] in positive black thinking, but [he] probably [produced] the first scholarly, serious socio-ethnological study by a Negro" (52), there has been little attempt to produce sustained comparative study within the larger history of the African diaspora of Vastey's efforts to document the habits of mind and daily experiences of the enslaved.[17]

Including discussions of Haitian authors within histories that study black people writing about other black people, which in many ways "followed the creation of the Haitian republic," to use Ifeoma Nwankwo's words (20), might seem like common sense. The striking reality is that early Haitian writers have been historically disregarded or dismissed as directly contributing to the development of the kinds of anti-colonial and anti-racist intellectual discourse more immediately associated with later black writers, including W.E.B. Du Bois.[18] This often occurs because of (mis)perceptions about early Haitian authors' usage of the French language and/or pre-conceived notions about the connection between their skin color or class and their political and ideological affiliations.

Vastey's own position as the son of an affluent French enslaver also complicates our understanding of the relationship of class and color to nineteenth-century black emancipationist and twentieth-century black radical writing and the genealogies that link them together. Baron de Vastey was the phenotypically white son of a French colonist from

---

[17] Passing comparisons of Vastey's writing to central figures of the Enlightenment, Négritude, and the U.S. American abolitionist movement can hint at the kind of rhetorical resonance that Vastey's style of writing calls forth in readers of his works. Vastey's centrality to theorizing a post-slavery Atlantic World has led scholar Laurie Maffly-Kipp to compare his writing style to that of the Enlightenment thinker Baron de Montesquieu and the abolitionists David Walker and William Lloyd Garrison (Maffly-Kipp, 62). David Nicholls, J. Michael Dash, and Chris Bongie have all seen similarities between Vastey's writing and the anti-colonialist thought of Frantz Fanon (Dash, *Literature and Ideology* 4; Nicholls, "Pompée," 130; Bongie, *Friends* 228). For my own part, I have written about Vastey in connection with both Aimé Césaire and Jean-Paul Sartre's much later theorizations of colonialism as a system (Daut 2008, 52–53).

[18] Haitian intellectuals have long been attuned to the importance of Vastey's writings. For example, the literary historian Duraciné Vaval (1933) once wrote, "One does not know history, if one is not familiar with the works of Vastey (129)." I suggest, however, that it is not necessarily Haitian intellectual historians who need to remember early Haitian writers, but rather that transnational American, transatlantic, and Afrodiasporic scholars from Europe and the rest of the Americas have been slow to include early Haitian authors in their considerations of early Caribbean and other Black Atlantic print cultures.

Normandy and a free woman of color from a wealthy plantation owning family in Saint-Domingue. Yet, despite having possibly owned slaves
himself as a young man in the French-controlled colony, Vastey aligned
himself with Dessalines's *armée indigène* during the war of Haitian independence and subsequently became one of the most important officials
in the government of the only sovereign, free and black state of the
Americas under King Henry Christophe I. Nevertheless, assumptions
about Vastey's life, including his social and economic status, his status
as enslaved or free(d), as well as his race and skin color, have overdeter-
mined interpretations of his writings.[19]

In scholarship on the Caribbean and the Atlantic World as a whole,
where Vastey is discussed at all, he is most often discursively referred to
and sometimes even dismissed as an "ideologist," a "propagandist," or a
mere "publicist."[20] These characterizations highlight a tension in interpretations of Vastey's works. Because radical European intellectual traditions often view themselves as completely removed from the violence of
state power, scholars have had a difficult time thinking about how to read
the works of a phenotypically white and European educated Haitian intellectual who was also a member of the Haitian state. Vastey's works need
to be seen, however, as a part of a tradition of Black Atlantic humanism
that can be traced to post-independence Haiti and which reflects the
complicated positions of power occupied by the former slaves and free
people of color of the first black independent state of the Americas.

---

[19] Although I aim in this work to present the most comprehensive biographical information available on Vastey to date, this work is not a biography and cannot purport to provide
anything more than a speculative assessment of the relationship of Vastey's life in colonial
Saint-Domingue under slavery to his works. But Vastey's personal history is central to this
analysis of his role in the origins of Black Atlantic humanism, if only because his life helps
to partially explain why a phenotypically white writer who became one of the most ardent
and popular anti-slavery and anti-colonial writers of the nineteenth-century Atlantic World,
fell into virtual obscurity in twentieth-century histories of race and decolonization.

[20] The idea that Vastey is a "propagandist," "ideologist," "publicist," and/or an "ideologue" is repeated in nearly all works that discuss him at length. See, Sepinwall, "Exporting
the Revolution;" Dain 125; Cole 1967, 220; Griggs and Prator, 44; Dash, "Before and
Beyond Negritude," 53; S. Fisher, 311 ftn13; Lewis, *Main Currents in Caribbean Thought*,
218; Maffly-Kip 56; Castera 45; Davis, *Inhuman* 174; Garraway, "Introduction" 17ftn12.
Vastey's biographer refers to him as an "idéologue implacable" (Quevilly 244), and the
twentieth-century translator of Vastey's *Le Système colonial dévoilé*, Chris Bongie, calls
Vastey the "principal ideologue" of the northern kingdom (*Friends* 227).

Vastey's *Le Système* can provide a material example of the possibilities and the complications of such post-revolutionary collaboration of the state with both an intellectual class and the broader mass of people in Haiti. Even though Vastey had never been enslaved, he claimed that he had spoken to the dead as well as to the formerly enslaved (including consulting their maimed bodies) to produce what he called "these testimonies" in *Le Système* (40). In using his writing to collaborate with the dead and those who lacked the opportunity to publish their own words, Vastey spoke both from a position of power and produced intimate knowledge from below of the physical, social, and spiritual ramifications of enslavement. His methodology, which combines oral history with textual analysis, provides a unique example of adaptive strategies of narration that have come to be associated with diasporic and indigenous forms of storytelling. Vastey's writings collectivize the experience of slavery to ground a critique of colonialism and racism in a form of witnessing that approaches the collaborative genre of the "testimonio," usually associated with twentieth-century Latin American writing.

This form of collaboration—a writer using his own privileged voice as a stand-in for the relatively powerless one of the people—also makes Vastey's *Le Système* both similar and dissimilar to prior black writing about slavery. Nicole Aljoe has written that one distinguishing feature of Anglophone slave narratives from the Caribbean is the "floating 'I,'" which she says "has the grammatical status of what linguists call a 'shifter', a linguistic function that can be assumed by anyone" (18). This "shifter" is important to Aljoe's analysis of eighteenth and nineteenth-century "creole testimonies" from the British-claimed Caribbean because, as she contends, "every West Indian slave narrative is explicitly mediated in some way—by a white transcriber, editor, or translator" (14). What makes Vastey's writing different from these Anglophone "creole testimonies" is that it is not just Vastey who acts as a mediator between the enslaved and the never enslaved, but the anti-slavery Haitian state also fills in the role of mediator, at least metaphorically.

In *Le Système*, Vastey suggests that he had collected his descriptions of slave tortures and punishments from the formerly enslaved themselves in service of the king. His use of the royal *we* makes him, as a member of the Haitian state, similar to literary history's other mediators, such as those found in Anglophone slave narratives. But Vastey officially makes the depredations of the slave's life a metonymy for the history of all Haitians by channeling these narratives through the state. In *Le Système*

Vastey states, "we watered the soil with our sweat and our blood" (37) and in another section he writes, "Thus, there existed on each plantation a *white despot*, who wielded the barbaric right to life and death [...] abusing this atrocious privilege, death hovered over our heads as if we were the most vile animals" (*Système* 63). Statements such as this one have likely led to the scholarly confusion concerning whether or not Vastey had ever been enslaved himself[21] and also reveal the Haitian state's complicated relationship to people who themselves formerly owned slaves and to the slave-labor based economies of the Atlantic World.

Vastey was genealogically bound to both enslavers and the enslaved, and, as with many early Black Atlantic writers, including Equiano and Louverture, and all white people living in the colony, including abolitionists and other anti-slavery activists, he was materially bound by the capitalist economics of slavery. This is not only because his father owned slaves, but because Vastey was a free person living in a slave colony. To a large extent, all free people, regardless of their political leanings, class affiliations, or skin colors, benefitted from slavery in a dichotomous society marked starkly by the gulf between the enslaved and the free(d).

Vastey's racial, political, and economic biographies can at least partially account for the difficulty some scholars have had incorporating him into narratives of early Afro-diasporic writing, which often tie the emergence of black (slave) literacy to black (slave) liberation.[22] The connection between black writing and black emancipation arises because the achievement of literacy is narrated as a precondition for personal liberty in many slave narratives, or at the very least, it provides the impetus for the recognition of one's own humanity (see Hager 3), as is the case in Frederick Douglass's *Narrative of the Life of Frederick Douglass, an American Slave* (1845).[23] And in many abolitionist speeches of the period the former enslaved person's literacy, instead of preparing him to

---

[21] See, Chap. 2 of the present volume for a discussion of this mis-conception.

[22] In one of the first essays to be written about Vastey, David Nicholls asked, for example, "Into which category does Vastey fall: true radical—pointing to a firm foundation for a new national identity—or opportunistic spokesman of a new, self-serving elite?" ("Pompée" 108).

[23] The equation of literacy with humanity is a longstanding association. Dain writes, "The very idea of writing oneself free was typical of the eighteenth century, when writing seemed to be the visible sign of reason and imagination" (4). Hager adds, "For those newly freed, learning how to write symbolized the end of their enslavement" (3).

assume a role in state governance, turns him against the government participation from which his blackness had already a priori excluded him. This is precisely the argument made by Douglass in his later speech, "What to a Slave is the Fourth of July?" (1852):

> Fellow-citizens, pardon me, allow me to ask, why am I called upon to speak here to-day? What have I, or those I represent, to do with your national independence? Are the great principles of political freedom and of natural justice, embodied in that Declaration of Independence, extended to us? [...] This Fourth of July is yours, not mine. You may rejoice, I must mourn. To drag a man in fetters into the grand illuminated temple of liberty, and call upon him to join you in joyous anthems, were inhuman mockery and sacrilegious irony.

Unlike Douglass, however, not only had Vastey never been enslaved, but after Haitian independence he began to immediately work for, and therefore to profit from, the state. And while the Kingdom of Hayti was intellectually anti-racist and anti-slavery, Christophe's government had deep trading ties with both the United States and England, two slave-labor based economies. This fact probably made early nineteenth-century Haiti what José Carlos Mariátegui called in 1927, in another context, "economically colonial" (175).[24]

This contradiction between the economic and intellectual biographies of individual writers (and the individual states to which they belonged), might be viewed as a contest between statism and non-statism. Statist intellectual positioning can be understood as contributing to or bearing (consciously or not) the benefits of the global capitalist economics that supported both slavery and other forms of unfree labor, while non-statist perspectives represent radical breaks with the economics of state formation and the unequal labor policies they necessarily support. Non-statist philosophies emerge when authors begin to write and live against their own economic interests in capitalism, or more broadly, profiting at the expense of others. As such, purely non-statist writing is rare, if it exists at all. In fact, within the tradition of Black Atlantic letters, statist and non-statist writing often exist in a highly fractured state of tension. The life

---

[24] Mariátegui noted that even though nationalism was "revolutionary" in "colonial peoples" and that they often boasted of their "political autonomy," they still found themselves mired in global capitalism. This state of affairs would continue, Mariátegui observed, until they could reach what he viewed as the irreducible and inevitable goal of instituting "socialism" (175).

and works of Baron de Vastey demonstrate precisely the complications of writing that is both statist and non-statist at the same time, and that reflects the contradictions of a state that is simultaneously anti-slavery and capitalist.

The tense relationship of Black Atlantic humanism to the nation state and the global capitalism it supports also manifests itself in the uneasy slippage that lies between propagandistic writing and intellectual writing. Where intellectual writing is seen as pure and removed from the influences of state power, propagandistic writing is figured to be an arm of state authority. Anti-slavery writing, propagandistic though it may seem in that it is produced with a singular goal of persuasion in mind, is almost always divorced from direct state interference in nineteenth-century Europe and in the antebellum United States, where slavery and the slave trade were still in practice.

All of Baron de Vastey's writing, even those publications principally directed at destroying Alexandre Pétion's rival state,[25] can be characterized as anti-slavery and anti-color prejudice. At the same time, however, Vastey's nineteenth-century anti-slavery writing also linked him to the government of Henry Christophe, particularly, his most compelling anti-slavery work, *Le Système colonial dévoilé*, which includes a dedicatory epistle, "To the King." I suggest, in any event, that the tension apparent in Vastey's works between populist protest and state authority is not something we should ignore or condemn but requires our analysis.

The simultaneous affirmation of (black) state power and condemnation of (white) colonial power that Vastey articulates is also invariably characteristic of the lives and works of much later philosopher-politicians from the African diaspora like Aimé Césaire and Léopold Sédar Senghor,[26] both of whose writings are genealogically connected

---

[25] After the assassination of Dessalines in 1806, Christophe and Pétion, both former generals of the Haitian war of independence, became engaged in a civil war, which eventually led to the division of Haiti into three separately governed states (see, p. 18 for more information).

[26] John Patrick Walsh, for instance, has detailed the relationship he sees between Césaire's efforts to promote Martinican departmentalization, which permanently changed the colony of Martinique into a *département* of France, and Toussaint Louverture's desire to have French Saint-Domingue remain "free and French," per the latter's 1801 Constitution. Nesbitt also explores some of the complications that exist between freedom from enslavement and postcolonial sovereignty in the Caribbean in *Voicing Memory* (141–143). For Senghor, see the chapter, "On Poet-Presidents and Philospher-Kings" in Ali Al'Amin Mazrui's *Power, Politics, and the African Condition* (2004).

to the same discourse of Black Atlantic humanism that produced Vastey as an ardent defender of "the black man." Vastey's simultaneously statist and non-statist political writing may therefore require us to re-consider some of the subtle ways that later Afro-diasporic "poet-presidents" and "philosopher-kings" (Mazrui, "On Poet-Politicians" 13), can be linked to an earlier tradition of Black Atlantic humanism stemming from the early states of Haiti. Re-positioning Vastey within the fields of both Afro-diasporic and transatlantic studies, as well as hemispheric American studies, requires us to adopt a more nuanced (but not necessarily less unencumbered) view of Black Atlantic writing as at once populist and authoritative, radical and conservative. Coming to terms with the constraints of black sovereignty in a hostile world of chattel slavery in this way contains the capacity to transform our understanding of not only the origins but the meaning of modern humanism.

The goal here, then, is less to indelibly link Vastey's writings to his life than it is to thoroughly use both his writing and his life to analyze the relationship between national sovereignty and decolonization in the Caribbean. In so doing, my hope is that *Baron de Vastey and the Origins of Black Atlantic Humanism* will contribute to the necessary work begun by literary critics and historians of both early Caribbean and early Afro-diasporic print culture.

Nicole Aljoe, for example, contributes to the archive of slave narratives in her book, *Creole Testimonies* (2012), by focusing on little known orally transcribed dictations by enslaved peoples from the British-controlled Americas; Deborah Jenson provides her own literary history of Haitian independence by examining the Kreyòl writings of Haitian revolutionary leaders and free women of color in *Beyond the Slave Narrative* (2011); Faith Smith's timeless *Creole Recitations* (2002), analyzes the life of the nineteenth-century Trinidadian linguist John Jacob Thomas (1841–1889) to probe the way that "newer Caribbean writers are connected to earlier generations of writers" (xii); Christopher Hager's *Word by Word* (2013) expands our definition of the slave narrative by considering the connection between semi-literacy and slave emancipation in the antebellum U.S.; in their edited collection, *Biography and the Black Atlantic* (2014), Lindsay and Sweet have urged us to "approach[…] the Black Atlantic through the lens of life stories," paying attention to the way that life writing can "move readers' emotions by helping them to imagine being someone else" (2); and the contributors to Laurent Dubois and Julius Scott's *Origins of the Black Atlantic* (2010) call attention to the multiple rather than stable foundations of Black Atlantic history, while the editors urge us to be attentive to the "perspectives, daily lives, hopes and especially the political ideas of the enslaved who played such a central role in the making of the Atlantic World" (2).

In addition, the essays in Lara Cohen and Jordan Stein's collection, *Early African American Print Culture*, "showcase the variety of discoveries scholars might make when they ask what early African American literature looks like when read with an attention to its material conditions, and what print culture looks like when it turns its attention to African American archives" (4); and most recently, David Kazanjian's *The Brink of Freedom* (2016) uses a form of connected histories to bring to light linkages between the writings of "black settler colonists in Liberia" and "Mayan rebels in the Yucatan" (5).

Weaving Vastey into these histories of emerging Black Atlantic voices can only enrich our knowledge of the personal and political lives of Black Atlantic actors and demonstrate the Haitian state's compelling role in exposing the horrors of an Atlantic world-system that depended upon degrading *black people*.

A Word About the Words Black and Humanism

My usage of the term black as an adjective describes the humanist philosophies emanating from the Atlantic World and their connection to the "black positivist" discourse introduced by Vastey, which would later be formally written into hemispheric American intellectual history by the Haitian ethnologist Anténor Firmin. I use the term "positivist" precisely in the sense offered by Firmin in his *De L'Égalité des races humaines: anthropologie positive* (1885). Firmin referred to his research as a "positivist anthropology" because it challenged the "doctrine of inequality" put forth by philosophers and scientific materialists.[27] Firmin argued that teaching the world about racial justice may have been the cosmological destiny of Haitians when he wrote that Haiti's greatest act of participation in "the flourishing of progress, will be, above all, to develop a sense of justice with more force, and at the same time, more generosity" than the Europeans (655). Firmin continued by proclaiming:

---

[27] For a more in-depth explanation and reading of Firmin's notion of black positivism, see Bernasconi (2008).

the more that we have suffered, the more that we are prepared to understand and practice justice. And really, we do not even know how wonderful will appear before the eyes of the philosopher and the thinker this family of men emerging from the most profound intellectual and moral misery, having been brought up under the influence of hardened prejudices; but having engendered, in any case, a flower of virtue made of courageous strength and ineffable kindness, two qualities that tend at the same time towards promoting and tempering justice. (656)

The fact that blackness could be a signifier of humanity and justice rather than inhumanity and savagery recalls Manthia Diawara's astute commentary about the contributions of black people and their thought to modern humanism:

> For people of African descent, blackness is ... a way of being human in the West or in areas under Western domination. It is a compelling performance against the logic of slavery and colonialism by people whose destinies have been inextricably linked to the advancement of the West, and who have therefore to learn the expressive techniques of modernity: writing, music, Christianity, and industrialization in order to become uncolonizable. They have to recuperate the category black from the pathological space reserved for it in the discourse of whiteness, and reinvest it with attributes valorized in modern humanism.[28]

My understanding of the "modern humanism" sparked and encouraged by eighteenth- and nineteenth-century anti-slavery writers is, therefore, not derived from eighteenth-century *philosophes*, whose belief in probing the meanings of humanity extended only to white people. Rather, my sense of the meaning of the word "humanism" is derived primarily from Black Atlantic writers of the twentieth century who used the term.

Much like Baron de Vastey in *Le Système colonial dévoilé*, in his own *Discourse on Colonialism* (1955), Aimé Césaire describes colonization as an outgrowth of a disastrous Enlightenment philosophy that sought more to know in order to dominate the Other rather than to feel in order to have compassion and tolerance for difference. Césaire writes, "no, in the scales of knowledge all the museums in the world will never weigh so much as one spark of human sympathy" (72). This observation led Césaire to the conclusion that "at the very time when it most often

---

[28] http://www.blackculturalstudies.net/m_diawara/callaloo.html.

mouths the word, the West has never been further from being able to live a true humanism—a humanism made to measure the world" (73). Césaire hinted toward an outline of this presumably better humanism when he finished the *Discourse* by suggesting that what the world truly needed "in Africa, in the South Sea islands, in Madagascar (that is, at the gates of South Africa), in the West Indies (that is, at the gates of America)," rather than neo-imperialism, was "a new policy founded on respect for peoples and cultures" (Césaire 61). Césaire's gesture toward a different form of humanism buttressed by a pluralistic national policy founded on "respect" for the indigenous rather than upheld by colonial policies founded on the death of the colonized was one less tied to Enlightenment knowledge and more attentive to subjectivity and affect.

In *Black Skin, White Masks*, Fanon took on racism in service of a similar affective deconstruction of colonial discourse. In a combination of poetry and prose, Fanon outlined how in his estimation combatting racism depended not only upon appealing to human *feelings*, but depended upon a principled faith in the inherent goodness of humankind to want to lessen the suffering of others. He wrote that he was working, therefore:

Towards a new humanism...
Understanding among men...
Our colored brothers...
Mankind, I believe in you...
Race prejudice...
To understand and to love...

From all sides dozens and hundreds of pages assail me and try to impose their wills on me. But a single line would be enough. Supply a single answer and the color problem would be stripped of all its importance. (9–10)

Still, even with these explanations, a precise definition of this "new humanism," as equally as a "humanism made to measure the world" is hard to clarify, principally because of the ambiguity involved in the nouns we have to describe what a true humanism might entail: respect, understanding, love, belief. Similarly, for some, it may be difficult to determine whether or not Vastey as an arm of the Haitian state (and therefore of inevitable state violence) should be considered a humanist because it remains an open question as to whether a depoliticized and decontextualized humanism can exist. The humbling experience of trying to know

Vastey, nevertheless, has taught me to embrace what I cannot understand, as much as what I can, as well as to trust the way Vastey's writing might make us feel newly about the contributions of people of color to modern philosophical thought. I hope I am following in the wake of Édouard Glissant, then, when he argues that "exalting the right to opacity, another form of humanism, is to renounce the idea of bringing back truths measured only by a sense of transparency, which is my own, and which I would impose" (*Philosophie* 69).

Since there is little that can be known definitively about the feelings of any author at the moment of writing, my method here aims more toward the documentary and often journalistic style of the literary historian rather than the theoretical and uniquely argumentative fashion of the literary critic. By placing forward evidence about Vastey's life and the myriad readings of his works performed throughout the nineteenth- and twentieth centuries, my goal is to encourage students and scholars alike to become similarly fascinated by the contributions of this particular Haitian author to the discourse of Black Atlantic humanism. The hope is, at the very least, to cultivate acceptance of Vastey's limitations as a writer and a human being (something we all deserve), but also to move us towards a simultaneous embrace of Vastey's talents as a thinker and a politician.

It is precisely because Vastey is no longer well-known outside the halls of academia that in this book I want to bring his voice to the readers' attention. I have, therefore, quoted Vastey and his interlocutors at length throughout these chapters. Vastey's unique rhetoric of argumentation fascinated and infuriated those who engaged with his works in the nineteenth century, and I hope that twenty-first century readers find a similar sense of challenging delight in reading the words of one of the first Black Atlantic philosophers.

This is the story of Baron de Vastey and the many people who have used and learned from his writings, as well as those who criticized them. It reflects the tortured tale of Vastey's passion to produce black people as subjects rather than objects, as speakers for themselves rather than as people spoken for. It is also the tale of the many journalists, abolitionists, politicians, playwrights, and poets who engaged with his works for their own purposes.

In the end, although Vastey and his allied readers' quests to prove the humanity of black people will likely be considered outmoded by many twenty-first-century readers (particularly, the desire of these authors to use literacy as the principal sign of humanity), in many respects, such a discourse has never been more timely and necessary. We live in an era when we must still proclaim, at the cost of human lives, the essential worthiness of African Americans, as did U.S. Black Lives Matter activist Sandra Bland before she mysteriously died in a Waller County, Texas jail on 13 July 2015 after being arrested in the course of a routine traffic stop.

If the Black Atlantic humanists of the twentieth-century *négritude* movement left themselves open to charges of Afro-centricity (Gilroy, *Black Atlantic* 190), today's proponents have been labeled by white supremacists as themselves racist. Former New York mayor, Rudy Giuliani, appearing on CBS's *Face the Nation* on 23 September 2014, described the Black Lives Matter movement, for example, as "inherently racist," calling it also "anti-American" (Chan 10 July 2016).[29] The Black Lives Matter Movement, a contemporary iteration or extension of Black Atlantic humanism, is only "anti-American" if the word American itself can be equated with white supremacy. Black Atlantic humanists did not argue for the supremacy of any particular racial, ethnic, or national group. Instead, they sought to promote racial, ethnic, and national equality, even if by doing so they often reified the idea that race, ethnicity, and nationality are useful categories of human organization. A writer like Baron de Vastey fought against ideas of white supremacy for his entire adult life, and it is my hope this book can play a small part in contributing to the legacy of Black Atlantic humanism that he and other writers like him charted before us.

Charlottesville, USA   Marlene L. Daut

---

[29] http://time.com/4400259/rudy-giuliani-black-lives-matter/.

CHAPTER 1

Introduction: Baron de Vastey in Haitian (Revolutionary) Context

Tout le monde crie contre la révolution, et tout le monde en a profité.
—Baron de Vastey, *Réflexions politiques*

One of Baron de Vastey's major goals was to contest the racist assumptions of western philosophical discourses that rendered Africans and Afro-diasporans as at once people without history and as people who had never contributed to history. Vastey believed that this kind of European "Enlightenment" needed to be countered by Haitian writers not only because of the general support for slavery and colonialism embedded within early modern texts (see, Duchet, *Anthropologie* 138–139; Reinhardt 24–28, 39; Miller, *The French Atlantic* 73), but also because of the generally racist ideas produced about Haiti in nineteenth-century attempts to write the country's early history. Vastey wrote,

> What Haiti needs is a general history written by someone native to the country; the majority of historians who have tried it have been Europeans who concerned themselves primarily with the part of our history that involves them; and when they were led, by the subject at hand, to speak of the natives, they did so with that spirit of prejudice and bias that they never seem to be able to abandon. [...]

(*Essai* 1)

© The Author(s) 2017
M.L. Daut, *Baron de Vastey and the Origins of Black Atlantic Humanism*,
The New Urban Atlantic, DOI 10.1057/978-1-137-47067-6_1

The history of the Haitian Revolution had not yet been faithfully told, in Vastey's estimation, because European writers had "enveloped the truth" in "the darkness of lies" (*Essai* 2). Living in an age of slavery, however, Vastey hardly found joy in refuting tales of African savagery or revising inaccurate descriptions of Haitian history: "if I am experiencing in this moment any deep regret," Vastey wrote, "it is because I have been reduced to using my pen in order to redress this bloody outrage, and I have not been able to find any other way that would be better than words to convince [Europeans] that our kind is not inferior [to theirs]" (*RM* 5).

Vastey's comments demonstrate that Black Atlantic humanism has perhaps always been "vindicationist," to a certain extent, to use David Scott's term. Scott defines "vindicationism" as the "practice of providing evidence to refute a disagreeable or incorrect claim and a practice of reclamation, and, indeed, of redemption of what has been denied" (Scott 83, italics in the original). The purpose of this book is precisely to explore the way that the vindicationism evident in Vastey's writing links him to a larger Black Atlantic humanistic discourse that continues to this day. In many ways, Paul Gilroy's struggle to force recognition of black people as thinkers by showing them to have been indelible actors in western history marks a continuation of the strategies produced by earlier Black Atlantic writers like Baron de Vastey: "The struggle to have blacks perceived as agents," Gilroy writes, "as people with cognitive capacities and even with an intellectual history—attributes denied by modern racism—that is for me the primary reason for writing this book" (6).

As the most publicly visible and outspoken member of Christophe's administration, Vastey's particular quest of vindication can be linked to both dismantling the theories of race that became popular during the European Enlightenment, and the theories of colonialism developed by early nineteenth-century French ex-colonists aimed at destroying the sovereignty of Haiti and restoring colonial rule. Vastey's writing shows, in fact, that anti-black Enlightenment discourse was wholly linked not only to pro-colonial arguments, but to early nineteenth-century external aggression against the newly formed state(s) of Haiti. This aggression was both material and theoretical.

Vastey directly linked European theories about the degradations of blackness to the material practices of slavery and colonialism. "Posterity will never believe that in an age of Enlightenment, like ours," he lamented, "men who call themselves savants, philosophers, would have wanted to turn other men into animals solely in order to conserve their atrocious privilege of being able to oppress another part of humankind" (*Le Système* 30).[1] Vastey used vindicationism, then, to deconstruct such writing not simply because the claims were personally hurtful to him (he once wrote, "having been given life by an African woman, I very much identify with being African" [*RM* 31]), but because some French ex-colonists were using theories of black racial inferiority to justify their continued desires and attempts to re-conquer France's lost colony (see p. 165 of this monograph). With respect to the ex-colonist Mazères's claim that black Africans were uglier and therefore less intelligent than white Europeans, Vastey responded by pointing out that "the same prejudice exists among black people with respect to white people":

> They believe themselves to be more beautiful and more favored by nature; this belief is strengthened by frequent examples that they have before their eyes. Europeans arrive in the tropics in vigor and great health, with rosy skin, and at the end of two or three-months residence, they fall into the most deplorable state of heath. The white skin that was once their pride, becomes pallid, dirty, and spotted, the whiteness of their eyes cannot support the rays of our sun [....] the white man becomes only in [the natives'] eyes, then, an ambulant specter, disgraced by nature, who cannot even stand the influence of their climate, nor thrive in their beautiful country. (*RM* 21)

Vastey concluded that Mazères's claim that "the animal with the most beautiful form [...], is ordinarily inclined to be more kind and generous, stronger, and more intelligent" (qtd. in Vastey, *RM* 17) was a part of a compendium of statements used solely to "justify [Mazère's] theory of slavery" and "in order to perpetuate the abominable colonial system" (*RM* 26, 31).

The idea that the abolition of slavery and the dismantling of the colonial system in Haiti was good not only for Africans but for all of

---

[1] In his 1787 *Thoughts and Sentiments on the Evil and Wicked Traffic of the Human Species*, Cugoano, whose work Vastey would have known about due to his familiarity with the Abbé Grégoire's *De la littérature des nègres*, had written something similar when he asked, "Is it not strange to think, that they who ought to be considered as the most learned and civilized people in the world, that they should carry on a traffic of the most barbarous cruelty and injustice, and that many think slavery, robbery and murder no crime?" (112).

humankind found some of its earliest expression in the writing of Baron
de Vastey. He argued that the goal of liberty through revolution had not
fully been achieved by the (U.S.) American War of Independence the
way that it had been in Haiti: "The independence of the United States
of America has been a source of goodness for Europe[…]; ours will contribute to the Happiness of the human race, because of its moral and
political consequences" (*RP* 15). Vastey argued that although the (U.S.)
American Revolution may have introduced Europe to a useful and previously unknown political philosophy and form of democractic governance for white people, the Haitian Revolution put into practice the moral
ideals of freedom and equality that underpinned such a democratic philosophy. The Haitian state had created both a philosophically and materially free political institution for people of color. Moreover, because the
Haitian Revolution led to the abolition of slavery for all people in the
territory, it was good for all humanity, having "thrust us into civilization
and enlightenment" (*RP* 25).

In his *Notes à M. le Baron de V.P. Malouet* (1814), Vastey went even
further with this strategy of deconstructive reversal when he argued
that the Haitians and the French had derived completely different lessons from their particular histories of Revolution. Speaking directly to his
French readers, Vastey wrote, "The revolution produced the same effect
for us that it did for you, but in the *inverse* sense; the revolution led you
to commit every crime; it taught you to violate everything sacred and
saintly among men [….] it made you commit aggressions and injustices
of which your ancestors could never even have conceived" (*Notes* 22).
Because Haitians were the only ones in the Age of Revolutions to derive
lessons about racial equality from their own history of revolution, it
was therefore, the Haitian Revolution and not the (U.S.) American or
French Revolutions, that proved the means of violence could justify
the ends of freedom, Vastey called this the "triumph of humanity"
(*Système* vi).

Vastey's most important insight on this account comes in his
Réflexions sur une lettre de Mazères (1816) when he suggests that it was
not Haiti that needed philanthropy, but that Haitians, as a truly free people, could instead provide "a base of support where the philanthropists
will be able to plant the powerful lever which will lift up the moral world
against the enemies of the human race" (*RM* 41). People who were pro-
slavery were not just the enemies of Africans and their enslaved descendants in the Americas, but enemies of the "human race." It was their

Anglo-European world, not the Haitian one, that needed to be uplifted by anti-slavery and anti-colonial activists.

Vastey's usage of deconstructive reversals and vindicationism to attack the philosophical foundations of slavery, colonialism, and racism continued a tradition of pamphleteering evident in French Saint-Domingue on the eve of the Revolution. Although these early Haitian texts, produced largely by free people of color in revolutionary Saint-Domingue were written and published before formal Haitian independence, they contributed to the later development of anti-slavery writing by Vastey and other official members of the Haitian state.

The rationale for designating writing from revolutionary Saint-Domingue as part of early Haitian intellectual history is partially because of the similarity in form that characterizes the writing and also because this connection promotes an understanding of the link between the writing from people of color in Saint-Domingue and the pro-sovereignty defenses of early Haiti to be found in post-independence works. While the Haitian Revolution did result in rupture in many ways–for example, with the style of governance that had existed in the colony prior to independence—it did not immediately create a vastly different literary culture among people of color. In fact, eighteenth-century writers of color from French Saint-Domingue, including Julien Raimond, were among the first people of African descent to devote their political writing to systemically (as opposed to personally) tackling the problem of color prejudice. They were far more interested in changing the laws of the colony than in changing the minds of the people living there who exhibited prejudices towards them.

My periodization of early Haitian writing begins precisely with the late eighteenth-century pamphlets published by Julien Raimond (1744–1801) in French controlled Saint-Domingue.[2] Raimond was a wealthy free man of color from Aquin, who like Baron de Vastey, was the son of a French man who had emigrated to Saint-Domingue, and the daughter of free woman of color from a wealthy plantation owning family. Even though Raimond was perhaps the wealthiest person of color in the "southern peninsula" (Garrigus, *Before Haiti* 182), he made it is his mission to respond to the racist writing of French colonists such as M.L.E. Moreau de

---

[2]The first printing presses arrived in the colony in 1763, but the flourishing of writing produced by free people of color does not appear to have begun before the early 1790s.

Saint-Méry, himself a Martinican-born colonist, most famous for his two-volume *Description topographique, physique, civile, politique et historique de la partie française de l'isle Saint-Domingue* (1797). In his first pamphlet, *Réponses aux considérations de M. Moreau, dit Saint-Méry* (1791), Raimond wrote that his principle aim was to "destroy all the falsehoods of Mr. M—concerning the origins of the people of color, their population, their release from slavery" and to "prove the necessity of restoring to them their rights as active citizens" (2). Raimond also produced what is likely the first political memoir of the early days of the Revolution written by a person of color. His *Mémoire sur les causes des troubles et des désastres de la colonie de Saint-Domingue* (1793) was given first as a speech in defense of the *hommes de couleurs* in 1791. The principal goal of Raimond's *Mémoire* was to refute the popular notion that the Haitian revolutionists, both the enslaved and the free(d), were the perpetrators of violence and betrayal and the French planters and white colonists were the unfortunate victims.[3] In the *Mémoire* Raimond blamed "le préjugé de couleur" instituted by the white colonists, rather than the violence of enslaved Africans, as the principal cause of all the "political crises that this colony has experienced" (5).

In 1797 General André Rigaud published his own memoir of the Revolution entitled, *Mémoire du Général de Brigade, André Rigaud, en réfutation des écrits calomnieux contre les citoyens de couleur de Saint-Domingue*. Rigaud was a free-person of color who had been educated in Bordeaux. He participated in the (U.S.) American Revolutionary War, most notably at the battle of Savannah and soon became a general in the French army and eventually one of the principal Haitian revolutionists (L. Dubois, *Avengers* 121). In his *Mémoire*, Rigaud refutes the notion that the free people of color deserved the violence used against them because they were traitors who had refused to fight for France. "Are the men of color the ones who have betrayed their country?" Rigaud asked,

---

[3] Raimond also authored what may very well be the first work of critical race theory by a writer of African descent with his *Observations sur l'origine et les progrès* [sic] *du préjugé des colons blancs contre les citoyens de couleur* (1791). His other publications include, *Réflexions sur les véritables causes des troubles et des désastres de nos colonies, notamment sur ceux de Saint-Domingue; avec les moyens à employer pour préserver cette colonie d'une ruine totale* (1793); and *Lettres de J. Raimond, à ses frères les hommes de couleur. En comparaison des originaux de sa correspondance, avec les extraits perfides qu'en ont fait MM. Page et Bruelly, dans un libelle intitulé: Developpement des causes, des troubles, et des désastres des Colonies françaises* (1794).

"Have they invited enemies onto the territory of the republic? Without a doubt, no. On the contrary, they fought the enemies." (iii) Rigaud, like Raimond, sought to prove that the free people of color were willing to be loyal to France—"their country"—as long as they were treated on equal terms with the white colonists.

The political memoirs of Raimond and Rigaud anticipate and refute the first person writings of the colonist Gros who penned a quasi-captivity narrative entitled, *Isle de Saint-Domingue, province du Nord. Précis historique; qui expose dans le plus grand jour les manœuvres contre révolutionnaires employées contre St. Domingue; qui désigne et fait connoître les principaux Agents de tous les massacres, incendies, vols et dévastations qui s'y sont commis* (1793). Gros's pamphlet, along with J.P. Garran de Coulon's lengthy report on the Saint-Domingue revolts entitled, *Rapport sur les troubles de Saint-Domingue* (1797), quickly became the authoritative sources on the first two years of the insurrection (Popkin 515). Both works, however, blamed the free people of color and enslaved Africans for the cruelty of the Revolution.[4] Rigaud and Raimond's writings, on the contrary, sought to vindicate free people of color, in particular, from the notion that they were merely insurgents who chose to collude with the enslaved in order to obtain revenge (rather than equality under the law) against the French colonists.

The claim that the free people of color were merely ungrateful and naturally vindictive was incredibly widespread among the French colonists of Saint-Domingue in the late eighteenth-century. In 1792, the governor general of Saint-Domingue, Philibert François-Rouxel de Blanchelande, wrote of the free people of color in the colonial journal, *La Feuille du Jour:*

> Up until this point, I have used gentle and moderate tactics to remind you of your duty; your conduct proves that I have presumed too much of you [...] Instead of embracing those who once made all of France esteem you, and the entire colony cherish you; What avenue have you taken? That of true scoundrels, who dare everything, because they believe they have everything to gain. (1–2)

---

[4]The colonist Gros, for example, who had been taken as a prisoner by Jeannot, claimed that "evidently...the slaves have been excited to revolt by *the mulattoes*" (qtd. in Ardouin 1: 50).

Blanchelande refers here and throughout his article to the participation of the free people of color in various uprisings in the colony, admonishing them for "betraying" France in supposedly siding with the enslaved. Blanchelande's statement also attempts to induce feelings of guilt on their part by suggesting that France had always "cherished" and "esteemed" them and, as a result, it was their "duty" to remain loyal.

Blanchelande's public admonishment of the free people of color as traitors to the French and responsible for the revolt of the enslaved represents the government's official position towards them, and also reflects widespread public opinion in France, the United States, and the rest of the Americas. "Many of the accounts of the event [the insurrection of 1791] that were soon produced and disseminated throughout the Americas and Europe," Laurent Dubois writes, "presented tales of savage and unthinkable atrocities committed by the slaves" (Dubois, *Avengers* 110); while Jeremy Popkin tells us, "Descriptions of the insurrection in the local press followed a rigid ideological formula [...] the white colonial orthodoxy emphasized the cruelty and destructiveness of the insurgents whose actions were categorized as crimes against the paternal plantation owners" (Popkin 514). Gordon S. Brown adds that U.S. journalists, too, "almost always expressed sympathy for the colonists and horror at the revolt" (51).

Free people of color in St. Domingue had at least a handful of newspapers after 1789 through which they could respond to the kinds of accusations made by Blanchelande and the other royalists against them (Desquiron 24–25).[5] Raimond, whom Hénock Trouillot refers to as "the head of the free people of color," often acted as a "spokesperson," particularly in the newspaper *Le Patriote français*, when Raimond wrote: "They live like strangers in their own country [...] they are treated as slaves even in the midst of their supposed liberty" (qtd. in H. Trouillot 88). Raimond's comment was designed to create a *rapprochement* between the situation of the *hommes de couleur*, free in name only according to him, and enslaved peoples by suggesting that the former had been subjected to conditions that rendered them equal in status to the latter.

---

[5] For a complete list of these publication see, also Justin Emmanuel Castera, *Brèf coup d'oeil sur les origines de la presse haïtienne* (1986).

We should note that the material gulf between the lives of free people of color and enslaved Africans was often quite large, even if the affective experience of color prejudice was sometimes shared. Slavery was, nevertheless, a powerful and ambiguous metaphor for a variety of non-desirable social conditions in the eighteenth and nineteenth-centuries.[6] And free people of color, even those who had once been enslaved, often equated color prejudice with "but another form of slavery itself," to use the former fugitive slave and U.S. abolitionist William Wells Brown's words (*Clotel* 171). This comparison, in fact, became an effective argumentative strategy in the mid-nineteenth-century transatlantic abolitionist movement, but since such a metaphor was used by writers who had been enslaved and then free(d) like Brown, we cannot entirely dismiss the metaphor when it appears in black writing as purely rhetorical. Wells Brown wrote about the affective register of color prejudice as operating so as to make it worse than the material register of slavery when he said that the free people of color of the U.S. "*felt* their degradation even more keenly than the bond slaves" (*The Black Man* 94, *italics mine*). In *The Condition, Elevation, Emigration, and Destiny of the Colored People of the United States* (1852), Martin Delany, a U.S. free man of color (who was the son of an enslaved man and a free woman of color), expressed similar sentiments with respect to the passage of the Fugitive Slave Law in the United States: "We are slaves in the midst of freedom, waiting patiently and unconcernedly—indifferently, and stupidly, for masters to come and lay claim to us, trusting to their generosity, whether or not they will own us and carry us into endless bondage. The slave is more secure than we; he knows who holds the heel upon his bosom—we know not the wretch who may grasp us by the throat" (n.p.).

---

[6] In the *Social Contract* Rousseau famously refers not to chattel slavery, but to a figurative slavery that "for Rousseau as for Montesquieu" was a "metaphor for the debased condition of man in society *in general*, that is to say in Europe" (Miller 69, italics in original). And as Elizabeth Colwill has written:

"French and colonial commentators, journalists, deputies, missionaries and pamphleteers defined civilization—and by extension the new citizenry—against an astonishing parade of transgressive bodies. In political pamphlets, 'seductive' financiers, 'immodest' clerics, 'infamous courtesans', 'vile prostitutes', unnatural nuns, sinful celibates, and lusty 'nègres' illustrated the state of savagery produced by centuries of real and metaphorical slavery" (Colwill 200).

Like Raimond before him and Wells Brown and Delany after him, Vastey, too, made a more than rhetorical case that racism represented an extension of slavery and he devoted an entire section of *Le Système colonial dévoilé* (1814) to the chimera of freedom enjoyed by the free people of color:

> we are now going to sketch the sad situation of those who one called, in these times of horror, impudently, the freed. We will not make any distinction between these so-called free people [and the slaves], because even if they didn't have distinct masters, the *white* public was their master, and by all counts, they suffered the same humiliations and the same infamies that the slaves did; we will consider them as such. (74)

These supposedly free people in French-claimed Saint-Domingue certainly had reason for complaint. In 1769 a new law forbade these men from serving as ranked officers in the military and in March of 1780 Saint-Domingue's acting governor, Reynaud de Villevert, ordered the creation of the *Chasseurs Royaux*, a militia based on forced conscription of all men of color between the ages of 15 and 16 or who could not present proper manumission papers (Garrigus, ibid., 211). In *Le Système colonial devoilé*, Vastey supported his claim about the "deplorable" treatment of the free people of color by offering the French government's own "Règlement des Administrateurs concernant les Gens de Couleur Libres" of June 24, 1773. The cited decree forbade free people of color from using the names of their white fathers, from dressing like whites (including wearing shoes in some instances), and from occupying any public function or profession such as priest, schoolteacher, surgeon, pharmacist, or doctor (76–77). Vastey also wrote that free people of color were "obliged to undertake forced labor [*corvées*] of all types" and that French colonial laws made it legally possible for a white person to perpetrate a crime against a free person of color without any real punishment. These new laws, as reactions to the ascension to economic power of many wealthy free people of color in the middle part of the eighteenth century, had the effect of sanctioning color prejudice and of denying the rights of citizenship that Louis XIV's 1685 *Code Noir* had, at least in theory, indicated that all free people should enjoy.

These new colonial laws also had the effect of causing many free people of color, including Vastey and Raimond, to link the prejudices directed at them to the continuation of slavery. Rather than merely projecting a sense of false equivalency between the prejudices experienced by free people of color and the daily oppressions and degradations of slavery, the works of Vastey and Raimond demonstrate how they eventually became aware of the powerful connection between the dehumanization of enslaved peoples and the theories of African inhumanity that supported racism against all people of color in the colony.

In his *À Mes Concitoyens* (1815), Vastey explained in some detail the effect that developing a consciousness about race had on his own life when he describes why, after fighting against the Haitian revolutionists, he suddenly joined them in 1803. In response to Leclerc and Rochambeau's genocidal tactics instructing French soldiers to drown or otherwise kill the entire population of color in Saint-Domingue (Ribbe 2005), Vastey who had been previously fighting on the side of France, wrote:

> in order to avoid the death that our executioners were preparing for me, I fled into the woods to look for my salvation. Did I not find within the bosom of my maternal roots, fathers, mothers, brothers, friends who greeted me with transports of joy and the most pure friendship? Could I forget this moment where I threw myself into the arms of my brothers that I had unfortunately combated! What remorse did I not feel in their midst when instead of receiving the reproaches that I believed I deserved, forgetting my ingratitude or rather my error, they welcomed me among them with a truly paternal tenderness! From that moment forward I uttered an oath never to separate my cause from that of my fellow men, and I will perish in these sentiments. (*Concitoyens* 18)

The relationship of color prejudice to black death, a relationship that ultimately caused this son of a former slave owner, Vastey, to join the side of Dessalines's *armée indigène*, illustrates a fundamental clash between one's economic interests in slavery and a personal belief in the rights of all people to live with dignity. This clash would ultimately convince Raimond, Rigaud, and Vastey, all from slave-owning families of color, to turn their backs on their properties and join the Revolution.[7]

---

[7] This appears to have also been the case with Vincent Ogé who led an ambiguous, but failed revolt of the free people of color in October 1790, resulting in his execution. I wrote at length about the conflict between Ogé's attempt to at first preserve his property interests in slavery and achieve equal rights for free men of color in *Tropics of Haiti* (557–559).

It was not only free-born people of color in Saint-Domingue who had the experience of being a part of the plantation and slave-owning class while also being subject to the degrading reality of color prejudice. Toussaint Louverture, who lived in slavery on the Bréda plantation until he became part of the *anciens libres* in 1776 at age 33, also owned slaves (Bell 71–73). This likely accounts for his focus on the affective experience of color prejudice in his memoirs rather than the material conditions under which he had both been enslaved and had enslaved others.

The *Mémoires du général Toussaint-Louverture, écrits par lui-même*, were first published in a unified form by the Haitian historian Joseph Saint-Rémy in 1853.[8] Within the pages of his *Mémoires*, Louverture only directly refers to his own enslavement once (90), focusing instead on painting himself as the loyal, but unjustly dishonored son of "la mère-patrie" (88), who had been betrayed by France because of his "color." Writing after having been kidnapped and forcibly taken to France during the Leclerc expedition, Louverture accused General Leclerc of behaving "with methods which have never been used even with respect to the greatest criminals." "Without a doubt I owe this treatment to my color," Louverture wrote, "but my color...my color, has it ever prevented me from serving my country [*ma patrie*] with diligence and devotion? The color of my skin, does it compromise my honor and my bravery?" (85). Louverture admonished the French government, and Bonaparte in particular, for not fairly resolving the dispute between he (Louverture) and Leclerc, who led the ill-fated expedition to restore slavery to French Saint-Domingue. Louverture asked, "If two children are fighting one another, does not their mother or their father have a duty to prevent them from doing so, to find out which one of them is the aggressor, and punish him or punish them both in the case that they are both wrong?" (88). Instead of censuring what he believed to be Leclerc's rather than Bonaparte's attempt to restore slavery, Louverture claimed that he, himself, was assumed to be the guilty party and was subsequently imprisoned without a trial "in a dungeon," while "General Leclerc enjoys his liberty" (89).

---

[8] I refer here and throughout this monograph to the 1853 version established by Joseph Saint-Rémy because that is the version with which nineteenth-century readers would have been familiar. For more on the literary history of his document, see, Desormeaux's introduction to the *Mémoires*, p. 19.

One feature that the pre-independence political memoirs of Rigaud, Raimond, and Louverture share with the post-independence Haitian writing of Vastey is what Daniel Desormeaux has referred to as, "the well-known historical dialectic of inserting individual protest into the transmission of history as a principle of truth" ("The First of the Black Memorialists" 134). Louverture claimed that his memoirs would allow him to finally reveal the true nature of his conduct towards France when he wrote, "At last, I will tell the truth, even if it will be used against me" (29). He further stated that he was penning his memoirs solely to counter the fact that, in his words, "the most atrocious of lies have been spread about me" (86). Rigaud, for his part, believed that his memoir might provide evidence against the French colonists, "Maybe even this Memoir," Rigaud wrote, "traced by the hand of truth, will serve to expose someone" (iv). While Raimond said of his purpose, "We are going to try to paint, without passion, without bile, without hatred, and above all, without partiality, all the facts" (*Mémoire* 6). These statements underscore the vindicationist elements of political writing in revolutionary Saint-Domingue and highlight the limitations of the political memoir as a genre of historical discourse.

In the eyes of many scholars, the amorphous nature of the political memoir marks its distinction from "professional historiography" and renders it unrelated to formal historical work (Egerton, *Political Memoir* 349). This is because the political memoir is ordinarily based not on extensive archival resources but rather on the writer's personal involvement in the political events being described. George Egerton defines it as a "polygenre" not easily defined precisely because of its polymorphous nature. "The parameters marking political memoir off from other genres or types of writing," Egerton writes, "often appear indistinct as it appropriates autobiography, biography, diary, history, political science, journalism, and pamphleteering, to name but its nearest literary literary neighbors" (223).

Political memoirs are narrated not from the supposedly healthy distance of historical objectivity but rather from the intimacy that comes from living through the experience of the events being narrated themselves. These lived-experiences become the evidence that buttress an author's claims to writing the *truth* in the vein of what Joan Scott has called "the evidence of experience" (Scott 382). Scott writes that modern historiography often opposes these forms of life writing because this makes it easier to dismiss the experiences of *difference* that such personally sourced narratives offer. It is exactly the Other's "appeal to experience as incontestable evidence," Scott argues, "that weakens the critical thrust of histories of difference" (382). Her logic helps to explain the critical hesitancy towards using political memoirs as secondary, rather than primary sources.

A principal example of how early Haitian political memoirists used their status as political insiders to produce counter-histories of the Revolution comes to us from Louis-Félix Boisrond-Tonnerre, Dessalines's most important secretary. In his *Mémoire pour servir à l'histoire d'Haïti*, published immediately following independence in 1804, the infamous secretary of Jean-Jacques Dessalines and a co-author of the Acte de L'Indépendance, attempted to establish a version of Haitian history that could be considered official. To urge belief in his account of the events Boisrond-Tonnerre wrote, "I must state, first of all, that there is not a single fact, a single crime, or a single action mentioned in this work that does not carry with it the mark of the utmost veracity" (13). Boisrond-Tonnerre's political memoir attempts to undermine dominant accounts of the Haitian Revolution that voiced prejudices against people of color. He combats earlier colonial histories of the Revolution by creating his own narrative, one where Dessalines emerges as a hero. Boisrond-Tonnere's memoir represented a determined and deliberate attempt to re-shape the vision of a past that was already becoming distorted for the purposes of propaganda and silenced because of its damning implications for the plantation economies of the New World.

In Boisrond-Tonnerre's eyes, producing a history of Haiti written by a Haitian (even one like him who had never been enslaved) would not simply revise earlier narratives, but also prove that the nation-state of Haiti existed independently and should be viewed as a powerful country capable of influencing the foreign policies of other nations. In the passage below, Boisrond-Tonnerre speaks of the best way to persuade the nations of the world that it is the French who are the criminals and the Haitian people the victims:

> And what, said I to myself a thousand times before undertaking this work, this repertory of French crimes, what being could add more veracity to the truths that I am recounting? What sensitive soul, especially after having lived during the storm of the revolution, will believe that the French had improved upon their crimes in the most beautiful as in the most unfortunate of their overseas possessions? How to persuade the nations of the

world that the French contagion had not yet won, that a tyrant who had usurped the throne of the master, whose power was founded only upon liberty and equality, who even set himself up as the restorer of civilization and religion, had decreed, in cold blood, the massacre of a million men, who only wanted liberty and equality themselves; that they will defend against the entire universe? (15)

By alluding to Bonaparte's duplicitous attempt to use Leclerc to restore slavery to Saint-Domingue, Boisrond-Tonnerre implicitly asks the nations of the world to believe his account of the events on the strength of his personal testimony, which was based on his experiences as a member of Dessalines's inner circle. Boisrond-Tonnerre suggested furthermore that the truth of these experiences would shine through in the very style of his unadorned prose, "if the colors are missing from my painting, it is because they are too strong for my feeble pen" (*Mémoire* 14). This kind of apology will be recognizable to anyone familiar with the (U.S.) African American slave narrative where such publicly performed self-consciousness was practically a publication requirement.

The political memoirs of early Haiti do not simply illustrate critical counter-histories from below that could oppose the more dominant histories from above written by white European authors. They also demonstrate an adaptive hermeneutic. Many early black writers had been excluded from pursuing the kind of formal education that their European interlocutors had received and they also lacked access to many formal state documents. Writing from the cold, bare cell of a dungeon in the Fort de Joux of the Jura Mountains, Louverture was particularly worried that uneven access to corroborating documents might affect his ability to vindicate himself and therefore to disseminate the truth about his political relationship to the French state. He said, referring to his French captors:

They took all of my papers away from me in order to attribute to me crimes that I had not committed; but I have nothing to fear; this correspondence will suffice as my justification. They sent me to France stark naked; they took all of my belongings and my papers; they spread the most atrocious lies with respect to me. Is this not to cut a person's legs and then order him to walk? Is it not to cut out his tongue and then tell him to speak? Is it not to bury a man alive? (86)

That his own ardency and personal protest could match and even rival the official (French) archive demonstrates Louverture's principled faith in the idea that his affect alone could reveal the genuine nature of his conduct and produce the kind of outrage associated with the exceptional violence described in many Anglophone slave narratives.

In stark contrast to Anglophone slave narratives, which often feature graphically detailed scenes of brutal punishment of enslaved peoples at the hands of enslavers, early Haitian political memoirs are ordinarily scant on personal details and tell us little about the daily lives of people of color in the colony. Yet these Haitian political memoirs are, nonetheless, a form of life-writing as crucial to our understanding of attempts to make black lives matter in the eighteenth and nineteenth-centuries as those texts we more traditionally understand to be slave narratives. Examining them as a distinctive part of the world of Black Atlantic biography, however, requires unlearning much of what we think we know about the emergence of Afro-diasporic writing in the eighteenth and nineteenth centuries.[9]

In *Beyond the Slave Narrative* (2012), Deborah Jenson has argued that the great focus on Anglophone black writing in slavery studies has led to an under-nuanced analysis not only of the relationship between slavery and sovereignty in the Age of Revolutions, but of the connection between literary form and personal emancipation. "The privileging of a single form of literary testimony, in one language," Jenson observes, "disrupts our view of a longer continuum of multilingual New World African diaspo-ran expression and discourages comparative study of the African diaspora across language traditions" (3). Jenson continues by making the case that "the French colonial and early postcolonial tradition by the slaves and for-mer slaves [of Saint-Domingue] offers particularly detailed accounts of *un-becoming* the legal property of another human being—and, unfortu-nately, *becoming* the national equivalent of brigands on the international scene..." (3). Jenson's argument is important because it invites us to read the personal into the political. Although the Haitian revolutionaries under study in her monograph—Louverture, Dessalines, and Christophe, in particular—did not write formal autobiographies detailing the events of their daily lives, we can still view their written correspondence and politi-cal proclamations as primary pieces of the unfolding of sovereign personal identities that we glimpse in many Anglophone slave narratives.

---

[9] Jeremy Popkin has written, for instance, that "no memoirs [were] written or dictated by ex-slaves from this period [the late eighteenth-century], or even from the more literature mulatto group" (Popkin 512). However, if we include the political memoirs of Raimond, Rigaud, and Louverture we have a few more sources.

Baron de Vastey's own political writing is connected to the earlier traditions of the slave narrative, including the revolutionary writings of Dessalines and Christophe, and the pamphlets and political memoirs of Rigaud, Raimond, and Louverture, not only because Vastey uses a format where the political becomes personal, but also because of his awareness of the aesthetic and politically uneven ground upon which he would compose his works. Vastey had read the Abbé Grégoire's 1808 *De la littérature des nègres*, which he quoted from in his own *Le Système colonial dévoilé* (13 ftn). Reading Grégoire's work would have meant that Vastey was familiar with the writings of not only Julien Raimond, but Wheatley, Equiano, Ignatius Sancho, and Ottabah Cugoano, all of whom Grégoire also cites (*De la littérature* 190). Vastey's reading of Grégoire is important because in *De la littérature des nègres* Grégoire mentioned Thomas Jefferson's famous statement that Wheatley's poetry was "below the dignity of criticism" (qtd. in Grégoire, *De la littérature* 262). Vastey, in turn, appeared to worry about the (in)comparable aesthetic grounds upon which a writer like Phillis Wheatley had been discounted, and upon which he sought to inscribe his version of Haitian history. He preemptively defended himself by warning, "my Haitian pen will, without a doubt, lack eloquence, but it will be truthful; my pictures will be without ornaments, but they will be striking [...]" (39). The putative absence of literary elements contributes to his claim to the truth and supports the argument that he has not embellished for the sake of painting a better picture. The purpose of political writing for him was to "enlighten" his "compatriots" about the disastrous effects of slavery and the slave trade, colonialism, and color prejudice upon human beings (Vastey, *Le Système* viii), not to render beautiful or more easily digestible certain facts or memories.

Black Atlantic studies may continue to be in need of a more generous sense of what both life writing and political writing entailed for writers of color—the enslaved, the formerly enslaved, and the never enslaved—in the early modern world. And what I hope to prove with this book is that the political and historical writings of Vastey, which at first glance appear wholly unlike the more novelistic genre of the slave narrative, are important to understanding other writing from African-descended peoples in the eighteenth and early nineteenth-centuries. It is my hope that bringing the life and works of Baron de Vastey to a wider audience will help us to gain a better sense of the capaciousness of early Black Atlantic writing so as to allow us to view nineteenth-century Haiti as connected to rather than isolated from modern political and philosophical thought.

*

Historicizing Vastey and Black Atlantic Humanism

Although the story of its Revolution needs no recitation here, the history of the early sovereign state(s) of Haiti is much less well-known and deserves a few words of explanation. The political inner workings of early Haiti are absolutely central to any understanding of Vastey's life and works.

After Dessalines formally declared the independence of Haiti on 1 January 1804, he became Governor-General of the island, which he had renamed Haiti after the indigenous name, *Ayiti* (see, Geggus, "The Naming of Haiti"). By 1805, Dessalines had declared himself an emperor and issued a new constitution. Among the most famous articles of the 1805 constitution are its laws forbidding foreign "white" property ownership (Article 12),[10] its mandate that all Haitians shall be considered "black," and its designation of all Haitians as brothers and sisters, whose father was the head of state (Article 14). Despite Dessalines's attempt to organize a unified state, factions appeared in his administration almost from the beginning and led to a conspiracy against him that resulted in his eventual assassination on 17 October 1806.

After Dessalines's murder, Haiti was divided into three separately run provinces in the control of three former generals of the Haitian Revolution: Henry Christophe rose to power in the north, Alexandre Pétion assumed governance of the south, and André Rigaud initially ruled in southwest Haiti until his death in 1811, after which time the provinces he controlled first came under the power of General Borgella, and later in 1812 fell to the jurisdiction of Pétion. In the meantime, Pétion had declared himself president and created a democratic republic,

---

[10]Article 12 is actually much more complicated than it might initially seem. For, Article 13 subsequently clarifies that the interdiction against "white" property ownership does not extend to "white" people already living in the empire, and in fact, Article 14 essentially outlawed the recognition of color difference, making it so that even "white" Haitians had to be considered "black" as well. The property exclusion therefore only applied to foreigners. To this day, the generic word for man in Haitian Kreyòl is *nèg*, derived from the French word *nègre*, and the word for foreigner is *blan*, derived from the French word *blanc*. Therefore, all Haitians had to be recognized as *black* and all foreigners as *white*, regardless of skin tone or phenotype.

modeled (at least, in theory) after that of the United States. By 1811, Christophe would convert his state to a constitutional, but hereditary monarchy. After the death of Pétion in the spring of 1818, Jean-Pierre Boyer, also a former general, became president of the southern republic. Christophe and Pétion, and later Christophe and Boyer, would spend their entire administrations staving off continuous threats from the French to retake its former colony, as well as internecine threats from one another.

Following years of civil war between the north and the south of Haiti, an intellectual class of writers closely tied to the administrations of their respective governments rose to prominence. Among these writers were Juste Chanlatte (the Comte de Rosiers), Baron Dupuy, and Baron de Vastey from the north, and Noël Colombel and Jules Solime Milscent from the south. The political and intellectual disagreements between these two governments and their respective intellectual elites sparked an entire discursive tradition all its own. Five of Vastey's early works are almost entirely devoted to attacking the government of Pétion and/ or Vastey's own intellectual adversaries from the south.[11] These works were, in great measure, devoted to trying to convince the citizens of the southern part of Haiti that they should tie their fates to the leadership of Henry Christophe. In order to urge this reunification, Vastey provided evidence that supported his claim that Pétion may have been open to restoring Haiti's status as a French colony. He also accused Pétion of secretly harboring his own prejudices against "blacks" and supporting their re-enslavement.

Writers from the South completely refuted Vastey's account of Pétion's relationship to France and denied wholeheartedly that their president held color prejudices or wanted to bring back slavery. Milscent and Colombel, in particular, countered these claims by suggesting that Christophe was a despotic ruler whose subjects constantly and continuously defected from his kingdom to join the southern republic.

---

[11] *Le Cri de la conscience* (1815); *Le Cri de la patrie* (1815); *À mes concitoyens!* (1815); *Réflexions adressées aux Haytiens de partie de l'ouest et du sud, sur l'horrible assassinat du Général Delvare, commis au Port-au-Prince, dans la nuit du 25 décembre, 1815, par les ordres de Pétion* (1816); and *Communication officielle de trois lettres de Catineau Laroche, ex-colon, agent de Pétion* (1816).

In the summer of 1819 King Christophe suffered from what was likely a stroke, which reportedly left him severely mentally impaired. At the same time, Christophe was also fighting opposition within his own government, and soon after, a rebellion broke out in St. Marc, resulting in an attempted coup. Perhaps still suffering from the lingering effects of his neurological problems or perhaps afraid of losing his throne, Christophe committed suicide in October 1820. Shortly thereafter, many of Christophe's most prominent cabinet members like Baron de Vastey, who had not defected to the side of Boyer (like Juste Chanlatte), were murdered. Boyer would subsequently reunite both the northern and southern regions of Haiti, as well as the eastern part previously controlled by Spain, into one state in 1822.

The royal offices held by Vastey during these political and discursive struggles are important. They highlight how deeply and personally anchored the Haitian baron was in postcolonial state governance precisely during the period in which he composed his most famous attacks on colonial power. From 1804 to 1811, under Dessalines and Christophe, respectively, Vastey was secretary to André Vernet, Haiti's Minister of Finance (Vastey 1819, 202ftn). He was then made a baron sometime after Christophe created the armorial of Haiti in 1811 and definitely before 26 December 1812 (Cheesman 12).

Two years later, according to the 1814 edition of the *Almanach royal d'Hayti*, Vastey had not only become one of the many "secretaries" of Christophe (12), in addition to being a member of the "privy council of the king" (29) but he was also the "chief clerk" (*greffier en chef*) of the Sovereign Court of Justice (*Cour Souveraine de Justice*) and one of the actors in Christophe's Théâtre Royale (126). According to the 1816 *Almanach*, Vastey had also become by that time the tutor of the "royal prince" (12) and had been promoted to the rank of knight on 28 October 1815 (29).

Vastey's upward mobility appeared to have continued. Aside from having assumed at some point between 1815 and 1816 the editorship of the official newspaper of Christophe's kingdom, *La Gazette royale d'Hayti*, an edict published in the *Gazette* on 28 December 1818 also lists Vastey as a member of the newly created *Chambre Royale d'Instruction Publique* (1).[12] The *Almanach* from 1820 adds that Vastey was one of the chancellors of the king and describes in great detail his new duties, which included "keeping the register of the records of birth, marriage, death, and all of the other *actes* of the members of the Royal Family" as well as "the safeguard and deposit of the archives of the Royal Family" (40).

If Christophe's government was fighting two wars, one on the home-front and one abroad, Vastey was engaged in both of these contests with his political writing. Despite holding no formal diplomatic title, many of his book-length treatises are laden with implicit attempts to convince not only France but the United States and England, that they must recognize Haitian independence. Vastey's writings are also characterized by a form of discourse analysis, whereby the baron deconstructs French colonial writing in an effort to show how it disingenuously purported to prove that "Africans" were not human solely "in order to turn the black man into a material thing" (*Le Système* 30). According to Vastey, furthermore, the French government's disavowal of Haitian independence was of a piece with broader philosophical attempts to dehumanize black people in service of preserving slavery in the other colonies of the Atlantic World and restoring both slavery and colonial status to Haiti. This is the argument that we find in Vastey's earliest publication, *Notes à M. le Baron V.P. de Malouet*, and in his *Réflexions sur une lettre de Mazères, ex-colon français,* [...] *sur les noirs et les blancs, la civilization de l'Afrique, le Royaume d'Hayti*, etc. (1816), as well as in his *Réflexions politiques sur quelques ouvrages et journaux français concernant Hayti* (1817).

Vastey can also be considered to be, along with Boisrond-Tonnerre and Juste Chanlatte, one of independent Haiti's first historians.[13] Vastey

---

[12] According to Karen Racine, "Christophe's state of the union address of 1 January 1816 specifically had identified public instruction as the state's 'prime duty' and declared that his administration was seeking learned professors from abroad to undertake the eduction of youth" (215). Subsequently, Christophe with the help of abolitionists like Thomas Clarkson, Prince Saunders, and Zachary Macaulay adopted Joseph Lancaster's "monitorial method of education which promised to educate large numbers of children quickly and inexpensively" by "[o]lder pupils who had mastered a certain amount of basic literacy" (Racine 217).

[13] In 1810 Juste Chanlatte published a work entitled, *Le Cri de la nature, ou, Hommage haytien au très-vénérable abbé H. Grégoire, auteur d'un ouvrage nouveau, intitulé De la littérature des Nègres, ou, Recherches sur leurs facultés individuelles, leurs qualités morales et leur littérature; suivies de notices sur la vie et les ouvrages des Nègres qui se sont distingués dans les sciences, les lettres et les arts.*

authored a short journalistic work called, *Relation de la fête de la Reine S.M. D'Hayti* (1816), and later he published a daunting history of Haiti, *Essai sur les causes de la Révolution et des guerres civiles d'Hayti* (1819). Although Vastey's *Essai* can be considered the first full-length Haitian history written by a Haitian, and his *Réflexions sur une lettre de Mazères* is part of the genesis of what we now call critical race theory, his most important contribution to modern humanism is undoubtedly *Le Système colonial dévoilé* (1814). *Le Système* is the text in which Vastey most clearly uses postcolonial reversals to upset the association of colonialism with European benevolence. It is also where Vastey's marriage of the personal with the political becomes most evident as he develops a new adaptive hermeneutic to address the absence of traditional first-person narratives of slavery that plague all French Atlantic slavery scholarship.[14]

Chapter 2 of *Baron de Vastey and the Origins of Black Atlantic Humanism*, "What's in Name?" begins precisely by dealing with the incompleteness and/or absence of the archive. My 2012 essay in *Research in African Literatures* entitled, "From Classical French Poet to Militant Haitian Statesman: The Early Years and Poetry of Baron de Vastey," questioned whether or not this Haitian statesman might have authored several dozen poems under the name and initials of "Pompée Valentin Vastey" in revolutionary France before joining the Haitian wars of independence. The article also included a discussion of Vastey's previously un-consulted baptismal certificate located in the Archives Nationales d'Outre-Mer in Aix-en-Provence, France. Based on the evidence available at the time of the 2012 article, I concluded that Jean-Louis Vastey (the name listed on the baptismal certificate), and Baron

---

[14] At this time, there are no known traditional first-person slave narratives from Saint-Domingue or from any of the other French colonies, (Miller 35; Reinhardt 5–7). What writing from enslaved Africans we do have exists in letters. While Deborah Jenson has found implicit literary value in these documents (see, *Beyond the Slave Narrative*), Christopher L. Miller has drawn a different conclusion in writing, "as compelling and moving as they are, [these letters] cannot compete with the comprehensive value of the slave narratives published in the United States in the nineteenth century" (36). It is not just the French Caribbean that has been perceived as a space devoid of first-person slave narratives. Aljoe has written, "To date, not a single self-written slave narrative has been discovered in the Caribbean. Every single West Indian narrative is a collaborative text, drawing on more than one voice" (14).

de Vastey (who is listed as the author on nearly all of Vastey's post-independence prose works), and Pompée Valentin (de) Vastey (the name that is assigned to Baron de Vastey's works in virtually all international library catalogues since 1839 and who signed the French poems), could be reasonably considered to be the same person. Since the time of my earlier article's publication, however, further research complicates this picture. In this chapter, consequently, I hypothesize how Baron de Vastey, whose given name was indeed Jean-Louis, came to be associated with the name of the poet, Pompée Valentin. Importantly, the implications of Baron de Vastey having perhaps been (mis)identified as Pompée Valentin for nearly two-hundred years is also addressed, along with Vastey's rival Noël Colombel's accusation that as a young man the Haitian baron had been involved in the infamous *noyades de Nantes* (1793–1794) during the Reign of Terror in revolutionary France. Ultimately, this analysis of the various genealogical, political, revolutionary, and intellectual identities assigned to Baron de Vastey will occasion more tentative questions than it will provide definitive answers as we continue to analyze the life of this son of a plantation owner turned Haitian statesman, turned prolific anti-colonial essayist.

Chapter 3 positions Vastey in relation to a series of favorable nineteenth-century reviews of his works that were published in France, Great Britain, and the United States, where abolitionists and other anti-slavery activists used the baron's writing, along with that of Phillis Wheatley, Ignatius Sancho, Ukawsaw Gronniosaw, and Olaudah Equiano, to prove that Africans were capable of civilization and humanity. The famous English translation of Vastey's *Reflections on the Blacks and Whites* (1817), a text which represents Vastey's most direct contribution to the field that that we now call critical race theory, demonstrates the remarkable interest of abolitionists in showing how Vastey and his writings could be used as a functional component of both transatlantic anti-slavery thought and pseudo-scientific racial debates. Abolitionist writers from Europe and the United States often strategically compared *Réflexions* [...] *sur les noirs et les blancs* (1816), along with Vastey's *Réflexions politiques* (1817), with the writings of pro-slavery advocates like Malouet, Drouin de Bercy, and Mazères, suggesting that Vastey's writing was superior to that of these French colonists and therefore that black people could not be inferior to whites. Through widely circulated and cited commentaries of these two works, in particular, Vastey became attached to, and identified with, some of the most important debates of the era, including: how a nation-state should be governed, the meaning and consequences of revolution and universal emancipation, the emergence of national literary traditions, the capacity of former slaves for self-rule, and the issue of international trade. Notably, Vastey's ideas were critical to the development of international attitudes towards Haitian independence after 1816 and provided crucial momentum for many U.S., British, and more surprisingly, French authors who were engaged in ardently urging their governments to formally recognize Haitian sovereignty.

Chapter 4 argues that Vastey's works have often been judged according to many of the æsthetic and intellectual values of western Europe, which deny that history, not to mention art, could ever have an official relationship to state power without being pernicious. To understand the importance of Vastey's works, I contend that we need to consider alternative vocabularies that do not rely upon already established, sanctified, and fully approved genres of the western literary canon. The language used by John Beverley to describe "testimonio" as a form of protest against the violence of modernity, "a revulsion for fiction and for the fictive as such" (Beverley, "Margins" 15), can be useful to us in understanding early Haitian prose works and their seeming refusal to adopt or conform to established literary forms, such as the novel and the slave narrative. Rather than simply being coeval with the sentimental and gothic literary traditions of the Atlantic World in which he lived, Vastey's brutal account of slave punishments and tortures in *Le Système colonial* emerges as a deeply personalized text that is both a state-sanctioned version of Haitian colonial history and a methodologically novel use of collective slave memory to create a "history from below." In comparing Vastey's works to a tradition of sentimentality and gothicism more immediately associated with the British and U.S. American abolitionist movements, I argue that Vastey's desire to publish a Haitian-produced account of collective atrocities in colonial Saint-Domingue stems not from a desire to scare, please, or evoke pity from his readers. Instead, Vastey pursues an indictment of the French colonists that, similar to testimony given in a courtroom, could have significant legal ramifications.

Beginning with May Miller's *Christophe's Daughters* (1935), Chap. 5 discusses representations of Vastey as a dramatic character in several theatrical works about Haitian Independence from the early twentieth-century. In addition to Miller's play, Baron de Vastey appears as an important character in Selden Rodman's *The Revolutionists* (1942); Dan Hammerman's *Henri Christophe* (1945); Césaire's *La Tragédie du roi Christophe* (1963); and in two of the plays that make up Derek's Walcott's *Haitian Trilogy* (2002). Although the ideological underpinnings of each of these dramatic representations is as variable as interpretations of the Haitian Revolution itself, I argue that the element they all share in common is an isolationist narrative of Haiti. These plays tend to obfuscate the *real* Baron de Vastey's argument about the neo-colonial circumscriptions of sovereignty after colonialism by portraying twentieth-century Haitian political problems to be almost entirely the result of internal Haitian policies rather than external, foreign political interference. Moreover, Vastey's sudden appearance as a character in the early to mid-20th-century theater of Haitian independence, after being completely absent from 19th-century fictions of the Haitian Revolution, suggests that his philosophical presence lingered on in the Afro-diasporic intellectual tradition in less direct, but perhaps no less important ways. As he began to increasingly disappear from historiography about Haiti in the twentieth century, Vastey emerged as a literary character in his own right, but this emergence seems to have more to tell us about how these writers used Haiti to express and hide anxieties about what we might call, using Yarimar Bonilla's phrase, the "non-sovereign future" (15) of the entire Caribbean archipelago than it does about Vastey himself. His life may have, thus, had more performative value in the early twentieth century than his works had intellectual value for readers and writers of the Haitian Revolution. Paying attention to the difference between performing and reading Vastey, this chapter questions how twentieth-century playwrights used Vastey to depict sovereign Haiti as having pursued a misguided (and failed) quest to prove the inherent humanity of black people through the creation of a black state.

The epilogue provides the first sustained critical examination of René Philoctète's 1975 play, *Monsieur de Vastey*. If the plays examined in Chap. 5 *use* Vastey to produce isolationist accounts of Haitian leadership and to criticize vindicationist black writing, Philoctète's play centers Vastey to suggest the more relational kind of reading of Haiti that Baron de Vastey had himself encouraged. *Monsieur de Vastey* demonstrates early sovereign Haiti's essential connectedness to the world powers of Great Britain, France, and the United States. In so doing, the play performs the kind of neocolonial criticism that is absent in earlier plays that depicted Vastey as a character. By portraying Vastey as a humanist rather than an opportunist, Philoctète's play also de-centers the theater of Haitian independence from its focus on "great heroes" by calling attention to the heroic intellectual legacy and the enduring validity of the Black Atlantic humanistic perspective wrought by Baron de Vastey's anti-colonial critiques.

CHAPTER 2

What's *in* a Name? Unfolding the Consequences of a *Mistaken* Identity

The tension between statist and non-statist readings of Vastey's writings, or propagandistic versus humanist understandings of his work, can be at least partly attributed to conflicting assertions about Baron de Vastey's personal history. A quick gloss of Vastey scholarship reveals numerous contradictions and inconsistencies, mostly in attempts to narrate his biography. According to the archive of Vastey scholarship, the future Baron was either born in 1735 (Vaval, 129; Berrou and Pompilus, 1: 73) or 1781 (Nicholls 1990; Daut 2008; Bongie 2014); and his name was either Pompée Valentin Vastey, the name which has been used in virtually every article published about him in the twentieth century (and is the name under which he appears in Walcott and Rodman's plays), or Jean Louis Vastey, the name listed on the baptismal certificate that I located in 2011 in the Archives Nationales d'Outre Mer in Aix-en-Province (Daut, "From Classical French Poet").

The date and nature of Vastey's death has also provided matter for controversy. Karl Ritter, a German geographer, who composed a "sketch" of Christophe's palace of Sans-Souci eight days after the king's death (Trouillot, *Silencing*, 35), wrote that Vastey had been murdered in October of 1820 and that his body was subsequently thrown into a well, "where I myself saw it" (*Foreign Quarterly Review*, 1838, 93). Ritter's observation is in some senses confirmed by the Swedish artillery officer, Johan Albrekt Abraham de Frese, who reported in his 1821 handwritten memoir, that after the execution of Christophe's son, Vastey had "prayed" and "begged" for his life, but to no avail. Vastey was subsequently "hit in the head with an axe" and then thrown into a ditch to be left for dead (qtd. in Thomasson).

© The Author(s) 2017   27
M.L. Daut, *Baron de Vastey and the Origins of Black Atlantic Humanism*,
The New Urban Atlantic, DOI 10.1057/978-1-137-47067-6_2

The British traveler James Franklin claimed, however, in his 1828 *The Present State of Hayti* that "De Vastey is now living at the Cape in retirement, and is exceedingly attentive to the English residents, for whom he has a very high respect and veneration" (198).

There also exists confusion concerning Vastey's social and legal status in Saint-Domingue under French rule. Many scholars have reported that Vastey had been enslaved in Saint-Domingue (McCune Smith 1841, 5; Farmer, *Aids* 156, *Uses* 479; Heinl and Heinl, 127; Wirzbicki 2014), but Vastey's baptismal certificate (see Fig. 2.2) lists him as the "fils légitime" of his father, Jean Vastey, and his mother, a free woman of color, Élisabeth "Mimi" Dumas. Moreover, recent research into Vastey's biography suggests not only that Vastey was born with free status but that he had been a slave-owner himself, rather than merely the son of a slave owner. Vastey's cousin, Michel Vastey, wrote of the future Haitian baron in 1802, for example, "The fortune of his wife, joined together with his own, which consists of five plantations, would have provided him with a great deal of revenue if it were not for these insurrections" (qtd. in Quevilly 249).[1] Finally, several sources, likely influenced by nineteenth-century writers, including William Woodis Harvey, assert that Vastey had been educated in Paris (Maffly-Kipp, 56; Griggs and Prator, 44; Harvey 221; Williams-Wynn, 188), while others suggest that Vastey was an autodidact ("Hayti," *North American Review*, 1821, 112; Esterquest 174). Vastey himself indirectly acknowledged having some formal education, intimating in his *Réflexions sur une lettre de Mazères* that he was at a disadvantage vis-à-vis his French adversaries since he had not even finished "sixième" or the first year of junior high (33).

The idea that Vastey had been an enslaved person with no formal education was partly supported by the circumspect way he wrote about (or rather did not write about) his life in colonial Saint-Domingue. Vastey rarely mentioned his personal life in his prose works but in November of 1819 he wrote a letter to the British abolitionist Thomas Clarkson stating that he had been born in 1781 in a small province of Saint-Domingue named Ennery and was therefore nearly thirty-nine years old. He also mentioned joining the revolutionary leader Toussaint

---

[1] Quevilly's biography is based on a rather miraculous gift to him of well over 100 letters from the French descendants of the Vastey family in Normandy dating from 1759 to 1835 (Quevilly 10). For an explanation of how these letters came into Quevilly's possession see Quevilly's *Le baron de Vastey* (9–13).

Louverture's army at the age of fifteen and having two daughters, Aricie and Malvina (rpt. in Griggs 181–182).[2]

Although Vastey reveals little else about his family in the letter to Clarkson, in his *Réflexions sur une lettre de Mazères*, he did speak of his mother, referring to her only as the "Africaine" who "gave [him] life" (31). This "Africaine," according to Vastey's baptismal certificate, dated 29 March 1788, was actually a free woman of color named Marie Françoise Élisabeth Dumas from the wealthy Dumas family of planters. Further information about Vastey's mother and maternal grandmother can be distilled from his parent's marriage certificate. This document, dating from 3 July 1777 (see Fig. 2.1), lists Vastey's mother, "Élisabeth dite Mimi," as a "Carteronne libre [sic]," "minor and natural daughter of Marie-Catherine, a free mulattress" ("Acte," 1777).[3] These seemingly minor details of the marriage certificate reveal that Vastey actually did write, although ambiguously, about his family in his published writings.

At one point Vastey mentions his mother in *Le Système colonial* without explicitly revealing his own connection to her when he tells a moving story about one "Élisabeth 'Mimi'," "fille naturelle" of "Dumas, settler, resident of Marmelade, and at present a property owner in France" (70). Vastey describes how this "Mimi" saved an infant slave named Laurent from being thrown into *le four à chaud* by her own father, Pierre Dumas (thus, Vastey's grandfather). Mimi apparently subsequently raised Laurent as if he were her

---

[2] The Vastey family letters suggest, on the contrary, that Vastey was forced into conscription through what is called the "corvée." Vastey's father wrote to his nephew, Pierre Julien Valentin Vastey, that the French troops under the leadership of Toussaint Louverture "bothered us a lot about joining the service. In particular, your cousin, *Cadet*, is burdened with a corvée tax" (qtd. in Quevilly, 223). In a later letter Vastey's father revealed that his son, Jean-Louis, *Cadet* (the future Baron de Vastey), had been "taken by command and suffered a terrible illness during the campaign" (qtd. in Quevilly, 227). An even later letter from October 1802 suggests that Vastey had actually initially fought against the "insurgents." His cousin, Michel Vastey wrote, "My cousin Cadet was almost killed. He has escaped death a thousand times. He received a gunshot wound to the leg about a month ago" (qtd. in Quevilly, 246). Thus, Vastey may indeed have fought under Louverture, but perhaps under less voluntary circumstances than he had intimated in the letter. Quevilly writes that Vastey, along with his father and his cousin, Louis, were forced to join the French army in 1802, otherwise, they would be required to serve "one month in prison or hard labor at the arsenal" (249).

[3] Following the custom of the colony for children of color who were born to fathers to whom their mothers were not married, Mimi's father, Pierre Dumas, is listed on the document only as a witness. The document is housed at the Archives Nationale d'Outre Mer in Aix-en-Provence, France.

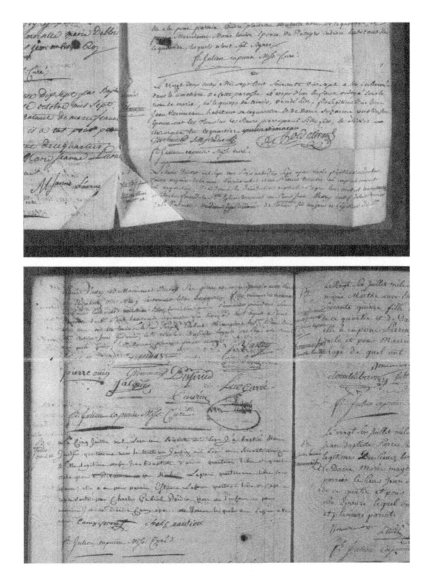

Fig. 2.1   Acte de Mariage de Jean Vastey and Élisabeth "Mimi" Dumas, 1777

own child so that the enslaved mother could return to work. Of his mother's attempt to lessen the degradations of slavery, Vastey writes: "Mimi, virtuous and good, you are no longer with us! But you rejoice in the bosom of eternal beatitude, as compensation for your noble actions. Your friend here consecrates your name and your virtues, as a symbol of veneration and friendship for all kind and tender-hearted souls" (70–71). Vastey's decision to refer to Élisabeth Mimi as his "friend" rather than his mother speaks to the tensions involved in representing one's self as connected to enslavers in a post-slavery society. Even if the story of Élisabeth Mimi might have moved Vastey's nineteenth-century readers outside of Haiti, one imagines that the revelation that Vastey was the grandson of a reportedly cruel slaveowner might have infuriated some of his Haitian readers.

The large number of conflicting accounts of Vastey's life documented in subsequent historical writings about him expose the inherent unreliability and relationality of all biographical narrative. Biographical details about Vastey's life have been shaped in manifest ways by the motives of those who have written about him.[4] In order to produce a vision of Vastey as wholly divorced from the slave-owning life into which he was born, for instance, James Vandercook, who penned a fictionalized biography of Henry Christophe in 1928, implied that Vastey's seemingly incongruous allegiance to black people was because he hated his white father. Noting that Vastey "could 'almost pass for a white man'" and that his skin "was the color of old parchment," Vandercook described Vastey as the "bastard son of a white father whose memory he scorned and a mulatto mother he had forgotten" (114). Vandercook's emphasis on Vastey's supposed bastard "mulatto" status and his suggestion that Vastey held his parents in mutual disapprobation—to say nothing of his reference to Vastey as "the 'white nigger'" who "loved the blacks with a fierce, consuming love" and "hated all whites with a double fury" (114)—is not simply mistaken and deeply prejudiced, it also tells us something about the need for congruity when examining black writing.

It is partially the need for coherence that led to the assumption that Vastey had been a formerly enslaved person. James McCune Smith, for

---

[4] The issue with Vastey's date of birth might have been easily cleared up without the baptismal certificate, owing to the letter that Vastey himself penned to the British abolitionist Thomas Clarkson in 1819, which confirms a birth date of 1781 (rpt. in Griggs 180–182, Nicholls 1990; Daut 2008).

example, claimed that Vastey wrote his *Réflexions politiques* "twenty five years after he had obtained his liberty" (5), and McCune Smith used the following passage of the English translation of the above work as evidence that Vastey had himself been "one of these slaves:" "We were one plunged…in the most complete ignorance," he quotes Vastey as writing, "we had no notion of human society, no idea of happiness, no powerful feeling; our faculties both physical and moral, were so overwhelmed under the load of slavery, that I myself, who am writing this, thought the world finished at the spot which bounded my sight, and all my countrymen were as ignorant, and even more so than myself, if that is possible" (qtd. in McCune Smith 4–5). Thus, Vastey's writing itself would also seem to encourage the belief that he was a part of the "we" narrative of the slave lives being described. Moreover, his œuvre might as well encourage a reading whereby the baron would appear to have been a self-taught intellectual. Vastey vaguely suggested that he had indeed educated himself when he wrote, "It is not useless to warn my readers that I have never undertaken official study of the French language. They will excuse, then, certain faults of speech and literature that will necessarily abound in the works of an islander, who never had any other teacher than his books" (*RM* 4–5). In another passage of the same work Vastey plainly stated, "I have not had the good fortune to attain an education" (*RM* 33).

Reconstructing the life of Baron de Vastey is crucial to any study of his contributions to Black Atlantic humanism. The ambiguities and contradictions in nineteenth-century era attempts to understand who he was as a person have much to tell us about how his contributions to the political and philosophical ideas of freedom and equality exalted in the modern world became silenced. In this chapter I suggest that the problems concerning Vastey's name, his age, his education, and his social and legal status in French Saint-Domingue, are directly related to assessments of his character as "mercenary," leading in turn to judgments of his writing as propaganda. What is partially under examination here are assessments whereby Vastey appears as merely a "mercenary scribe," (Colombel, *Examen* 7) to use the words of one of his fiercest rivals, Noël Colombel, a journalist from Pétion and later Jean-Pierre Boyer's republic.

Although it may seem of rather trivial importance whether Vastey died at the age of 85 or 39, whether he was educated in Paris, Rouen, or not at all, Colombel's more damning claim that Vastey had been a terrorist in Nantes, France during the reign of Jean-Baptiste Carrier (Colombel, *Examen* 11), appears to be directly linked not only to the many confused ideas about Vastey's life recounted above, but to contemporary readings

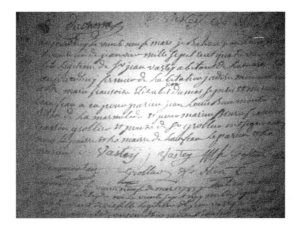

Fig. 2.2 Acte de Baptême, Jean Louis Vastey, 29 March 1788

of Vastey as a propagandist, an ideologue, and even a scribe—the very opposite of a humanist.

VASTEY AS POET

The issue with Vastey's *Christian* name has been and will likely continue to be difficult to adjudicate, precisely because of the longitudinal implications of this error. Vastey's first and middle names are listed in nearly every library catalog across the world as Pompée Valentin. The unearthing of his baptismal certificate (see Fig. 2.2), however, reveals that his given name was Jean-Louis Vastey. More importantly this *discovery* also puts into question when and whether he ever used the name Pompée Valentin. Vastey signed all of his published works in Haiti with his title of nobility, for instance: "le Baron DE VASTEY." The only exception to this was Vastey's first publication, *Notes à M. le baron de V.P. Malouet* (1814), which was signed in part with the initials of his apparent birth name and reads: "Le Baron de J.L. Vastey" (see Fig. 2.3).

Conflicting, erroneous, and often confusing information in the archive has led every scholar who has written about Vastey down the path of biographical imprecision. In 2009, encouraged by discovering some poems in the Bibliothèque Nationale de France, signed variously as V. Vastey and P.V. Vastey and attributed to Pompée Valentin Vastey, the name by which

NOTES

A

M. le Baron de V. P. MALOUET,

Ministre de la Marine et des Colonies, de Sa
Majesté LOUIS XVIII, et ancien Adminis-
trateur des Colonies et de la Marine, ex-Colon
de Saint-Domingue, etc.

EN

RÉFUTATION du 4ème Volume de
son Ouvrage,

INTITULÉ:

COLLECTION de Mémoires sur
les Colonies, et particulièrement sur
Saint-Domingue, etc.

Publié en l'An X.

Par M. le Baron de J. L. VASTEY. Secrétaire
du Roi, Membre du Conseil Privé de Sa Majesté
HENRY Iᵉʳ.

Au Cap-Henry, chez P. ROUX, imprimeur du Roi

OCTOBRE 1814, L'AN 11ᵐᵉ.

Baron de Vastey had come to be known in virtually every source about
his life, I suggested that Vastey had perhaps lived in France in the late
eighteenth century and had potentially authored those poems (see Daut,
"From Classical French"). Quevilly's biography of Vastey, however, sheds
serious doubt on the idea that Vastey could have authored the poems in
question or that he had ever used the name Pompée Valentin (326).

The primary letter writers in Quevilly's biography, Vastey's father, Jean
Valentin Vastey, and his uncle, Pierre Valentin Vastey, mention nothing
about "Vastey fils" having written poetry, and his relatives never refer to
him as Pompée Valentin, preferring to call him merely "Cadet," a reference to Vastey's status as a younger brother. The letters do reveal that

Vastey traveled to Rouen in Normandy with his father in 1791 where he stayed behind with his older brother to be educated under his uncle's roof until 8 March 1796 when the family traveled together back to Saint-Domingue (Quevilly 218). Quevilly is also able to place Vastey in Saint-Domingue in 1798, the year in which the first poem signed V. Vastey was published in France, owing to a letter signed "Vastey fils" from Ennery, Saint-Domingue and dated 23 May 1798 (Quevilly 222). An announcement posted by Vastey's father in the *Affiches Américaines* confirms the departure, but not the return, of Jean Valentin Vastey and two of his children (though the article does not mention the children by name): "M. Vastey, living in Marmelade, is leaving for France, with two of his children; he leaves his wife in charge of his affairs" (4 May 1791, 220).

Most of what we know about Vastey's father, "Vastey, jeune" or "Jean Vastey," is described on his *acte de mariage* to Élisabeth Mimi. The *acte* reveals that his father was born in Rouen, France and the elder Vastey's parents are listed as Pierre Vastey and Marianne Duval. While Baron de Vastey makes no direct or obvious mention of his father in his prose works, the baptismal certificate provides a few more details. The certificate confirms that Vastey's father was, in fact, a plantation owner in French-ruled Saint-Domingue. The elder Vastey is listed in the *acte de baptême* as "a planter in Marmelade, before that, at the minor Boutin's [plantation]." The certificate also reveals that Vastey's godparents were Jean-Louis Beaumont and Marie Françoise Gaston Grollier ("Acte," 1788). Although these Vastey family records from the Notariat de Saint-Domingue provide precious biographical information about a man whose verbosity rarely extended to his own personal history, they do very little to tell us how Baron de Vastey spent the early years of his life or how precisely he came to be known as Pompée Valentin.

The belief is so widespread that Baron de Vastey's *real* name was Pompée Valentin that the printed signature, "The Baron de Vastey," is scratched out of the title page of not only an original 1819 copy of Vastey's *Essai*, but also an original 1823 English translation, both held by the New York Public Library (see Fig. 2.4). It is precisely because Vastey's signature has been elided, crossed out, and written over that we must continue to sort out the genealogy of this biographical conflict.

Although this seeming case of mistaken identity is most manifest in library catalogs and contemporary scholarship, its roots appear in nineteenth-century French poetry; roots that would later indelibly link the militant Haitian statesman Baron de Vastey to Pompée Valentin Vastey's early career as a poet in metropolitan France. According to a poem entitled

Fig. 2.4   Baron de Vastey, *Essai sur les causes de la révolution et des guerres civiles d'Hayti* (1819)

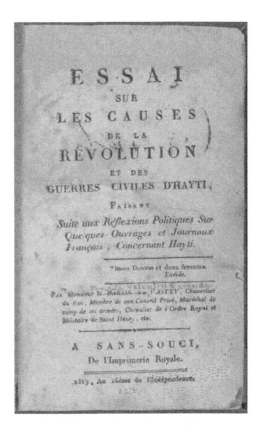

"Représaille" [sic], or "Revenge" (1803), published in the famous French journal *Almanach des Muses* and written by the French poet Etienne Vigée,[5] someone named Pompée Valentin Vastey was "author of a poem entitled la *Cotinéide* [sic], and of a collection of poetry published [in France] in 1800 under the title of *La Cruche d'Hippocrene* [sic]" (251).[6]

---

[5] Louis-Jean-Baptise-Etienne Vigée (1758–1820) was the brother of the famous French painter Élisabeth Vigée-Lebrun (May 73). According to an evaluation of his life in *Beautiful Thoughts from French and Italian Authors* (1875), Vigée's poetical "works [we]re of no value" (358).

[6] According to a fragment of a poem signed by P.V. Vastey entitled "Les trois sœurs ou le Parnasse moderne," published in 1808 in the *Journal des Arts, de Littérature, et de Commerce*, the collection was actually called *La Cotiniade, poëme en 10 chants*.

In his poem, Vigée accused this Vastey of having chosen for a "patron" the reportedly vicious French poet and critic the Abbé Cotin[7] and of simply being a "swindling rhymer" (251). In 1789, Vigée had become the editor of the *Almanach des Muses* (*Revue Encyclopédique* 1820, 7: 291), and in 1803 he used that platform to author an additional entry about *La Cruche* under the pseudonym Le C. Syntaxe, which read: "To Pompée Valentin Vastey, *Author of a strange collection of poetry, published under this strange title:* La CRUCHE d'Hippocrene, ou Mes Délassements. Bees, at every opportunity, have chased you from their hive, little WASP; go die in your jug" (64).[8]

The source of Vigée's ire and desire for "Revenge" against Pompée Valentin Vastey appears to be a poem published under the signature V. Vastey in the prominent opposition journal *La Décade Philosophique*: "Epître à Monsieur Syntaxe, *satire*: Sur Sa Rimomanie" (1802).[9] In this poem V. Vastey accused Vigée of a disease he called "rhymomania," compared him to the Abbé Cotin, and suggested that Vigée was simply boring everyone with his poetry: "...tell me, Is it not ridiculous that an entire group of people who treat you like a friend/Must, too often, be put to sleep by your verse" (lines 10–12).

Vigée and V. Vastey's equally provocative criticisms notwithstanding, the citation of a collection of poetry published under the name of Pompée Valentin Vastey, as well as a poem signed with these initials in one of the most controversial journals of the era (Trinkle 52–53), appeared to pose serious questions about a man who is usually believed to have lived all of his life in what is now present-day Haiti and who

---

[7] P.V. Vastey's poem *La Cotiniade* appears to be a reference to the Abbé Cotin. Simon-Augustin Irail's *Querelles littéraires, ou Mémoires pour servir à l'histoire des révolutions de la république des lettres, depuis Homère jusqu'à nos jours...* (1761) described the abbé Cotin as "le hibou de la littérature" or "the owl of literature" and claimed that "[t]oday none would dare to carry his name" (326).

[8] Frédéric Lachèvre's *Bibliographie sommaire de l'Almanach des Muses* (1765–1833) notes that such invective was common in the *Almanach des Muses*, which Lachèvre wrote had always been a "mean press" (9).

[9] For more on the press see, *The Napoleonic Press: The Public Sphere and Oppositionary Journalism (2002)* and *Un Millieu intellectuel: La Décade philosophique* (1965). V. Vastey's poem was reprinted in *Le Journal des Arts, de Littérature, et de Commerce* in 1807. In fact, many of the poems with this signature published after 1802 indicate that they are only fragments of earlier works.

many scholars have even speculated may have been a former slave.[10] Was the poet Vastey spoken of in Vigée's poem the same Vastey who would become Christophe's most valued administrator? Had Vastey, who never once mentioned traveling to France, let alone to Europe, lived in Paris and been a published and rather well-known *French* poet, as the attention from the *Almanach des Muses* suggests?[11]

Of a few things we can be reasonably certain: someone using the name Pompée Valentin Vastey was living in Paris and publishing poetry in the leading French journals in the late eighteenth and early nineteenth centuries. To that end, a *carte de sûreté*, which all citizens, residents and entrants to Paris were required to obtain after the law of September 19, 1792 (Faron and Grange 795), was registered under the name Pompé [sic] Vastey in 1794. The detailed *carte* lists the holder's height as five-feet tall, his profession as "commis" or "clerk," his address as Rue de Lappe, and states that *this* Vastey had already been in Paris for four years ("Carte"). The *carte* actually provides the first clue that the poet Vastey and the Baron de Vastey were perhaps not the same person at all. The *carte* lists Vastey's age as fifteen when he would have been only thirteen, and indicates that he was born in "Ducler [sic]" in Normandy when we know that our Vastey was actually born in Ennery in colonial

---

[10] In addition to those I earlier mentioned, a number of reviews of Vastey's works in the nineteenth century stated that he had once been a slave (Lewis 326; McCune Smith 5; Mahul 322), while the *Anti-Slavery Record* (1819) wrote of him that "we do not know whether he was originally a slave" ("Anecdote" 129). This same confusion persists today. Hutton refers to Vastey as an "ex-enslaved man" (116), Hall calls him an "ex-slave," Farmer says that Vastey was a Haitian who had grown up a slave (*Uses* 479; *Aids* 156), while Heinl and Heinl also note that "Vastey had lived half his life as a slave" (127). Vastey, for his part, implied that he had never left Haiti when he wrote that he was a simple "Haitian, raised on the mountain peaks in the middle of the forest" and not a "man of letters" (*Système* viii). According to Hénock Trouillot, however, Vastey traveled to London where he met the Abbé Grégoire, whom Trouillot says was "the object of a cult on the part of the Baron de Vastey" ("Le gouvernement" 72).

[11] The *Almanach des Muses* had also advertised Pompée Valentin Vastey's collection in 1801 as *La Cruche d'Hypocrène, ou mes Délassemens, essais poétiques; par Pompée Valentin Vastey*, providing only the following brief commentary: "*La Cruche d'Hypocrène!* Strange title *[singulier titre]*" (293). Incidentally, even though the *Almanach* was typically not favorable towards Pompée Vastey, his poem "Les fils de Mercure" did appear in the journal in 1814. Vastey's poem had already been published, however, in 1808 in the *Journal des Arts, de Littérature et de Commerce* and in 1809 in the *Journal de Paris*.

Saint-Domingue.[12] Moreover, four years after the *carte* was issued Pompée Valentin Vastey was still living in Paris since V. Vastey listed his address as Rue de la Loi, N. 26 in his 1798 poem "Derniers adieux."

Because fragments from Pompée Valentin Vastey's collections *Le Pays de Caux* and *La Cotiniade* appeared under the signature V. Vastey in *La Décade Philosophique* and *Le Journal des Arts, de Littérature et de Commerce*, respectively, we can infer that V. Vastey and Pompée Valentin Vastey were the same person. But were Jean Louis Vastey of the birth certificate, the man who would sign his first work as "Le Baron de J.L. Vastey," and each of his subsequent works as "The Baron DE VASTEY," and Pompée Valentin Vastey, the poet who lived in Paris, also the same person? This is the real question. And circumstantial evidence linking the two names abounds.

There is a fragment of *Le Pays de Caux*, "Les Cauchoises," which appeared in *La Décade Philosophique* in 1802, which was signed with the signature "J. Vastey." This could suggest that P.V. Vastey's *real* first name, like Baron de Vastey's, may have begun with the letter J. In addition, the head of the Imprimerie Royale du Roi in Cap-Haïtien was a man named P. Roux and many of Vastey's poems appeared in the

---

[12] However, due to the generally unreliable information on these identification cards, this discrepancy alone would not be enough to rule out a connection between these two names. According to L'Association Héraldique et Généalogique de Normandie, the most important indication on these cards was the date of entry in Paris since orthography, birthdates, and places of birth were often "random":

> Until 1792, the French had as their only identification their baptismal certificate, which was moreover the only permitted identification. It was only if they crossed borders that they needed a passport or a safe-conduct, which was always for a limited duration and limited place. In 1792 the revolutionaries took the view that [the baptismal certificate] was insufficient and that every good citizen should have a *carte* [*de sûreté*]. The distribution of the cards was essentially a Parisian phenomenon. Inclusion on the register and the delivery of the card were made by the committee of the civil section. Many of its representatives barely knew how to read and write, that is why there is a lot of creativity in the orthography. In addition, departmentalization was new and determining the precise districts where births took place was often random. The most important indication [on the cards] was the date of arrival in Paris. Anyone male over the age of 15 years old, arriving in Paris had to go and obtain a card. However, it should be noted that the *cartes de sûreté* were only distributed in certain major cities. The entire population was not obligated to have one as they were in Paris ("Cartes").

(For more about the inconsistent orthography of the *cartes de sûreté*, see also Faron and Grange, 81).

Journal typographique et bibliographique, publié par P. Roux.[13] Further circumstantial evidence appears in an entry in the nineteenth-century almanac *La France littéraire.* The entry reads that Baron de Vastey was, "at first, a writer in Paris, later a chancellor of the king of Haiti" (10: 65). The entry then lists Baron de Vastey's publications as two works of poetry: *Anaïde et Alcidore, poëme érotique en quatre chants* (1800) and *Délassemen[t]s poétiques, ou la Cruche d'Hypocrène* (1799). Three of Baron de Vastey's prose works are also listed in the same entry: *Essai sur les causes* (1819), *Réflexions sur une lettre de Mazères* (1815), and *Réflexions politiques* (1817). Joseph-Marie Quérard, the editor of *La France littéraire,* thus, believed that Pompée Valentin and Baron de Vastey were the same person, and he was definitely not the only one to have thought so.

At least one fragment of V. Vastey's poetry was reprinted in the collection of poetic jokes and puns by the vaudevillist Armand Henri Ragueneau de la Chainaye (1777–1856)[14] entitled *Brunetiana, recueil dédié à Jocrisse* (1802).[15] Poems signed with the name of Vastey in this collection led one early twentieth-century critic to surmise that "the negro Valentin Vastey, later a Haitian official," had been intimately involved in the creation of the collection and had been good friends not only with Ragueneau de la Chainaye, but with the vaudevillist Charles Henrion, the "future general

---

[13] P. Roux was the official printer, by turns, of Toussaint Louverture, Jean-Jacques Dessalines, and Henry Christophe until 1816 when he was replaced for unknown reasons by one known only as Buon (Tardieu 4–7; Esterquest 174). According to Patrick Tardieu, the curator of Haiti's Bibliothèque Haïtienne des Pères du Saint Esprit, there were two different P. Roux's publishing works around the same time period, one in Haiti and one in France (7). Tardieu concludes, nevertheless, that although he believes "they were not the same person, regardless, nothing would stop us from researching any links of ancestry or perhaps the origins of their houses of commerce" (7). Tardieu also reveals that "A third person held the same name, it was one of the signatories of our Declaration of Independence. The biography of the *chef de brigade* Pierre Maximilien Roux, leaves no doubt that he could not have been our printer, because our character [P. Roux, the printer] established himself at Cap beginning in 1791 and finished his career there under King Christophe in Sans-Souci in 1816. The signatory of independence was residing at that time in Port-au-Prince" (7).

[14] Ragueneau de la Chainaye was coincidentally the brother of Alexandre-Louis Ragueneau de la Chainaye (1779–1836) who, according to Brière, was eventually sent to be vice-consul of Cayes in Haiti (72).

[15] Brunet (1766–1853) was a French actor and comedian famous for his "bons mots," or jokes, according to Ragueneau (see the preface to *Brunetiana* iii, vi), and for starring in Dorvigny's play *Le Désespoir de Jocrisse* (1798).

Claparède,"[16] and the satirist André Jacquelin, who also appeared in the collection (Plon-Nourrit 326). Plon-Nourrit, the author of this later volume, makes these assertions likely because P.V. Vastey had published numerous poems alongside Jacquelin and Henrion in the short-lived satirical French literary journal *La Mouche*, whose motto was ironically, "Je pique sans blesser" or "I sting without injuring."

Even with Quérard's earlier and Plon-Nourrit's much later linkage of the statesman Baron de Vastey to the poet Pompée Valentin Vastey,[17] what remains missing is, as Chris Bongie has noted, something or someone who can connect the name Pompée Valentin to Baron de Vastey in *his* own lifetime (*The Colonial System*, 17). Even though catalogs and reviews of Vastey's works during his lifetime consistently refer to him as Baron de Vastey, by the mid nineteenth century, his publications were starting to be regularly cataloged under the name of Pompée Valentin in England, the United States, and France. This is evidenced in transatlantic context by historic entries in the 1850 edition of Édouard Marie Oettinger's *Bibliographie Biographique, ou, Dictionnaire de 26.000 Ouvrages* (283), the 1851 catalog of the Bodleian Library at Oxford University (953), and the "Alphabetical Catalog of the Library of Congress," dating from 1864 (1147). All of which suggests that Vastey only became known as Pompée Valentin after Quérard's dictionary entry yoked these two names, perhaps erroneously, together. Moreover, Baron de Vastey, had *dozens* of male cousins living in France, any one of whom could have been using the initials V. Vastey or P.V. Vastey to publish poetry. In fact, Vastey had several relatives with the names of Pompée and Valentin, and one of these male cousins was named Jacques Valentin Pompée Vastey. If the Baron de Vastey's cousin Jacques was the author of the poems in question, this could account for the outlying poem signed J. Vastey (Figs. 2.5, 2.6, and 2.7).

---

[16]Michel-Marie Claparède (1770–1842), incidentally, fought in Napoleon's army as a part of the failed Leclerc expedition (1802–1803), which the First Consul sent to the colony of Saint-Domingue in order to reinstate colonial rule.

[17]William Woodis Harvey, a Methodist preacher, also claimed that Vastey had written some poetry. He wrote, "Another piece had proceeded from his pen, in the form of a play; the object of which was to represent the more remarkable and meritorious parts of Christophe's life. Whatever were the abilities or acquirements of the author, this piece showed that he was totally unqualified to write dramatic poetry" (222). It is very possible that Harvey had confused Vastey with Juste Chanlatte who did write poetry and had authored several operas.

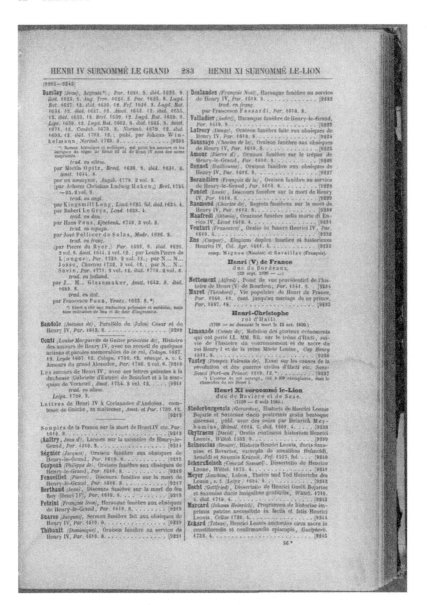

Fig. 2.5 1850 edition of Édouard Marie Oettinger's *Bibliographie Biographique, ou, Dictionnaire de 26.000 Ouvrages*

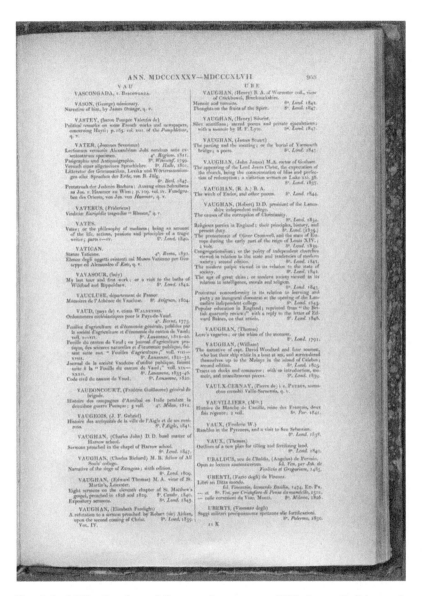

Fig. 2.6 1851 *Catalogus Librorum Impressorum Bibliothecae Bodleianae in Academia* Volume 4

1147

VARRO.   VAUGHAN.

VARRO, (Marcus Terentius) De Re Rustica. 16°. Parisiis, 1543. (Libri de Re Rustica, v. 1.)

VARTHEMA. See BARTHEMA.

VASARI, (Giorgio.) Opere, 8°. Milano, 1840.
—— Vite de' più eccellenti Pittori, Scultori et Architetti. 3 v. 4°. Bologna, 1647.
—— The same. Illustrate con note. 16 v. 8°. Milano, 1807–11.
—— Lives of the most eminent Painters, Sculptors, and Architects. Translated from the Italian, with notes and illustrations, chiefly selected from various commentators, by Mrs. Jonathan Foster. 5 v. 12°. London, 1850-52.

VASSA, (Gustavus.) Olaudah Equiano; or, Gustavus Vassa, the African. Written by himself. 12°. Boston, 1837.

VASTEY, (Pompée Valentin, Baron de.) Essay on the Causes of the Revolution and Civil Wars of Hayti. 8°. Exeter, (Eng.,) 1823.
—— Political remarks on some French Works and newspapers concerning Hayti. 8°. London, 1818. (Pamphleteer, v. 13.)

VATER, (Johann Severin.) Untersuchungen über Amerika's Bevölkerung aus dem Alten Kontinente. 8°. Leipzig, 1810.

VATTEL, (Emmeric de.) Droit des Gens, ou principes de la loi naturelle appliqués à la conduite et aux affaires des nations et des souverains. 3 v. 16°. Londres, (Neuchâtel,) 1758.
—— The same. Nouv. éd. 2 v. in 1. 4°. Amsterdam, 1775.
—— The same. Nouv. éd., par M. de Hoffmanns: précédée d'un Discours sur l'Étude du Droit de la Nature et des Gens, par Sir James Mackintosh. Traduit en Français par M. P. Royer-Collard; avec les notes et table générale par M. S. Pinheiro-Ferreira. 3 v. 8°. Paris, 1835-38.
—— Questions de Droit Naturel; et Observations sur le Traité du Droit de la Nature de M. le Baron de Wolf. 12°. Berne, 1762.
—— Law of Nations; or, principles of the law of nature applied to the conduct and affairs of nations and sovereigns. From the French. 4th ed. 8°. London, 1811.
—— The same. 8°. Northampton, 1820. (4 copies.)
—— The same. New ed., by Joseph Chitty. 8°. London, 1834.
—— The same. 4th Am. ed., from a new ed. by J. Chitty. 8°. Philadelphia, 1835. (2 copies.)
—— The same. 6th Am. ed., from a new

ed. by J. Chitty. 8°. Philadelphia, 1844. (4 copies.)
—— The same. From the new ed. by J. Chitty; with additional notes and references, by E. D. Ingraham. 8°. Philadelphia, 1852.
—— The same. 8°. Philadelphia, 1855.
—— The same. 8°. Philadelphia, 1857. (3 copies.)

VATTEMARE, (Alexandre.) Annual Reports of the Agents to the State of Vermont. 8°. Montpelier, 1850.
—— Exchanges between France and North America. 8°. Paris, 1846.
—— Proceedings in the City of Washington relating to Exchanges. 8°. Washington, 1848.
—— Report on the Subject of International Exchanges. 8°. Washington, 1848.
—— Reports and Resolves of the State of Maine. 8°. Augusta, 1847.

VAUBAN, (Sébastien Leprêtre de.) Traité de l'Attaque et de la Défense des Places. 4°. La Haye, 1737.

VAUCIENNES. See LINAGE DE VAUCIENNES.

VAUDORÉ, (J. F.) Bibliothèque de Législation et de Jurisprudence, pratique, rurale et urbaine. 3 v. 8°. Paris, 1856.

VAUGHAN, (Henry.) Sacred Poems and Pious Ejaculations: Silex Scintillans, etc. 16°. London, 1858.

VAUGHAN, (John.) Reports and Arguments in Special Cases in the Court of Common Pleas, 1665 to 1672. Folio. London, 1706.

VAUGHAN, (Robert.) Causes of the Corruption of Christianity. 8°. London, 1834.
—— History of England under the House of Stuart, including the Commonwealth. (A. D. 1603—1688.) 2 v. 8°. London, 1840.
—— John de Wycliffe; a monograph. 8°. London, 1853.
—— Memorials of the Stuart Dynasty, including the constitutional and ecclesiastical History of England. 2 v. 8°. London, 1831.
—— Revolutions in English History. 3 v. 8°. London, 1859-63.
    Vol. 1. Revolutions of Race.
    Vol. 2. Revolutions in Religion.
    Vol. 3. Revolutions in Government.

VAUGHAN, (Robert Alfred.) Hours with the Mystics; a contribution to the history of religious opinion. 2d ed. 2 v. 12°. London, 1860.

VAUGHAN, (William.) New and Old Principles of Trade compared. 8°. London, 1788.
—— Memoir of W. Vaughan; with miscellaneous pieces relative to docks, commerce, etc. 8°. London, 1839.

Fig. 2.7   *Alphabetical Catalog of the Library of Congress* from 1864

The question that remains is whether any of this purely circumstantial evidence can definitively tell us whether or not Vastey authored the poems in question and/or ever used the name Pompée Valentin? Somewhat ironically, the details provided in my earlier attempt to understand the connection between Baron de Vastey and Pompée Valentin Vastey are precisely what has allowed Vastey's biographer, Quevilly, to provide what he believes to be a final answer to this question: "Never in his lifetime, never," Quevilly writes, "was Baron de Vastey known under the pseudonym of Pompée-Valentin." (324).

Although many of Pompée Valentin Vastey's poems that appeared in French journals *after* Haitian independence had been previously published elsewhere or appear to have been merely fragments of his longer and much earlier published book-length works, Pompée Valentin Vastey was almost still certainly in France in the early nineteenth century, particularly in 1808, when Baron de Vastey had already assumed a prominent role in Dessalines and later Christophe's governments as secretary to the Minister of Finance, André Vernet. Gaspard Mollien, for instance, places Vastey at the home of Louis-Félix Boisrond-Tonnerre, secretary to Dessalines, in April of 1804 (23). There is also a document dating from May of 1804 and signed by "Vastey ainé"[18] who is listed as "Le Secretaire du ministre des finances" to André Vernet. Vernet was the Minister of Finance under Dessalines (*Lois et actes sous le règne de Jean-Jacques Dessalines*, 33). Moreover, in a footnote to his *Essai*, Vastey said he had worked for Vernet, a former owner of slaves himself, who had died in 1813 (Quevilly 95, 282), under not only Dessalines, but Christophe. Vastey wrote, "I was the principal secretary for seven years in the département des Finances et de l'intérieur," which accounts for the years 1804–1811 (*Essai*, 202ftn).

While Vastey was busy assuming his station as a member of the newly minted Haitian state, his poetical counterpart was busy publishing poems in metropolitan France. Only three weeks after the publication of a poem entitled "Satire," published on 26 April 1808 in the *Journal des Arts, de Littérature et de Commerce*, Pompée Valentin Vastey wrote a letter to the editors that appeared in the same journal on 16 May 1808. The letter asks the editors to insert a footnote indicating that the following line from Vastey's own poem was borrowed from a verse by the French

---

[18]Vastey's older brother had died by that time, making Vastey the oldest child.

poet Boileau: "The moment of which I speak is already far from me."[19] Quevilly's evidence rests primarily on the fact that none of Baron de Vastey's family members refer to him by the name of Pompée Valentin and that he himself never appears to have used this name in Haiti. Quevilly also relies on this painstakingly constructed timeline that places Baron de Vastey in Haiti at the very moment in which I revealed Pompée Valentin Vastey to have been in France. Quevilly concludes, "One sole argument will destroy at last the thesis whereby Baron de Vastey is the author of the poems published in France. On 16 May 1808, in Paris, our famous V. Vastey published in *Le Journal des Arts* a correction concerning one of his poems that had appeared in the review only a few [weeks] before. That Jean-Louis Vastey, who was at that time first secretary to Minister Vernet in Haiti, could be the author of this corrective is materially impossible" (326).

Even if the issue of whether or not Baron de Vastey ever published poems in Paris under the names of V. Vastey or Pompée Valentin Vastey may be resolved in Quevilly's eyes, many other questions remain. If it was Quérard who first made the direct link between Baron de Vastey and Pompée Valentin Vastey, what caused or encouraged him to make this association? What was known about the Vastey family's connection to Saint-Domingue that would make Quérard believe that a French poet would not only remove to independent Haiti, but would be capable of ascending to a high ranking political position under the reign of a king who had been fervently described as anti-French in much of the transatlantic print culture of the Haitian Revolution?[20]

Although there is little that directly links Colombel to this particular error of naming, Colombel is intimately involved in the case of Vastey's mistaken identity, a case that has everything to do with how Vastey has been read as not only an ideologue, and thus, the very opposite of a humanist, but as a terrorist.

*

[19]The line published in P.V. Vastey's original poem actually reads "Mais l'instant où je parle est déjà loin de moi" or "But the instance of which I speak is already far from me" (line 6).

[20]P.J.V. Vastey was apparently aware of his cousin Vastey's (Cadet) connection to Christophe (see, Quevilly, 308).

VASTEY AS TERRORIST

In November 1819, Noël Colombel, who described his own title as "Sécretaire Particulier de S. Ex. Le Président d'Haïti," published an indignant response to Vastey's *Essai sur les causes de la Révolution et des guerres civiles d'Hayti*, which had been published earlier that same year. In this pamphlet Colombel accused Vastey of having started a "war of words" [*guerre de plume*] (4) with Alexandre Pétion and later Jean-Pierre Boyer's governments, and of having perpetuated, in general, "the most virulent" and "incendiary" lies about the southern Republic of Haiti. Colombel also insinuated that Vastey was simply a "mercenary scribe" who "enriched" his pockets "through spying and duplicity."[21] He further suggested that Vastey, under Christophe's murderous influence, could only be considered a propagandist who wrote "for his wages under the most ferocious if not the most bloodthirsty of despots" (7). Colombel's ensuing descriptions of Vastey as a corrupt "scoundrel" would be immediately tied to this subsequent claim about Vastey's early years. In a passage that is worth quoting at length, Colombel charged Vastey with have been involved in the Reign of Terror that fell upon Nantes in late eighteenth-century France:

> Vastey, always following the impulse of his heart and attracted by his natural instinct to scenes where great misfortunes would afflict humanity, where crimes and monstrosities without number were to be committed, found in France at the time of the revolution, called the hour of terror, various theaters, where he was able to put his ferocity to good use. After having actively participated in the massacres of 2nd and 3rd of September[22] and having been among the assassins of those horrid days, he attached himself to such a one as Carrier, who fills our memories with horror. Returning to Nantes with this representative of barbarity, for whom he became a henchman and one of the most vile cronies, he found once again the opportunity to display his *savoir faire* in the arts of Néron or the Borgias. Nantes, because of its proximity to the Vendée, which had become the center of civil war, and was the administrative home of the

---

[21] Vastey had also used this word "scribe" to defame his enemies when he accused J.J. Dauxion-Lavaysse, a French spy, of being merely a "miserable scribe" (*À Mes concitoyens* 13).

[22] Colombel appears to have his dates mixed up. The *noyades* took place from November of 1793 to February of 1794. Carrier was tried and then convicted on the 2 and 3, respectively, of September 1794 and was subsequently guillotined in December of 1794.

Department, was to be the scene of terrible crimes. Only a little while after the arrival of Carrier in this city, thousands of individuals of both sexes [...] were thrown into prisons. The number of these innocent victims of the *réaction* grew every day with such a frightening rapidity that soon enough the jail could no longer contain them. Out of fear that some of them might escape, and in the absence of having any other place to lock them away, the cannibals of the Carrier clique came up with a way to accelerate their execution by killing a great number of these unfortunates all at once. To that end, they gave recourse to the *bateaux à soupape*[23]; they filled them with wretches who they had consigned to death, after having attached them two by two, woman and man, in what they call in their barbaric language, *les mariages républicains*[24]; afterward they abandoned the floating scaffolds to the river, and in a few short minutes, they were engulfed by the currents.

Colombel goes on to add, "In these days of death and destruction Vastey was under the influence of this murderous power who made everyone tremble!...Vastey was the favorite of Carrier!...What a great opportunity for him to deploy all the arts of his genius. For he was one of the first to disclose the appalling murders of which we have just spoken" (11).

Colombel's tale about Vastey's supposed involvement in the infamous *Noyades de Nantes* is shocking on many levels, not the least of which is that if these accusations were ever proven to be accurate, Vastey would only have been twelve years old at the time of his conscription. No, it is much more likely that the Vastey described in Colombel's work was one of the many Normand relatives of the Baron de Vastey and, perhaps, even the same relative who is the subject of Philippe Goujard's "L'homme de masse sans les masses ou le déchristianisateur malheureux" (1986).

---

[23] The *bateau à soupape* was actually an invention of Carrier's. In his *Nouveau dictionnaire français*, Richelieu described it as "A simple trap, placed horizontally at the bottom of the boat that could be raised or lowered by means of a hinge...After completely overloading the skiff and having arrived at the destination, one only needed to raise the trap so that an irruption of water would inundate the boat and drown at once the unfortunates who were crammed therein" (qtd. in *L'Intermédiaire des chercheurs et curieux*, 1896, 75).

[24] Another invention of Carrier's (see M. Berriat Saint-Prix as quoted in *L'Intermédiare et chercheurs curieux*, 1896, 75).

In this impeccably researched article, Goujard catalogs with detailed archival precision what he calls the "politique du terrorisme" of Pierre Julien Valentin Vastey (164), who was a paternal relative of Baron de Vastey's. Pierre Julien Valentin Vastey (hereafter referred to as P.J.V. Vastey) was the son of Jean-Valentin Vastey's brother (Pierre Valentin Vastey), and therefore he was Baron de Vastey's first cousin. P.J.V. Vastey, a functionary in the Pays de Caux, where many of Vastey's family members on his father's side resided at the time of the French Revolution (see, Quevilly 2014),[25] is also the author of some of the letters in Quevilly's possession. While Goujard owns that he had never been able to recover P.J.V. Vastey's movements during the Revolution of 1789, he does locate his Vastey as an actor in the Reign of Terror that struck the Pays de Caux beginning in November of 1793. Was Colombel's linkage of Baron de Vastey to the *terrorist* Vastey, then, merely another case of mistaken identity?

The French historian Alfred Lallié gives a detailed description of those closest to Carrier during these fateful events, including Carrier's apparent spy, Lamberty, a former "adjutant-général" named Fouquet, Laveau, a former prisoner, Robin, "son of a wise woman from Nantes," O'Sullivan, also a former soldier, and Foucault, who "ordered the last of the massacres" (10). A person named Vastey is not among the names listed.[26]

Regardless of whether any of these claims may be true, the declaration that Baron de Vastey had been a *terrorist* in revolutionary France, a story Colombel claims was revealed to him by Vastey himself (Colombel,

---

[25] According to Quevilly, Vastey did have a front seat to the events of the French Revolution, but as a spectator rather than an actor. Quevilly writes, "in Rouen, he resided in the shadow of the guillotine, situated only a few dozen meters from his window" (208).

[26] Perhaps it is ironic that even the tale that Goujard weaves out of his archive is plagued by prior biographical errors. In detailing how he came to know the proper first and middle names of the *déchristianisateur* under study in his article, Goujard writes, "In fact, one of the major difficulties that I experienced while undertaking this more biographical research concerns the identity of the personage—just as another rests upon his fate after his release from prison. The scholarly tradition of the late nineteenth century suggests that Vastey was a feudist....In reality, it seems that nothing could be farther from the truth. It was his father, Pierre Valentin, who exercised this profession in Bacqueville-en-Caux....it is possible to believe that our character [P.J.V. Vastey] had been helping his father in his profession as a feudist, and imagined, before the Revolution, that he would succeed him. However, some have confused the father and the son most likely because of the similarity of their first names, which has undoubtedly contributed to this confusion. If the father was called Pierre Valentin, the son was called Pierre Julien Valentin" (160).

Examen, 11–12), serves a statist reading of Vastey's works in a variety of profound ways.[27] Colombel uses this biographical detail not only to bolster his general claim about Vastey's essential moral depravity, but to prove his earlier assertion that the Haitian baron was a hagiographic opportunist who tied his fate to whichever power protected and paid him. Colombel wrote, "he is only doing his job, he uses his usual and favorite weapons in order to earn his infamous salary" (8).

As Colombel's charges reveal, there is much more than merely a potential historical or biographical error *in* the politics of Vastey's name. There is also an argument about *who* and *what* kind of person Vastey might have been; and therefore what kind of scholar he was in the past and can be for us today.

Vastey as Mercenary Scribe

In 1815 a pamphlet entitled, *Le Peuple de la République d'Hayti, à Messieurs Vastey & Limonade*, was sent to the northern kingdom of Henry Christophe.[28] The pamphlet styled itself as a response both to a letter written by Julien Prévost (Comte de Limonade), which was published as a part of *L'Olivier de la paix* (1815), and to Vastey's *Le Cri de la patrie* (1815). In Prévost's letter, which was addressed to Pétion, the Haitian count had urged the president to consent to reunite his republic under the rule of Christophe as their mutual and sovereign king. Alluding to the affair of Dravermann, Agoustine Franco de Médina, and J.J. Dauxion-Lavaysse,[29] the three French spies sent by France to the

---

[27] In contrast, the notion that Vastey had been an enslaved person, promulgated by many nineteenth-century reviewers of his work, has served non-statist readings, principally by portraying Vastey as one who had been wholly humanized not only by his self-taught literacy, but by Haitian independence.

[28] The pamphlet was signed by several dozen men living in Pétion's republic, including, Bazelais, Boyer, Magny, Borgella, B. Inginac, and D. Chanlatte (Juste Chanlatte's brother). Ardouin, however, identifies this pamphlet as having been authored by Sabourin under the orders of Pétion (8: 153–154).

[29] There is a discrepancy in the spelling of Lavaysse's name. Sometimes Vastey spells his name Lavayasse, for example, which is one of the spellings we find in the *Gazette royale d'Hayti* and which is the spelling adopted by some nineteenth-centruy reviewers of his *Voyages aux Iles de Trinidad, de Tobago, & de Paris* (1813) (see, for example, "Professor Rudolph's Elements of Physiology," 165; and volume 5 of Joseph Sabin's *Bibliotheca Americana*, 1873, 233). I have adopted the spelling Lavaysse because that is the way the French spy's name was spelled in a work he himself published in 1813 entitled, *Voyage aux*

island after the Bourbon Restoration to promote dissension between Pétion and Christophe and to gather information that would help France to recover the erstwhile colony, Prévost wrote that the recent events that had transpired between Haiti and France regarding these spies required the reunification of the Haitian people under one leader[30]: "The schemes of Haiti's implacable enemies having been discovered," Prévost argued, "can no longer allow Haitians any hesitation with respect to reuniting, and we must compose a massive force capable of defeating as swiftly as possible the next attacks with which our oppressors threaten us" (3). Prévost went on to say that it had been their ability—the constituents of Pétion and Christophe— to briefly unify in order to ward off the French that had secured continuing freedom from colonial rule for both Haitis: "Have you forgotten that it was only by reciprocal Haitian aid that the French were driven from Port-au-Prince and other places in the island?" (6). Yet, despite what seemed like a friendly overture from the north to the south—Prévost writes, "come, hasten to us our brothers, Blacks and Yellows; come, and you will be welcomed with open arms by our mutual father....King Henry only has one enemy: white French ex-colonists" (2)—the response from the south was not favorable.

The collectively signed letter to Vastey and Prévost unequivocally stated that the inhabitants of the southern republic would rather die than find themselves under the rule of Christophe: "we must repeat it, we have no desire for royal peace with your master, we do not desire any communication with him; we declare once again in the presence of God, in front of the entire universe, that we will never subject ourselves to the French nor to him, and we will never bow our haughty republican heads under the yoke of anyone, whomever that shall be" (7).

Part of the reason for this ire against Christophe—of whom the authors of the letter write, "At least, Christophe is not Haitian. He is

---

Iles de Trinidad, de Tabago [sic], *de la Marguerite, et dans divers parties de Vénézuela, dans l'Amérique méridionale, par J.J. Dauxion Lavaysse.*

[30] According to the testimony of Franco de Médina, who was captured and interrogated by Christophe's government in the fall of 1814, the three spies were sent to the island at the request of a letter they received in June of 1814, signed by Malouet (Vastey, rpt. in *Essai* 62). Médina was supposed to go to the northern part of the island, Dravermann to the south, and Dauxion-Lavaysse was supposed to stay in Jamaica to await a response from Pétion (rpt. in *Essai* 71).

a foreigner; this is without a doubt the reason for which he plagues [the country] with death and destruction" (2)—was almost certainly, at least in part, the insulting manner in which Vastey spoke of Pétion in *Le Cri de la patrie*. Not only did Vastey accuse Pétion of harboring a secret hatred towards "negroes" (*Patrie* 5) but he claimed that Pétion had a desire to be French, which for Vastey meant a desire to be "white." Vastey wrote, "Ah! Pétion, you are more French than white French people even" (*Patrie* 15). Perhaps, more seriously, Vastey had also claimed that Pétion had directly colluded with France in that country's failed attempt to restore French rule over independent Haitians.[31] Addressing himself directly to Pétion's constituents, on this score, Vastey said, "Haitians, my brothers of both colors, who did not have the intention to sell their citizens like general Pétion, read all of the newspapers and printed works published in Port-au-Prince under his orders" (16).

This "war of words," to use Colombel's phrase, which is at the heart of statist readings of Vastey's works, would continue all the way until the latter's death in 1820. In a separate pamphlet published in June of 1815, *Le Cri de la conscience, ou réponse à un écrit, imprimé au Port-au-Prince, intitulé Le Peuple de la République d'Hayti à Messieurs Vastey & Limonade*, Vastey responded to the letter addressed to him and Limonade/Prévost. In this response Vastey once again absolved his southern "compatriots" (5) of any involvement in what he saw as the crimes of Pétion vis-à-vis the three French spies: "Oh, no, it was not you, the work of a monster can not be imputed to all" (*Conscience* 11). For Pétion, however, no such absolution was in sight. Vastey wrote, "...the more I learn about the character of Pétion, the more I find him to be an unconscionable monster" (*Conscience* 31).

Enter Jules Solime Milscent, editor of the first Haitian review, *L'Abeille haytienne* and his sometimes collaborator, Colombel. In his *Essai*, Vastey had sharpened his verbal knives when he wrote that Milscent and Colombel, along with a series of "natives [*indigènes*], whose skin colors may have been black or yellow, but whose characters and principles were as white as that of the white French ex-colonists," (22) should be "treated like the ex-colonists, worse even, because they are traitors; they deserve to be slaves...we could only hope for as much!" (23).

---

[31] As evidence for this claim, Vastey described the contents of a pamphlet written under the "baroque name of Columbus," which he said had urged among other things, less ire towards the French (*Patrie* 57).

One of the principal reasons behind Vastey's manifest and even poisonous ire was that Milscent's review, *L'Abeille haytienne*, published twice per month from 1817 to 1820, contains page after page of damning testimony against Christophe. In the second issue of the periodical, dated 16 August 1817, the editors write, "Hardly a week goes by without some of Christophe's people coming to rally behind the banner of the Republic [of the South]. It has only been a few days since more than twenty of these unfortunates came to live among us; they painted a horrific portrait of the state of degradation and misery under which that despotic *Bacha du Cap* holds the people of the north" (12). This kind of incriminating rhetoric was often deployed not only against Christophe himself, but was often directed toward anyone associated with his monarchy. Of Christophe's nobility, the editors of *L'Abeille Haytienne* write in the issue dated 16 September 1817, "these nobles who were invented right next door to us amount merely to minions doing the bidding of Christophe. If there exist among them some men of good faith, they must be at constant war with their consciences. By accumulating privileges and riches for themselves, they have stripped their unfortunate compatriots of the most sacred rights and have condemned them to a new slavery" ("Suite des Considérations" 4). The same article continues, "this elect nevertheless gives the impression that they have all the comforts of liberty; they are free without a doubt, but at the cost of their serf brothers... who are so oppressed that they cannot even hear the voice that calls them to rally under the banners of the Republic, which is our mother and theirs" (4).

As if the discursive assaults that filled the pages of *L'Abeille haytienne* were not enough to get out the message about the putatively ineffective and despotic rule of Christophe, in 1818 Colombel published a pamphlet entitled, *Réflexions sur quelques faits relatifs à notre existence politique*. Here, Colombel not only accused Christophe of ordering the murders of pregnant women, but he charged the Haitian king with having almost killed his own infant son simply because the baby was crying: "His own son, Monseigneur le Prince Victor, when he was only a few months old," Colombel writes, "was sleeping in the room where his father slept. The baby, experiencing some need, started to cry. Furious that the cries of his noble progeny had interrupted his slumber, [Christophe] rushed upon the poor royal offspring, like a madman, grabbed him by one leg and was going to throw him out the window when someone, who was right next to him, stopped his arm and prevented him from committing infanticide" (13).

In many respects, Vastey's *Essai*, while providing a general survey of Haitian history that could combat European representations, is also a direct response to the competing *histories* of Christophe's kingdom produced in the pages of *L'Abeille haytienne* and in the works of Colombel. Vastey spends a considerable amount of time discussing both Milscent and Colombel and what he viewed as the various calumnies they were spreading through their writing. One particular mention of both journalists in Vastey's *Essai* deserves more attention than the others precisely because it provides the perfect context needed to understand Milscent and Colombel's own statist readings of Vastey's works:

> *Le Cri de la conscience* has never received, in the latest writings from Port-au-Prince, a response from our antagonists. They limited themselves to saying that it was a simple diatribe, fabricated in Sans-Souci; I agree with them that it is much easier to use this epithet than to be able to respond to it. (*Essai*, 300)

In other words, Vastey charges his detractors with using words like "scribe" and "ideologue" precisely so that they will not have to fully engage with his charges against them.

Although Vastey appeared to believe that Milscent and Colombel were behind the publication of *Le Peuple de la République*, Colombel and Milscent, who were not among the signatories of the document, denied any involvement. Colombel, in particular, claimed to have been in France at the time of the affair of Dravermann, Médina, and Lavaysse, and Colombel directly refuted the notion that he had returned to Haiti with the latter as a part of the Bourbon espionage (one of Vastey's charges against him) and declared that he was at that time totally "ignorant" of all political affairs in Haiti (22). Colombel's explanation of his whereabouts is in some senses supported by a brief biographical detail in a footnote written by Joseph Saint-Rémy in *Mémoires du Général Toussaint Louverture, écrits par lui-même* (1853), who notes that Colombel did not arrive back to Haiti from France until 1816 (129ftn). Nevertheless, if Vastey was dismayed to have never received an answer to *Le Cri de la conscience*, in November of 1819, Colombel certainly provided a spirited *réponse* to the former's *Essai* by publishing his *Examen d'un pamphlet, Ayant pour titre: Essai Sur les Causes de la Révolution et des Guerres Civiles d'Haïti, Etc.*

True to its title, Colombel, who claimed to have penned this work hastily and in a mere matter of days (1819, iiftn), described his motive for having undertaken such a project: "we must confess to [Vastey] that our conclusion about his work," Colombel wrote, "which is our object of study, is that it does not have any of the qualities that characterize a history; that we find on the contrary, that there are only libels, those of a most virulent and incendiary pamphlet..." (6). While Colombel would go on to accuse Vastey of producing with his *Essai* "elaborate sophistries, erroneous conclusions, and slanderous and untrue assertions," (10) the opening material of his *Examen* was actually devoted to describing Vastey as a morally bereft "mercenary scribe" who wrote merely at the behest of Christophe. In contrast, Colombel wrote that "my compatriot Milscent and I...do not write to please anyone in power, or out of this or that consideration, but only to promote the truth and to do so under the inspiration of our conscience" (7). Colombel is likely the first reviewer to suggest that the baron's œuvre had merely been written under the orders of the state. As such, it is important to recognize Colombel as a crucial part of the genesis of contemporary statist readings of Vastey's works.

The personal anecdotes that Colombel provides as evidence for his defamation of Vastey, including his claim that the baron had once admitted, "yes, I am a scoundrel" (9), promotes a picture of Vastey as the sort of "scribe" described by more contemporary critics, but that Vastey would primarily come to be known as *after* his death. As Chap. 3 of this volume will show, *during* his life (and for a long time afterward in anti-slavery and anti-racism circles), Vastey was considered to have been a voice of reason about anti-slavery issues and his writings were often used as examples of black humanity. Before moving on to consider how Colombel's reading of Vastey flies against the grain of most prior nineteenth-century reviews of his œuvre, it is important to briefly set up the ways that humanist readings of Vastey's works, which abounded *during* his lifetime, particularly in the transatlantic abolitionist movement, were undone by the kinds of statist readings performed by Colombel and that were reproduced largely *after* Vastey's lifetime.

After Vastey's execution in the fall of 1820, an entire cadre of historians and other chroniclers emerged, not only to banalize Vastey by claiming the unimportance, incoherence, and essential unreliability of his works, but to assault the baron's character in a manner that eerily resembles Colombel's writing. Starting with William Woodis Harvey's

Sketches of Hayti: From the Expulsion of the French, to the Death of Christophe (1827), Vastey's career as an author once again became linked to the charge of terrorism. As in the case of Colombel's similar accusation, this judgment would come largely as the result of determinations about Vastey's personality rather than the contents of his writing. Harvey wrote, "Had the character of Vastey been as consistent, as his abilities were respectable, he would have deserved our admiration; but this unhappily was not the case. His fierceness, his duplicity, and his meanness, rendered him at once despicable and odious. He cheated whenever an opportunity offered, and afterwards boasted of his dishonesty. The hatred which he entertained for whites of all nations rendered him sometimes an object of terror" (223). Harvey goes on to charge Vastey not only with the monstrous crime of having "wantonly imbrued his hands in the blood of his nurse" (223), but with having "during the struggle for liberty [of Haitians]…coolly assisted in the massacre of thousands," which "he alone was capable of executing" (224).

While both James Franklin who published *The Present State of Hayti* in 1828 and Charles Mackenzie in his two-volume *Notes on Haiti: Made During a Residence in that Republic* (1830) also throw proverbial shade on Vastey's character and reliability (Franklin, 91–92; Mackenzie, 7, 84, 92), in 1842 James Candler more forcefully linked Vastey's purportedly depraved psychology to the supposedly unreliable content of his works. In his *Brief Notices on Hayti*, Candler wrote that Vastey was "a man of respectable literary acquirements, as his history of Hayti shows, but of a base and dishonorable disposition" (37). A manuscript entitled, "The Last Days of Christophe," published in March of 1856 and purportedly written by one of Christophe's former physicians, Jabez Sheen Birt, continued to paint Vastey as morally bereft: "The fiend Vastey died a miserable coward, as he had lived a tyrannical villain. I never knew a man more generally detested" (803).[32]

---

[32] The note preceding this work published in *Littel's Living Age* notes that "the manuscript is furnished us by Mr. B.P. Hunt, a leading merchant at Port-au-Prince, and one of the most intelligent and cultivated of his calling in any country." The explanatory remarks lead to a second note by Hunt who detailed "the circumstances under which it came into his possession:" "The manuscript narrative of the death of Christophe, which I placed in your hands a few days since, was copied by me from the original about twelve years ago, at Cape Haytien. I found it in the hands of a shipmaster. The only account which he could give of it was, that it had been presented to him by a Haytian merchant of Port-au-Prince

Vastey's reputation, perhaps less surprisingly, was also surrounded by questions marks in metropolitan France. In 1819 a reviewer from the *Bibliotheque universelle* wrote of his *Réflexions politiques*,

> The author is, as you can believe, under the influence of an extreme rancor against the nation of France, in general, and against the writers who have acknowledged the possibility of a return of another order of affairs than that which currently exists in the kingdom of Haiti. This writing is almost from one end to the other, a violent diatribe against the French, the ex-colonists, and certain individuals who played a role in Saint-Domingue. The work seems principally designed to encourage in the heart of the young royal prince a vigorous hatred against anyone who could attempt to bring a system of oppression back to the colony. ("Civilisation" 58–59)

The French explorer Gaspard-Théodore Mollien penned a history of Haiti published in 1830 in which he not only detailed the supposed involvement of Vastey in several lugubrious Christophean plots, including spying, laughing at indiscriminate murder, and assassination attempts (Mollien 2: 23, 119, 157–158), but he also connected two of Vastey's writings to the kind of statist reading performed in Colombel's work. Mollien wrote that after Pétion had himself re-elected as Président in 1815, "Christophe could no longer take it; he ordered his secretaries, Dupuy, Vastey, [and] Préseaux [sic], to destroy his adversary with the stroke of their pens; the presses of Sans-Souci, of Cap, of the Citadelle, would henceforth only be used to print 'le cri de la conscience,' 'le cri de la patrie'" (2: 136).

The connection between Vastey's personal character and the character of his writing also found its way into mid-nineteenth-century Haitian-produced historiography, almost certainly because of the pervasiveness of the transatlantic print culture of the Haitian Revolution. Indeed, as I have elsewhere written, Vastey was the most discussed Haitian author of the early to mid- nineteenth century (Daut, *Tropics* 136). Passages concerning Vastey from the writings of mid-nineteenth-century's Haiti's

---

whose father, an American, had been in trade at Cape Haytien in the time of Christophe. This narrative is anonymous, but the text shows that it was written by one of the king's physicians, and on the making of inquiries of a Mr. Castel, an old officer of Christophe's household, I learned that the king had two physicians—namely, the Baron Stewart, a Scotchman, and the Chevalier Bird [sic]. The latter was no doubt the author" (799).

most important historians Thomas Madiou, Beaubrun Ardouin, and Joseph Saint-Rémy, are so telling with respect to how often they repeat, extend, and attempt to legitimate statist readings of Vastey's works that they are worth quoting at length. Beginning with Madiou, in volume five of his *Histoire d'Haiti*, the Haitian historian writes of Vastey, whom Madiou called "l'organe du Roi" (5: 421):

> Among the most prominent of those who made up his entourage, reports indicate that the most cruel and the most perfidious were above all generals Richard and Joachin and Baron de Vastey. This last, educated, industrious, [and] effective, made himself indispensable to Christophe who only kept him closest, over all of the rest, because of his talents. Vastey, *homme de couleur*, had even tried to bring down Prévost and Dupuy, of whom he was jealous. He slandered and defamed them. He was feared by families throughout Cap[-Haïtien], because they regarded him as the most dangerous of the king's spies. He was often evil merely for the sake of being evil, without even being able to obtain any immediate advantage. (5: 240)

Ardouin tied Vastey's corruption, for his part, not merely to the reign of Henry Christophe, but also to that of the Emperor Dessalines. In volume 6 of his *Études sur l'Histoire d'Haïti*, Ardouin writes,

> Most likely, the emperor had recognized that the corruption or negligence of certain functionaries had *compromised* the rights of public domain, and that the properties of the ex-colonists had passed into the hands of persons who were not qualified to receive them. But, in requiring a new justification of titles to be brought to the minister of finance, who was incapable on his own of understanding this material, he had to send the property owners back before Vastey, the author of this corruption of which we speak; this was, in effect, to give [Vastey] the ability to arbitrarily impose bribes upon the proprietors, even those who were entitled to a claim. (1856, 6: 164)

Later, in the same volume Ardouin paints Vastey, under Dessalines, as an opportunist, if not a manipulative thief:

> It must be said that Dessalines was often of the most cheerful humor, and that he liked to amuse himself by playing jokes, whether with words or with actions, which were inappropriate for the rank he occupied. For example, recognizing the incompetence of General Vernet, as minister of finance, he said one day: 'My poor comrade only spends his time making lunch and making love; he relies entirely on Vastey whose purse is filling more every day.' (240)

Nevertheless, Ardouin, while recognizing Vastey's superior capabilities as a writer and historian, also, like Madiou, tied the former's publications to statist rather than humanist aims. Ardouin concluded, "Vastey published the best of his writing in *Réflexions*, in the form of a letter to a colonist named Mazères, on the topic of Blacks and Whites, etc. But counter to the ardent republicanism of H[érard] Dumesle,[33] it was accompanied by all the platitudes of a mind subject to the yoke of an atrocious tyrant." (8: 254)

Saint-Rémy was even more ardent in his criticisms of Vastey than Madiou and Ardouin. In volume 4 of his *Pétion et Haïti* (1857), citing the previous listed passage from Harvey as evidence of Vastey's character, Saint-Rémy wrote, "Vastey was himself one of the most corrupt and corrupting of men." (103)[34] While in volume 5 of the same work published in 1864, Saint-Rémy described Vastey (along with Juste Chanlatte) as one of Christophe's "monsters who merely doled out pompous praise" for the Haitian king in his writings because he sought to "save his own life" (5: 48).

Perusing contemporary criticism of Vastey produces a qualitatively similar narrative. Vastey's own twenty-first-century biographer, Laurent Quevilly, for instance, appears to believe Vastey's most ardent critics when he calls the baron an "idéologue implacable" (244). The baron as ideologue has also been the conclusion drawn by many of those who find his works of the utmost importance for Haitian studies. Jean Casimir refers to Vastey as "the most important ideologue," (2013, 17) while the literary critic Doris Garraway has variously called Vastey Christophe's "principal polemicist" ("Empire of Freedom" 9) and "the leading ideologue and apologist for Christophe's kingdom." ("Empire of Freedom" 10) Vastey is similarly characterized in the work of Nick Nesbitt who has written that Vastey's *Le Système* "might ultimately be called an ideological war machine rather than a scientific critique" ("Afterword" 296;

---

[33] Dumesle was the author of a lyric prose poem entitled, *Voyage dans le nord d'Hayti ou révélation des lieux et des monuments historiques* (1824).

[34] Ralph T. Esterquest also appears to have been influenced by Harvey when he concludes of Vastey, "His writings show an intensity of love for the blacks and a fierce hatred of all whites" (178). Esterquest had elsewhere appeared to praise Vastey when he wrote, "The productions of the Royal Press [of Christophe] never got beyond the national propaganda stage, and yet, at least one royal author gave promise of literary ability, and it was the Royal Press that gave his writings to the world of books" (173).

Caribbean Critique 177). David Geggus has been more obviously critical of *Le Système* when he suggests, "Vastey's book is a litany of atrocity stories, which indicts a large portion of Saint-Domingue's famous names. As such it is easy to dismiss as a propaganda piece." ("The Caradeux" 240) The celebrated historian, David Nicholls, also labored to produce Vastey as "the official ideologist and apologist of the kingdom" (1979, 43).

The idea of Vastey as mere ideologue, in fact, has become the filter through which most scholars see all of Vastey's œuvre. Chris Bongie, for example, has produced several such statist readings of Baron de Vastey's writing, among them a chapter in his 2008 book *Friends and Enemies.* After referencing Colombel's categorization of Vastey as a "mercenary scribe," (qtd. in Bongie, *Friends* 32) Bongie proposes that both Vastey and Colombel, "double the rival politicians in whose name they speak." Bongie further argues that Colombel's explication of the relationship of Vastey's writing to the rule of Christophe "has much to tell us about the mutual dependency of (hierarchical) politics and (scribal) writing." "In the case of the two Haitis' deferent scribes and their political masters," he writes, "this dependency is so obvious that it is virtually impossible for us to recuperate either writer as an 'autonomous' intellectual (much less a stylistically interesting author)" (*Friends* 32).

In the preface to his translation of *The Colonial System Unveiled* (2014), Bongie continues with this primarily scribal line of inquiry by writing that Vastey is: "Neither a recognizable *author* nor a producer of 'authentically' Haitian culture." Instead, "Vastey as scribe exemplifies the discomfiting interstitial forms of 'literary life' that flourished in post/revolutionary Haiti" (9). Later in the volume, Bongie argues that we can *only* understand "Vastey as a *scribe*...that is to say as a writer whose subject-position can only with the greatest of difficulty be conceived of apart from the sovereign power it serves" (31). Bongie's evidence for this claim is a letter written to Christophe by the British abolitionist Thomas Clarkson on 20 July 1820. The letter provides Christophe with explicit instructions to give to Vastey in order for the latter to pen a *new* work about the Haitian kingdom that would show the monarchy and its people in a positive light. "Permit me to say a few words more," Clarkson writes,

> concerning this little work, which, though little, I consider to be of great importance. In the first place it must be written by the Baron de Vastey. No one of your Majesty's friends in England could write it, because all the documents are in Hayti; and no person could write it, who had not

witnessed the whole process of the improvement which has taken place in your Dominions, or who had not seen the wonderful change, which has been produced from the beginning of your Majesty's reign to the present time. Secondly, it should contain *a plain* statement of facts, without any extravagant embellishment from the flowery powers of oratory. Thirdly, it should be written in the most modest manner, and with the greatest temperance. Fourthly, nothing should be mentioned in it concerning Protestantism or any intended change of religion. Nothing of a political nature should appear in it. No reflection should be made upon France: indeed it would be better not to mention France at all, except in a respectful manner. (qtd. in Bongie, *The Colonial System* 34)

Bongie, who reprints a great deal of the letter, concludes, "What I hope emerged from my purposely detailed rendering of Clarkson's obsessively precise instructions is a clear sense of the institutional framework within which Vastey's œuvre was produced—or, in other words, a clear sense of the *scribal* conditions that...must be the starting point for any appraisal of him as a writer" (35).

We must remember, however, not simply that these instructions were given to Christophe only *after* Vastey had already produced 11 prose works that had circulated widely in the Atlantic World, but that Clarkson's mandates are actually themselves a *response* to Vastey's writings. While Bongie has linked these instructions to speculation about Clarkson's reading of *Le Système*, the British abolitionist is, at least in theory, responding to all of Vastey's written works by urging Christophe to instruct Vastey *not* to publish the kinds of works that he had already published. Vastey's publications, on the whole, perform every forbidden foible that Clarkson warned against, particularly, the *disrespectful manner* in which France is discussed throughout Vastey's writings, which Bongie acknowledged (*The Colonial System* 35). The letter itself, thus, suggests that Vastey's writings had not been entirely statist, even if commissioned by Christophe. Clarkson is clearly inferring that Christophe had not been able to properly rein in or instruct Vastey and that he *should have*. In fact, Vastey's already published response to previous calls for him to self-censor allows us to imagine precisely how he would have responded to Clarkson's later directives. In *Le Système* Vastey wrote, "What? They have had the right to publish base fabrications about us for centuries [...]! And good God! Now that we are capable of avenging and enlightening, you say that we do not have the right because we might offend white people, in general? What a miserable sophism, an absurd puerility!" (95).

Yet, in the end, the principal issue with *statist* readings of Vastey's works remains, as the next chapter will aim to show, that he was primarily read in this manner *after* Colombel's problematic and suspect designation of Vastey not merely as a "mercenary scribe" but as a terrorist. Much to the contrary, most readers prior to Colombel's published response to the *Essai*, who had no putative personal knowledge of Vastey's personality or character, read his works as the greatest expression of humanism and anti-slavery thought to have emerged in the Black Atlantic world. These early readings, in turn, greatly influenced nineteenth-century abolitionist accounts of Vastey's life and works in the broader transnational African American intellectual tradition.

What accounts, then, for the gap between the statist readings performed largely *after* his death by nineteenth-century travel writers, most of whom claimed to have known him or to have received first-person testimony about him, and the *humanist* readings performed largely during his lifetime by people who did not personally know him and only had his writings alone to guide their perceptions of his works? If, in fact, the error of Vastey's name may have unleashed the statist criticisms of his personal history enumerated by some nineteenth-century authors and repeated by many twentieth- and now twenty-first-century critics, Vastey's supposed immorality has negatively affected the importance of his writing.

CHAPTER 3

The Uses of Vastey: Reading Black Sovereignty in the Atlantic Public Sphere

In February 1817, Thomas Strafford returned to Kingston from the Kingdom of Hayti. Shortly thereafter he would be accused before and would go on to be convicted by the county of Middlesex Assizes for having published "several wicked, scandalous, malicious, seditions and inflammatory libels" ("Strafford Indictment" 347). Strafford was originally from Kingston but according to the detailed record of indictment, which amounts to about thirty-eight pages in length, he had recently been living in northern Haiti. While in Cap-Henry, Strafford had evidently made the acquaintance of King Henry Christophe, who is referred to in the indictment as the "usurped, accursed [...] person called Christopher to wit" (347–348). The allegations against Strafford had everything to do with his alleged connection to Christophe. The accused was charged with "being a malicious and ill disposed Person [who] unlawfully, wickedly, and maliciously devis[ed] and intend[ed] to aid further [...] the said Christopher in such designs and endeavours to excite disaffection and insubordination [...] amongst the Slaves of the said Island of Jamaica" (348). The defendant was, furthermore, accused of having attempted "to disquiet, molest, and destroy tranquility and the good order of the said Island of Jamaica in furtherance and aid of the said Person called Christophe" (348).

© The Author(s) 2017   63
M.L. Daut, *Baron de Vastey and the Origins of Black Atlantic Humanism*,
The New Urban Atlantic, DOI 10.1057/978-1-137-47067-6_3

It is not surprising that a person returning from independent Haiti to a colony where slavery still reigned might be vulnerable to charges of sedition in connection with anti-slavery activity.[1] In the early nineteenth-century, Haiti stood simultaneously as the pinnacle of black sovereignty and the nightmare of postcolonial rule. What is surprising about this indictment is the particular evidence provided to uphold these charges and therefore to justify Strafford's conviction.

What was this "wicked" document that Strafford had apparently so "maliciously" carried with him to Kingston, allegedly, with the goal of inciting slave rebellion? And what, if anything, did Haiti's King Christophe have to do with it?

The "seditious" material in question was written by none other than Baron de Vastey. In perusing the pages of the indictment, we learn in overly verbose and repetitive prose that on 13 December 1816, Strafford "unlawfully quit" Haiti, "with the purpose of clandestinely landing in the said Island of Jamaica" (348). After having arrived in Kingston on 6 January 1817,[2]

> the evil, dishonest Strafford did publish and cause to be published a most wicked, scandalous, seditious, and inflammatory libel of and concerning the condition of Slaves and of and concerning the existing state of Slavery, and of and concerning the conduct relation and Sentiments of white Persons towards Slaves, and of and concerning the insurrection and revolt in the said Part of the said Island of Saint Domingo, and which said wicked, scandalous, malicious, seditious, and inflammatory Libel is printed in the French language and purports to have been composed by the Descendant of an African called the Baron de Vastey [...] and which said wicked, scandalous, malicious, sedition and inflammatory libel is entitled in the French language, "Reflexions [sic] sur les Noirs et les Blancs [...]" [...]

---

[1] Documents standing almost entirely alone as evidence for the encouragement of slave rebellion may have been a common phenomenon in the Caribbean. In a recent article, Romy Sanchez has revealed that B.B. Thatcher's fairly innocuous 1834 *Memoir of Phillis Wheatley, A Native African and A Slave*, was among the documents listed in an indictment of the Cuban rebel, Jorge Davidson (467, 474). Davidson was a "mulatto" from Jamaica who was expelled from Cuba in 1837 under "suspicion of having diffused pernicious doctrine among the slaves of this island" (Sanchez 461).

[2] Despite the charges listed in the indictment, it is unlikely that Strafford was formally working for Christophe. The *Almanach Royal d'Hayti* for the years 1814, 1815, 1816, 1817, and 1818, do not list any Thomas Strafford as a member of Christophe's government.

meaning as these English words follow (that is to say) Reflexions on the Blacks and Whites. (348–349).

Strafford's sentence for having published a copy or copies of Baron de Vastey's *Réflexions sur une lettre de Mazères* (1816) (whose subtitle contained the words "on the blacks, the whites, the civilization of Africa and the kingdom of Haiti") was recorded as a fine of 500 pounds. Jail time was also mandated and Strafford was to "be and stand committed until such security be given" (384).

Almost the entire indictment, beginning on page 346 of the register and ending on page 384, is made up of handwritten passages copied from the original French of Vastey's *Réflexions*, which appear alongside original translations into English.[3] Although, it can hardly be considered a faithful rendition of the Haitian original, this Jamaican translation for the purposes of indictment is noteworthy, if only because it is entirely interventionist and inflected with the carceral aims of the court. Not only does the translator insert parenthetical asides into the middle of quoted passages (as above), but he often prefaces these translations with unequivocal judgment designed to stand as evidence for the charges at hand. The translator prefaces the following translation, for example, by noting that the passage contains "said wicked, scandalous, seditious, and inflammatory words" (354). Baron de Vastey is then quoted as having written of the logic behind the Haitian Revolution:

> Wearied with so many crimes and offenses, we ran to Arms, we measured our strength with our exertions, we fought body to body, Man to Man, with stones, with iron [...] to preserve our liberty, our existence, those of our Wives and Children:—After having spilt our Blood in Streams mixed with that of our Tyrants, we remained Masters of the field of Battle. Let Mazères (meaning the said Mazères),[4] that ferocious and treacherous Colonist, who has been [...] one of the instigators of the cruelties of all kinds which his Countrymen have exercised upon us, [...] let him recollect how many Victims he has caused to be sacrificed or he has massacred with his own hands, then he will see if we have a right to that liberty and

---

[3] I first learned of this document from a footnote in Jonathan Dalby's *Crime and Punishment in Jamaica* (2000) (50; 70 ftn68).

[4] Vastey's *Réflexions* was directed toward a publication that appeared in France in 1814 under the title, *De l'Utilité des colonies*, which was signed "M. Mazères, colon."

independence which we have conquered at the price of so much Blood
[…] I am far from wanting to dispute the right that other Nations have
had to render themselves independent, but I dare affirm without fear of
being contradicted that no people has had more right to liberty and independence than the people of Hayti. (364)

So, it was that the first English translation of Vastey's *Réflexions sur une
lettre de Mazères* was commissioned solely in order to put Strafford in
prison.

It will perhaps not be difficult for the modern reader to imagine what
was perceived to be so dangerous and threatening to the colonial government in Jamaica about Vastey's rather singular, and in some ways,
exceptionally violent claim to sovereignty on Haiti's behalf. Baron de
Vastey was a black identified writer from a sovereign black state that sat
in the middle of a decidedly non-sovereign Caribbean archipelago. This
was a space controlled primarily by four white empires: Spain, France,
England, and the Netherlands. The act of the self-identified descend-
ant of an "African"[5] defending the sovereignty of a (black) postcolonial
nation was always going to be perceived by (white) colonial ruling powers as seditious, dangerous, and even malicious.[6] Moreover, at the time
Vastey published his *Réflexions*, Haitian independence had not been officially recognized by any other nation.

Haiti was not merely being passively ignored by the other world powers so much as it was being consciously disavowed, as colonial governments worked to actively "suppress certain memories of the Haitian
Revolution" (Fischer 38). Early Haitian writers often tasked themselves
with countering attempts at suppression by publishing performative
memories of Haitian independence. Doris Garraway has written, to that

---

[5] Recall that in his *Réflexions sur une lettre de Mazères*, Vastey referred to his mother as
the *"Africaine"* who "gave him life" (31).

[6] Writing of Vastey's, *Le Système colonial dévoilé* (1814), and its "stunningly detailed critique of 'the injustice and inhumanity of the colonial system,'" Chris Bongie suggests that
"[f]irst time readers of the text today will no doubt be struck by the incendiary contents of
Colonial System as were readers and reviewers in the 1810s" (Bongie, *The Colonial System*
64). Vastey's postcolonial reversal on the title page of *Le Système* would likely have seemed
particularly incendiary to the French colonists. Mocking the former French colonist, Baron
de Malouet, the title page of Vastey's *Le Système* reads: "At last, the secret full of horrors
is known: the Colonial System is the domination of the Whites, It is the Massacre or the
Enslavement of Blacks."

end, "writing and crucially print were the indispensable means by which Haitians attempted to declare and make manifest Haitian sovereignty by publicly disseminating defenses of that sovereignty as so many textual speech acts" ("Print, Publics" 82). Vastey's *Réflexions sur une lettre de Mazères*, as merely one of these numerous "textual speech acts," was as much a defense of Haiti's sovereignty as it was the indisputable evidence. If Haitian sovereignty represented a continuation of the Haitian Revolution's threat to the Atlantic World, (black) Haitian writing was the proof.

Reading Vastey's words as deadly weapons is not entirely out of keeping with the Haitian baron's own argumentative strategy. After all, he had made the argument that the Haitian print public sphere itself could rival the threat of violence that led to Haitian independence. Vastey wrote that he sought to prove to Mazères with his *Réflexions*, "morally and physically, with the pen and with the sword, that we are not inferior to their type" (*RM* 13).

Despite the indictment's inflammatory characterization of Vastey's defense of black humanity and Haitian sovereignty, the vast majority of contemporary Anglophone reviews of his writings were exceedingly positive. One laudatory example comes from Moses Thomas's Philadelphia-based *Analectic Magazine*, which published praise for Vastey and the very same text that Strafford stood accused of having used to incite slave rebellion in Jamaica. The reviewer not only recognized Haitian sovereignty through Vastey's book, but made the case that England, the United States, and the other world powers should do so formally, as well. Vastey's writing, according to the review, "cannot but leave a favourable impression on the minds of our readers relative to... the state of the people in Hayti [...] the most cogent arguments which his Majesty [of Haiti] could urge, in favour of such a recognition [of Haitian independence], would be, to present the other powers with a copy of le Baron de Vastey's Reflections" ("Article V" 403).

The *décalage* is quite large between the interpretation of Vastey's work, and by extension Haitian independence, in the Strafford indictment as "wicked" and "seditious," and the interpretation of his work in the *Analectic Magazine* as the best argument for Haitian sovereignty. This difference can serve as the impetus for understanding how *unofficial* arguments for black sovereignty in the nineteenth-century Anglo-European world were channeled to a large extent through the *official* writings of Baron de Vastey. After publication of the first full length

English translation of *Réflexions sur une lettre de Mazères* in March of 1817, Vastey gained an international reputation in anti-slavery circles not only as the foremost defender of Haiti's sovereignty, but as the foremost defender of (black) human rights. The same damning critiques of slavery, colonialism, and color prejudice that appeared threatening to colonial authorities in Jamaica helped to cement Vastey's image as, in one nineteenth-century natural historian's terms, "a practical demonstration of what the negro is capable of doing," after having "gained and maintained their liberty by striking manfully with the sword" (Ewcorstart 272).

By looking at largely contemporaneous nineteenth-century writing from England, the United States, and France, I want to both make the case that Vastey's books became the signs and symbols of the promises of black sovereignty in the Atlantic World and understand why they had such an important impact. To this end, I consider three early nineteenth-century readings of Vastey's works performed by his British translator, the botanist William Hamilton; the U.S. journalist and future Attorney General Caleb Cushing; and the French anti-slavery historian, Antoine Métral, in order to document how Vastey's ideas positively inflected international attitudes towards Haitian independence.

Although influence is notoriously difficult to measure, these three writers have been chosen because their reviews and judgments seem to have greatly contributed to the impact of Vastey's work in the early nineteenth century. Their engagements with Vastey's writings demonstrate how the case for Haitian sovereignty was mediated through several separate but related realms, including, literature, literacy, history, science, and the law. Following Hamilton's translation of *Réflexions sur une lettre de Mazères*, Vastey's works became available for use not only by Anglophone abolitionist writers and activists but by natural historians, many of whom used Vastey's words to both affirm Haitian sovereignty and to make arguments about the capacity for all black people to rule themselves without colonial intervention.

Judging by subsequent citations and references, the writings on Vastey by Hamilton, Cushing, and Métral, also provided crucial momentum for many other U.S., British, and more surprisingly, French authors, who were engaged in ardently urging their governments to formally recognize Haitian independence. Nineteenth-century reviews of Vastey's writings also help us to see how his efforts to study the meaning and consequences of black identity became part of the same transatlantic Afro-diasporic network of translation and circulation that would claim Phillis

Wheatley, Ignatius Sancho, and Olaudah Equiano as the primary signs and symbols of African literacy, and therefore, of African humanity.[7] The major difference here, however, is that Vastey's writings are not only made to stand as evidence for "African" literacy as humanity, but they represent the justification for Haitian, and by extension, black sovereignty.

One question I am also asking in this chapter is what accounts for these positive interpretations of Vastey's writings as humanist, which so vastly diverge from the majority of those discussed in Chap. 2 where Vastey was painted as a propagandist? Beyond understanding varying critiques of his writing along the binaries of pro-slavery or abolitionist thought, colonialist or anti-colonialist arguments, how do we account for the same works being read and *used* in such directly conflicting ways by people whose ultimate goals might otherwise be largely aligned? These are crucial questions for the examination of Vastey's role in the development of Black Atlantic humanism.

One of my contentions is that the nineteenth-century readings, whether they render his works as propagandist or as humanist, have influenced twentieth-century and contemporary readings of Vastey's work. I am particularly interested in what the practices of generous reading under study in this chapter, as opposed to the skeptical readings discussed in the previous chapter of this volume, teach us about understanding the legacy of Vastey's works for the philosophical and material discourse of Black Atlantic humanism for which nineteenth-century Haiti was not merely the symbol but the argument.

*

SCIENCE AND SOVEREIGNTY

In Liverpool on 26 March 1817 there appeared in publication a formal, full-length English translation of Vastey's *Réflexions sur une lettre de Mazères* under the title, *Reflexions on the Blacks and Whites [...]*

---

[7] In 1808, the Abbé Henri Grégoire published his famous, *De la littérature des nègres* (a work which Vastey cites in his *Réflexions sur une lettre de Mazères* [18–19]), which would be almost immediately translated into English, where it would appear in Brooklyn in 1810 under the title, *An Inquiry Concerning the Intellectual and Moral Faculties, and Literature of Negroes.* Wheatley, Equiano, and Sancho, as well as Saint-Domingue's Julien Raimond, are all discussed in Grégoire's book as proof of African literacy as the sign of African humanity. The entire point of chapter VII entitled, "Littérature des Nègres" is to prove "that with Negroes the intellectual faculties are just as susceptible to development as they are with the Whites" (178).

Translated from the French of Baron de Vastey, which was dedicated "[t]o the Philanthropists of every country" (n.p.). The translator signed his name only W.H.M.B, but I have elsewhere identified him as a British botanist named William Hamilton (Daut, *Tropics*, 140–141 ftn20), an assertion I will return to in just a moment. Seeming to almost be in dialogue with the Strafford indictment, Hamilton defended Vastey's "Bloody" linguistic style from any possible reading of the latter's motives as malicious when he wrote:

> If in some parts the language of wounded feelings appear too strong, or too acrimonious for English ears, let the reader cast his eye over the latter pages, containing a few specimens of the humanity of the ex-colonists, when power was on their side, and he will there find an apology which no feeling heart can hesitate to admit. (11)

Here, Hamilton, certainly influenced by Vastey's own discussions of the barbarity of the ex-colonists, uses irony to call into question what kind of humanity can exist in a system of torture like slavery. Hamilton implores his ostensibly male British readers, therefore, to forgo harsh judgment of Vastey's violent prose by putting themselves in the place of the formerly enslaved Africans of Haiti: "Let him for a moment imagine himself in the situation of a Haytian, witnessing the barbarities exercised upon a Father, Mother, Brother, Sister, Wife, or Friend *torn to pieces by blood hounds, roasted by fire, thrown alive in sacks into the sea, or smothered in the holds of ships with the vapor of sulphur*" (12).[8] Hamilton continues by making an appeal to the sentimentality of his audience, which was fast becoming a popular strategy of abolitionists and other anti-slavery activists: "Let him call to mind these and a thousand other greater barbarities which cannot be enumerated," Hamilton writes, "and the frown of criticism cannot

---

[8] Hamilton is here quoting from (in italics) and paraphrasing passages from Vastey's *Réflexions sur une lettre de Mazères*, which I have left in the original French: "des centaines de victimes enfermées dans le fond de cale des bâtiments, périssaient asphyxiées par les vapeurs du soufre" (96–97). Elsewhere Vastey describes Rochambeau's infamous usage of starved dogs trained to "devour" alive the Haitian revolutionaries (99–100). Another passage details the kidnapping and arrest of Toussaint Louverture, along with "his wife, his children, his family," as well as the executions of Generals Jacques Maurepas and Charles Bélair, who are both described as having "meurent dans les supplices," in front of, and in the case of Bélair with, a spouse (102). Vastey's account of these events was repeated by Thomas Madiou in his daunting *Histoire d'Haïti*: "In the great harbor of Port-au-Prince and in that of Cap [Français] warshps had become floating prisons where *des noirs* and *des hommes de couleurs* were suffocated in the hold" (2: 433) Victor Schoelcher described

but be relaxed into a tear—the severity of reproof lost in the overflowing of compassion" (12).

Hamilton's reading and translation of Vastey's writing encouraged and enabled not only a broad readership for the Haitian baron's works but the adoption of precisely the sentimental views toward Haiti that the British botanist desired. Even though in Chap. 4, I argue that Vastey's writings do not so much seek to evoke sympathy for the enslaved, as they promote the idea that the ex-colonists deserved to be legally punished, Hamilton's writing is an extension of certain other facets of Vastey's Black Atlantic humanist arguments. Hamilton not only encourages his readers in the Atlantic World to manifest sympathy for the plight of Haitians, but he argues for the irrefutability of their inherent humanity, and, most importantly, their right to sovereignty in the region. As a botanist, Hamilton was, however, interested in Haitian independence for scientific and agricultural reasons as well. These reasons fly against the grain of our understanding of the relationship between colonialism and science, empire and sovereignty and, thus, demonstrate why many European, and especially British natural historians, became unlikely allies of early nineteenth-century Haiti.

Previous research by James McClellan (1992), Londa Schiebinger (2004), and others (Hulme 1986; Young 1995; Iannini 2012) both assume and argue that science, and especially natural history, wholly supported colonialism and empire in the eighteenth and nineteenth-centuries. New research, nevertheless, has begun to put such assumptions into question. Julie Chun Kim, has asked, "what happened when the agents of scientific inquiry themselves possessed little commitment to the upholding of imperial order?" ("John Tyley"). The case of William Hamilton, who spent several years living in the West Indies and who was the principal translator of Haiti's Baron de Vastey,[9] provides an

---

these *bateaux à vapeur* as well in his *Vie de Toussaint Louverture* (1889) when he wrote, "They had invented floating prisons called *étouffoirs*" (143). For a more recent account of the genocidal tactics of the French, see Claude M. Ribbe, *Le Crime de Napoléon* (2005).

[9] According to Howard et al., Hamilton visited Nevis in April 1812 and from May–June 1814. From May–July 1815, Hamilton was on the island of Dominica, and in January 1816, he can be placed in Guadeloupe. Although Hamilton "did not specify the year" that he visited Haiti, an article published in the *Liverpool Mercury* on 3 April 1818, establishes that he was "residing at Cape Henry" at that time, while the publication of the English translation of Vastey's *Réflexions sur une lettre de Mazères*, published in 1817, had noted that the translator was a resident of Haiti, putting him in Haiti in the years 1817 and 1818.

interesting perch from which to consider this question. Hamilton's profession as a scientist is key to his ability to use Vastey's writing to make multivalent agricultural arguments in service of British empire. But these arguments were also laden with anti-slavery and anti-colonial rhetoric, which supported rather than undermined the sovereignty of Haiti that the British government would not officially recognize.

Before he published his botanical observations of the Caribbean, Hamilton, who lived at Cap Henry in the Kingdom of Hayti from at least 1817–1818, translated three publications of Baron de Vastey's: *Reflexions on the Blacks and Whites* (1817); *Political Remarks on some French Journals and Newspapers* (1818); and the posthumously published, *An Essay on the Revolution and Civil Wars of Hayti* (1823).[10] The purpose of publishing these works in translation was, in Hamilton's words, to "furnish a most impressive and valuable illustration of the *impolicy*, no less than the *injustice* of slavery, and the evils which unavoidably flow from the *colonial system*" (*An Essay* i, *emphasis in original*). Since these translations were signed only with the initials W.H.M.B. (with the exception of *Political Remarks on some French Works and Newspapers*, which was initially published unsigned), a few words are in order that can help to establish William Hamilton, the botanist, as the translator.

The title page of Hamilton's first known English translation of Vastey's writing, *Reflexions on the Blacks and Whites* (1817), reveals that the book was "[s]old by J. Hatchard [...], Bookseller to the African Institution[11] and may be had of the Booksellers in general" for the price

---

[10] A "*postscript*" apparently written by the publisher notes, "The following work was within a few pages of being ready for publication, when the melancholy intelligence of the death of the patriotic Henry, and the unfortunate overthrow of his wise system of administration, arrested the progress of the press, and put a stop to the completion of the translation. Anxious however to give the work in a perfect form, to a few of the more zealous friends of the African Cause, the Translator has ventured to complete a limited impression of only One hundred copies, for private distribution—not for sale, hoping that the interest which its perusal can hardly fail to excite, at the present period more especially, may eventually lead to its more extensive circulation, through the medium of a larger impression. *Stonehouse, July 1st, 1823.*"

[11] According to Junius P. Rodriguez, the African Institution was created in 1807 after England abolished the slave trade in the Commonwealth, and it was "the premier national British anti-slavery group during the early nineteenth century." Among its members were noted abolitionists, William Wilberforce, Thomas Clarkson, and Zachary Macaulay. The institution closed its doors in 1827 (Rodriguez 12).

of eighteen pence (n.p.). An advertisement from the publisher, F.B. Wright of Castle Street in Liverpool, tells us "[t]he following work, with the English version, was transmitted by the Translator to a friend in this country, with directions to submit the same to consideration of a British public" (5). Providing only a few more clues about the translator's identity, the publisher notes that "the Translator is an Englishman, of a liberal profession, resident in the Island; who appears to have engaged in the task solely with the view of promoting a cause so dear to the interests of freedom and humanity" (5). The section called, "Translator's Preface," adds that the translator considered himself to be a mere "volunteer" (11), and, thus, not officially employed by the government of either Christophe or Great Britain.

The first item that helps identify William Hamilton, the nineteenth-century British botanist, as Vastey's primary translator is an article entitled, "Original and Interesting State Papers," from the *Liverpool Mercury*, dated 3 April 1818. The author of the article states, "We have been favored by a most respectable and intelligent friend, Dr. William Hamilton, now residing at Cape Henry, with the following interesting proclamation, which has not, we believe, appeared before now in any British print." After reprinting Hamilton's translation of Christophe's proclamation,[12] the author inserts a "Note of the translator," which reads, "Owing to the indisposition of Baron Vastey, preventing his attending to public affairs, a small error has crept into this proclamation ...." This article allows us to identify someone named William Hamilton as having lived in Haiti, as well as having been interested in translating Haitian documents, in addition to being aware of

---

[12] The piece was simply entitled, "Proclamation: The King to the Haitians." It bears the strong influence of Vastey's *Réflexions politiques*, particularly, in its argument for what we might call, after Gayatri Spivak, a form of "strategic silence." The proclamation states, for instance, "we will meet [our calumniators] with dignified silence and profound contempt." Furthermore, the king also makes an appeal to what Vastey had called the "civil death" of Haitians during the era of slavery and revolution. The proclamation states, "Robbed of every right, civil, natural and political, we were destitute of everything—without country—asylum—or possessions. Bent beneath the yoke of tyrants we were detested, we held no rank in the scale of men, but were, in effect, civilly and politically dead to the world." For Vastey's similar statement, see Chap. 4 of the present volume.

Vastey's crucial role as the most important of Christophe's political writers.[13]

In volume 5 of *The Gardener's Magazine and Register of Rural and Domestic Improvement* (1829), the botanist Hamilton, this time signing his name as "William Hamilton, M.B.," also translated and quoted from *Réflexions politiques* by the "late Baron de Vastry [sic]" ("Vines"). The initials M.B. stood for Hamilton's medical degree in botany. According to his application for a Radcliffe Travelling Fellowship signed "William Hamilton, M.B. And corresponding Member of the Medico-Botanical Society for London," our botanist was a "Master of Arts and Bachelor of Medicine of the University of Oxford" (1832–1835, 1). The reference to the Vastey translation in the *Gardener's Magazine* helps us to identify the William Hamilton, M.B. of the 1829 article as the "W.H.M.B." referred to in two of the translations. And because the citation is from *Réflexions politiques*, it also establishes Hamilton as the translator of that unsigned publication ("Vines" 100). Although the English translation of Vastey's *Political Remarks* was the only one of the Vastey translations that originally appeared unsigned, Hamilton's translation of it in *The Gardener's Magazine* allows us to also connect him to this publication.[14] Hamilton cross-referenced the earlier translation of *Réflexions politiques* yet again in his English translation of Vastey's *An Essay on the Causes of the Revolution* (v). Further cementing the connection, the British botanist would also reference Vastey as his "talented and lamented friend" in his *Memoir on the Cultivation of Wheat in the Tropics* (1840), which was also signed

---

[13] Hamilton also wrote about having traveled extensively in the Caribbean. According to Howard et al., "We know from articles cited in his bibliography that Hamilton was on Nevis on April 27, 1812, and again in May and June of 1814. In May, June, July, 1815, he was on Dominica, and in January, 1816, on Guadeloupe. He wrote of being in Haiti in the months of January through July, but did not specify the year" (213).

[14] The translation appeared in London in 1818. The title page notes that it was "Translated exclusively for the Pamphleteer" (n.p.). The inaugural issue of the British *Pamphleteer*, which appeared in 1813, gives some clues to the broader aims of the publication set to appear "an average of four or five numbers annually" (n.p.): "we have considered the better sort of those compositions, which, under the appellation of *Pamphlets*, burst forth upon the public, on every new object of inquiry, as stars; which, for the purpose of concentrating their rays into a more durable, as well as convenient, focus for observation, we propose to collect and combine together into distinct volumes, like so many constellations, by means of which these guides through the obscurity of transient opinions will be made mutually to reflect their light upon each other" (iv).

William Hamilton, M.B; while in the *Memoir* itself, Hamilton included yet another passage in translation from *Réflexions politiques* (90).

Hamilton's interest in Haitian affairs went far beyond using Vastey's works to decry the "injustice of slavery." This is evidenced by a letter that Hamilton wrote to Baron Dupuy, which mentions his personal correspondence with Joseph Banks (see, "To Joseph Banks;" and Howard et al.).[15] In the undated letter that Hamilton transcribes for the benefit of Banks, the botanist implores Dupuy to send him several specimens of two specific plants, namely the "Krameria ixina" and the "Théophraste américain," "for the gardens of his Majesty at Kew." Hamilton had explained to Dupuy in rather broken French, "I took with me two types of plants from your country, which are very beautiful and of interest, because this is the first time that they have been brought to Europe." Hamilton wrote, nevertheless, that he was disappointed because as he explains, "[t]he seeds that I brought have not given at the present time any indication of growth, which greatly upsets me."[16]

Hamilton's interest in the astringent plants, often used to color wine, can be partially explained by the natural curiosity of a botanist. But he was interested in the agriculture of Haiti for more philosophical reasons as well. Hamilton consistently sought to make the argument that developing and encouraging sustainable crops, such as wheat, to grow in the "tropics" would help to combat slavery by making the forced labor of enslaved Africans unnecessary, or at the very least, less profitable. In the section entitled, "To the Reader," from his *Memoir on the Cultivation of Wheat in the Tropics* (1840), Hamilton explains,

> The increased facilities afforded to the culture of the [sugar] Cane, by the introduction of the Slave Trade, operated so powerfully to the exclusion of

---

[15] Sir Joseph Banks was a famous botanist and natural historian. For over forty years, he presided over the Royal Society, the oldest scientific institution of England. He also established the Kew Botanical Gardens, one of the most noteworthy centers for the study of botany in the world (P. Edwards, "Sir Joseph Banks and the Botany of Captain Cook's Three Voyages"). Baron Dupuy is listed as "sécretaire interprète du Roi" in the *Almanach Royal d'Hayti* (1814) (12). Dupuy was also a member of the Privy Council of the King (29) and was a knight of the royal order (32).

[16] "j'apportais deux especes de plantes de votre pays qui sont tres [sic] jolies, et tres interessantes, car c'est la premiere fois qu'elles ont été apportées en Europe," but, he writes, "Les graines qui [sic] j'apportais n'ont pas données jusqu'à ce temps aucune apparence de la vegetation, qui me fait bien facher."

Wheat, as to create an almost total oblivion of its former flourishing existence, and give birth to an unfounded prejudice; the effect of which has
been to render the modern inhabitants of these very regions dependant
for their supply of this necessary article of human sustenance, upon distant
countries, and far less favourable climates. (9)

Hamilton consistently likens what he calls the prejudice against wheat in
the tropics to prejudices against Africans and their descendants in that
same ecological space. He goes on to explain how slavery in the colonies had created broad food dependencies in the West Indies by making
these islands (even where slavery had already been abolished by 1840)
reliant upon metropolitan centers for basic commodities such as wheat
and other popular foodstuffs like wine and corn. Hamilton found his evidence, in part, in the works of Baron de Vastey:

> Other causes appear to have concurred with the African Slave Trade, in
> excluding not only the culture of the Cerealia,[17] but likewise the manu-
> facture of wine and other objects of European industry, from Haiti, under
> the Colonial Regime, which are fully explained in the following passage
> extracted from the 'Reflexions Politiques' of my talented and lamented
> friend, Baron de Vastey, [...], and upon which comment is unnecessary:
> "Government has made many experiments: already it has *sown*, and *reaped*
> *Wheat*, Barley, and *Oats*; and we have ample proof that our having been so
> long without these substantial productions, has arisen only from the malice
> of the ex-colonists, and the identification of their interests with those of
> the mother country. The Carthaginians, the firmer to impose their yoke
> upon the Sicilians forbade the cultivation of Wheat under pain of death. In
> like manner, under the Colonial system, the cultivation of Wheat, or of the
> Vine, for the manufacture of Wine, was prohibited under the most severe
> penalties." (qtd. in Hamilton, *Memoir* 10; original in Vastey, *RP* 108–109)

Hamilton viewed antipathy to the production of wheat, corn, and wine,
as commodities in the tropics, as a mirror to the same prejudices that
situated Africans as the forced laborers of an economy dominated by the
sugar trade. He quotes Vastey to prove his point: "M. de Soleil, a Planter
of Gonaïves, having made some pleasant wine, gave a portion of it to
M. de Bellecombe, who was then Governor, to taste; who rewarded his
zeal and industry by fine and imprisonment" (qtd. in Hamilton, *Memoir*

---

[17] The scientific term for wheat.

10; original in Vastey, *RP* 109 ftn). Apparently, not only suggesting that wine could actually be produced in the colony but going ahead and manufacturing it, was regarded by colonial authorities with as much suspicion as Strafford's dissemination of Vastey's *Réflexions sur une lettre de Mazères*, the punishment having been nearly identical.

Hamilton was clearly influenced in his assessment of the legacy of food dependency left to the former colony by Baron de Vastey's thoughts on the matter. In his *Réflexions politiques* (the work from which Hamilton quotes above), Vastey had written that what he called this "impolitic system" (*RP* 110) had been designed to enrich the plantation owners, at the expense of everyone else. "[*L*]*e colon* only envisioned sugar, coffee, indigo, and cotton," Vastey wrote: "in short, the colonial goods, which could provide him with capital; it hardly mattered if poor farmers lacked subsistence, [and] perished from hunger and poverty" (*RP* 110).[18] Vastey described these "colonial goods," then, as merely a method for the planters to "buy food and slaves [*des nègres*]" for themselves and therefore to "fuel metropolitan commerce and the slave trade," (*RP* 110) at the expense of everyone else living in the colony.

Twenty-three years later, Hamilton made an almost identical argument, tying the monopoly of the colonial sugar trade, in particular, to the slave trade, in general. In his *Memoir*, Hamilton detailed what he would call, "A Remedy for the Slave Trade" (2). This "remedy" involved his argument about "lessen[ing] the demand for human labour" (1) required to cultivate sugar cane. Focusing less on the production of sugar cane, and more on the production of wheat, he asserted, would undermine slavery as an economic system that depended upon human (and mostly, enslaved African) labor that only benefited the rich planters:

> it has been objected to the culture of Wheat in the West Indies, that its introduction will have an injurious effect upon the black population, by

---

[18] Vastey's sense that the colonists had promoted the cultivation of only four crops at the expense of "farming substantial products, so necessary, and so indispensable to the existence of man" (*RP* 110), is in many respects confirmed by the pamphlets produced during the Saint-Domingue grain crisis of 1789. These pamphlets have been translated and curated by Abby Broughton, Kelsey Corlett-Rivera, and Nathan Dize as a part of the digital humanities project, *A Colony in Crisis*. The project can be accessed in English translation: https://colonyincrisis.lib.umd.edu/the-translations/ (Accessed 18 May 2016).

lessening the demand for their labour; and were it proposed to convert the whole of the arable land in that quarter into fields of Wheat, there might be some plausible ground for the objection: since a Wheat Farm of a thousand acres may be fully cultivated by from 40 to 50 able-bodied men, aided by half as many women and children; whilst a similar extent of land under the culture of the cane requires at least one able-boded negro for every acre under tillage. (1)

Although, he explicitly mentioned the "negro" here, it was actually all forms of unfree labor that informed Hamilton's argument. Slavery had already been abolished in the British colonies by the time that Hamilton published this *Memoir*, but unfree labor had not (see, for example, Emmer 2000). For Hamilton, maintaining and promoting the sugar trade as the primary colonial export meant to ensure the kind of caste system that would divide society into the ones who labored and those who stood to profit from it. The manufacturing of sugar offered a microcosm of class: "the culture of the Cane," Hamilton argued, "is a lottery exclusively restricted to the wealthy" (1).

Hamilton's critical take on the inequalities of the colonial food supply juxtaposed with his criticisms of slavery are important primarily because how much of his analysis appears to anticipate later critiques of capitalism. Hamilton's deconstruction of the relationship of human labor in the colonies to capital in the metropole seems to anticipate Marx's later writing about "estranged labor." In 1844, Marx wrote,

On the basis of political economy itself [...]we have shown that the worker sinks to the level of a commodity and becomes indeed the most wretched of commodities; that the wretchedness of the worker is in inverse proportion to the power and magnitude of his production; that the necessary result of competition is the accumulation of capital in a few hands, and thus the restoration of monopoly in a more terrible form; and that finally the distinction between capitalist and land rentier, like that between the tiller of the soil and the factory worker, disappears and that the whole of society must fall apart into the two classes – property owners and property-less workers. (137)

In much the same way, Hamilton was concerned that laborers—enslaved Africans and ostensibly sharecroppers—were consistently alienated from the products that their hard work produced. Hamilton uses as evidence a letter he received from a friend still living in the colonies: "'We could employ,' says my correspondent, in a letter as recent as the 1st of January, 1840, 'half as many more labourers as we have. The position which masters now stand in is an unnatural one: instead of labourers courting employment, the masters have to search for and make a favour of their services'" (1).

In short, Hamilton's friend suggests that the colonies were in need of *more*, not less, human labor in order to continue to produce the awesome amount of sugar necessary to keep up with demand. Hamilton viewed this economic state of affairs as especially problematic. "This is an evil which the introduction of Wheat tillage will correct," Hamilton writes, "by restoring the balance between the supply and demand to a more healthy state, and promoting that mutual dependence between the employers and the employed which forms the only cement of the social system, and has for this purpose been wisely ordained by a beneficient Providence" (1). Hamilton's vision was of a Caribbean economy facilitated not only by free labor, but by choice of labor. He writes that he would like to see a tropics that could "give the industrious labourer a choice of occupation, [...] enabling him to obtain wages proportionate to the degree of his toil" (1), and he finishes by making the argument that wheat is essentially more democratic. Wheat was democratic for Hamilton not merely as a metaphor for the fantasy of this more egalitarian agrarian society, whose exports would be entirely determined by the volition of its laborers rather than its proprietors, but as an agricultural fact:

> While the costly outlay of capital, the length of time consumed in its growth, and the great fluctuations in the amount of its return, necessarily restrict the culture of the cane to the wealthier class of proprietors; the infinitely smaller capital required for wheat tillage, the lighter amount of labour to be expended upon it, the diminished risk of loss, and the greater promptitude of return, place it as fully with the reach of the ten acre cultivator in Barbados, as of the wealthiest planter in Jamaica: nay, even the poor and hitherto despised and persecuted black, in the intervals of his daily toil, may be able to till his half or quarter acre of wheat, take the produce to a neighbouring mill, feed his little family with wheaten bread, the produce of his own labour, and thus add, at the cheapest possible rate, to the amount of their little comforts. (64–65)

Hamilton's ability to *use* Vastey's works to weave together agricultural and anti-slavery arguments certainly complicates (but does not resolve) the idea that natural historians necessarily colluded (either deliberately or unwittingly) with their home governments to consistently uphold colonial rule and to prevent the kind of sovereign rule established by the ex-slaves and former free people of color in Haiti.[19]

*

HAITIAN SOVEREIGNTY AS HUMANISM

In the Strafford indictment, the sovereign rule of Henry Christophe is mentioned disparagingly over a dozen times. Such repetition underscores the colonial Jamaican government's argument that Strafford's connection to the "usurper" "Christopher" could only mean that the former was conspiring to bring Haiti's slave rebellion to Jamaica, and therefore, to bring about the end of both slavery and the British empire. While sovereign rule may have represented a huge problem for colonialist Britain, nevertheless, many of England's storied abolitionists such as William Wilberforce and Thomas Clarkson, and natural scientists like Joseph Banks and Hamilton, used Vastey's writings to ardently plead for formal recognition of Haitian independence. Hamilton argued, in this respect, that political sovereignty was already an incontestable reality in Haiti, and he found that Vastey's writings could furnish the proof. In his preface to the English translation of Vastey's *An Essay on the Causes of the Revolution*, published in Exeter in 1823 (three years after Vastey's execution), Hamilton writes that Vastey's history "*practically* demonstrates,

---

[19] Even though Hamilton was thoroughly anti-slavery, noticeably, he is not actually anti-empire, which is to say that unlike Vastey, slavery and empire were not locked into a mutually dependent relationship. For example, Hamilton described the goal of his reforms as a plan that could "awaken the planters, so long slumbering on the verge of ruin, to a sense of their true interests and convert the West India islands, from a fatal millstone about the neck of Great Britain, into what a bountiful providence designed they should be, a terrestrial paradise, and a source of benefit to the parent state" (qtd. in Howard et al. 236). In addition, in his Application for a Radcliffe Traveling Fellowship, Hamilton enumerates rather unequivocally his historical willingness to support empire: "Upon the first appointment of British Consuls to South America," he writes, "I eagerly availed myself of the opportunity to attempt the introduction of the various valuable productions of those diversified, even now but imperfectly explored regions, into our own Colonies, for the mutual advantage of those Settlements and the Parent Country" (2). He continued by saying, "I am at this moment endeavouring also to establish the *Pita* Plant […], in Jamaica, with the double view of improving the agriculture and commerce of our Colonies, and rendering Great Britain independent of foreign nations for the supply of those essential maritime stores, canvass and cordage" (2).

that superiority of both *intellectual* and *moral* power, is *not* confined to any one complexion, and that *generous* and *virtuous feelings* are *not* the exclusive privilege of Europeans" (ii, *emphasis in original*). He connects his recognition of Haitian humanity to an argument for the country's sovereignty when he contends that it is precisely "[i]n the instructive records of such a history [of Haiti], [that] we should see [in] a people [...]after their emancipation from bondage, those dormant energies of the soul, and those latent virtues of the heart which we had been taught to believe them incapable of possessing, and, not only forming themselves into an organized and well regulated community, but starting, almost *per salute*, into notice, as statesmen, legislators, and historians" (ii). Here, sovereignty, rather than literacy, stands as the more dominant sign of humanity.

Unlike the characterization we found in the Strafford indictment, Christophe's ability to establish a government of people of color signified *humanness* for Hamilton in as much as Christophe's ability to organize the Haitian people into "statesmen, legislators, and historians," provided the botanist with proof that "blacks" were capable of ruling *and* writing. Hamilton wrote, to that end, that Henry Christophe was clearly the most preeminent of the "statesmen, [and] legislators" to have emerged in independent Haiti:

> As a statesman and a legislator, no less than as a warrior, the illustrious hero who sways the sceptre of the North, stands pre-eminently conspicuous, and the code of laws which bears his name, the wholesome regulations he has established in the administration of the state, the order and punctuality which he has introduced into all the details of office, and above all, the institutions he has founded for diffusing the light of moral and intellectual improvement throughout his dominions, are so many splendid monuments of the extent of his genius, and the liberality of his heart. (iii)

Hamilton's assessment of Christophe as a humane ruler echoes that of another Anglophone botanist and natural historian who consistently championed the Haitian monarch as both an executive power and a legislator: Sir Joseph Banks. Banks was not only corresponding with and supporting the research of Hamilton, but he was also in contact with a New England schoolteacher of African descent who had briefly emigrated to Haiti named Prince Saunders. In 1818, Saunders, who had

been in Haiti at the same time as Hamilton,[20] had written and published
a letter addressed to him from Joseph Banks as a part of the following
work, *A memoir presented to the American Convention for Promoting the
Abolition of Slavery, and improving the condition of the African Race,
December 11th, 1818: containing some remarks upon the civil dissentions of
the hitherto afflicted people of Hayti, as the inhabitants of that island may
be connected with plans for the emigration of such free persons of colour as
may be disposed to remove to it, in case its reunion, pacification and independence should be established: together with some account of the origin and
progress of the efforts for effecting the abolition of slavery in Pennsylvania
and its neighbourhood, and throughout the world*. According to Colleen
C. O'Brien, "Saunders first published the book in London to enlist the
financial support of wealthy British philanthropists who could underwrite
his American emigration project, then reprinted it in the United States
in 1818 and began lecturing, primarily to northern free black organiza-
tions who might be interested in emigrating to Haiti" (32). Before the
letter begins, Saunders refers to Banks as "that illustrious personage"
whose opinions "will serve to evince the views and sentiments [...] of
the abolitionists generally in Great Britain, upon the subject of Haitian
affairs" (18). Like Hamilton, Banks also argues for the kinds of agricultural reforms that Hamilton would suggest in his 1840 memoir—relying on free rather than forced, coerced, or other forms of unfair labor.
Banks asks Saunders to relay a message to that effect to Julien Prévost,
the Comte de Limonade: "I hold the newly established government of
Hayti in the highest respect," Banks wrote. Speaking more directly of the
Code Henry, Banks continued, "It is without doubt in its theory, [...]
the most moral association of men in existence; nothing that white men
have been able to arrange is equal to it" (qtd. in 18).

What Banks found so admirable was precisely the portion of the Code
dealing with the equitable treatment of laborers and their compensation.
A statement following Saunders' reproduction of the Banks letter directs
us to the former's English translations of some of the very articles of
the Code governing the conduct of both the proprietors and the laborers. These codes in English translation had been published as a part of

---

[20]The same April 1818 article from the *Liverpool Mercury* that placed Hamilton in
Haiti, also placed Prince Saunders there. The "Note of the Translator" states that "Prince
Sanders, Esq. [sic]" was the director of a school at Sans Souci.

Saunders's earlier *Haytian Papers* (1816). The first article listed under "Law Respecting the Culture," maintains, "The proprietors and farmers of land are bound to treat their respective labourers with true paternal solicitude" (vii). The second article states, "The law exacts from the labourers in return a reciprocal attention to the welfare and interest of the landlord and farmer" (viii). The third article requires that "In lieu of wages, the labourers in plantations shall be allowed a full fourth of the gross product, free from all duties" (vii).

Arguing that these codes could prevent the alienation of the worker, Banks claims: "To give the labouring poor of the country a vested interest in the crops they raise, instead of leaving their reward to be calculated by the caprice of the interested proprietor, is a law worthy to be written in letters of gold, as it secures comfort and a proper portion of happiness to those whose lot in the hands of white men endures by far the largest portion of misery" (18). The Code Henry was not just a beacon for Haitians, then. According to Banks, the Code was ultimately a humanist rather than merely a Haitianist document. Banks wrote that "in due time," the Code could help to "conquer all difficulties, and bring together the black and white varieties of mankind under the ties of mutual and reciprocal equality and brotherhood, which the bountiful Creator of all things has provided for the advantage of both parties". Banks alludes here to an argument for the recognition of Haitian sovereignty by the (white) world powers: "I grieve therefore," Banks wrote, "that the governments of white men have hitherto conceived it imprudent to acknowledge that of their fellow men of Hayti" (qtd. in Saunders 19).

In contrast, Hamilton did not appear to be merely grieving non-recognition of Haitian sovereignty. If Banks had simply thought that the ability for France to recover its lost colony was improbable—Banks wrote, "We must admit, that the French have a right to re-conquer if they are able; but this, in my view of the subject, is not within the bounds of the most extensive probability" (qtd. in Saunders 19)—Hamilton considered it more than imprudent and completely unwise. "May France then be wise enough to profit by the experience of the past—resign pretensions which she has no longer the power to maintain—and by the prudent forbearance of her future conduct with respect to Hayti," Hamilton wrote, "entitle herself to the gratitude of a people who only require to be known to be admired" (*An Essay* ix). The admiration that Hamilton felt for Haiti, particularly, in connection with Baron de Vastey's works, spread throughout metropolitan England, at least partially because of Hamilton's own translations. These translations clearly enabled the circulation of Vastey's rhetoric of the goodness of the Haitian king to the Anglophone world, and by extension, the transmission of his ideas about what it meant to be sovereign after colonialism.

The circulation effect of Hamilton's translation is evidenced by several British reviews of Vastey's works, which praised him with a language similar to that which we find in Hamilton's writing. The *British Review* (1820), for example, applauded Vastey's writing (via Hamilton's translation) by saying that "a black" who had once been "deplorably illiterate" stood as a "specimen of the native black genius" ("History, Literature"), while the *Monthly Repository of Theology and General Literature* (1819) wrote of Hamilton's translation of Vastey's *Réflexions*, "We have here a great curiosity, a vindication of the Negroes by a Negroe." Going on to quote Vastey's touching "I am a man" passage, the *Monthly Repository* reviewer was even "most pleased with [Vastey's] expression of indignation at having such a task to perform" ("History, Literature, and Present State of Hayti," *British Review and London Critical Journal* 15 [1820]) 74; and rpt in "Article VI," *Monthly Repository of Theology and General Literature* 14 [1819]: 329). The *Quarterly Review*, however, most clearly echoes Hamilton's writing on Vastey in claiming, "Under every point of view, any fresh attempt of the French government to disturb the island would deserve the reprobation of mankind. The progress made by the inhabitants in agriculture and all the arts is quite extraordinary, but more particularly in education and general literature" (457). The writer's proof lay in the work of Vastey: "Of this we have an interesting account given by the Baron de Vastey," the author writes, citing Hamilton's English translation of "his 'Political Reflexions on certain French Journals concerning Hayti'" ("Past and Present" 457–458).

Such support in the British press for both Haitian sovereignty and for a writer like Vastey may appear unsurprising in the abolitionist England of Clarkson and Wilberforce where slavery was fast becoming wildly unpopular. Yet support for the writing of Vastey in a country that was much more apologetic about slavery appears to provide a different sort of paradox. In the next section, we witness not merely praise of Vastey's writings as an *African* "curiosity"—although there is a great deal of that as well—but we witness distinct political urgings toward the recognition of Haitian sovereignty in the northern U.S. press and made in the name of U.S. nationalism.

*

READING HAITIAN SOVEREIGNTY THROUGH VASTEY'S RECEPTION IN THE U.S. PRESS

The perceived radicalism of Vastey's arguments for Haitian sovereignty conjoined with the idea that "African" literacy was an exceptional phenomenon, probably accounts for the parenthetical doubt about authorship expressed by the author of the Strafford indictment. In quoting the following lengthy passage, the writer refers to the author of the *Réflexions sur une lettre de Mazères* as "the Person purporting to be the Baron de Vastey" (364):

> Happy, if by my endeavours I, (the person purporting to be the Baron de Vastey) have been able to dispose of the prejudices which have been hovering over us for Centuries and to contribute to the happiness and improvement of my fellow Creatures. Mazères (meaning the said Mazères) defends the cause of the Ex-Colonists, of that Cast of Men, whose horrid System, and unheard of Crimes make nature shudder, and [...] the cause which I defend is that of humanity at large; White, Brown and Black, we are all Brothers, all Children of the Eternal Father, all interested in the Cause of Man whatever may be the Colour of thy skin, whatever may be thy Station and Religion thou professes, thou are interested in the triumph of the Haytians, unless thou has smothered every Sentiment of Justice and Equality which God has engraved in all hearts. Thou canst not place the interests of a Cast of Men who are tarnished with Crime in the Scale with the interests of mankind. (qtd. in "Strafford Indictment" 364)

Somewhat remarkably, the author of the indictment found a way to interpret the above passage, which might in other hands merely seem like an argument for universal humanity, as being "[i]n contempt of our said Lord the King and his Laws." The mere claim that "White, Brown, and Black" people were "Brothers" is positioned as a "great danger [to] the Rule of Government, good Order, Peace, and Tranquility, of the said Island of Jamaica" (364) precisely because Haiti's sovereign present signaled a possible sovereign future for Jamaica as well.

Vastey's sights were not on the future sovereignty of Jamaica though. Instead, his eyes were turned toward the present sovereignty of the United States. Vastey consistently used the United States as the only other independent nation of the American hemisphere as a point of political comparison and departure for Haiti. For him, the revolutions that had occurred in the United States and Haiti were both products of a "torrent and … coincidence of events" that had eventually culminated in the termination of a "bad marriage" with the metropole (*RP* 31). Vastey pointed out in his later publication *Réflexions politiques sur quelques Ouvrages et Journaux Français* (1817) that Haitian independence was hardly exceptional in a comparative historical sense because "all the changes that have taken place in Europe" since the classical age had been "the result of revolutions, revolts, wars, force" (*RP* 22, 23). The culmination of the Haitian Revolution in Haitian independence was in his mind simply a part of the natural, and somewhat inevitable, historical progression that had produced countless other changes to the maps of the world, including the creation of the United States (and ostensibly, the one that could have and did eventually, result in a change for Jamaica).

What was exceptional, according to Vastey, was that when Switzerland separated itself from Austria, the United States from England, and Portugal and the seven provinces of the Pays-Bas from Spain, these changes were "undertaken under the aegis and sanction of European public opinion" (*RP* 22). The Haitian revolutionists' creation of a new nation-state, in contrast, was equated with "a political fiction" (*RM* 90). Thus, begins Vastey's assiduous documentation of how Haitian exceptionalism as a discourse promulgated by European colonists to mask their "negative contributions" (M. Trouillot, "Odd and Ordinary") worked to make the commonplace in Haiti extraordinary and the extraordinary mundane. To the suggestion that Haitians should monetarily compensate the French colonists for the loss of their plantations as U.S. American proprietors did for the English as part of Jay's Treaty (1794), Vastey pointed out that the Americans did this in a state of relative peace, as propertied men who themselves sought compensation from the British for the loss of their slaves and for the confiscation of (U.S.) American ships (*RP* 48). Haitians, for their part, had been "deprived of everything… possessed nothing … were nothing, and … counted for nothing." (*RP* 50) Consequently, Haitians had a right to the properties of the former French colonists since, in Vastey's words, "we have conquered all over these vampires: country! liberty! independence and property" (*RP* 50). Though Vastey acknowledged that the laws of modern warfare, as opposed to ancient practices, protected both the persons and the property of the vanquished, he pointed out that "we do not find any comparable example to ours in the annals of nations" (*RP* 52).

Though Vastey's statement above may seem like a contradiction of his earlier position that Haiti was not so different from other newly formed countries, it actually reflects his acute awareness that comparison must always move upon a shifting axis of sameness and difference. Although the U.S. and Haitian Revolutions had similar historical antecedents, according to Vastey, there was an immeasurable difference between U.S. and Haitian independence. This was because there was no equalizing comparison to be made between the material conditions of Haitians and U.S. Americans at the specific moments of independence in the two countries. Vastey observed that at the time of the Haitian Revolution Haitians had been "mort civilement" or "civilly dead" and "inhabited this earth as if they did not really inhabit it; ... lived as if they were not really living" (*RP* 49–50). Vastey then asks, "Is it not a wish to distort everything, to find examples in subjects that are completely dissimilar?" (*RP* 49). On the contrary, Vastey pointed out that those who would become immediate citizens of the United States "were themselves white Englishmen, free and propertied [who] enjoyed their natural civil and political rights, [and] no one disputed them these rights" (*RP* 49).

In other words, the U.S. American Revolution focused solely on the question of independence, not emancipation. And because Haitians had been what Orlando Patterson would later describe as "socially dead" beings,[21] any comparison between the two acts of independence that sublimated the racial distinctions of Haiti as a country populated mostly by Africans who had been, "black and enslaved, without country, without property, deprived of their natural rights" (*RP* 49), only contributed to Haiti's threatened position in the New World, while the United States enjoyed economic and political prosperity as one of the privileges of whiteness.

Vastey's comparison of Haiti to the United States did not go unnoticed in the Atlantic public sphere. Even if the composer of the Strafford indictment doubted variously Vastey's "Africanness" and/or his authorship of the document published under his name, by 1817 Vastey was already fairly well known in the United States as a famous black author. Vastey's budding notoriety was a result of the publication of his most famous work, *Le Système colonial dévoilé* (1814), which circulated heavily in the northern United States in the early nineteenth century, even

---

[21] Patterson, *Slavery and Social Death*, 38.

without having been fully translated into English (See, Daut, "The 'Alpha and Omega'").[22] Vastey's name would have also been familiar to U.S. readers on the basis of a later publication, *Le Cri de la conscience* (1815), characterized by a reviewer for the *Boston Daily Advertizer* as having a "great zeal and ingenuity" ("Boston: Friday Morning, Sept. 15, 1815," 2).[23] A brief review of Vastey's *Notes à M. le Baron de V. P. Malouet... en réfutation du 4ème volume de son ouvrage, intitulé: Collection de mémoires sur les colonies, et particulièrement sur Saint-Domingue* (1814), published in the *North American Review* in May 1815, refers to Vastey's work as "well and eloquently written" ("Miscellaneous and Literary Intelligence," *North American Review* 1.1 [May 1815]: 134). Vastey's name would also have been known to readers of U.S. newspapers due to the publication of *Le Cri de la patrie* (1815), the work where Vastey most ardently attacks the southern Republic of Haiti and which at least one U.S. newspaper chided for its "false defamation of Pétion" (*Weekly Recorder*, July 10, 1816).

Later, the future U.S. attorney general, Caleb Cushing, a journalist whose anti-slavery and pro-Haitian sovereignty arguments helped Vastey's words to spread across the U.S., provided a lengthy and much reprinted and referenced review of Vastey's *Réflexions politiques* (which had been translated into English by Hamilton in 1818)[24] in the *North American Review*. Cushing wrote, "The works of M. de Vastey are very favourable specimens of the native mental force of a Haitian" (Cushing, "Article VI—*Refléxions politiques*," 112).[25] Cushing even began to internalize Vastey's own understanding of the meaning of Haitian independence for the hemisphere repeating Vastey's very own words about Haitians needing time to produce esteemed writers and politicians such as Benjamin Franklin and George Washington (Vastey, *RP* 31). Cushing echoed Vastey's words again when he wrote that the French were responsible for all civil strife in Haiti (131), and he also bought into Vastey's ideas about the unreasonableness of requiring the Haitian

---

[22]The first full English translation of *Le Système* appeared in 2014 with Liverpool University Press.

[23]Reprinted in the *Alexandria Gazette*, September 26, 1815.

[24]Cushing, in any event, quotes from Vastey's original French rather than from Hamilton's English translation.

[25]Cushing's article on Vastey was either referenced or quoted several times in the northern U.S. See, for example, "Review of New Books," *Literary Gazette; or Journal of Criticism, Science, and the Arts*, February 17, 1821; "From the Catskill Recorder:

government to compensate the French colonists when he wrote: "No man of course but a colonist can seriously think the king of Hayti was under the least obligations to restore the lands of the planters, or even give them an equivalent" (124).

A more radical adoption of Vastey's language and rhetoric occurs when Cushing defends Christophe's monarchy:

> A nation, which has attained considerable refinement, which is tranquil within and threatened by nothing but ordinary dangers from abroad, can enjoy a free and republican government; but when a country has been plunged for two centuries in the lowest degradation, when its inhabitants have been sunk below the level of ordinary political oppression, and when, although exalted to the rank of a nation, it has continued to be harassed by restless and able enemies,—in such a country, the firm hand of kingly power is needed to stifle faction, repel aggressors, and give energy, dispatch, and secrecy to the public measures. (116)[26]

Cushing continued by repeating Vastey's very own words: "Little does it matter, indeed," he wrote, "what is the form of a government, if it be sagely conducted, and its only aim be the public happiness and peace" (119; see also, Vastey, *RM* 73).

Not everyone in the U.S. print circuit agreed with Cushing's enthusiastic assessment of either Haiti or Vastey. On February 17, 1821, *The Literary Gazette, Or, Journal of Criticism, Science, and the Arts*, published a review of the very issue of the Boston-based *North American*

Revolutionary Incidents. St. Domingo," *Rhode Island American*, February 13. 1821; "From the Catskill Recorder: Revolutionary Incidents. St. Domingo," *Essex Patriot*, August 18, 1821. The invaluable *Index to the North American Review*, published posthumously in 1877 by William Cushing, lists Caleb Cushing as the author of this unsigned piece (124). For further confirmation of Cushing's authorship of this article and further contextual discussion of it, see Belohlavek (10).

[26] *The North American Review* was not the only U.S. newspaper to print positive reviews of Christophe after 1817, as evidenced by the following extract from a letter written by a U.S. person from Virginia who lamented the glowing reports of the Haitian monarch in the northern press: "It astonishes me a great deal to see that the editors of our newspapers treat the name of that monster, Christophe, the soi-disant king of Hayti, with the shadow of respect" (*Boston Daily Advertiser*, June 26, 1816; repr. *Enquirer*, July 6, 1816).

Review in which Cushing's review of Haitian publications, including those of Baron de Vastey, was produced. The author of the review published in *The Literary Gazette* was evidently not impressed by the *North American Review*'s most recent issue, observing, "There is less good writing and rather more pretension, less novelty of thought or variety of style" (100). When the reviewer arrives at "Article VI," Cushing's piece, we are told that in this section: "We find a view of the present condition of Hayti, derived from a long list of publications placed at the head of the article,[27] and it would seem from some personal knowledge possessed by the writer of the country" (102). The reviewer wasted no time in getting to the heart of the critique, as the very next sentence reads, "The Baron de Vastey, the Alpha and Omega of Haytian intellect and literature, has furnished the principal materials for this review, as we perceive he has done for similar articles in the Quarterly and British" (102).[28] In an effort to read Vastey's race as a legend for reading his writing, the reviewer makes use of the trope of monstrous hybridity. Vastey is subsequently described as a "coloured philosopher," who, borrowing Cushing's language, "is 'a yellow man either a mulatto or mestizo' and therefore not quite so high in the scale of humanity as the unmixed African race" (102; Cushing 113). Such an assessment of Vastey's lack of "humanity" in connection with his "mulatto or mestizo" identity did not bode well for the rest of the review. Suspicion appears to have been the reviewer's dominant hermeneutic when the reviewer writes that Cushing, "gives a long detail of the barbarities inflicted upon the negroes by the French colonists, the authority for which we may remark is rather suspicious, as it seems in part derived from the Quarterly Review" (102). The reviewer for *The Literary Gazette* sought to cast aspersion not only on Vastey, but on Henry Christophe in contesting Cushing's claim that "[t]he late King Henry [...] was a person of 'fine features, noble presence, and accomplished manners,' and was considered by his subjects in the light of

---

[27]The publications under review in Cushing's article for the *North American Review* included three of Vastey's works, *Réflexions Politiques* and *Réflexions sur les Noirs et les Blancs*, *Relation de la Fête de S.M. la Reine d'Hayti*, and six additional publications from Haiti: *Acte de l'indépendance*, *Code Henry*, *Gazette Royale d'Hayti*, *Des Almanachs Royals d'Hayti*, *Des Ordonnances, Déclarations, Proclamations, &c. du Roi d'Hayti*, and *L'Entrée du Roi en sa Capitale, Opéra Vaudeville, par M. le Comte de Rosiers* (Cushing 112).

[28]The author is speaking of the previously mentioned articles about Vastey in the *Quarterly Review* and *The British Review, and London Critical Journal.*

an affectionate father" (qtd. in 102). "The late revolution," in contrast, the reviewer writes, "has unfortunately affected the soundness of this latter opinion, and confirmed the truth of the old observation respecting the difference between the good qualities of a living and dead monarch" (102).

This sentence perhaps unwittingly captures both the temporal and subjective nature of nineteenth-century critiques of Vastey's works (and by extension, Henry Christophe's reign). During his life, and in the immediate aftermath of both Vastey's death and Christophe's own suicide, Vastey was almost universally praised in both England and the United States for arguments that writers thought transcended either blackness or whiteness, Africanness or Europeanness/Americanness. In the U.S. public sphere, specifically, Vastey was even considered a visionary, whose works proved the righteousness of Haitian sovereignty, the ability for "Africans" to achieve civilization, and an undeniable common humanity. It was primarily in the decades after Christophe's death, in some senses anticipated by the assessment of both Vastey and Christophe in *The Literary Gazette*, that the tide of positive public opinion, bookended in certain ways by Cushing's writing, would change for Vastey as well. This change can be meaningful to us when juxtaposed with the greatly contrasting arguments used by Cushing to promote Haitian sovereignty as beneficial for U.S. nationalism.

*

READING HAITIAN SOVEREIGNTY THROUGH U.S. NATIONALISM

Cushing selected the nine works under review in his article because, as he wrote, "Some of these works have considerable intrinsic merit; and we have therefore resolved to place them before our readers, not only because they are little, if at all, known in this country, but also because they were written by the descendants of negroes, and by nobles of the late kingdom of Hayti" (112). He went on to explain why he planned to focus primarily on Vastey:

> The writings of M. de Vastey, which consist of a chief part of the works at the head of this article and of a few pamphlets of less importance, are very favourable specimens of the native mental force of a Haytian. Self-educated, as are most of his countrymen of any distinction, struggling constantly for the first thirty years of his life against every thing which could

damp or stifle a literary ambition, he has nevertheless acquired a respectable style, a correct knowledge of his language, and a store of information
of considerable variety and extent. (112–113)

Cushing believed that these works stood as evidence for Haiti's potential
to flourish as a sovereign state and he tied this assessment to the concept of racial regeneration. Regeneration was a crucial point for Cushing
because, as he wrote, "We consider the single fact of their regeneration
as decisive in favour of the blacks. Never was a servitude more complete,
never was abasement more hopeless, never was ignorance more deplorable, than that of the slaves of Saint Domingo" (115). He connected
Vastey's writings to the post-Enlightenment discourse of regeneration and degeneration circulating in the Atlantic World. Because he saw
Vastey as "self-educated," Cushing applauded the fact that the Haitian
baron had arisen out of what he called the "lowest moral and intellectual degradation, by the force of his own powers." On the strength of
such a belief Cushing wrote that "the vehemence of the once oppressed,
but now victorious soldier, the fire of an emancipated slave, the vigor-
ous pride of a regenerate African are all wrought into the style" of his
works (114). Cushing concluded on this score that Vastey's writing
proved "the regeneration of Hayti," saying, "we may hope that before
long they will have wiped away all the disgraceful stains contracted in a
life of bondage" (120).

The word "regeneration" had a particular meaning in the late eighteenth and early nineteenth centuries. By "the [French] Revolution,
regeneration had become an extremely popular and more general
word, referring to improvement, a freeing from corruption, or societal
renewal" (Sepinwall, "Exporting the Revolution" 45). By the nineteenth century, regeneration was equally connected to both the abolition
of slavery and racial "miscegenation."[29] According to Robert Fanuzzi,
early nineteenth-century U.S. writers were distinctly affected by the
French discourse of "the elevation of the African race" through "struc-
tural" and "institutional philanthropy" (580). The idea that slavery had
caused a corruption of humankind that only abolition and philanthropy
could cure would become a favorite claim of abolitionists like the Abbé

---

[29] Buffon's naturalist writings were premised on the assumption that blacks represented
a "degenerate" form of the white race, for instance. The French author even proposed
racial mixing to speed up the process of regeneration, writing that if such "amalgamation"
were promoted, "the Mulatto would have only a light trace of brown that would disappear
altogether within the next generations; it would only take therefore 150 or 200 years to

Grégoire, who claimed that slavery corrupted equally the masters, slaves, and the free people of color (*De la noblesse*, 52, 82).

Vastey had also internalized the idea that slavery had resulted in a complete corruption of humanity, and he therefore understood Haitian independence as a part of a larger post-Enlightenment project of rehabilitating humankind. Vastey wrote that after the Haitian Revolution, humanity had triumphed and "the regeneration of a large part of the human race [was] beginning" (*Système* vi). Not only did Vastey believe that humankind was being "regenerated," but he also believed that whatever happened in Haiti would mean something for the world and not just for "Africans" (*RP* 1). This a priori conflation of literacy with humanity and civilization may have been part and parcel of the Enlightenment and the burgeoning science of race,[30] but it also formed a crucial element in early U.S. American as equally as Haitian assessments of postcolonial Haiti's potential as a sovereign state.

American writers like Cushing appear to have been open to accepting Haitian writing, in general, and Vastey's writing, in particular, as proof of black capacities for nationhood precisely because they were involved in their own project of national consolidation through the development of a specifically American U.S. literary and political tradition. In the United

---

clean the skin of a Negro by this method of mixing with white blood" (*Histoire naturelle générale et particuliére*, 14: 313–314). It was not long before racial mixing was proffered as a possible solution to help end slavery and to hasten the "regeneration" of the black race. In his *Études des races humaines*, Michel-Hyacinthe Deschamps wrote, for example:

"The *regeneration* of the *human species*, or the return of all the colored races to the white type, is possible, suppressing the odious prejudice, by means of perpetual crossing of the métis with the primordial white, now European, race. We could whiten the natives of an island, of a country, of a vast colony. The Negroes would not have to be born slaves, our *inferior brothers*, they are our equals in the order of creation; they have the right—as do we—to the sun, to liberty, and to the banquet of life.... Glory to the promoters of the emancipation of the slaves!" (135, *emphasis in original*)

A reviewer of John R. Beard's biography of Toussaint Louverture also encouraged *miscegenation* as a way to help end slavery in the United States, writing that "many sensible men who have lived in Hayti are of opinion that an increase of the mulatto stock, by legitimate and permanent sanctions would vastly improve it, in as much as the public interests fare well at the heads of these men of mixed blood who are not, as we commonly supposed, faded copies of both black and white, but specimens of an original ability as yet but imperfectly displayed" ("Toussaint L'Ouverture," *North American Review*, 1864, 596).

[30] For literacy as humanity, see Chukwudi, Introduction, 5; and Aravamudan, *Tropicopolitans*, 270.

States this project of literary sovereignty as humanity was intimately connected to a "cultural milieu" that "sought alternately to solidify and to signify across the unstable boundaries of nation and race within a New World arena characterized by its transnationality" (Brickhouse, *Transamerican 7*).

Yet the consolidation of U.S. American identity was also formed in conjunction with a fantasy of imperialism paradoxically bound in certain ways to the recognition of Haitian independence. An article in the *Boston Commercial Gazette* argued that it would be in the best interests of U.S Americans to recognize Haitian independence so that the Haitian government might allow "our ships of war" to be stationed in the port of Môle-Saint-Nicolas (*BCG* et al.). The expression of this desire to station U.S. troops in Caribbean waters seems now like a dangerous precursor of what Paul Farmer has called "the uses of Haiti." Almost immediately after Christophe's death in 1820 and again after the United States formally recognized Haitian independence in 1862, the United States "began showing great interest" in Môle-Saint-Nicolas (Farmer, *Uses of Haiti* 72). The long term desire to station U.S. troops somewhere in Haiti was immediately coupled with the stability and validity of U.S. democracy when the author of the article in the *Boston Commerical Gazette* continued:

> Under the influence of reason and sound sense, a more enlightened policy than has yet existed towards the Haytiens will arise, and the declaration of our bill of rights, that 'ALL MEN ARE BORN FREE AND EQUAL', [will] be considered as having some weight in the scales of justice and humanity. When this period arrives, it will become our duty, as a moral people, to seek their alliance, that we may the more readily aid them in the advancement of learning and Christian philanthropy. (*BCG* et al.)

The article oscillates uncertainly between patrimony and militarization of Haitian-U.S. relations, coming dangerously close to proposing a civilizing mission of "Christian philanthropy." This civilizing mission would perhaps provide closure to the project of the American Revolution that the continuation of slavery in the United States had stifled.

The United States's revolution was supposed to have brought liberty to the hemisphere, but as the Abbé Grégoire observed, the United States would have to do something about its enslavement of more than "one million six hundred thousand Africans" "to conciliate, as republicans, this contradiction of their principles, and to justify, as Christians, this profanation of evangelical maxims" (*De la noblesse* 86). If it was true that, as Brissot de Warville observed during his visit to the United States, "Americans, more than any other people, are convinced that all men are born free and equal" (qtd. in Fanuzzi 582), then the philosophical underpinnings of U.S. identity were threatened by a policy toward Haiti that was viewed as devoid of "reason and sound sense." The very existence of masses of rebelling enslaved Africans and Haitian revolutionists who would write their own Declaration of Independence, as Nick Nesbitt has written, "presented freedom to the world as an absolutely true logic," and one that had to be made "universal": the Haitian Revolution had meant that "no humans can be enslaved" (Nesbitt, "Idea of 1804," 8, 17). If no humans could be enslaved and Haiti was both the argument and the proof, then the United States's revolution was not just incomplete (Fanuzzi 582), but, as Sibylle Fischer has noted, was of spurious virtue (*Modernity Disavowed* 9).

Vastey acknowledged that U.S. slavery confounded the meanings of liberty and revolution for the world when he wrote: "The independence of the United States of America has been a source of goodness for Europe and the entire world; ours will contribute to the Happiness of the human race, because of its moral and political consequences" (*RP* 15). In Haiti (in great contrast to the United States), a life out of chattel slavery was not just for people of certain complexions or social stations, but was for everyone.

Moreover, Vastey's argument illustrates what Ralph Bauer has called two different and competing conceptions of the nation-state in the Americas as it developed into the twentieth century: one as "the agent of hemispheric or global hegemony" and the other as "a protection against United States cultural, economic, and military expansion" (Bauer 236). If the U.S. as a nation was defined and indeed "imagined" in terms of a limitless expansion, the nation-state in early Haiti was conceived of in terms of clearly defined unity within the border of Hispaniola. In other words, in nineteenth-century Haiti, "cultural nationalism" might be considered what Simon During has called in another context "a mode of freedom" that was "developed *against* imperialism" (139, *emphasis in original*). There was surely a desire in Haiti to unify the north and the south and even the eastern parts of the island, as Vastey noted in his 1819 letter to Clarkson (rpt. in Griggs and Prator 180–181), but there was not an evident wish to expand the borders of the country beyond the limits of the island; nor was there any considerable effort made to transfer the Haitian ideals of universal emancipation and liberty for all human beings to other countries in any way that accorded with the U.S. American belief that it has to the right to "violently export" (Moten, "Democracy" 77) its democracy to other countries. Vastey vehemently argued against the slave trade and the horrors of colonialism in *Réflexions sur une lettre de Mazères*, *Le Système*, and *Notes*, but simultaneously affirmed that Haitians were not going to meddle in the affairs of the other countries in the hemisphere. Furthermore, Vastey pointed out that the Codes of Christophe, as Dessalines' 1805 Constitution had already done, expressly prohibited Haitians from interfering with "affairs outside of our island" (*RP* 36).[31] Vastey also explicitly noted that Haitians did not desire to create a Caribbean empire when he wrote: "The revolution did not transfer from the whites to the blacks the question of control of the West Indies.... Haiti is one of the islands of this archipelago and is not itself the Caribbean" (*Notes* 7).[32] Vastey's point was that Haitian nationalism was not going to be defined by or based upon its ability to expand its territories, but rather upon Haitians' own particular claim to sovereignty over a small part of the region.

The above gloss of certain key tenets of Vastey's writing is crucial for understanding his influence on Cushing's assessment of Haitian independence and right to sovereignty. Cushing's understanding of Christophe's Haiti derives entirely from his reading of Vastey. Like Banks and Saunders, Cushing praises Christophe for the "compilation of the Code-Henry," which he called an "act of equal wisdom with the establishment of royalty in Hayti" (122), and lauds the country for being non-imperialistic, both assertions being allusions to Vastey's reading of the monarchy. Cushing writes: "Content and happy to live in peace, satisfied with their lot, they felt no desire to disturb the tranquility of their neighbors" (122).

---

[31] For an intriguing argument about Dessalines's desire to export the revolution in Haiti elsewhere in the Americas, see Jenson, "Before Malcom X" (340).

[32] Here, Vastey specifically refutes the writing of the former French colonist Malouet, who had written that "the [Haitian] revolution has transferred from the whites to the blacks the question of control over the Caribbean, and our unfortunate rivalries must give way in the face of the great interest in the region that is obviously developing" (*Collection de mémoires*, 4: 2). Christophe's Code had followed in the stead of Dessalines's constitution, which had mandated, "The Emperor will never form any enterprise with the view of conquest or of troubling the peace or domestic regimes of foreign colonies" (Art. 36).

Also, like Vastey, Cushing understood the Haitian Revolution to have been a beacon for humanity that was without precedent in the Atlantic World. "What revolution has the world ever beheld," Cushing asked, "that was comparable to this in the credit which it does to the aptitude and perseverance of its leaders? Other revolutions were conducted by men who were free...who had before enjoyed the rights of men and knew how to prize them; who were comparatively speaking enlightened and civilized" (115). The Haitian Revolution, in addition to Haitian independence, was proof of African humanity for Cushing as well: "Surely not more convincing argument in proof of the capacity of blacks could be required, than their achievement of such a revolution" (115). He offered as evidence, "A few extracts from the Baron de Vastey," which he said, "will show the sufferings of his countrymen to have been without any thing similar in revolutionary annals, and will justify us in the severe terms in which we have alluded to the colonists" (116). Perhaps, most importantly, Cushing, much like Hamilton, did not believe that France stood any chance of reconquering Haiti and noted that though "France has never ceased to long for the restoration of her colonial dominations," "Hayti, not withstanding her divided and fluctuating governments, continues and probably ever will continue independent" (118).

If Christophe's monarchy was a huge problem for a French abolitionist like the Abbé Grégoire (as we will see in the final section of this chapter), it was not at all a problem for Cushing. The U.S. writer told his readers,

> It is impossible, therefore, not to praise the design which established a monarchy in Hayti, strengthened the king by the grant of adequate power and endowed him with revenues and military forces for his defence against foreign and domestic assailants. The recent death of the king has, it is true, been followed by a revolution in the government; but, as we shall take occasion to remark hereafter, this circumstance neither proves the king was bad, nor that a monarchical government was ineligible in Hayti. (119)

A fascinating defense of monarchy as a potentially more fruitful form of government than a republic follows the above defense of Christophe when Cushing writes, "Hayti, we doubt not, enjoyed more prosperity under the scepter of an absolute king, than she could ever have hoped for from republican institutions" (119–120).

Other northerners were similarly bold in their argument that Haiti had a right to, at the very least, choose its own system of governance, even if the choice was ultimately a monarchy. This is a point to be found in a toast given by Rufus King, who, like many Federalists, was "unabashed" in his "defiance of Jeffersonian policy towards Haiti." King reportedly stated, "To the government of Haiti, founded on the only legitimate basis of authority—the people's choice" (qtd. in Zuckerman 194).[33] The prior review of Vastey's work in May of 1815, also published in the *North American Review*, had a more semantic reason for defending Christophe's monarchy: "There is as pretty and numerous a collection of Princes, Dukes, Counts, Barons as any country in Europe could produce," the article states; "indeed England is quite outdone; she has produced only one Black Prince, but in St. Domingo there are many. These titles sound as well as any similar appellations; and may wear as well as older ones. If the colour of the heart be right, that of the skin is of inferior importance" ("Miscellaneous and Literary Intelligence" 134). Finally, an additional U.S. journalist even went so far as to defend the "military attitude" of the north of Haiti by writing that it was "necessary, perhaps, as a preservative against the attempts of France" ("Article V" 406).

It might at first seem astonishing that a monarchy, with its attendant "collections of Dukes, Counts, Barons" and "Black Prince[s]" was so openly defended in a country whose origin story rests upon the opposition between monarchy and democracy. John Adams's very own "Defense of the Constitutions of the Government of the United States" (1787) had provided a harsh critique of "kingly power" by suggesting that the "American people" were too "enlightened" to ever allow

---

[33]Thomas Jefferson, once a proponent of "Toussaint's Clause," which allowed the United States to continue to trade in arms and other goods with Toussaint Louverture during the Haitian Revolution, changed his tune remarkably after Haitian independence, when he began attempting to have a bill imposing a trade embargo on Haiti passed in Congress. The Logan Bill was passed in February of 1806, and it forbade U.S. merchants from trading with any portions of the colony not in possession of France. See Matthewson, "Jefferson and the Nonrecognition of Haiti" (32). Official trade statistics (which do not take into account the illegal trade, of course) show that U.S. exports to the French islands stood at $6.7 million in 1806 but fell to $5.8 million in 1807 and to $1.5 million in 1808 (ibid., 35). When the trade embargo expired in 1810 and was not renewed, trade resumed between the two countries. For a table indicating the trade statistics after 1810, see Logan, *Diplomatic Relations* (194–195).

the "executive power" to rest with "one single person." The force of Vastey's influence over U.S. reviews of his work, however, lay in his recognition that international democracy in its more metaphysical possibilities rather than in its actual literal applications rested not in imposing one nation's government on another but in accepting that different peoples might choose to be governed in different ways.

To that end, in his *Réflexions politiques*, Vastey pointed out the hypocrisy of those who criticized Haiti's black king while they showed deference to their own white king (17). In so doing, he clearly spoke to a European audience. His defense of monarchy as a system of government, however, was also explicitly directed at the United States. Vastey knew that if he wanted to appeal to his U.S. audience, he would have to defend the monarchy on racial, as well as theoretical grounds. This is why he devoted an entire chapter in his *Essai* to defending the monarchy as a system of government. In his earlier *Réflexions sur une lettre de Mazères* he had already taken up the topic, writing that the method of government hardly mattered as long as it was "wise, just, enlightened, and benevolent, and the governees have religion, virtues and good morals!" (*RM* 73). Vastey further wrote that since no two peoples were exactly alike, no single form of government could suit all nations. To that end, he paraphrased Montesquieu to prove that it would be an error to think that a republican government was always better than a monarchy since "the best constitution is not the one that is most beautiful in theory, but the one that suits itself the best to the people for whom it has been made" (*Essai* 147–148). This statement seems specifically aimed at the United States since Vastey appeared to view the country as having a democracy that was an exceptionally good form of government with "sage laws" that were specifically suited to the U.S. mindset. His point, nevertheless, was that such a democracy might not be exportable. Remarkably, this idea of democratic relativity was implicitly accepted by many of those in the early United States who both read and published responses to Vastey's words, and even adopted some of them, to defend the Haitian government of the north.

*

Vastey and Abolitionism in Nineteenth-Century France

Cushing imagined a Haiti not only politically divorced from France but also linguistically and culturally separated from its francophone origins. He wrote that Christophe "could not hesitate in adopting that language, which now possesses a literature unrivaled by the proudest in ancient or modern times, which is making rapid strides to a diffusion almost universal, and which is spoken in the first instance by two nations of which one is the noblest in the old and the other the noblest in the new world" (125). Cushing, in fact, argued for United States recognition of Haiti on the grounds that Haiti wanted to be more like the United States, with its "unrivaled" Anglophone literature. He invited Haitians to join in the imagined solidarity of England and the United States by adopting the English language and by degrees its literary tradition. This invitation hardly reflects the kinds of isolation and non-recognition—cultural, diplomatic, and commercial— described by many scholars of early Haitian-U.S. relations (Leyburn, *Haitian People*, 11; and Mintz, Foreword to Leyburn, *Haitian People*, vi). Rather, it indicates that many writers from the Atlantic World, through their engagement with Haitian writing, imagined and even acknowledged the independence of that country—a fact that somewhat complicates the fable of non-recognition.

New research shows that nineteenth-century Haiti cannot be fully characterized as operating within a "century of isolation," (Leyburn 11) specifically, with respect to England and the United States. Julia Gaffield's *Haitian Connections in the Atlantic World* (2015), for example, thoroughly complicates the so-called "isolation thesis" (qtd. in Gaffield, 198 ftn5). Gaffield writes that approaching nineteenth-century Haiti from the perspective of "isolation" fails to "capture the many and varied ways that foreigners interacted with Haiti during and after the period of diplomatic non-recognition" (2). If isolation signifies a lack of contact, my own research also challenges the popular belief that Haiti was culturally isolated by non-recognition in the first two decades of independence. In fact, Vastey—like King Henry Christophe, who addressed a letter to American merchants in the *Republican Watch-Tower* on July 28, 1809—understood the power of the press to influence popular ideas about Haiti and often used it to his own advantage.[34]

---

[34] For Dessalines in the U.S. press, see Jenson, "Before Malcom X," 331. In 1809 King Henri Christophe sought to counteract his negative image abroad by issuing a heart-felt plea to U.S. merchants. The article stated that its purpose was "to make known the truth, and to bring to light the falsity of the infamous impostures my enemies have spread with so much profusion against me." Christophe's letter was reprinted in the *Observer*, July 30, 1809, and the *American*, August 4, 1809. An additional article in the *New-England Palladium* on August 4, 1809, which made reference to this letter, stated that Christophe's address to the merchants was brought to the United States by a "gentleman from the

Although new scholarship has begun revising earlier narratives about Haiti's relationship to England and the United States in the nineteenth-century with more nuance than the "isolation thesis" ordinarily allows, there continues to be a void with respect to historical treatments focusing on Haiti's relationship with its formal colonial occupier, France. There is, nonetheless, evidence of some support for Haitian independence in early nineteenth-century metropolitan French publications.

In fact, the most surprising defense of Vastey's work, viewed by many writers in the Atlantic World as a distinct argument for Haitian sovereignty, came from France. Despite his country's exceeding hostility to the Kingdom of Hayti in the early 19th century,[35] in 1819, historian Antoine Métral penned a laudatory article in two separate installments for *La Revue encyclopédique* entitled, "De la littérature haïtienne." Referring to Vastey's "magical eloquence" (533), Métral wrote of *Le Système colonial dévoilé*, Vastey's most ardent work attacking the French colonists: "M. de Vastey's exclamations are sometimes biting and impetuous like those of J.J. Rousseau. He refutes in the same manner all those who claim that the civilization of Africa is impossible" (Part 1, 534). Métral had earlier said that Vastey's "anger is dignified" before going on to quote him, to that effect, from *Réflexions politiques*: "Strength, courage, virtue, and vice," Vastey wrote:

> do they derive from the skin or from the heart of man? Well then, if that is the case, if it is only the difference in color that is a crime in your eyes..., arm yourselves, revolt against the vision of the Creator who wanted for there to be different types of man on earth. (qtd. in Métral, 1: 528; original in Vastey, *RP*, 18–19)

Métral concludes of Vastey's œuvre:

> The work from which I have drawn these proofs of the genius of a black writer, is a refutation of the system of colonization proposed in a

---

West-Indies." This last article was also reprinted several times. See *Boston Patriot*, August 5, 1809; *Providence Gazette*, August 5, 1809; *Massachusetts Spy; or Worcester Gazette*, August 9, 1809; and *Rutland Herald*, August 19, 1809.

[35] In the words of the Abbé Henri Grégoire, speaking specifically of the north, "The creation of nobility in the North of Haiti has made [France] rain, if I can say that, with criticisms and sarcasms" (*Observations* 149).

huge volume by M. Leborgne de Boigne.[36] Did Baron de Vastey spare any vehemence in his attack? He employs, without a doubt, thunder-bolts of eloquence. His path is bold, frank, and new; he has risen to the heights of his subject and he only allows his adversary to live in order to fight him person to person. Whoever judges with impartiality these two works, will see just how much the black man has bested the white man in point of style, with the power of his thought, and above all with the eloquence that follows. The white man writes with his mind, but the black man writes with his heart. He writes for liberty, and it is from liberty and from the heart that the great inspirations of genius flow. (534–535)

Despite Métral's bold defense of Vastey's writing, the early nineteenth-century France of Christophe's era can be character-ized by its hostility to both anti-slavery thought and the abolition-ist movement (Hoffmann, "Lamartine, Michelet" 343; Heuer 537; Kadish 669–70). In his "Observations sur la constitution du nord d'Haïti" (1819), the Abbé Grégoire recognized as much when he wrote that, while England abounded with "friends of the blacks" such as Clarkson, Wilberforce, James Stephen, and Zachary Macaulay, he was very well alone in France.[37] He also declared that as a result of his almost singular anti-slavery activism, "supporters of trafficking and slavery have especially directed against me their persecutions and their anger" (152).

In his earlier *De la Traite de l'esclavage des Noirs et des Blancs* (1815), Grégoire alluded to the way that the current and former colonists, as well as other metropolitan pro-slavery apologists, had attempted to nega-tively characterize the philanthropic abolitionist movement of which he was a part. "They even tried, without succeeding, to stigmatize the word Philanthropy," Grégoire wrote. "Then, according to the language as it was in usage at that time, it became routine to repeat that the princi-ples of equality, of liberty, were metaphysical abstractions, or even mere ideology, because despotism has a logic and a slang that is all its own"

---

[36] Claude Pierre Joseph Leborgne de Boigne, *Nouveau système de colonisation pour Saint-Domingue* (1817).

[37] Recall that Jacques Pierrot Brissot de Warville, the founder of the Société des Amis des Noirs, was executed during the French Revolution in 1793.

(16).[38] In this same publication, he praised the northern kingdom of Haiti for its stellar government and legislations directly in service of his anti-slavery argument: "In the north of the Island, which is the most important part," Grégoire said, "the blacks have a completely organized government. It is evident that a legitimate legislation presides over all the branches of the administration" (43).

Despite characterizing his opinions on both Haiti and the abolition of slavery as extraordinary, Grégoire had two friends in France who were also generally anti-slavery. Civique de Gastine, who died in Haiti on 12 June 1822 (Rahul 97–99; Benot, "Grégoire contre Christophe," 145), published a generally sympathetic history of Haiti entitled, *Histoire de la République d'Haïti ou Saint-Domingue, l'esclavage et les colons* (1819). Grégoire's other friend, Antoine Métral (Benot 144), more closely followed in Grégoire's stead, writing about nineteenth-century Haitian literature. Grégoire had published his *De la littérature des nègres* in 1808, which argued for the ultimate humanity of "negroes" by demonstrating their capacity for literacy. In contrast, Métral's articles affirmed a specifically Haitian relationship to literacy and by extension, a defense of Haitian sovereignty.

Métral acknowledged the influence of Grégoire's earlier publication on his own work when he wrote that Haiti's progress toward "civilization had been announced in advance by M. l'évêque Grégoire, in his book on the literature of the Blacks, a work filled with new and erudite research" (526). Métral further stated that in *De la littérature des nègres*, "L'auteur," meaning Grégoire, "had proved that the Blacks were men, and these men had intelligence, and that their intelligence made them capable of solving the most difficult problems" (526). Speaking of the "burning eloquence" of Dessalines, Métral claimed that the founding documents and speeches of Haitian independence could similarly be used to contest the dehumanization of "black" people found in much of eighteenth-century European writing.

---

[38] A character in Hugo's 1826 novel about the Haitian Revolution, *Bug-Jargal*, alludes to French disdain for the word "philanthropist" with its implied connection to anti-slavery thought: "the *philosophes* fathered the philanthropists, who gave birth to the *négrophiles*, who produced the eaters of the whites," concluding, "these purportedly liberal ideas of which we are intoxicated in France are a poison in the tropics" (68).

Métral appears to have understood nineteenth-century Haitian literature with the more capacious definition of the literary, as promoted by
Deborah Jenson in *Beyond the Slave Narrative* (2011). Speaking of the
letters, memoirs, constitutions and other official documents issued by
Toussaint Louverture and Jean-Jacques Dessalines, Jenson writes: "I
contend […] that the words of Toussaint Louverture and Jean-Jacques
Dessalines are literary in the degree to which they harnessed poetics to
persuade large audiences, represent the stakes of freedom and domination,
and engage in political construction of themselves and their constituen-
cies" (9). If historian David Geggus has had trouble with Jenson's assig-
nation of sole authorship to Dessalines (Geggus, "Haiti's Declaration of
Independence"), Métral found no such problem.[39] Métral observed: "We
find the same nobility of thought in the correspondence of Dessalines
with Rochambeau during the time when the French army was forced to
abandon Saint-Domingue" (140). After quoting a lengthy passage from
a speech that Dessalines gave shortly after he declared Haiti independent,
Métral characterized the former's "veneration for the ashes of his ancestors," who had died in the name of Haiti's independence, as "this sublime
impulse" (529). Métral characterized another of Dessalines's speeches as
having offered "a new form worthy of the epic" (529).

Métral reserved special acclaim, however, for the proclamations
and speeches of Christophe of whom he wrote: "The many proclamations of Christophe are filled with original beauties" (530). The French
writer also viewed the Haitian king as having a nuanced understanding
of tone and audience: "We could not write such touching truths with
more simplicity, nor with more force; and with an inimitable candor, he
forgets that he is the king to get closer to the spirit and heart of the simple people […] He takes on another tone when he addresses himself to
the magistrates" (530). Métral quotes Christophe as having written to
these magistrates: "Be the organs of the law, be just, be unblinking like
it; always defend the rights of the weak and the oppressed against the
unjust attacks of the powerful" (qtd. in Métral 530).

Métral's reading of the humanist Christophe is a far cry from the
kind of despotism described in accounts of the Haitian leader describing

---

[39] Geggus writes, "Deborah Jenson has made an interesting case that Dessalines should
be regarded as [the Haitian Declaration of Independence's] 'political author' and that
Boisrond Tonnerre's role was merely 'secretarial'," but in Geggus's estimation, "The first
proposition seems to me convincing; the second perhaps goes too far" (27).

Christophe as a "black emperor" who was "imitating his white brother [Napoleon]" in committing "robberies" (*Evening Post* May 25, 1810). Métral referred to Christophe in a much more paternal light in writing: "These exhortations are filled with a gentle sensitivity; this is a father who speaks with tenderness; but what a difference in language when this same chief lets loose his indignation against a powerful enemy who threatens the liberty and independence of his States" (530).

Despite their friendship, by 1819 Métral's assessment of nineteenth-century Haiti, and specifically, of the northern kingdom of Christophe, differed remarkably from that expressed in the later writings of his friend, Grégoire. Speaking of both the north and the south of Haiti, Métral wrote: "These two peoples are walking together towards civilization; enemies by their constitutions, they are united in their common defense" (525–526). Speaking more particularly of the northern government, Métral found: "Justice is here rendered with impartiality. Laws are written in codes that are clear and precise, a regular finance system prevails that requires taxes to be paid more by the rich than the poor" (526). If the laws of the Kingdom of Hayti could stand as evidence of its civilization, so, too, did the writing of Baron de Vastey. "The works of M. de Vastey," Métral writes, "that we have already cited, are filled with instructive details about the progress of the civilization of the blacks, about the manner in which they are educated and made useful to perform all of the different functions of society" (145).

Grégoire similarly esteemed the writing of Vastey. He said in the 1819 publication that "Vastey's *Réflexions politiques* [...] reveal a very distinguished talent" ("Observations" 151). But although Grégoire had praised the northern kingdom of Haiti in the 1815 publication, by the time he wrote the "Observations," his opinion about Christophe had undergone a forceful change. Whereas he refrained from criticizing the institution of a monarchy in Haiti in the 1815 text, in 1819 Grégoire wrote of Christophe's kingdom: "This form of government is all the more shocking as it contrasts with the principles currently in circulation in the two hemispheres, and which are everyday growing more forceful, and will gradually change the face of the political world" ("Observations" 149). Grégoire continued, observing that it was curious that while the Americas were generally moving away from the "despotism" and decadent wastefulness of royalty ("Observations" 149, 150), Haiti was moving precisely in that direction: "We ask ourselves how," Grégoire writes, "they could have instituted an absolute monarchy next to a republic, which sanctions all rights, and in the vicinity of the American continent, which has republics in every corner" (149). He further claimed that monarchies were inherently prejudicial: "The nobility of the scrolls is just as absurd as that of the skin, which the colonists wanted to award exclusively to the color white" ("Observations" 150).

Alyssa Goldstein Sepinwall confirms that the Abbé Grégoire was "disgusted with the return of monarchy" in northern Haiti, and for this reason was an ardent supporter of Pétion. In Sepinwall's words, Grégoire was "appalled that as much of the world was slowly adopting republican principles, the North of Haiti was abandoning them. He was especially incensed at the irony of blacks' creating a system based on arbitrary titles" ("Exporting the Revolution," 48). While Métral viewed the laws that reigned in both governments of Haiti as equitable and fair, in his 1819 "Observations" Grégoire argued, much to the contrary, that Pétion's style of governing was far superior to Christophe's. The French priest wrote: "Now, of the two constitutions in use, one in the North, and the other in the Southwest of Haiti, the latter established in 1806, revised and improved in 1816, is the only one that contains the fundamentals required to assure the rights and consequently the happiness of the people" ("Observations" 149). Because of this and similar statements made by Grégoire in the "Observations," Yves Benot has argued that the purpose of Grégoire's text appears to have been to refute the obviously more conciliatory stances towards Christophe of Civique de Gastine and Métral. Benot writes,

> we will see that the points of view about the regime [of Christophe] that Grégoire refutes here are those of Civique de Gastine in a book published in 1818, and those expressed in articles in the *Revue encyclopédique* in the first half of 1819, by Métral, principally. In both of these cases, we are talking about Grégoire's friends, and he writes precisely in order to help them to see more clearly. However, although these writings were explicitly addressed to his French friends, we might ask ourselves if, indirectly, he does not also have in mind the pro-Christophe sympathies of his English friends, James Stephen, the Tory, but also Clarkson. (144)

The differential readings of nineteenth-century Haiti by Grégoire and Métral provide an opportunity to think about encounters with historical subjects like Vastey—and by extension, the Kingdom of Hayti—from multiple rather than singular perspectives. A broad range of possible explorations of the meaning and consequences of nineteenth-century

Haitian sovereignty for Black Atlantic humanism manifest in the constellation of conflicting readings of Vastey and contradictory reports about Christophe's government. The following fraught question posed by David Nicholls could easily be also posed about Christophe's kingdom: "Into which category does Vastey fall: true radical—pointing to a firm foundation for a new national identity—or opportunistic spokesman of a new, self-serving elite?" (108). This question represents an attempt to find certainty where ambiguity exists. We would like to know, and often think we can know, the *real* Vastey, in the same way that many of our attempts to historicize the era of Christophe lead us down the path of trying to determine whether his government was as despotic (or benevolent), as some reports suggest.

Glissant's theory of opacity offers a much different approach to historical analysis, one that can help us move us away from positivism, empiricist fact-finding, and ultimately, our potentially misguided quests to uncover *the truth*. The Martinican philosopher, in conversation with Manthia Diawara remarked, "There's a basic injustice in the worldwide spread of the transparency and projection of Western thought. Why must we evaluate people on the scale of transparency of the ideas proposed by the West?" (14). Glissant likens the demand for such transparency to a form of barbarity: "Everyone likes broccoli but I hate it," he says,

> But do I know why? Not at all. I accept my opacity on that level. Why wouldn't I accept it on other levels? Why wouldn't I accept the other's opacity? Why must I absolutely understand the other to live next to him and work with him? That's one of the laws of Relation. In Relation, elements don't blend just like that, don't lose themselves just like that. Each element can keep its, I won't just say its autonomy but also its essential quality, even as it accustoms itself to the essential qualities and differences of others. (15)

Perhaps, we, too, need to remain more open to the elements of Vastey's writing (and nineteenth-century Haiti) that unsettle and even disturb us. That is to say, those elements that strike us as contradictory or propagandistic—is he a radical or an opportunist?—distasteful and possibly out of character for a humanist.

Can we find peace in understanding Vastey as both one of the earliest and most ardent defenders of black humanity in the nineteenth century and also a faithful proponent of a monarchical government in independent Haiti? As Alexander Weheliye has asked, "Why are formations of the oppressed deemed liberatory only if they resist hegemony and/or exhibit the full agency of the oppressed? What deformations of freedom become possible in the absence of resistance and agency?" (2). In essence, I am asking if we can we consider the statist actor (Vastey) also as an agent of black (humanistic) radicalism?

This question about whether we can accept a certain level of opacity when evaluating Vastey's works (and Christophe's government) is one that must necessarily be posed to us living as we do within a system where "black" and "human" when joined together are words understood to present not only a paradox, but an impossibility. The difficulty that many writers have had in acknowledging Vastey's *philosophie* as populist, in both the past and the present, bespeaks a continuation of the same hermeneutic circle that has silenced Haiti's revolution in mainstream world history. Thinking about Vastey as primarily a Christophean scribe, and therefore *not* as an autonomous intellectual, paints an impossible picture of black writing. If the western world was incredulous at a "crown on the head of a black man!" (Vastey *RP* 17), it appears to have remained equally nonplussed at humanist arguments flowing from the pen of a person of color working under a "black man" with a crown on his head.

It continues to be difficult to assess black writing (read: black sovereignty) in the context of a world that continuously said it was as impossible as a crown on the head of a "negro." How can a sense of writing as a purely aesthetic vocation emerge in an era when black people existed in the broader imaginary, as much as in reality, as commodities to be bought, and sold, and traded?

For nearly the entire nineteenth century, people of African descent were those one spoke "for" rather than "with." In as much as they contested the idea that "Africans" were not human by promoting awareness of their literacy, and their sovereignty, Métral and Grégoire also affirmed the extraordinary consequences of viewing blackness as incompatible with humanity in the first place. Entire philosophical discourses had been devoted to disproving the humanity of "Africans," and now entire narratives were being and would continue to be created that proved the opposite, the essential humanity of people without white skin, using mountains of cultural artifacts to bolster these counter-narratives. Imagine the enormous global effort that to this day continues to be exhausted in service of Black Atlantic humanism.

Haiti's entry into the republic of letters provided some of the earliest material that supported these counter-narratives. "When an emerging people shows such love and aptitude for letters, is there anything that we cannot hope for its destiny?" Métral asked, "Letters are the soul of a civilization; without them, a nation remains ignorant and barbaric, and with them its glory shines for future generations to come" (148). His beautiful statement demonstrates precisely the quandary of Haiti as the scene of an impossible aesthetic. Métral wrote that with Haitian authorship, "the world will be offered for the first time the spectacle of black men, who had until now been savages or brutes, stolen from their native land, led into servitude across the Ocean, breaking their chains, forming a new society, creating in their midst the *beaux-arts*, and cultivating them with a success that will stun posterity" (148).

This is the signaling of an aesthetics of impossibility. Colonialists have never been stunned into humanity by black writing. Recall Frantz Fanon's famous maxim: "colonialism will never blush for shame by spreading little known culture treasures before its eyes." (*The Wretched of the Earth* 223) Glissant, for his part, was even more disheartened by the impossible humanity signaled by Haiti's extraordinary artistic output. Of Haiti's attempt to create itself into existence in a world that continued to reject and attempt to destroy it, Glissant said, "it's shattering to see a people massacred to this degree and still producing great painting, fantastic Caribbean music, and a literature. I think there's a question mark there as well. What's happening there? And can a people be purely and simply annihilated in this way?" (Diawara Interview 14)

As long as we attempt to understand Haitian writing using a vocabulary designed to deny agency and even to eliminate the possibility of people called Black or African to be considered human, the ultimate meaning and legacies of early nineteenth-century Haitian sovereignty will continue to elude us. In the end, the kind of Black Atlantic humanism in operation in Vastey's work marks both the philosophical tradition and the legacy of a nineteenth-century aesthetics of sovereignty that we may never fully comprehend.

CHAPTER 4

Baron de Vastey's *Testimonio* and the Politics of Black Memory

Although Baron de Vastey's writings were well known in the nineteenth-century Atlantic World, scholars of the period have been slow to include his works in their assessments of transatlantic print circulation and translations. The majority of recent comparative work about Haiti has been undertaken by early Americanists, who, in the words of Michael Drexler, seek to "critique the insular and exceptionalist analyses of U.S. culture" by "open[ing] up new avenues for research" into the connection between the United States and the Caribbean basin ("Haiti, Modernity, and U.S. Identities" 453).[1]

Yet even so, most studies concerning U.S.-Haitian relations have remained, to a large extent, very "U.S.-centric," to use Carol Boyce Davies's term (99). In the context of Haitian-U.S. studies, this has meant that attention has focused largely on U.S. reactions to and readings of the Haitian Revolution—or what Mimi Sheller has called the "Haytian Fear" (Sheller 286)—at the expense of analyzing Haitian narratives of these events, on the one hand, and their reactions to global readings of their revolution, on the other. Much of the scholarship on U.S.-Haiti relations, in fact, addresses the perspectives of scared

---

[1] See the work of Sean Goudie (2006), Monique Alleweart (2013), James Alexander Dun (2016), Christopher Iannini (2012), Matthew Clavin (2009), Ashli White (2010), for instance.

© The Author(s) 2017
M.L. Daut, *Baron de Vastey and the Origins of Black Atlantic Humanism*, The New Urban Atlantic, DOI 10.1057/978-1-137-47067-6_4

southerners, northern abolitionists, or African American activists, but rarely do early Haitian authors significantly figure in these accounts.[2]

In many studies of early Haitian-U.S. relations, the importance of the Haitian Revolution is viewed almost exclusively for how it impacted U.S. American lives and the politics, history (especially slave history), and literature of the United States. This reflects "a constantly expanding" center "logic" that, to use Boyce-Davies' words again, in taking the United States as its primary and "most important" object of study, finds it increasingly difficult to imagine "multiple and *equal* centers" (96, my emphasis). Such a center "logic" also places the United States and its authors, politicians, and historians in the forefront while forcing Haitian actors of this revolution into a secondary position. In so doing, Haitian people operate behind the scenes of an independence movement that they not only scripted and staged but for which they suffered and died.

When Baron de Vastey and other Haitian writers have figured into Atlantic World scholarship, it has often been in ways that elide the shifting axes of sameness and difference needed to understand the significance of their contributions to Black Atlantic humanism. The literary critic Matthew Clavin, for instance, invoking the English translation of Baron de Vastey's *An Essay on the Causes of the Revolution and the Civil Wars of Hayti* (1823) (Clavin 12), has written that whether authored by "British abolitionists or French proslavery zealots, American merchants or Haitian politicians" (6), narratives of the Haitian Revolution "fall into one of two ideological camps" (2). He writes that "[p]roslavery authors warned of a repetition of the 'horrors of St. Domingo'" while abolitionists proposed a "radically different reading" in which they found enslavers and "white soldiers culpable [...] arguing that whites who brutally enslaved Africans sowed the seeds of their own destruction" (2). Clavin finds, however, that both strains of writing the Revolution tend to narrate these events as grotesque in a fashion that coincides with the rise of the "Gothic romance at the turn of the nineteenth century" (4). He further argues that biographers, chroniclers, and story-tellers of the

---

[2] For southerners, see Sidbury, "Saint Domingue in Virginia," 539–541; Hunt, *Haiti's Influence on Antebellum America*, 101; Sheller, "The Haytian Fear," 287; and White, "Limits of Fear," 363. For northern abolitionists, see Sheller, "The Haytian Fear," 286; and Clavin, *Toussaint Louverture*, 118. For African Americans, see Fanning, "Roots of Early Black Nationalism," 63; and Dixon, *African America and Haiti*, 8.

Revolution "capitalized" on the idea of the Haitian Revolution as a "Gothic tale" in order to feed the desires of the nineteenth century reading public for sensationalistic stories, and he goes on to make the case that these authors also used the events as a didactic tool to either promote or encourage the end of slavery, urging their readers to believe that they were performing an important public service (25).

While it is true that nineteenth-century Haitian writing on the Revolution shares many of the elements of European and U.S. American writing on the events—a stated "unwillingness to publish their work" (Clavin 6), insistence on their impartiality (Clavin 8), desire to authenticate the narrative by claiming personal experience (Clavin 10), and the gothic convention of "indescribability" (Clavin 18)—to suggest that Haitian authors wrote merely to entertain, instruct, or improve salability (Clavin 12) is to miss a crucial point. As this chapter will attempt to show, a writer like Baron de Vastey explicitly noted that he was writing *against* the gothic and sentimental literary spheres that characterized much of European and U.S. writing of the time. In other words, although many U.S. and European writers published gothic renderings of race and revolution in the nineteenth century because "the market demanded them" and because "the journey 'delighted' them" (Clavin 29), the same cannot be said of Haitian authors without nuance or qualification.

Making such an argument discounts a postcolonial project of writing back to empire developed by early Haitian authors that challenges dominant European discourses. As Lara Cohen and Jonathan Stein have recently observed of early U.S. African American print culture: "The print-capitalism thesis possesses undeniable explanatory power. Yet [...] its model is not as generalizable as scholars tend to imagine, for the circulation of early African American print proves not to have been strictly (or even necessarily) an economic issue" (14). Like many early (U.S.) African American authors, Haitian writers attempted to publish in a global public sphere where they were not supposed to have had access. This lack of access is illustrated by the sheer number of U.S. and European texts published on the Haitian Revolution compared to the relatively minuscule number of Haitian texts produced and/or published. This disparity in publications did not go unnoticed by Vastey who observed that "[t]he majority of historians who have written about the colonies were whites, colonists even" (95). The unevenness of writing about Haiti was also noticed by an author from the United States who reviewed *Le Système* for *The Port-Folio*:

The object of this Haytian nobleman is to lay before his countrymen a number of important facts, which, though possessing the authority of foreign historians [...] had not till now been given to Haytians in the language of one of themselves [....] of the cruelties practised by the French in St. Domingo, Europe had, in a great measure, till now, been totally ignorant. The mask has, however, been withdrawn, by the liberty which the Haytians have given themselves, and perhaps the most signal vengeance they can now take of their ancient oppressors, is to give an impartial history. ("State of Hayti" 315)

For Vastey, the subsequent publication of an ostensibly black history of slavery and revolution in Saint-Domingue constituted a powerful reversal of power relations by which Haitians could finally force access into the global public sphere through print rather than purely through violence. Vastey believed that he could speak for the former slaves and others unable to speak for themselves and understood the collection of the testimonies gathered in *Le Système* as a part of a serious and urgent undertaking whose goal was to "awaken the ashes of the numerous victims whom [the French colonists had] precipitated into the tomb, and borrow their voices to unveil [...] heinous crimes" to the public (*Système* 35).

One of the reasons that studies of Vastey have only begun to be included within the broad fields where rightful examination of his works belong (Atlantic, early American, Caribbean, Afro-diasporic, and European Enlightenment studies, as well as postcolonial and critical race studies) is that they are often judged according to aesthetic, critical, and racial values which deny that history, as well as art, could ever have an official relationship to state power without being pernicious. To understand the importance of Vastey's works, however, I suggest that we need to consider alternative vocabularies not reliant on already established, sanctified, and fully approved genres of the Western literary canon.

As a first gesture, the language used by John Beverley to describe "testimonio" as a form of protest against the violence of modernity, "a revulsion for fiction and for the fictive as such" (99), can be useful in understanding early Haitian publications and their authors' seeming refusals to adopt or conform to established anti-slavery literary forms, such as the abolitionist novel and the Anglophone slave narrative. Rather than simply being coeval with the sentimental and gothic literary traditions of the Atlantic World in which he lived, Vastey's brutal account of slave punishments and tortures in *Le Système* emerges as a hard to define text that is both a state-sanctioned version of Haitian colonial history and a methodologically novel use of collective slave memory to create a "history from below."

It is precisely because Vastey's *Le Système* ties the personal to the political in a methodologically new way that it is important to consider Vastey's *Le Système* first on its own terms rather than tying it to a literary genealogy that foregrounds sentimental and gothic discourses. Including Vastey within these dominant traditions of Atlantic world print culture would mark him as merely a "cosmopolitan," subordinating what Srinivas Aravamudan would call his tropicopolitanism to some larger "meta-narrative" (Aravamudan, 10). This would situate Vastey not in the nationalism that Aravamudan formulates but in a kind of trans-Atlanticism that paradoxically erases difference for the sake of inclusion and thereby instead promotes sameness. Vastey's desire to publish a Haitian-produced account of collective atrocities in colonial Saint-Domingue stems not from a desire to scare, please, or evoke pity from his readers but from his wish to provide an indictment of the French colonists that, like a testimony given in a courtroom, could actually have significant legal ramifications.

Though the opening of *Le Système colonial* reads like a historical essay (we learn about the *discovery* of the island by the Spanish, the subsequent extermination of the Amerindian populations, and the institution of colonial slavery by the French), the subsequent text is a testimony or catalogue of abuses that aims to simultaneously expose colonialism as a system of barbarity and cruelty and to register the "secret" histories of former colonists for public opprobrium and ostensible legal punishment. The epigraph of *Le Système* reads: "At last it is known, this secret full of horror: the Colonial System means the domination of Whites, it means the Massacre and Enslavement of blacks." Vastey writes that in order to reveal this "secret" he had conducted numerous interviews of ex-slaves and he suggested that it was their "borrowed voices" which provided the source for these testimonies "full of horror." "For centuries," Vastey tells us, "the voices of my unfortunate compatriots could not be heard beyond these shores" (39), but now with the help of "my Haytian pen," the truth about the many "crimes" of colonialism will finally be told and "the brutal colonists will shake and tremble upon seeing [their] cruel deeds brought to light" (39).

Vastey's notion of borrowing voices from former slaves and the dead, and using them as *témoins* (40), makes *Le Système* an important precursor to the Latin American *testimonio*, a hard-to-describe genre that was, nonetheless, famously defined by George Yúdice in 1991 as an "authentic narrative, told by a witness who is moved to narrate by the urgency of a situation" (17). The official rules of the annual literary contest held by the Casa de las Américas, which added *testimonio* as one of its categories in 1970, shows the fluidity of the term, even as they try to provide a strict definition of it. The rules state, "Testimonios must document some aspect of Latin American or Caribbean reality from a direct source. A direct source is understood as knowledge of the facts by the author or his or her compilation of narratives or evidence obtained from the individuals involved or qualified witnesses." The rules also state that the author must produce "reliable documentation, written or graphic" (qtd. in Beverley, 98 [fn. 6]).

For John Beverley, one of the best-known analysts of the genre, the emergence of *testimonio* as a tool against colonial oppression in Latin America in the 1960s served to question the "existing institution of literature as an ideological apparatus of alienation and domination at the same time that it constitutes itself as a new form of literature" (40).[3] In other words, *testimonio*, as stories of the oppressed by the oppressed, emerged because most novels, epic poems, and romances had historically been written by people who were, at the very least, unwittingly complicit in a world-system that made possible the traumatic and momentous events described in *testimonio*. As a kind of proto-*testimonio*, *Le Système* stands in opposition to the more commercial, alienating, and complicit literary genres of Vastey's own era, namely the sentimental abolitionist narratives and gothic romances that became popular at the turn of the nineteenth century, which were designed to "satisfy readers' demands for sensationalistic descriptions of unimaginable acts of violence" (Clavin 2007, 25) by titillating, scaring, delighting, and horrifying them (and ultimately profiting the authors).

Unlike Leonora Sansay's *Secret History; or the Horrors of Santo Domingo* (1808), whose narrative strategy focuses on the incongruity of the "life of pleasure" pursued by the white Creoles of Saint-Domingue and the horrific violence of the raging insurrection (Sansay 80), Vastey's text proposes to disclose the "secret history" of slavery and colonialism

---

[3]There has been a lot of debate in recent years over whether or not *testimonio* is, in fact, anti-literary by people like Linda Brooks and David Stoll, but it is not necessary to enter into that debate here. Instead, we might more fruitfully ask if *testimonio* provides a solution to the incapacity of Western discourse (and really any discourse at all) to provide an adequate vocabulary for traumatic events. If we read *testimonio* instead, like Stoll and Brooks, as simply one of many kinds of (now canonized) fiction, are we doing violence to a form of writing that cannot be understood using established literary genres? When we try to classify these works in relation to existing genres, what might we be missing?

without recourse to Sansay's sentimental romanticism and her gothic voyeurism. *Le Système colonial*, in fact, is able to evade the notion of slavery as a tragic but entertaining fiction that "invites us to enjoy, not to think" (Wood, *Blind Memory* 238), principally because the events recounted by Vastey are not tied together by any unified or sequential sense of time, location, or biography.

Often the reader of *Le Système* simply gets a brief recitation of an atrocious event committed by a particular colonist followed by a list of other colonists who committed similar crimes. In other words, Vastey does not use the literary devices of personification, drama, climax, and intrigue to create suffering characters like the *tragic mulatto/a* or the kinds of slave narratives to be found in the Anglophone African American literary tradition that detail the individual lives of escaped or rebellious slaves, for whom readers might feel affinity and, in the end, sympathy.

In *Gothic America*, Theresa Goddu writes that Harriet Jacobs's *Incidents in the Life of a Slave Girl* (1861) represents a diversion from the sentimental abolitionist texts of her day since it "specifically indicts northern readers [in the U.S.] for their voyeuristic pleasure in and appropriation of the slave's suffering" (151). Yet, even *Incidents* ends on an incongruously hopeful and triumphant note that invites the reader to rejoice when Linda Brent exclaims, "Reader, my story ends with freedom... I and my children are now free! We are as free from the power of slaveholders as are the white people of the north; and though that, according to my ideas, is not saying a great deal, it is a vast improvement in *my* condition" (259). Vastey's text resists caving into the reader's need for even a quasi-heroic ending by simply cataloguing slave death after slave death and torturous event after torturous event while making sure to name, at every turn, the specific colonists guilty of these crimes.

In the introduction to *Le Système*, Vastey states that his goal in recording or chronicling in this fashion, rather than fictionalizing, the violent history reported in his book is not "to aspire to the glory of being recognized as a man of letters," but "to convey information and be useful" (viii). He explains his ardent commitment to the memories of the formerly enslaved therefore as a rejection of the genre of fiction itself: "It is not a novel that I am writing, it is an exposé of misfortunes, long sufferings and unheard of tortures" (39). Vastey even suggests that fiction might never be able to provide an adequate medium to describe the violence of colonial slavery: "Flowers and adornments suit those paintings of which man does not have to be ashamed," he writes. However, "for such a somber subject, to sink into a cesspool of crimes, they are useless. I will do nothing but retell" (40).

In his explanation of how *testimonio* works, Beverley suggests that "there are experiences in the world today that would be betrayed or misrepresented" by certain forms of literature since "there has been a complicity between the rise of 'literature' as a secular institution and the development of forms of colonialist and imperialist oppression" (29). Beverley's reasoning may help us understand Vastey's desire to compose a testimony of colonialism and slavery that rejects fiction, and ultimately the pleasures of narrative, in general, as a technique for telling the story of trauma.

Like the collaborative authors of *testimonios*, which Beverley characterizes as an "extraliterary or even an antiliterary form of discourse" (42), many Haitian authors in the early days of independence, including Vastey and Louis-Félix Boisrond-Tonnerre, repudiated travel writing, the novel, and poetry precisely because of their potential to disguise the atrocities of colonialism with ornate words. Vastey identified the colonial tendency to obfuscate with language when he wrote that French colonists and travel writers had "entered into the smallest of details on the production, the climate, the rural economy, but they took much care not to reveal the crimes of their accomplices. Very few," he adds, "had the courage to speak the truth, and even in saying it, they looked for ways to disguise or attenuate with their expressions, the enormity of these crimes" (38–39).

If fiction is merely another way to attenuate with its "expressions" the "cesspool" of colonialism, then the eponymous heroine of Émeric Bergeaud's 1859 historical romance of the Haitian Revolution, *Stella*, who asks the two dueling brothers, Romulus and Rémus, "What could pity do for you?…You evidently attach too much esteem to a sterile sentiment" (43), clearly reflects Vastey's point. The testimonies revealed in *Le Système* reject the rhetoric of sentimental abolitionism and what Marcus Wood calls "the promiscuous emotional dynamics of sentimental empathy" (*Slavery, Empathy* 13).

By reporting events rather than fictionalizing them, Vastey evades the pitfalls of what Amy Dru Stanley has called in the context of Victorian America, the "cult of feeling" (Stanley, 22). The "cult of feeling" in abolitionist discourse was problematic precisely because, as Lynn Festa has written, "the sentimental text enables the reader to pay the tribute of a tear and thus to dismiss his culpable participation in the broader system" (199). An example of Vastey's rejection of such a strategic and hollow

use of the "sentimental text" and its "cult of feeling" can be found in
Le Système where he writes: "Europeans who are not acquainted with
this horrific system, who cannot even imagine it, all you men who feel,
do not weep too soon over this portrait... Hold back your sighs and
tears: you have seen and heard nothing yet!" (35) Although Vastey per-
mits himself to "shed tears of pity and sympathy" (3) as he describes the
extermination of the indigenous population of Hispaniola in a kind of
vanishing Indian narrative, he maintains that abolitionist sympathy and
sentimental tears are of no real use for understanding the horrors of slavery and colonialism.

Throughout the text, therefore, Vastey does not ask his readers to
"weep" or to perform acts of sympathy for enslaved peoples by sighing
and shedding tears. On the contrary, drawing on the description of the
miserable state of the African slave trade described in Raynal's *Histoire
des deux Indes* (1770–1780), Vastey directly inserts into *Le Système*
Raynal's own opposition to sentimental tears: "We do not have enough
tears to lament these horrors; and what tears we have are useless!" (qtd.
in Vastey 24). Vastey later explains the purpose of his rejection of sentimentality when, specifically addressing the ex-colonists, he writes: "In
tracing the outline of these horrors, I do not hope to soften your hearts,
for, we know only too well, your hearts are more hardened than bronze
and steel: we know that your degraded souls are incapable of remorse
and pity; [...] we know that you will never change" (35). What Vastey
does want vis-à-vis the colonists is for their crimes to enter into the public sphere in a highly visible way that recalls the courtroom as spectacle.

One of the many goals of *Le Système* is to put on public trial the cruelty of the French colonists and in the end the entire colonial system.
The very act of referring to the planters' actions as "crimes" reveals
Vastey's own attitude toward the events he recounts: these are actual
breaches of humanity that deserved to be punished by the law. Vastey
laments, in fact, that "not a single one of the[se] monsters... has suffered the consequences that his cruel deeds merit; not a single one has
experienced even the slightest punishment for his crimes" (62). Since the
French government will never properly punish the former enslavers of
Saint-Domingue, the only hope, he writes, is to commit the names of the
guilty colonists to paper "so that they might be held in opprobrium by
all future generations" (35); he solicits, in short, the negative judgment
of public opinion.

Vastey publicly admonishes the former enslaver Venault de Charmilly, for example, when he exposes the planter's practice of burning his slaves alive and his torture of a particular enslaved man named Jean-Phillippe: "Slanderer of the blacks, undoubtedly you believed that your crimes, like those of all the other colonists, your accomplices, would have been buried into nothingess" (56). Vastey's wish to shame the former French colonists of Saint-Domingue extended even to his own grandfather— a "property owner" currently living in France in Marcilly-sur-Seine, according to Vastey—whom he called "barbarous" for condemning a newborn baby to death presumably so that the baby's mother could return to work more quickly (70–71).[4] It is precisely the relentless cataloguing and naming of the perpetrators of such monstrous offenses, an attempt to keep them from being "buried into nothingness," that lends a truthful rather than a gothic effect to Vastey's narrative.

Testimonio is different from other forms of oral history because of both its legal quality and what Beverley calls the "truth effect" (33) generated by the speaker. The "truth effect" of Vastey's narrative was generated to such an extent that *Le Système* actually furnished information that abolitionists used against the former French colonists. The author of an article entitled "The Namesakes" from *The Baltimore Patriot* (19 May 1815; 2) provided a translated version of a long passage from "*the colonial system unveiled*, by the baron de Vastey," which describes the horrific crimes of the settler called de Cockburne: "Among all the inhabitants of St. Domingo, few were more notorious for cruelty than was M. de Cockburne... He was in the habit of burying his slaves upright, leaving their heads out, *at which he amused himself with rolling cannon balls!*" This article was given national distribution when it was subsequently republished in the Baltimore-based *Niles Weekly Register*, providing

---

[4] For this particular enslaver as Vastey's grandfather see page 29 of the present volume. Vastey's father, Jean Valentin Vastey, was an admittedly cruel enslaver, and Vastey may have witnessed his father's own torture of slaves firsthand. The elder Vastey wrote to his brother back in France on 10 December 1773 that he had purchased his first two slaves and that, "These slaves cost us a lot. 3000 pounds a piece! But they make our fortune with their labor. We ride them like horses with great clacks of the whip" (qtd in Quevilly 73). In the *Noms de Lieux d'époque coloniale en Haiti* of J.B. Romain, we learn that Pierre Dumas, who was originally from Bordeaux, also had a plantation in Fort-Liberté (74).

immediate circulation of the "truth effect" within a year of *Le Système's* original date of publication.[5]

The "truth effect" that Vastey hoped to produce was not merely transitory but continued to operate nearly fifty years after the publication of *Le Système*. On 12 December 1859, the abolitionist Charles K. Whipple, in a letter to the Boston *Atlas and Daily Bee* entitled "Falsehood in Support of Slavery" (eventually reprinted in his colleague William Lloyd Garrison's *The Liberator*, 20 January 1860; 10), remarked that former Massachusetts governor and senator Edward Everett's statement in a speech delivered a few days before at Faneuil Hall—in which Everett stated that the slaves of Saint-Domingue had been "heureux comme un nègre de Gallifet"—had to be ignorant or disingenuous since "I have before me a pamphlet of 96 pages... written by Baron de Vastey, entitled—'Le Système Colonial Devoilé' (The Colonial System Unveiled)." Vastey, Whipple writes, "understands the importance of giving details, and he specifies the names and the individual acts of some of those planters and agents who were most distinguished, at the time of the insurrection, for hideous and atrocious cruelty to their slaves." Whipple uses Vastey's testimony to prove that the statement "heureux comme un nègre de Gallifet" was ironic at best, and a total falsehood at worst.[6] He quotes Vastey's portraits of Gallifet, who "was accustomed to cut the ham-strings of his slaves," as well as his description of the Gallifet

---

[5] See *Niles' Weekly Register*, Supplement to Vol. 8 (March–October 1815), 172. The author of the original article clearly believed that the de Cockburnes who were famous for their cruelty in Saint-Domingue were the same de Cockburnes then living in Baltimore and "lately rendered illustrious by feats of arms on our shores." "The similarity of the two namesakes," the author notes sardonically, "removes all doubt of the relationship subsisting between them, and we shall make the extract [from Vastey] with the simple remark, that in few families are there two such worthy characters."

[6] The idea that the "proverbial" phrase "heureux comme un nègre de Gallifet" was a testament to the kindness of enslavers, appears to have originated in the abolitionist Benjamin Frossard's two-volume *La Cause des esclaves nègres et des habitans de la Guinée portée au Tribunal de la Justice, de la Réligion, de la Politique ou Histoire de la Traite & de l'Esclavage des Nègres, Preuves de leur illégitimité, Moyens de les abolir sans nuire ni aux Colonies ni aux Colons* (1789, 2: 332). Yet the phrase was almost certainly made popular by Bryan Edwards in his widely referenced *An Historical Survey of the French Colony of St. Domingo* (1797), later published as a part of the 1801 edition of his *The history, civil and commercial, of the British colonies in the West Indies*. Edwards writes, "The largest sugar plantation on the plain was that of Mons. Gallifet, situated about eight miles from the town, the negroes belonging to which had always been treated with such kindness and liberality, and possessed so

plantation's dungeons "where the victims perished lying in water, by a cold and dampness which suppressed the circulation of the blood" in order to clarify the true "meaning of the fearfully sarcastic proverbial expression—'*as happy as a slave of Gallifet!*'" The Gallifet family, like the de Cockburnes, was, thus, indicted on a grand scale since, not only did *Le Système* circulate broadly in the early nineteenth-century Atlantic World, but Whipple's letter was reproduced or referenced in several mid-nineteenth-century publications in addition to *The Liberator*, including James Redpath's 1860 *Echoes of Harper's Ferry* (254–256; see also *Harper's Weekly*, 28 September 1861; 610).

By publicly exposing the names and cruelties of individual planters, Vastey succeeded in forcing what we might call a memory "from below" into a global public sphere dominated by those who were the very generators of memories from above.[7] In *Le Système* Vastey claimed to even have consulted the memories of dead people who had been enslaved and whose testimony therefore quite literally came "from below." He writes:

---

many advantages, that it became a proverbial expression among the lower white people, in speaking of any man's good fortune to say *il est heureux comme un nègre de Gallifet* (he is as happy as one of Gallifet's negroes)" (3: 74). The influence of Edwards's analysis of the phrase (whether contested by abolitionists who refuted its meaning or affirmed by those who accepted Edwards's rendering) is quite obvious, for example, in Marcus Rainsfords's *An Historical Account of the Black Empire of Hayti* (1805, p. 135); Georgette Ducrest's 1829 *Mémoires sur l'impératrice Joséphine, ses contemporains, la cour de Navarre et de Malmaison* (3: 188); John Glassford Hopkirk's *An Account of the Insurrection in St. Domingo, Begun in August 1791* (1833, p. 17); Henry Peter Brougham's *Albert Lunel; or, The château of Languedoc* (1844); Theodore Edward Hook's *Precepts and Practice* (1857); and in his pro-slavery *Appeal to Commonsense and the Patriotism of the People of the United States* (1860), Louis Schade fully evoked the terms of the debate over the phrase's meaning when he wrote that U.S. abolitionists had tried to "pervert the meaning of those words, by insinuating that Gallifet treated his negroes so badly that the above expressions are used ironically." Going on to reference Edwards himself, Schade writes, "My authority, however, is older than that of Abolitionists; I quote literally from a book published in 1801, by a gentleman who visited Hayti at the beginning of the rebellion" (27). See also an 1806 review of Marcus Rainsfords' *An Historical Account of the Black Empire of Hayti* (1805) published in the *Edinburgh Review* wherein the reviewer contests Edwards's understanding of the phrase (Art III, p. 57).

[7] I am influenced here by George Rudé's concept of "history from below" as the history *of* the oppressed, but I suggest that *Colonial System* offers us a history produced *from* the oppressed. For history from below, see the articles collected in Krantz (1988); and, in the context of the Haitian Revolution, Fick (1990).

Colonists who still exist, listen to me! I am going to awaken the ashes of the numerous victims whom you precipitated into the tomb, and borrow their voices to unveil your heinous crimes. I am going to exhume those miserable victims whom you buried alive. I am going to ask the souls [*mânes*][8] of my unfortunate compatriots whom you have thrown alive into blazing ovens; those whom you have stabbed, macerated, impaled, and a thousand other diverse torments invented by hell! (35)

Vastey's interest in the dead as *témoins* demonstrates and, indeed, shows us how we can surpass, what Marcus Wood has called "the testimonial limits of slavery" (*Slavery, Empathy* 8). With its testimonies of the dead, *Le Système* poses a broad challenge to the idea that, in Wood's words, "the experience of the slaves is, in a very real sense, lost to the conventional resources of historical reconstruction" (9). Wood writes, "when black authors decide to go back into the history of slavery, they still usually find themselves dependent on white sources, white propagandas, white journalisms, white theory as a starting point" (9).[9]

Vastey's *Le Système* lies both inside and outside of "the conventional resources of historical reconstruction," since he draws on the works of authors as various as Moreau de Saint-Méry, Raynal, Baron de Wimpffen, and the Abbé Grégoire. The vast majority of the colonial crimes he recounts have come to him, however, directly through the disquieting testimony of deceased and former slaves as well as their living ancestors whose veracity and integrity, he believes, should not be doubted. Vastey writes: "The facts I will recount bear the marks of the greatest truth [...] I collected them from the survivors of families whose relatives experienced the acts of torture I am going to try to describe

---

[8]Vastey may be drawing on the classical usage of the term *mânes*, notably by Virgil in the *Enéide*, whom Vastey cites on the title page of *Réflexions politiques*. In the *Enéide*, Virgil uses the term *mânes* at least a dozen times to describe the souls of the dead. See, also Henry S. Frieze and Walter Dennison's *Virgil's Aenid* (1902), pp. 120 and 259. An entry on *mânes* in the *Routledge Dictionary of Cultural References in Modern French* also defines the term as the "souls of the dead in the Roman religion" (Mould 192).

[9]Wendell Phillips also lamented the problem of relying upon "white sources" in his famous 1861 speech, "Toussaint L'Ouverture:" "I am about to tell you the story of a negro who has left hardly one written line. I am to glean it from the reluctant testimony of Britons, Frenchmen, Spaniards,—men who despised him as a negro and a slave, and hated him because he had beaten them in many a battle. All the materials for his biography are from the lips of his enemies" (476).

here, as well as from those unfortunate enough to have lived through them. These witnesses are irreproachable" (40). In his works, collective slave testimonies form part of a larger alternative epistemology that places less emphasis on individual biography or narration, as in the U.S. African American slave narrative, and emphasizes more how collective memory from below might provide a deeper explanation of the history of both slavery and colonialism.

Vastey's decision not to reveal that the story of "Élisabeth Mimi" was that of his own mother is, perhaps, the best example of his preference for collective memory rather than individual autobiography. By withholding this intimately personal revelation, his mother's heroic and benevolent actions in saving the slave infant Laurent from certain death becomes merely another piece of evidence in the trial of the colonial system told to him by witnesses of the events themselves (in this case his mother and/or the former slave Laurent) rather than a sentimental ploy for readerly identification or sympathy. Vastey's text, therefore, sets up an alternative way of knowing about the history of slavery that does not rely solely upon the documentation of explicitly personal experience valued in the genre of the immensely popular and marketable slave narrative.[10]

By interrogating ashes and tombs, Vastey instead interprets the past through examining the lives of what Benedict Anderson has called "anonymous dead people." Anderson writes that the French historian Jules Michelet's claim "to speak on behalf of large numbers of anonymous dead people" was "probably unprecedented," along with Michelet's insistence, "with poignant authority, that he could say what they "really" meant and "really" wanted, since they themselves 'did not understand'". Anderson continues that, because of this supposedly new epistemological technique, after Michelet, the "silence of the dead was no obstacle to the exhumation of their deepest desires" (202). "In this vein," Anderson concludes, "more and more 'second-generation' nationalists, in the Americas and elsewhere, learned to speak 'for' dead people... This reversed ventriloquism helped to open the way for a self-conscious *indigenismo*, especially in the southern Americas" (203).

---

[10]Vastey's methodology, in some senses, challenges Hortense Spiller's claim that "[i]n a very real sense, a full century or so 'after the fact', 'slavery' is *primarily* discursive, as we search vainly for a point of absolute and indisputable origin, for a moment of plenitude that would restore us to the real, rich, 'thing' itself before discourse touched it" (qtd. in Aljoe 24).

Vastey, in any event, had already adopted such a hermeneutic by 1814, making Michelet less the progenitor of indigenous history than one of its beneficiaries. Indeed, in *Le Cri de la conscience* (1815) Vastey warns his readers that the dead do not always stay that way since their interminable memories live on through the people who are the very embodiments of history. He writes, "generations may die, but the people live on, and history encourages the memory of men's actions" (91). While Michelet's intervention in the field was "unprecedented" from a European standpoint, Vastey had earlier dismantled "Enlightenment" historiography that focused upon logic and reason to explain the past, focusing instead upon collective memory from below as well as narratives describing the enslaved body and its physical pain.

Because of the need in legal testimony to provide verifiable evidence, Vastey supplements the voices of the dead with the bodies of the living. He writes that, "as evidence in support of these testimonies," the victims of these tortures showed him "limbs mutilated by iron or scorched by fire. I have obtained these facts," he adds, "from a great many people who are notable and trustworthy" (40). Disembodied evidence in the form of ashes and voices is here doubled by the living body, which becomes the very repository of empirical evidence. The maimed and scorched limbs of former slaves presented by Vastey, as Diana Fuss has written of the corpse poem, "remind us that even the most abject body has a story to tell" (21).

In a sense, these tortured bodies say more than Vastey or their owners ever could. The living body succeeds where language fails since, as Elaine Scarry has written, physical pain cannot be objectified: "physical pain—unlike any other state of consciousness—has no referential content. It is not *of* or *for* anything. It is precisely because it takes no object that it, more than any other phenomenon, resists objectification in language" (5). By simply testifying to the existence of these bodies, still experiencing the lingering physical effects of slavery, rather than trying to represent the pain of the bodies themselves, Vastey recognizes that he will never be able fully to disclose the "secret history" of slavery. In other words, while we might be able to adequately describe the way bodies look while in pain, we can never fully represent the way that the pain itself feels. This ultimately suggests that slavery might be susceptible to representation as well, but that its physical anguish is far more difficult to capture.

While for Vastey there is no available vocabulary that can adequately represent the physical pain of slavery, verbally expressing the myriad kinds of torture perpetrated by the colonists presents different communicative obstacles. When recounting a tale involving a certain *dame Langlois*, who casually remarks—upon hearing from her overseer that he had to chop off a female slave's arm to prevent her entire body from passing through the sugar mill—that this "wouldn't have perhaps been such a disaster at the end of the day" were it not for the possibility that the slave's blood "might have spoiled my cane-juice" (61), Vastey says that this episode pushes the limits of his task as a compiler or recorder. He writes, "No, it is impossible for me to continue to describe such atrocities. What courage and what strength of spirit would it require to record the numerous crimes of the colonists during the colonial regime. I could fill entire volumes" (61–62). Although Vastey continues to relate these grisly events, he periodically stops himself to let us know that, if his language is failing him, it is because the tortures that he is describing are "above all expression" (66).

Vastey earlier lamented his very incapacity, and more importantly, his *unwillingness*, to describe slavery in writing: "What sort of writing would be required of me to describe crimes until now unknown to humanity? When depicting these myriad horrors, what form of expression could I possibly employ? I do not know" (40). Part of *Le Système*'s circumvention of the gothic tradition of "indescribability" (Clavin, "Race, Revolution" 18) is its author's resolve no longer even to look for turns of phrase that can describe the horrors of slavery. This is partially because, for Vastey, continuously describing "crimes until now unknown to humanity" holds the distinct possibility of lessening rather than increasing their horror by sheer desensitization. Also, according to Vastey, his vocabulary does not even contain "expressions" or idioms appropriate for capturing the many degradations of slavery.

Many scholars and artists, in the wake of Theodor Adorno, have written about the challenges of communicating traumatic events like the Holocaust and lynching in verbal terms.[11] Geoffrey Hartman has written

---

[11] In 1951 the German philosopher Theodor Adorno famously wrote that "to write poetry after Auschwitz is barbaric" (188), suggesting that to compose something beautiful out of something as horrible as the Holocaust was unthinkable. Adorno explains the logic behind this statement in writing that "no art" of the Holocaust could "evade" the fate of attempting to "styliz[e] and titillate readers" into attaining some form of enjoyment out of an event that had no transcendent, abstract meaning for humanity. Adorno writes: "The aesthetic principle of stylization, and even the solemn prayer of the chorus makes an unthinkable fate appear to have had some meaning; it is transfigured, something of its horror removed. This alone does an injustice to the victims: yet no art which tried to evade them could confront the claims of justice. Even the sound of despair pays its tribute to a hideous affirmation [...] When genocide becomes part of the cultural heritage in the themes of committed literature, it becomes easier to play along with the culture which gave birth to murder" (189).

that what complicates the relationship between literature and trauma is "our wish to achieve a perfect verbal marker by way of language, a successful verbal fixative of the real," an "orphic quest or communication-compulsion [that]...is always disappointed, always revived" (541). This disappointed "quest" for markers of the "real" emerges most clearly in *Le Système* when Vastey avoids using the French noun for rape, *viol*. The most immediate literal cognate of *viol* in English, *violation* (also related to *violence*), underscores the frustrating inappropriateness of any single term to capture the fundamental horrors of rape, which involves not merely violence and violation but also powerlessness and objectification. Although Vastey does use the verb *violer* to describe the colonist's violation of "all of the laws of nature" (69; "ce maître orgueilleux, violait sans pitié, sans remords, toutes les lois de la nature"), he is not solely talking about sexual assault here, which once again underscores the inadequateness of the French verb *violer* to signify rape. As a verb, the word *violer* rather innocuously (when compared to actual "rape") could refer to violating a law or a simple rule or anything else for that matter. Vastey's frustrated search for a more specific language for rape that could avoid downplaying its seriousness and/or turning the act into pornography is all too apparent when, alluding to incest, he vaguely tells us that the colonists were guilty of "the most crapulous forms of debauchery" and "even disrespected the laws of nature with respect to their illegitimate daughters" (89); while in another passage he writes, "Haitian women were at the mercy of these disgusting men, who abused them in the most horrific manner imaginable. I shudder when I think of the numerous unfortunate victims sacrificed to these jealous rages: on a mere suspicion, they would be whipped or lashed to death" (68–69).

The horror is communicated to the reader by the physiological reaction of Vastey's own body rather than any forcefulness of language. The trauma is so terrible that it makes him "shudder" even to think about it. This is yet another subversion of the gothic convention described by Matthew Clavin where the author hopes to produce a physical response in the reader to communicate the horror ("Race, Rebellion" 17). In his *Réflexions politiques* (1817), Vastey had similarly called forth the embodied terror occasioned by remembering not only the lives of those who have been raped but thinking about the rapists themselves: "We could name a great deal of planters," Vastey writes, "who rendered themselves guilty of incest and other crimes against nature; but the horror that we are experiencing, in writing these lines, prevents us from reporting them" (100). In both the passage from *Le Système* and the one from *Réflexions politiques*, the physical reaction is Vastey's own and captures an embodied idea of the horror of rape that cannot be expressed by verbal language alone. Moreover, Vaster's unwillingness to specify any of the names of these rape victims or their perpetrators, as opposed to his usual practice in *Le Système*, emphasizes the wholly inevitable and inadequate "orphic quest" of testifying to the act of rape, a form of communication that often re-victimizes the victims by forcing them very publicly (and pornographically) to re-live the trauma (and often to confront the traumatizer) over and over again.

The idea that the anguish of slavery could not ever (and perhaps should not ever) be fully communicated by spoken or written language was perhaps best expressed in the nineteenth century by the U.S. American abolitionist William Wells Brown (a former escaped and fugitive slave), who in 1847, anticipating Gayatri Spivak, said in a lecture to the Female Anti-Slavery Society of Salem: "I may try to represent to you Slavery as it is;... we may all represent it as we think it is; and yet we shall all fail to represent the real condition of the Slave... Slavery has never been represented; Slavery never can be represented... The Slave cannot speak for himself" (108). As Keith M. Botelho has written, "The quandary Brown faced was not how to represent slavery, but how to effectively represent slavery as it is. His turn to drama and performance protests minstrelsy, white benevolence, and perceived notions of racial superiority" (194). Yet, even in his *Clotel; or the President's Daughter* (1853), another hard to define text that makes use of oral history, newspaper stories, and contains elements of the slave narrative, Brown, like many black writers of his time, is forced to cater to the demands of a literary marketplace that valued sentimentality and near-white heroines. As Paul Gilmore has written, "In attempting to 'speak for' the slaves still in bondage, the former slave entered into public debates over race and slavery. But to do so he had to cast off the markers of both his past enslavement and his racial difference and take up the language and figures articulated by the dominant culture" (45–46).[12]

---

[12] The sentiment that the slave could not speak, and therefore that slavery could not really be known by *whites*, was also articulated early on by Elizabeth Hart Thwaites, "the first known black woman in the Caribbean to write against slavery" (Ferguson 5). In her "Letter to a Friend" (1794), Thwaites wrote of slavery, "It does not suit me to say the worst I know concerning it: only I assure you it comprises a mystery of iniquity, an endless list of complicated ills, which it is not likely you will ever know. You will not, perhaps, find the sufferers disposed to complain of their case. Not many are capable of *explaining*, however keenly they may *feel*, their disadvantages" (20).

While Brown may have felt constrained by the "dominant culture" in his fictional texts, the genre of oration allowed him to rely upon a different epistemology, one that was perhaps less exploitative, to communicate the suffering of enslaved peoples. Brown told his audience: "When I begin to talk of Slavery, the sighs and the groans of three millions of my countrymen come to me upon the wings of every wind; and it causes me to feel sad, even when I think I am making a successful effort in representing the condition of the Slave" (110).

Vastey, too, ostensibly freed from the alienation and domination of the Euro-American literary market place, speaks of slavery as a system that produces millions of testimonial "groans" (*gémissements*). He writes that in Saint-Domingue the "groans" and "useless cries" of the enslaved "would vanish into air, they would merge with the sound of the whip that echoed throughout our mountains" (65). These sounds of slavery or testimonial groans, from which it is practically impossible to derive enjoyment, would be transmitted across the oceans by the Haitian printing press. In Vastey's estimation, this was the best revenge that post-independence Haitians could take against the colonists.

Vastey writes that "the friends of slavery, those eternal enemies of the human race, have written thousands of volumes freely; for centuries now, they have made all the [printing] presses of Europe groan under the weight of their lies and their attempts to degrade the black man below the level of brutes" (94). He goes on to add, however, that whereas Haitian history had once been written by white colonists alone, "now that we have Haytian printing presses, we can reveal the crimes of the colonists and respond to even the most absurd calumnies invented by the prejudice and greed of our oppressors" (95). By releasing the "stifled" voices and guttural "groans" of former slaves and confronting the colonists with the "irreproachable" testimony of their scarred bodies, Vastey contests the memory factory of colonialism, and in essence requires his readers to confront the everyday brutality and dehumanization attendant in the colonial system itself.

Vastey's relentless insistence on cataloguing the many abuses of slavery and naming the perpetrators of these crimes, both collectively and individually, indicts enslavers while also refusing to give the reader the kind of satisfaction or even the opportunity to mourn that one might experience from a death described in a novel or a poem. He does not let us feel as if the slaves whom *dame Delorme* nailed alive to a wooden board could have experienced any joy before their deaths (57), nor does he let us feel that death is a symbol for eternal rest and peace. Instead, Vastey's compilation of corpse after corpse paints slavery as what Orlando Patterson has referred to as a "social death" (8), or alternatively, what Giorgio Agamben has called, "bare life."[13] In his *Réflexions politiques*, Vastey writes that at the moment of the Haitian Revolution, the slaves had been "civilly dead": "they inhabited this earth as if they did not really inhabit it; they lived as if they were not really living" (49–50). Such an explanation of the life of enslaved peoples had already been expressed in *Le Système*:

> Is it any wonder if we resorted to suicide, to poisoning? And if our women extinguished in their hearts all the sweet feelings of motherhood, when with cruel pity they caused the deaths of the dear, sad fruits of their lovers? In fact, how do you support life when it has reached the final limits of degradation and misery? When you must die a thousand times in one life by undergoing the most cruel tortures, when you are reduced to this deplorable situation, without any hope of escaping from it; to want to go on living, would that not be the utmost symbol of cowardice? Oh, why give life to such unfortunate beings, whose entire existence would condemn them to lead a pithy existence of torture and opprobrium in a long tissue of death without end; to extinguish such an odious life, was that such a great crime? it was compassion, humanity!!! (71–72)

Death represents life for the slave since the slave socially dies a thousand times before his physical death, a reversal of Shakespeare's famous phrase in *Julius Caesar* that it is "cowards" who "die many times before their deaths, the valiant never taste of death but once" (II.ii. 32–33). Standard

---

[13]There has been much debate in the historiography of societies of enslavement about whether slavery in fact constituted a "social death." Yet even if slaves created communities and complex systems of communication and resistance as well as diverse, alternative webs of kinship, all of which calls into question whether slavery actually constituted a social death, the many texts about slavery produced in the nineteenth-century Atlantic World often portray slavery as ultimately reducing human life down to the mere biology of "bare life." The emptiness of "bare life" is lucidly and eloquently captured in Ewa Ziarek's words as "damaged life, stripped of its political significance." For challenges to Patterson's argument, see Philip D. Morgan (1998), Richard Brent Turner (2004), Frederick Cooper (2005), and Vincent Brown (2008). For a reading of Agamben's idea of "bare life" in the context of twentieth-century Haiti, see Fischer (2007), and for a reading of Patterson and Agamben together, see Ziarek (2012).

notions of life and death and their intrinsic meaning cannot be used to describe the condition of an enslaved person who lies outside of such definitions of heroism and valor. Vastey writes, "What liberal feelings could possibly grow in hearts that were fertilized with endless misery! Could a life lived in such odious conditions of endless torture give birth to the sweetest moral affections of religion, humanity, virtue—those sentiments that are the source of happiness for all civilized men?" (71).

Compassion for one's fellow beings, when characterized as the total protection of human life, to Vastey, referred only to the world of the socially alive and could not be retrofitted to describe an enslaved person's experiences. Thus, he describes snuffing out the life of a newborn baby destined only for slavery as ordinary compassion and humanity rather than extraordinary barbarity and cruelty. While Marcus Wood writes that Toni Morrison in *Beloved* was able to develop a novel out of a "genuine case of slave mother infanticide" (Wood, *Slavery, Empathy* 10), for Vastey such infanticide was not fantastic, as it is portrayed in Morrison's novel. Like the other events that he described in *Le Système*, infant murder, suicide, and abortion, were ordinary components of the depredations of Atlantic slavery. Vastey's point was that the ordinariness rather than the extraordinariness of such events made them horrific. A slave's life, then, had such little meaning that the reader was denied the platitude that even the most abject human life has an ultimate purpose and is therefore worth living.

Vastey's images of slave torture, burnings, live burials, infanticide, rape, and suicide, in the end, perform what Fuss might call a "radical" subversion of the "more serene romantic portraits of corpses slumbering in the grave" that characterize the genre of the elegy (10). In *Le Système* slave corpses are "abject" precisely because they lie "beyond the scope of the possible, the tolerable, the thinkable" (Kristeva 1). Yet, because Haitians who serve the *lwa* or gods do not believe that the dead are "soulless," the souls or spirits of these slaves who died unquiet deaths still remain to be accessed and probed. As Colin (Joan) Dayan has written, "the landscape of Haiti is filled not only with the spirits of the dead seeking rest and recognition but with other corporeal spirits who recall the terrors of slavery and the monstrous, institutionalized magic of turning humans into pieces of prized and sexualized matter" (264).

Vastey's evocation of the voices and bodies of slavery's mutilated victims marks their almost total abjection but, like an ancestral spirit who mounts his corporeal horse in the Haitian religious tradition of *sèvi lwa* (or serving the gods), Vastey's testimony brings them to life once again.[14] In *Le Cri de la conscience*, the dead suddenly appear not to mourn or to complain, but to celebrate the victories of the Haitian Revolution. Vastey writes:

> We have avenged the spirits of our brave companions who died gloriously for liberty and independence; the ghosts of our fathers, our mothers, our sisters, who were victims of the French, have arisen from the ashes of the pyres, from the depths of the seas, from the intestines of rapacious dogs, to applaud us and chant with us, vengeance! vengeance! (10)

Vastey's glee and celebration of both discursive and physical vengeance may seem a far cry from (and may paradoxically appear to confirm) the kinds of deeply personal and parricidal "mulatto vengeance" narratives attributed to monstrous hybrids by the likes of Drouin de Bercy in the post-revolutionary Atlantic World (Daut, *Tropics* 110–151). Yet, Vastey's brand of vengeance was not motivated by the kinds of monstrous racial thinking attributed to people of mixed race in the work of Drouin de Bercy.

At least one of Vastey's early reviewers acknowledged that the vengeance for which he advocated had nothing to do with the supposed innate barbarity of "Africans" or the propensity for "mulattoes" to want to kill their white fathers; instead, it had everything to do with the kind of justice and "imprescriptible right to resist oppression" ostensibly encouraged by the radical Enlightenment thinkers who authored the *Declaration of the Rights of Man and the Citizen* (Article 2). The following account of *Le Système* published in *The Antijacobin Review* in 1818 acknowledged the humanity of the Haitian revolutionists and decried the inhumanity of the colonists:

---

[14] The practice that I describe above is often referred to as Vodou but, as Kate Ramsey notes in *The Spirits and the Law*, "In Haiti the word Vodou has traditionally referred to a particular mode of dance and drumming, and has generally not been figured as an inclusive term for the entire range of spiritual and healing practices... For many practitioners, the encompassing term is not Vodou, but rather Ginen, a powerful moral philosophy and ethical code valorizing ancestral African ways of serving the spirits and living in the world" (7).

Fig. 4.1 *Le Roi Henri 1er, Le Baron de Vastey* (1953) by Evans Pierre Augustin. Courtesy of Figge Museum

> In reading over the tract before us we have doubted whether we were in the society of men or of wild beasts; but a little reflection easily convinced us that the brutes of the field could not act as the monsters we have been placed in company with. ("*Système*" 243)

Vastey's writing causes the author not only to doubt that blacks are "wild beasts," but to perform exactly the kind of subversion of categories that *Le Système* urges when the reviewer asserts that it is the colonists who are "the monsters." Thus, Vastey ultimately succeeded in convincing many of his readers in the Atlantic World that the Haitian brand of "vengeance" during the revolution (and Vastey's daring exposé of the monstrosity of the colonists afterwards) was wholly justified and even occasioned by the greater violence of colonialism (Fig. 4.1).

CHAPTER 5

Baron de Vastey and the Twentieth-Century Theater of Haitian Independence

In his 2005 interview with scholar Françoise Vergès, Aimé Césaire, who wrote in his famous poem, *Cahier d'un retour au pays natal* (1939), that revolutionary "Haiti was the place where *négritude* stood up for the first time" (24), pointedly criticized postcolonial Haiti. "In Haiti," Césaire told Vergès, "I saw above all what should not have been done! A country that had supposedly conquered its liberty, which had conquered its independence, and which I saw more miserable than Martinique, a French colony! The intellectuals 'intellectualized,' they wrote poems, they took positions on this or that question, but with no connection to the people themselves. It was tragic, and it was something that could well happen to us too" (*Nègre* 56). In his collection of essays, *What the Twilight Says* (1957), Nobel prize winning author Derek Walcott, who hails from the island of St. Lucia, also had something critical to say about Haiti when he referred to its revolutionary leaders and eventual statesmen, Jean-Jacques Dessalines and Henry Christophe, as "squalid fascists who chained their own people" (12). This opinion about Haiti's first political leaders was also shared, to some extent, by Césaire, who published a famous play in 1963 entitled, *La Tragédie du roi Christophe*, in which the Haitian king, in Césaire's own words, appears "as a ridiculous man," having "installed a monarchy" that Césaire called, "grotesque" (Césaire, *Nègre* 57). In 2002, Walcott decided to publish together as *The Haitian Trilogy* the three plays he wrote about the events that led to Haitian independence: *Henri Christophe* (1948), *Drums and Colours* (1958), and *The Haitian Earth* (1984). In the foreword to the volume, Walcott

© The Author(s) 2017   135
M.L. Daut, *Baron de Vastey and the Origins of Black Atlantic Humanism*,
The New Urban Atlantic, DOI 10.1057/978-1-137-47067-6_5

doubled down on his own criticism with a backhanded compliment when he offered what has since become a much maligned assessment of the relationship between revolutionary Haiti and independent Haiti. "The Haitian Revolution," Walcott wrote, "as sordidly tyrannical as so many of its subsequent regimes tragically became, was an upheaval, a necessary rejection of the debasements endured under a civilized empire, that achieved independence" (vii–viii).

Although the statements of Walcott and Césaire have been roundly criticized by scholars of Haitian revolutionary literatures (Bongie, *Friends* 226; Kaisary 135; Figueroa 23; Walsh, *Free and French* 108), it is Kaiama Glover's estimation of Haiti's isolated position in the global literary marketplace that may be most useful for our thinking. Representing Haitian rulers as beyond the pale of humanity has contributed to the marginalization of Haitian poets and intellectuals. Glover writes: "Haiti has in many ways been relegated to the periphery of the so-called 'New World'—historically and contemporarily, politically and literarily. Marked by exceptionalism, the voices of some of its most important writers have been muted by the geopolitical realities of the nation's fraught post-revolutionary history" (vii).

As a corrective to this relegation towards the periphery, Glover's monograph, *Haiti Unbound* (2010), marks one of the first attempts to study the literary form of "spiralism," created in 1965 by Haitian authors Jean-Claude Fignolé, Frankétienne, and René Philoctète (1932–1995). Spiralism is a movement that implicitly challenges the more well-known political and literary schools of *négritude, antillanité,* and *créolité,* by drawing inspiration from "certain region-specific elements of Haitian reality" (Glover viii). "The very idea of the spiral," Glover writes, "recalls the foundations of the Caribbean oral tradition, according to which stories unfold cumulatively or cyclically; are relatively unconcerned with any purely narrative structure or horizontal, linear development; and are subject invariably to the frequent and spontaneous interventions of the public" (viii).

Aside from providing the most in-depth critical inquiry to date into the work of Spiralism, the aim of Glover's research is also to "question certain exclusionary practices at work within the already frustratingly peripheralized space" of Caribbean letters (xviii). "While the revolution marked an aggressive bid on the part of the newly independent Haitians for inclusion in a global—if reconfigured—world order," she writes, "the event has had an ironically isolating effect on Haiti's positioning with respect to other parts of the Caribbean" (16). It is this isolation, reflected rather bleakly in the commentaries of Césaire and Walcott above, to which I direct our attention as we begin to consider in this chapter what we can learn from performances of Vastey on the stage rather than readings of him on the page.

It is very likely that the majority of today's students of Caribbean literature are now more familiar with Baron de Vastey as a literary character in Walcott and Césaire's famous plays than with him as a historical writer. This, I suggest, makes it important to think about the differential understandings of Baron de Vastey's legacy that might arise when we know of him primarily as a postcolonial literary character rather than as a postcolonial author or even as a historical personage.

I will return to the importance of performing rather than reading Vastey and its consequences for understanding the development of Black Atlantic humanism later in this chapter. For now, it is important to clarify that the concept of isolation is of interest primarily because the portrayal of Vastey as a character in Walcott's *Henri Christophe* and *The Haitian Earth* and in Césaire's *La Tragédie du roi Christophe*, anticipated by the appearance of Vastey in the much less well-known plays of May Miller, Selden Rodman, and Dan Hammerman,[1] rests ultimately on the depiction of Haitian independence as politically impotent. In these plays, Haitian sovereignty is rendered null because of the implied despotism of Haitian rulers, and ultimately, the incompetence of the Haitian people themselves.

Portrayals of Haitian leaders and the Haitian citizenry as primarily to blame for Haiti's dire economic and political crises are problematic principally because the country's troubles since independence are presented as having occurred in isolation of other factors. Factors such as trade embargoes, the disastrous indemnity from France, the creation of food dependency, the lack of formal, diplomatic recognition, and most importantly, France's continuous attempts to re-take the former colony in the first two decades of Haitian independence. All of this neo-colonial[2]

---

[1] Respectively, *Christophe's Daughters* (1935); *The Revolutionists* (1942) and *Henri Christophe, Man for Freedom: An Historical Drama* (1945).

[2] I operate from a definition of neocolonialism that is derived, in part, from Kwame Nkrumah's "Neo-Colonialism, the Last Stage of Imperialism" (1965), wherein Nkrumah explains, "The essence of neo-colonialism is that the State [...] is, in theory, independent and has all the outward trappings of international sovereignty. In reality its economic system and thus its political policy is directed from outside."

interference contributed to the problematic leadership under scrutiny in what Walcott considered to be the "sordidly tyrannical" regimes of Jean-Jacques Dessalines, Henry Christophe, Alexandre Pétion, and Jean-Pierre Boyer. None of this interference is, however, *performed* satisfactorily in the plays of Walcott, Césaire, Miller, Hammerman, or Rodman. Indeed, in discussing in his book of essays, *What the Twilight Says*, his representation of Haitian rulers in *Henri Christophe*, Walcott called Christophe and Dessalines, those "slave-kings" who "structured *their own* despair" (11, *italics mine*). Even though the last play in Walcott's trilogy, *The Haitian Earth*, appears to argue on behalf of the Haitian masses, in the words of one literary critic, the play still manages to "convey visions of tragic circularity, senseless violence, and history as eroticized fantasies" (Kaisary 2). In much the same manner, in Césaire's *La Tragédie*, Christophe is presented as having isolated himself from his own people. In fact, the plays of both Walcott and Césaire present Christophe as a fatally tragic character undone by his own inadequacies rather than rendered impotent by an Atlantic world that continuously sought to disavow Haitian sovereignty.

Each of the plays under study here use Baron de Vastey as a vehicle to pursue this isolationist thesis of Haitian political leadership. Examining the portrayal of Vastey in the early to mid-twentieth-century theater of Haitian independence exposes the broader exclusionist stances of Haiti narrated within these plays, as well as the ways in which these kinds of representations end up reproducing a colonialist mentality with respect to understanding Haitian sovereignty. In other words, Baron de Vastey can be read in these renditions as someone who makes critically apparent the perils rather than the promises of postcolonial (black) sovereignty.

Even if Vastey can be considered "the most important ideological figure in early Haitian history" (Dash, *Literature and Ideology,* 4), his appearance in these twentieth-century dramas of Haitian independence has yet to come under wholistic interpretive scrutiny. In this chapter, by focusing on performances rather than readings of Vastey, my goal is to ask: What understandings of Haitian independence, Haitian sovereignty, and the Black Atlantic humanism that they both buttressed, can we glean by thinking about how Vastey, an intellectual, became a central figure in theatrical representations of Haitian revolutionaries by twentieth-century writers? I probe this question by first exploring the meaning and consequences of isolating and blaming Haiti for the troubles with black sovereignty (in Sect. 1) in twentieth century theater dramatizing the country's first years of independence. I then pursue this thread more specifically by examining how Vastey was used to isolate Haiti from Black Atlantic thought in the theatrical representations of him produced by Walcott (in Sect. 2), Césaire (in Sect. 3), and Miller, Rodman, and Hammerman (in Sect. 4). I argue that what we derive from these six performances of Vastey on stage is a pointed critique of Haitian leadership and ultimately, Haitian sovereignty; one that tends to isolate rather than include Haiti in a history of the Americas marked by both neo-colonialism and global capitalism. In their own ways each of these plays *uses* Vastey to produce a performance documenting the troubles with sovereignty after colonialism.

Isolation and Blame in the Theater of Haitian Independence

Attempts to produce isolationist narratives of Haiti are a longstanding feature of writing about the country. Paul Farmer writes, "journalistic and even scholarly commentary on Haiti has tended to depict the country as isolated and disconnected—a static country of backward peasants in a time warp" (*The Uses* 49). A "systematic perspective" on the "larger social and economic system" that brought Haiti into being, Farmer adds, while it may be "an approach common enough in the field of Caribbean studies," remains "curiously absent from much commentary on Haiti" (50). Farmer contests the implied *otherness* of Haitian society in political and economic histories of the Americas when he observes that "depicting Haiti as divorced from 'the outside world' turns out to be a feat of Herculean oversight, given that Haiti is the creation of expansionist European empires—a quintessentially western entity" (59–60).

One reason for nineteenth-century Haiti's peripheral status in many studies of the Caribbean region may be that early Haiti *was* different from the rest of the circum-Caribbean in that it was independent and sovereign. Such early sovereignty does not often fit into neat periodizations of the Caribbean that could sharply delineate a colonial past in contrast to a postcolonial present. Haiti's early postcolonial era is further complicated by the country's neo-colonial present. In a certain very real sense, the Haiti of today, due to the interference of the United States and France, in particular, shares much more in common with its colonial past than with the *soi-disant* postcolonial present of the majority of the Caribbean archipelago.

Portraying Haitian rulers in fiction as disconnected from the politics of the "expansionist European empires" that continue to greatly affect life in the Caribbean turns out be a part of the same tropology that drives ongoing political narratives of Haiti. While all of the plays of Haitian independence[3] under study in this chapter have much to say about the horrors of the colonialism and slavery of Saint-Domingue's day, none of the plays adds much at all to the critique of neo-colonialism that structures the economic, social, and political relationship that Haiti had and continues to have with "the West."

One reason for the lack of relational representations of Haiti may be that plays about the Haitian Revolution and Haitian independence usually fixate on singular heroic figures like Toussaint Louverture, Dessalines, and Christophe, who, in the words of Césaire, wrote the "first Negro epic of the New World" (qtd. in Kaisary 26). This is evident in the titles of many of these plays, which appear to be much more about Haitian revolutionary leaders than about the Haitian Revolution or Haitian independence, even though both can only be fully understood in the context of the transatlantic political and economic crises that brought them into being.

In addition to Walcott and Césaire's plays about Christophe, Langston Hughes's play, *The Emperor Dessalines* was performed in 1936. C.LR. James also staged a play entitled, *Toussaint L'Ouverture* in 1936, followed by a revised play about Louverture entitled, *The Black Jacobins* in 1967. Hammerman produced his historical drama, *Henri Christophe*, in 1945 and Édouard Glissant presented *Monsieur Toussaint* in 1961. Even plays that do not use the name of a "great man" in the title, more often than not still focus on Louverture, Dessalines, or Christophe. This is the case in John Matheus' play about Dessalines, *Ouanga: a Haitian*

---

[3]For the purposes of this essay, I make no fine distinction between dramas about the Haitian Revolution, proper, and dramas about the first two decades of Haitian independence. Most of the plays under consideration here merge these separate eras together. In fact, Corbould tells us that the vast majority of early twentieth-century plays about Haiti concern the Revolution and the regimes of Christophe and Dessalines. She writes, "Stage writers of the interwar years all but ignored the period of Haitian history from about 1820 to the 1920s and 1930s" (260).

Opera in Three Acts (1932), William Dubois's Christophe-centric, *Haiti*, produced as a part of the Federal Theatre Project in 1938; and Rodman's *The Revolutionists* (1942), which, in three separate acts, dramatizes the lives of Louverture, Dessalines, and Christophe, respectively.[4]

The attractiveness of focusing on great "heroes" of the Revolution was acknowledged by theater scholar, Errol Hill, who, incidentally, played Baron de Vastey in Walcott's *Henri Christophe*: "The Haitian revolution engendered more plays by black authors than any other single event in the history of race," Hill writes, "The principal leaders of the insurrection are the granite from which legendary heroes are hewn" (414). Clare Corbould adds that the "fascination, obsession even, with the Haitian Revolution, and with Haiti itself [...] was due to the need to tell the stories, again and again, of strong black men who resisted white colonial authorities, who bore arms and who governed themselves in a black nation" (280).

Understanding Haitian independence and its subsequent universal impact (namely, unequivocally outlawing slavery), as the culmination of the work of the enslaved and the formerly enslaved who populated Dessalines's army—rather than as the work of military and state leaders like Dessalines himself— is a historiographical and epistemological contest made visible by Carolyn Fick's groundbreaking monograph, *The Making of Haiti: The Saint-Domingue Revolution from Below* (1990). Fick wrote that "the mass of black slave laborers who participated in this revolution on their own terms and with interests and goals embodying their own needs and aspirations" were "often at variance with, if not in direct opposition to, the path being staked out by those in positions of leadership and control." At the time that Fick wrote *The Making of Haiti*, however, as she acknowledges, "very little research, at least

---

[4]Two notable exceptions to the "great man" narrative in twentieth century dramas about the Haitian Revolution occur in May Miller's *Christophe's Daughters*, which focuses on the monarch's two daughters, Améthiste and Athénaire, and features Vastey as a character, and Helen Webb Harris's *Génifrède* (1922), a play about Louverture's eponymous fictional daughter, which was likely inspired by Harriet Martineau's *The Hour and the Man* (1841). Martineau's play also gives Louverture a fictional daughter named Génifrède. Both Harris and Miller's plays were published as a part of a 1935 anthology, edited by Miller and Richard Willis, entitled, *Negro History in Thirteen Plays* (1935). Miller authored four of the plays in the anthology herself, including *Christophe's Daughters*. Miller's other plays were, *Harriet Tubman*; *Samory*; and *Sojourner Truth*. For more on Miller, see, Perkins (14).

from the standpoint of primary archival sources" had been devoted to the lives of the enslaved during the Revolution in Saint-Domingue (1). More recent scholarship has sought to affirm Fick's conclusion that the enslaved and formerly enslaved people of Saint-Domingue were the true heroes of the Revolution and were therefore the *real* authors of the racial universalisms brought about by Haitian sovereignty. Laurent Dubois writes, to that end, "if we live in a world in which democracy is meant to exclude no one, it is in no small part because of the actions of those slaves in Saint-Domingue who insisted that human rights were theirs too" (Dubois, *Avengers* 3).

It is Michel-Rolph Trouillot who has most clearly described the stakes of such an argument when he assesses the difference between understanding Haitian independence as the result of a series of texts with individual authors transcribed and then codified into law—for example, the Haitian Declaration of Independence—rather than as a series of deeds, collectively performed, which themselves performed Haitian independence and the end of slavery into existence—for example, the burning of Cap-Haïtien. Trouillot writes,

> The Haitian Revolution expressed itself mainly through its deeds, and it is through political practice that it challenged Western philosophy and colonialism. It did produce a few texts whose philosophical import is explicit, from Louverture's declaration of Camp Turel to the Haitian Act of Independence and the Constitution of 1805. But its intellectual and ideological newness appeared most clearly with each and every political threshold crossed, from the mass insurrection (1791) to the crumbling of the colonial apparatus (1793), from general liberty (1794) to the conquest of the state machinery (1797–98), from Louverture's taming of that machinery (1801) to the proclamation of Haitian independence with Dessalines (1804). (*Silencing* 89)

The literary inscriptions marking the process of "unbecoming a slave" (Jenson, *Beyond the Slave Narrative* 4), glimpsed through the Kreyòl writings of Dessalines, Christophe, and Louverture, and expertly described by Deborah Jenson in *Beyond the Slave Narrative* (2011), therefore, only become possible in Trouillot's orbit after "the mass insurrection" of 1791.

Reading the Haitian Revolution less as the result of what I have elsewhere called, the "enlightenment literacy narrative" (Daut,

Tropics 4), and more as a result of the volition of enslaved Africans themselves, upsets a common genealogy of the Haitian Revolution that marked it as the logical outgrowth of the French Revolution's *Déclaration des droits de l'homme* (1789). Even Vastey drew a genealogy from the French Revolution to the Haitian Revolution writing: "The French Revolution of 1789 is the primary cause of the revolutions in Haiti, the rights of man proclaimed in front of the entire universe, resounded in the hearts of *blacks* as it did in that of *whites*" (*Essai* 389). Responding to the related idea that the French abolitionist Société des Amis des Noirs had also incited slave rebellion in colonial Saint-Domingue with similar rhetoric of the rights of man, Julien Raimond, a former wealthy free person of color from the colony, contested this genealogy when he remarked, "Oh! When the insurrection happens, will we really have to go so far as to point to the existence of this society in order to explain the cause?". "[W]ould it not be natural," Raimond asks, "to fear that the blacks, in thinking about their own situation would have wanted to demand their liberty?" (*Réponse aux considérations* 12).

Even though Raimond foreshadows what to to him seems like an inevitable "insurrection," at the time that he published these words, he was a part of a small elite cadre of free people of color who initially argued only for the extension of civic rights for *free* people but not for the enslaved. In his *Réponse aux considérations de M. Moreau, dit Saint-Méry* (1791), Raimond made the utmost distinction between his struggle for rights as a free person of color and that of enslaved people in Saint-Domingue: "I begin by declaring that I will take much care to distinguish the cause of the citizens of color from that of the slaves [....] who are as distinct from one another as light is from darkness" (2). While Raimond appears to make a populist plea in arguing that abolitionist philosophy is not necessary to bring the enslaved to righteous rebellion, he makes the argument in service of elitist principles; whereas Vastey's seemingly elitist argument in tying the Haitian Revolution to the French Revolution is made in service of promoting the populist principle of Haiti's right to sovereignty. The different ideological trappings that accompany Vastey and Raimond's narratives of revolution and rebellion in Saint-Domingue demonstrate the importance of reading texts in relationship to the political institutions they uphold or undermine, a notion that will become important when analyzing the meanings assigned to the performance of Baron de Vastey in the twentieth-century theater of Haitian independence.[5]

In my first monograph, *Tropics of Haiti* (2015), I explored a broad terrain of fictional and non-fictional publications about the Haitian Revolution from the late eighteenth- to the mid-nineteenth centuries. While the book considered writing in all genres, fictional representations of the Haitian Revolution made up a considerable part of the texts under study. Nineteenth-century depictions of the Haitian Revolution, of which there are more than 200, are noteworthy in the context of Baron de Vastey studies, precisely because Vastey does not appear even once as a character in such a body of works.[6]

In some respects, Vastey's absence in nineteenth-century fictional representations of the Haitian Revolution is not surprising. We are only beginning to learn, for instance, with the publication of Laurent Quevilly's 2014 biography of Vastey, about the future baron's involvement in the Revolution as a soldier for France before the kidnapping of Louverture and about his relationship to the *armée indigène* during the latter part of Dessalines's war of independence.[7] In other respects,

---

[5] Philip Kaisary sees these kind of radical representations of the Haitian Revolution that might be in service of conservative arguments about Haitian sovereignty as endemic to twentieth-century literary representations of Haitian independence. He writes that "narrating 'through the people' does not necessarily give rise to a radical discourse, just as narrating through great individuals can be considered elitist, but not necessarily conservative" (138). Kaisary's example is Walcott's *The Haitian Earth*, which Kaisary views as celebrating the people of Haiti, mostly living in the rural countryside, over the leaders of Haiti, presented as big city politicians. Kaisary writes that "The *Haitian Earth* strives to make the Haitian people the play's major subjects" (151), and in so doing, it "sets up between the country and the city" a "binary" familiar to anyone in Haitian Studies: "the countryside and a rural way of life is presented as being authentically Haitian, whereas the city is associated with vice and the colonists" (154).

[6] For an expanding bibliography of nineteenth-century fictions of the Haitian Revolution, see http://www.haitianrevolutionaryfictions.com.

[7] Vastey wrote in an 1819 letter to Thomas Clarkson that he had served under Toussaint Louverture at the age of fifteen (rpt. in Griggs 181–82). Vastey's claim is in some senses confirmed by the future baron's own father. Jean-Valentin Vastey, the future Baron de Vastey's father, wrote to his nephew back in France circa 1798, "we are being harassed a lot about joining the service. Especially, your cousin [Jean-Louis Vastey] charged with paying taxes for the *corvée*" (qtd. in Quevilly 223). According to an additional letter written by Vastey's father on 9 Feburary 1801, the future baron had indeed eventually been forced into conscription, fighting against "les noirs:" "We are doing well, thank God," the elder Vastey wrote, "There is only your youngest cousin who has been been officially drafted and won his first campaign at the price of a serious illness. We were very worried

Vastey's absence in historical fictions of the Haitian Revolution until May Miller's *Christophe's Daughters* (1935), might strike us as more surprising, particularly, given the frequency with which his writings were discussed in the nineteenth century.[8]

In the first part of the nineteenth century, Vastey was, undoubtedly, the most familiar Haitian intellectual to the reading public on both sides of the Atlantic. I scrutinized Vastey's early nineteenth-century popularity in Chap. 3 when I examined the relationship between print circulation and reading practices with respect to Vastey's contributions to the discourse of Black Atlantic humanism.[9] At the very moment, however, in which Vastey's works began to be relatively forgotten in historical discourse, he experienced resurgence as a theatrical character. While several dozen publications mention Vastey's writing during the early decades of the nineteenth-century alone, there is noticeably less engagement with his work by early-mid twentieth-century writers outside of Haiti. Yet, what we lack in quantity we do not lack in quality. A handful of high profile references to the baron in the works of several prominent Anglophone African American intellectuals of the early twentieth century deserve brief mention because they represent the medium through which Vastey most likely became well-known to twentieth-century playwrights.

In 1905 W.E.B. Du Bois included the English translation of Vastey's *Reflections on the Blacks and Whites* (1817) in his *A Select Bibliography of the Negro American*, a work compiled after the tenth conference for the "study of Negro problems," which took place at Atlanta University on 30 May 1905. Two decades later, Alain Locke included one of Vastey's writings, *Réflexions politiques* (1817), in his own bibliography called, "A Selected List of Negro Americana and Africana," published as part of his famous edited collection, *The New Negro* (1925). Also, in

---

for quite some time that he would not live" (qtd. in Quevilly 227). Vastey was apparently wounded by a gunshot in the course of "fighting the insurgents" in October 1802. Vastey's cousin, Michel, who was also living in Saint-Domingue wrote home to say that his cousin "was almost killed yet again. He has escaped a thousand times from death. He received a bullet in the leg about a month ago. He remains in pain" (qtd. 246). For more on this, see Chap. 2 of the present volume.

[8] While Miller's play represents the first drama in which Vastey appears as a character, the first novel to feature the baron appears to be Bruce Graeme's *Drums of Destiny* (1947).

[9] See also, my article, "The 'Alpha and Omega' of Haitian Literature" (2016).

1925, Arthur Schomburg used Vastey's writing to make a Black Atlantic humanist argument in his famous essay, "The Negro Digs up his Past." Schomburg wrote that "Julien Raymond's [sic] Paris exposé of the disabilities of the free people of color in the then (1791) colony of France, and Baron de Vastey's *Cry of the Fatherland* [*Le Cri de la Patrie* (1815)], the famous polemic by the secretary of Christophe," could demonstrate the inherent intelligence of black people, concluding that the "cumulative effect of such evidences of scholarship and prowess is too weighty to be dismissed as exceptional" (671). In addition, Rayford W. Logan, author of *The Diplomatic Relations of the United States with Haiti-1776–1891* (1941) used Vastey's *An Essay on the Causes of the Revolution and Civil Wars of Hayti* (1823) in his 1935 article, "Education in Haiti," published in the *Journal of Negro History*, a periodical edited by Logan and Carter G. Woodson.

Perhaps it was because of these highly visible mentions of Vastey's writing by Du Bois, Locke, Schomburg, and Logan, that the Haitian baron was brought to the attention of Mercer Cook. Cook, like Logan and Locke, was a Howard University professor who traveled to Haiti from 1942–1944 to organize and direct a program designed to train Haitian professors in modern languages. Although Cook was an ardent Francophile and a specialist in French literatures, he is most well-known among scholars of the Caribbean for having translated, along with Langston Hughes, the famous Haitian author Jacques Roumain's *Gouverneurs de la rosée* (1944) into *Masters of the Dew* in 1947. Cook was well-versed in Haitian letters, which makes it unsurprising that he cited Hamilton's English translation of the baron's *An Essay on the Causes of the Revolution and Civil Wars of Hayti* (1823) in his 1948 book, *Education in Haiti*. After he returned from Haiti, Cook authored several additional historical works about the country, among them, *An Introduction to Haiti* (1951), which mentioned Vastey's *Le Système colonial dévoilé* (1814).[10]

---

[10]Cook authored several works published in Haiti while he continued to live in the country, including a *Handbook for Haitian Teachers of English* (1944); and *The Haitian American Anthology: Haitian Readings from American Authors* (1944) (Lubin, *In Memoriam*, 157).

Given that the theater of the Haitian Revolution was dominated by black writers in the early twentieth century (Corbould 260),[11] these references to Vastey in the works of such prominent scholars of color may be connected to the baron's appearance in *Christophe's Daughters*, the first in the extended genre of the theatre of Haitian independence to feature Vastey as a character in his own right. Miller's play, which presents Vastey as a tutor to Christophe's son, Prince Victor, disrupts the idea that the history of Haitian independence is the history of Haitian men by focusing on Christophe's daughters and their unfailing loyalty to their father in his final hours as king. The play was published as a part of a 1935 anthology, edited by Miller and Richard Willis, who at the urging of Carter G. Woodson, co-edited the collection, *Negro History in Thirteen Plays* (1935) (Perkins 144).

Although Miller's work differs from other plays about Haiti from her era in focusing on women, it does not diverge from these other plays when it essentially blames internecine racial strife *within* Haiti for the downfall of Christophe. One of Christophe's daughters, Améthiste, for instance, tells his other daughter, Athénaire, that the conspirator Richard is "[s]omewhere down there [...] talking to our men, promising them money and free rum to drive out their king. Our father called him a dirty yellow soul, and he's worse than that" (251). Because Miller's play seeks to portray Richard's complaints against Christophe as owing to his *color* rather than to his politics, *Christophe's Daughters* contributes to a broader "mulatto/a vengeance" narrative that extends from the nineteenth-century literature of the Haitian Revolution and Haitian independence to its twentieth-century counterpart.

This notion that behind Haiti's political struggles was both racial strife and political corruption undergirds many theatrical readings of both the Haitian Revolution and Haitian independence. Even though Hill called the Haitian Revolution, "[t]he most epic struggle to end slavery in the Americas" (414), he also acknowledged that "[t]he notion that power corrupts underlies many of the plays [about Haiti]" (415). Hill continued by generally echoing the precise sentiments expressed by Walcott:

---

[11] Hill tells us that "[f]rom the year 1893, when the black playwright William Edgar Easton wrote his drama, *Dessalines*, through Aimé Césaire's *The Tragedy of King Christophe* published in 1963, to Derek Walcott's *The Haitian Earth* produced in St. Lucia in 1984, over a dozen black dramatists have turned out plays dealing with aspects of the revolution" (414). See also Corbauld (281, ftn2).

"Faced on the one hand with the glorious triumph of the most successful slave revolt in history, and on the other with the disappointing reality
of what Haiti has become," Hill writes, "black writers are understandably preoccupied with the question: what went wrong?" (415).[12] Hill's
usage of the word "understandably," here, reveals that he is in general
agreement with those playwrights like Walcott, who found that independent Haiti had disappointed the efforts of revolutionary Haiti. Hill
could only vaguely gesture towards an answer to the question of "what
went wrong?" when he surmised, "[a] black-ruled nation could not be
denied; but a peaceful and prosperous black nation becoming a model
to the world of freedom and justice was not to be endured by the powers and principalities who saw profit in the spectacle of an impoverished
Haiti" (415).

Although, it is not clear whether those "powers and principalities"
who sought Haiti's destruction include agents of foreign governments,
on the whole, Hill's assessment of Haiti offers the same oblique outlook
observed in Walcott's foreword to *The Haitian Earth* and in *What the
Twilight Says*. Hill was likely influenced in these opinions both by the
many plays about the Revolution that he had read and studied, as well as
his own performance of Vastey, the principal character who isolates the
Haitian king in Walcott's *Henri Christophe*. "Prior to Césaire's tragedy,"
Hill writes, "the West Indian poet and playwright Derek Walcott had
also written a play called *Henri Christophe*, the first of his two dramas on
the Haitian Revolution. I had the privilege of directing and acting in this
drama as a student in London in 1952" (417). Because he was the director, Hill would have had an immediate role in determining not merely
his own performance of Vastey, but in interpreting for the stage the generally isolationist tenor and tone of the play.

A note accompanying Walcott's *Henri Christophe* in *The Haitian
Trilogy* (2002) revealed that the play was first produced for the stage
in 1949 by the St. Lucia Arts Guild at St. Joseph's Convent, located in

---

[12]While it seems obvious after reading the plays that many black writers were critical of
sovereign Haiti's first leaders in their attempts to dramatize the events, it is worth thinking
about whether or not the viewers, spectators, and readers of these plays necessarily shared
the sentiment that Haiti's leaders were ultimately tragic. Corbould, for example, has written that in the early twentieth-century theater of the Haitian Revolution, "the characters'
faults were not fatal to their fans, just as Brutus Jones [from Eugene O'Neills's famous play,
The Emperor Jones] had been warmly received in the early 1920s" (280).

Castries, St. Lucia. The initial performance was directed by Walcott himself and in 1952, Walcott's play appeared on the stage once again, this time with Hill directing and playing Baron de Vastey. Notably, the voice of the narrator was the famous Barbadian author, George Lamming.[13] Chris Bongie, the only critic of the play to pay specific and sustained attention to Walcott's characterization of Baron de Vastey, argued that what he viewed as a negative portrayal of both Vastey and Christophe was the result of Walcott's co-optation of historian David Nicholls's theory of the "mulatto legend of history." Bongie writes, "Given that nineteenth-century Haiti was in many respects the invention of the inheritors of Pétion, the 'mulatto elite', it is hardly surprising that the reputation of Vastey—a light-skinned intellectual who insisted on the need for Haiti to be ruled by a black king—was given a highly negative slant over the course of the century" (227–228).[14] Bongie continues by evoking the "war of words" between Vastey and Noël Colombel, discussed in Chap. 2 of this volume: "Walcott's representation of Vastey, as we will see," Bongie argues, "contains trace elements of this negative portrayal, being genealogically attached to the 'mulatto legend' for which the publicists of Pétion such as Colombel laid the foundation" (228).

Yet, there is an essential fictiveness to the theory of the "mulatto legend" itself that disrupts such an attempt to see Walcott's play as being in collusion with it. As many portrayals of the Haitian Revolution show, the critique and often outright demonization of Haitian political leaders occurs across the ideological spectrum of the theater of Haitian independence. Isolating and blaming Haitian rulers (whether described as *black* or *mulatto*) is as likely to occur in the texts of writers who profess sympathy for Haitian sovereignty as in the writing of those who voiced criticism of the country in the immediate post-revolutionary era.

The best example of a writer laying blame at the feet of Dessalines comes from Langston Hughes's *The Emperor of Haiti*, a play ordinarily

---

[13] Among Lamming's most well-known works are a novel entitled, *In the Castle of My Skin* (1953), and a collection of essays called, *The Pleasures of Exile* (1960).

[14] According to Nicholls, in historical writings that fall prey to "the mulatto legend of history," "Dessalines is portrayed as despotic, barbarous, and ignorant; Christophe was also despotic and prejudiced against the coloureds. Pétion, on the other hand, was everything that is virtuous: liberal, humane, democratic, mild, civilized, honest, as was Boyer, his lineal successor" (*From Dessalines* 91).

read in a sympathetic light.[15] Lindsey Twa, for instance, views Hughes's play as one in a long list of examples of "Dessalines's extreme sanitization at the hands of African-American writers" (October 2011). It is important, however, to consider the following scene in which one of Dessalines's initial supporters, a character named Martel, tells the emperor that he dreams "of an island where not only blacks are free, but every man who comes to Haitian shores." "Jean Jacques, I'm an old man," Martel tells him, "But in my old age, I dream of a world where no man hurts another. Where *all* know freedom, and black and white alike will share this earth in peace. Of such, I dream, Jean Jacques" (302). Dessalines acerbically replies to such an expression of humanism: "Too big a dream, Martel. If I could make Haiti a land where *black* men live in peace, I'd be content" (302).

The problem with Dessalines's vision of a Haiti for "*black* men" is revealed in the dialogue that follows this exchange when he explains why he decided to name himself emperor: "The French Napoleon gave himself the name of Emperor," Dessalines states, "I, too, am Emperor by my own hand. (*He snaps his fingers*) We might as well get a little glory out of life" (304). Such a statement exposes the essential ephemerality of political titles, as equally as titles of nobility, since both can be achieved here by a simple snapping of the fingers. This is just as blackness can be achieved through simple baptism in Aimé Césaire's *La Tragédie* when Christophe tells the character Richard, "Little *griffe*,[16] you are not a negro [....] In the name of cataclysm, on behalf of my heart which brings me back to life with a hiccup of disgust, I baptize, name you, coronate you, a negro" (150). Titles of nobility, as in the Abbé Grégoire's estimation, might be seen, then, as just as arbitrary and dangerous as

---

[15] According to Kaisary, "the 1936 play was published and performed as both *Emperor of Haiti* and *Troubled Island*, sketches for which were written during Hughes's six-month stay in Haiti in 1931, and the libretto for the opera *Troubled Island*, which was based on the earlier play and was nearly ready for performance by 1938" (39). The play premiered at the Karamu Theater in in New York City in November of 1936, where it was only performed eight times (Kaisary 43).

[16] Césaire's note reads that a "griffe" is a "Variété de métis haïtien" or "variety of Haitian of mixed-ancestry" (150). The term is a part of a larger compendium of pseudo-scientific terms used in the eighteenth and nineteenth-centuries as a part of racial taxonomies (see, Daut, *Tropics* 89).

titles of race (for Grégoire's writing on the matter, see, Chap. 3 of this volume).

Dessalines's statement about the ease with which he had become an emperor, nevertheless, also suggests that he is power hungry (a "glory" seeker), even to the point of becoming an autocratic leader. In a scene near the end of the play, Dessalines tells Martel,

> Long ago I dreamed a dream that I want to carry through. If you won't help me willingly—then I'll make you. I'm the Emperor! Your Liberator! Jean Jacques Dessalines, who came up from a slave hut to a Palace, to a crown on my head and an ermine cape covering my scars, to this jeweled scepter in my hand. I did it by fighting. The whites called me The Tiger! (*Fiercely*) If I have to be a tiger to you, too—I will be! (318)

Dessalines's increasing estrangement from his very own supporters in Hughes's play, thus, also offers an isolationist reading of the the first Haitian state, even while it valorizes Dessalines. Such an attempt to portray the first post-independence leader as estranged from the people of Haiti was noticed by Kaisary who, despite arguing that Hughes' play represents a radical stance on Haiti, observes that "[t]he play also communicates Dessalines's increasing political isolation, demonstrating that his failed attempts to woo the mulatto elite served only to alienate him from the black peasantry, hastening the loss of the bedrock of his political support, and provoking vodou priests to stir up the peasants against him" (47). Moreover, Hughes's portrayal of Dessalines also likens independent Haiti's first sovereign ruler not only to a dictator, but to an enslaver. In what is the most damning critique of Dessalines in the play, Martel tells the emperor, "It's not wise to ever be a master, Jean Jacques" (320). This statement suggests that Dessalines has become in the eyes of his own people exactly what he despises, a slave master. Suggestively, then, the people of Haiti over whom Dessalines rules, are his slaves, meaning that it is ultimately *he* who has alienated himself from the "black peasantry."

In the majority of plays about the Haitian Revolution it is actually Christophe who is the most likely to be accused of having instated a form of pseudo-slavery. This is precisely what we see, for example, in Césaire's *La Tragédie du roi Christophe* and in Selden Rodman's *The Revolutionists*. A character called Première Dame in Césaire's drama tells us, to that end, that Christophe's attempt to force Haiti's entry into the modern world through labor, "confounds liberty with slavery" (99). The Deuxième Dame chimes in by telling Vastey, "In short, King Christophe serves freedom by means of bondage!" (99). Rodman's Prévost is even more direct in *The Revolutionists* when he tells the character Richard, "But the worst is that!/That Citadel, that life-consuming fortress–/ To stop the French, he says—what is it to us/Whether the French or even Pétion's mixed-bloods crack the whip" (167); to which Richard responds, "Exactly! We are slaves/In everything but name again" (167).

Some contemporary literary critics have also unequivocally charged Christophe with the crime of having enslaved the very people he once helped lead into freedom. In *Prophetic Visions of the Past: Pan-Caribbean Representations of the Haitian Revolution* (2015), Victor Figueroa writes, "Henri Christophe virtually re-enslaved his people before they rebelled" (13). Nick Nesbitt, in his examination of Césaire's *La Tragédie* similarly finds that in Césaire's play "Christophe ends up re-enslaving his subjects" (*Voicing Memory* 127), while in another passage Nesbitt refers to "the construction of Christophe's palace by slave labor" (*Voicing Memory* 134). All of this is articulated without any consideration of the very real material differences between forced or unfree labor, perhaps of the stripe present in Christophe's kingdom, and the well-documented brutalities of the chattel slavery of Saint-Domingue. Although scholars are only beginning to explore the appropriate vocabulary needed for analyzing the labor regime authorized by Haiti's many rural codes in the nineteenth century (see, Hodgson, "Internal Harmony," 178–192), it seems reasonable to infer that, however hard life was under Christophe, the people of his kingdom were not in any sense his property to be bought and sold and traded away from their families for the king's own personal re-numeration.

While Christophe and Dessalines may be equally, although differently, demonized in fictions about the Haitian Revolution, Pétion does not significantly appear in any of the plays under study in this chapter. In the broader literary history of Haiti, this is not an extraordinary elision. According to Corbould, during the interwar years of the early twentieth century, "[p]lay after play focused on three men: brave, tragic Toussaint Louverture, betrayed by the French; self-proclaimed emperor Jean-Jacques Dessalines, deposed by a coup that brought Henri Christophe to power in the north, who in turn completed the triumvirate in twentieth-century black Americans' memory" (260). Analyzing writing about the Revolution without an analysis of the impact of other events of the era is as deeply problematic as is understanding in isolation representations of the events themselves. Both limitations lead to the belief that single omissions or broader historical anachronisms (such as Pétion's general absence or unimportance in these plays) are uncannily indicative of authorial frame of mind rather than the result of a host of other more interesting possible sociological inferences, such as a black king perhaps being more aesthetically legible in Atlantic World literary culture than a black president.

A good example of how isolating aesthetic decisions and historical representations from the broader transatlantic print culture of which they are a part can create interpretive obstacles comes at the end of *The Revolutionists*. Rodman includes a statement outlining in detail his sources for the play. In so doing, he explains some of the play's historical anachronisms, omissions, and elisions by writing,

> Beyond the published memoirs and histories of the writers of the day, no original documents were consulted in the preparation of this play. The two most helpful and brilliantly penetrating studies of the revolutionary period are C.L.R. James's *The Black Jacobins* and Lorthrop Stoddard's *The French Revolution in San Domingo*. One is by a radical Negro. The other is by a believer in White supremacy. John W. Vandercook's *Black Majesty*, though written in a semi-fictional style, is by far the best account of the rise and reign of Henry Christophe. Among general works, M.J. Herskovits' *The Myth of the Negro Past* and James G. Leyburn's *The Haitian People* were most suggestive. (195)

Rodman's subsequent and lengthy justification for not closely following the historical record charted in his admittedly problematic sources is important because of what it reveals about the politics (and difficulties) of writing historical fiction, especially, that which deals with the infinite complexities of revolution. Rodman detailed at length how he confronted, or rather, erased these nuances when he followed this explanation up with:

> The history of any revolution, and especially this one with its infinite racial complications, is confusing. I have paid only the broadest respects to Time, and tried to simplify the bewildering number of important characters by merging Toussaint's historical masters, Libertas and Count Breda, with Governors Laveaux and Blancheland [sic], and by giving General Leclerc

the earlier mission of General Galbaud, rather than merely the second on which he was sent by his brother-in-law, Napoleon. (195)

One of the "racial complications" that Rodman resolved by virtually erasing it has to do with Baron de Vastey. In great contradistinction to his sources, he portrays Vastey as black rather than mulatto. We know that Rodman gets his information about Vastey primarily from Vandercook's *Black Majesty* (1928) because this text is the only of Rodman's stated sources to deal with the history of the future baron.[17] Within the pages of *Black Majesty* Vandercook writes unequivocally that Vastey is "the bastard son of a white father whose memory he scorned," and later, Vandercook refers to the baron as a "white nigger" (69). Rodman's contrasting portrayal of Vastey in *The Revolutionists* as black and as a former enslaved person allows the playwright to simplify what were for him the confusions of a revolution that has often been painted as promoting racial revenge with whites, blacks, and mulattoes, all neatly aligned on opposing sides.

Organizing the Haitian Revolution, and subsequent Haitian independence, along the lines of race, allows Rodman to refer, without any nuance, to "Pétion's Mulatto State," for example (163), even though Baron de Vastey estimated that all three territories of Haiti, "the *North*, the *South*, and the *West*" contained a population that was "more or less" "mixed." Vastey wrote that in all regions of Haiti the "proportion" of "blacks" to "people of color" was virtually the same, standing at approximately "14/15th black" and "1/15th people of color" (*Essai* 124).

The choice to unequivocally paint mulattoes against blacks reflects stereotypical portrayals of Haitian independence, which quite often pit Pétion as a *mulatto president* against Christophe, as a *negro king*, thus, using race to describe what could otherwise be painted as a uniquely political division, i.e. a monarchy versus a republic. Rodman's portrayal of mulattoes against blacks in *The Revolutionists* may, therefore, tell us much more about the lasting effect of pseudo-scientific understandings of race on our modern world than it tells us about Rodman's own relationship to the racialized narratives of the Revolution that he repeats. This is an important reminder

---

[17] Leyburn's *The Haitian People* (1941) is the only other text cited by Rodman to even mention Vastey, and Vastey appears in this work only as a source without any other descriptive or biographical information (22, 254, 326).

that questions of authorship and intent are difficult to trace in the trans-atlantic print culture of the Haitian Revolution, precisely because of the grossly derivative nature of many representations of the struggle.

After having read hundreds of fictional representations of the Haitian Revolution, each filled with myriad historical anachronisms and passages directly copied from the works of others, I have had to re-think my reading of this literature. This has meant adopting a mode whereby I let the text tell me about the author's world rather than the other way around. I have been influenced in this way of thinking by Roland Barthes, who, in *On Racine* (1960) writes, "history will never tell us what is happening inside an author at the moment he is writing" (156). "Literary history is only possible if it becomes sociological," Barthes contends, that is, "if it is concerned with activities and institutions, not with individuals" (161).

Reading these plays for what they can tell us about the racism, classism, and sexism of the author's day, instead of the racism, classism, or sexism of the author him or herself, produces a form of reading that can be much more attentive to the value of performance itself. That it so say, we can see Vastey more clearly in these plays as a character rather than as a writer, as someone to be watched rather than to be only read, if we remain attentive to the ideological struggles not only of his times and that his writings represent, but also those that he came to represent for these dramatists who later staged his life. This kind of reading asks us to be much more attentive to the impression a theatre-goer, who most likely would know little about each individual character or even broader Haitian history, might experience of the story of Haitian independence based on the performance itself.

My own reading of Vastey in Walcott's *Henri Christophe* in the following section treats the Haitian baron much more as the literary embodiment of isolationist understandings of Haitian history common in Walcott's era rather than as a psychological manifestation of Walcott's problems with elitism. In other words, I hope we can move beyond viewing Vastey, the character, as Walcott's "problematic double," that is to say, as one who can "serv[e] as a sounding board for the young playwright in his attempts at thinking about the relation between the writer and the state and between the literate colonial subject and the public(ist) representations that his literacy might make possible" (Bongie, *Friends* 245). I think it is more valuable to see Vastey, the remorseful character that Walcott paints him to be in this play, as a vehicle for producing an isolationist critique of Haiti. Isolationism, unlike racism, sexism, and classicism has not been subject to criticism often enough in Caribbean studies. Walcott's plays give us an opportunity to expose the consequences of isolating Haiti's history to the extent that the country is rendered an example of the troubles with black sovereignty.

ISOLATING BARON DE VASTEY IN DEREK WALCOTT'S *HAITIAN TRILOGY*

The dominant mood of the entire kingdom during the last days of Christophe in Walcott's first play about the Revolution, *Henri Christophe*, is a sense of impending regret. Introspection and self-reflexivity abound, particularly, on Vastey's part, as the characters in the play begin to wonder if their toils to help Christophe create a "black kingdom," were worth the cost. Such toils, in a certain sense, mirror the *real* Vastey's own struggles to create an image of black humanity in the midst of a white polity that denied blacks the agency not only to be *sovereign*, but to be *human*. While it is Christophe who most clearly voices the goals of Black Atlantic humanism to counter these prevailing perceptions, it is Vastey's voice that punctuates the despair involved in realizing the limitations of Christophe's efforts to promote racial equality through the creation of a black monument that could serve as the symbol of black sovereignty, and therefore, black humanity.

Christophe tells Corneille Brelle, a French priest living in the kingdom and working for Christophe, "...what I wanted/Was memory, which no worm bites; this summer flesh/Wrapped in comfort around the arctic bone/Will crumble my work; you understand, white man,/This nigger search for fame/Dragged like a meteor across my black rule/Apart from that I have no ease,/No gods, Haitian or Christian; my primer is blood or honour" (65). Christophe's stated desire to create a black past by constructing a black future, signals the tense relationship between black sovereignty and Black Atlantic humanism. Walcott's Christophe believes he can forge black monuments in service of black sovereignty through the creation of the Citadel, which he claims had to be built as an example of Haitian, and therefore, black humanity. The Citadel is as much a weapon against racism as writing or literacy had been and remains in Black Atlantic humanist thought. Christophe tells Vastey, to that end, "To build these citadels for this complexion/Signed by the sun./Yes, for that we killed, because some were black,/And some were spat on./For that I overturned the horn of plenty,/ [...]/Against the King. I made this King they hate,/Shaped out of slaves.../What have I done, what have I done, Vastey, to deserve all this?" (101).

Vastey directly criticizes the idea that the Citadel could ever prove the worth of one's "complexion," when he tells the king, "In death, Henri, the bone is anonymous;/Complexions only grin above the skeleton; Under the grass the dust is an anthology of creeds and skins./Who can tell what that skull was?/Was it for that we quarreled?" (101). While this conversation existed only at the level of abstraction until this point, Vastey's next line reveals the human cost of using black work to combat white racism. Vastey directly answers Christophe's question pertaining to what the monarch has done to deserve the abandonment of his people, blaming the king for "Dessalines, Brelle,/The violent love of self that kills the self/Cathedrals and cruelties/[....]/poured from the sides of ships./Oh, Henri, we are guilty; admit, admit, it's time" (101).

Fanon's statement in *The Wretched of the Earth* seems to capture the essence of Walcott's portrayal of the problems with Christophe's philosophy of Haitian work as the measure of black humanity: "At the very moment when the native intellectual is anxiously trying to create a cultural work," Fanon writes, "he fails to realize that he is utilizing techniques and language which are borrowed from the stranger" (*Wretched* 223). One of the last pronouncements that Vastey makes to Christophe, "We were a tragedy of success" (103), may articulate the ultimate costs of nineteenth-century Black Atlantic humanism when conceived as an attempt to produce "cultural achievements" that might be valorized by Europeans in service of combatting colonialism and racism (Fanon, *Wretched* 223).

Whereas, later iterations of this concept, such as *négritude*, focused on valorizing the difference and even essential qualities of blackness that made it distinct but no less worthy than whiteness, nineteenth-century Haiti's version involved proving that blacks were ultimately the *same* and therefore the equals of whites. Césaire once said that in *négritude*, "there was an idea of an African specificity, a black specificity" (*Nègre* 28). What this meant for him was not that he should adopt what he called, "black racism," but that he hoped to guard against "assimilation," which was for Césaire, a form of "alienation, the most terrible thing" (*Nègre* 28).

Baron de Vastey, in contrast, writes in *Réflexions sur une lettre de Mazères*: "We write and we print. Even in our infancy, our nation has already had authors and poets who have defended its cause and celebrated its glory. In truth, we do not yet find here the skill of a Voltaire, a Rousseau, or a De Lille, but we have not yet lived like their nation a thousand years of civilization" (84). For Vastey, the yardstick by which to measure a Haitian writer's worth was still European, even French. In the world of Walcott's play, such an outwardly looking humanism meant that Haitians were tasked with proving that they could do everything that Europeans could do, including building monuments to their own power.

In *What the Twilight Says* Walcott wrote of West Indian writers, "Once we have lost our wish to be white, we develop a longing to become black, and those two may be different, but are still careers" (18). Christophe's actual "career" was to maintain Haitian sovereignty but this was not enough for him in Walcott's portrayal. Christophe tells Vastey that the "epilogue of Eden," would be "a prosperous Haiti,/My kingdom where I, a king, rule/Mine mine, Vastey! Once a slave,/Then after that Napoleon can envy,/With the Antilles mine, the whole archipelago overturning/Cauldrons of history and violence on their master's heads,/The slaves, the kings, the blacks, the brave" (74). At first, Vastey fully intends to help Christophe overturn the "cauldrons of history," even to the point of framing the innocently presented Brelle and therefore causing the latter's execution. By the end of the play, however, Vastey, who was once so willing to exchange dignity and decency for money— he had initially stated, "I am tired of war; I want a little money./But I'd make war to get money" (30)—now appears as the voice of philosophical reason. Musing on his own role in isolating the Haitian leader from his people, Walcott's Vastey bemoans, "My own paralysis/Creeps somewhere between my will/And my regret. There are broken statues/On my tongue, dead stale civilizations/Breeding in my brain/[....]/... the vocabulary of ruin/Littered on lawns" (99). Vastey's additional comments revel in even further self-pity: Vastey states he is "[d]rinking remorse in a spoonful of soup," because "[w]hen I think of the past/God!" (99).

Christophe's goal to create a past for Haiti by constructing its future in the Citadel's stonework, therefore, has failed. He may have created a monument for Haiti but it is one that even his strongest supporter, Vastey, seeks to forget. What Vastey ultimately regrets at the end of the play is his own role in subjugating the Haitian people when he tells Christophe: "Tomorrow has no comfort; we must wage war against the dark/In all of us, and make our chaos light/Regret, King, time..."

(105). Christophe's major flaw, in comparison to Vastey, is that he denies until the end that he has anything to regret. He tells the Haitian baron, "Do not regret, Vastey" (106). Yet Vastey's own regret is what allows us to see Christophe's fatal flaw as his inability to be reflexive about his own role in creating the political realities of his country.

Walcott's primary method of framing Vastey as suddenly and remorsefully estranged from the Christophe administration relies on an isolationist narrative that paints Corneille Brelle, the French Catholic priest involved in Christophe's administration, as one of Vastey's victims. Walcott allows the French and, ostensibly white Brelle, to appear as completely innocent, with respect to Christophe's decision to create a monarchy. (Brelle states, "Only god makes kings" [64]). Yet it is Brelle who charges Christophe with racism. Brelle tells Vastey, to that end, "…Let war adjourn; we are tired/Of bitter separations between complexions/That grin above the skeleton/All flesh is similar" (60). Instead of showing how France had colluded to ensure those "bitter separations between complexions," Walcott posits these racial problems as Haitian rather than European ones, a representation that will be carried over into *The Haitian Earth*.

Although in my reading, the central role of Vastey in Walcott's *Henri Christophe* proves far more isolationist than his marginal and ambiguous appearance in *The Haitian Earth*, the newly racialized nature of his identity in the later play deserves a few words. *The Haitian Earth* was also first produced for the stage in Castries, St. Lucia and was directed by Walcott himself. The performance of the play, supported by the St. Lucian government to commemorate the 150th anniversary of the end of slavery on the island, was staged from August 1–5, 1984. Of all the representations of Vastey under discussion here, his appearance in *The Haitian Earth* most immediately bears the influence of the eighteenth- and nineteenth-century pseudo-scientific debates about race that influenced the vast majority of nineteenth-century fictional narratives about the Revolution.

In *The Haitian Earth*, Walcott dramatizes the troubling relationship between mulatto vengeance and black radical thought by portraying Vastey as a student of mixed-race, who is primarily an intellectual nemesis of Christophe's, rather than one of his main collaborators. While in *Henri Christophe* Vastey's race is not represented, in *The Haitian Earth* Walcott's Christophe refers to Vastey as a "philosophical monkey" who is "always pronouncing big words" (318). Vastey—who himself wonders, "Why was I born into this tribe of mongrels?" (317)—responds by calling Christophe an "[a]pe...you illiterate black ape" (318). The racialized conflict between Christophe and Vastey escalates when the former implores the latter: "Tell me more, Excellency./I am here to learn, mulatto./..., you don't want to be free,/You just don't want to be black. Right?/.../Wouldn't it be nice if your children were white?/But making children is not a whore's business,/Any more than making revolution/Is a mulatto's" (319). Not only does Vastey have a "greatly diminished" role in *The Haitian Earth* (Bongie, *Friends* 248), but Walcott's portrayal of the Haitian baron as a "mulatto" who ultimately shares a disdain for "blacks" reanimates the eighteenth- and nineteenth-century anxieties of monstrous hybridity for a twentieth-century audience. Christophe tells a table full of people of mixed-race, including Vastey: "One day you will all have/To make up your minds if you're white or black" (320). Walcott's representation of the antagonistic relationship between Vastey and Christophe also revives the legend that there was something innately vengeful about people of mixed race when Vastey lunges at Christophe with a knife (319), naturally missing his supposed rival, which only adds to the stinging satire of the scene.

Ultimately, the portrayal of Vastey and Christophe as *inherently* divided by their skin colors, reflects an isolationist critique of Haiti that situates its early political problems as the result of internal *Haitian* prejudices, rather than *European* interference. There is a kind of myopia in viewing the political divisions of Christophe and Pétion, not only as racial divisions—the *real* Vastey asked, "what difference could exist between a man from the North, from the West, or from the South?' (*RP* 153)—but as divorced from the colonialist and neo-colonialist policies of France that sought to promote actual racial dissension.

Exposing France's desire to encourage color prejudices in Haiti, for example, was one of the primary aims of Vastey's *Réflexions politiques*. Vastey maintained that it was with the "childishness" of "these injurious epithets" of "negroes of the north" and "mulattoes of the South" "that our enemies count upon to divide us." Alluding more directly to France's involvement on that account, Vastey wrote, "They have been the constant architects of our civil wars and political troubles; on both sides, they can always be seen, with the same fervor and the same zeal occupying themselves by lighting the torches of discord, embittering and agitating our minds, stoking the fire, encouraging violence; and never have they been more happy and more satisfied than when they have watched Haitian blood flow because of Haitian hands" (55).

If, in *Henri Christophe* Vastey's voice was the vehicle through which the critique of Haiti's political leaders was achieved separate from France's involvement, in *The Haitian Earth*, all the good lines about Haitian political problems being caused by Haitians themselves are voiced by a former black slave named Pompey. Pompey tells Christophe:

> I remember, under the old coachman, and that talk was not who was king but who would make each man a man, each man a king himself; but all that change. We see them turn and climb and burn and fall down like stars that tired, and cut my hand, my head, my tongue out if you want, Your Majesty, but my life is one long night. My country and your kingdom, Majesty. One long, long night. Is kings who do us that. (431)

Even as he argues the value of the humanist universal of equality among "each man," Pompey critiques the black king for being no different from a white king. The black man in Pompey's estimation, is no different from the white man when it comes to his ability and/or the propensity to rule despotically, making equality negative rather than positive. His voice mirrors the kind of problematic Black Atlantic humanism marked by Vastey's wish, in Walcott's depiction, to prove to Europeans that "I am not an animal" (320).

Vastey's attempt to prove his lack of animality, and therefore, his humanness, represents what feminist scholar Sarah Hoagland calls, "conceptual coercion of dominant rationalities." Hoagland has written that arguing that the dominant narrative is "false" is futile precisely because "it is nevertheless to agree that the statement in question is intelligible, indeed possibly true—that is worth debating. Thus, at a deeper level we validate it. When one continues to respond to the dominant discourse one continues to reinscribe it" (129). If Hoagland's analysis was extended to the entire discourse of Black Atlantic humanism, this would mean that the efforts of (black) writers like Vastey had not only been circumscribed by the dominant (white) discourse, but undone by their own responses to it.

Walcott appears to deny the Vastey of *The Haitian Earth* the introspection, reflexivity, and remorse he expressed in *Henri Christophe*, which is precisely what allowed Christophe's isolation to become apparent. Yet, because Walcott believed that Pompey was also Vastey's first name (revealed in scene twelve [410]), the original contest between Vastey and Christophe in *Henri Christophe* simply finds its outlet in what Bongie has called the "doubling" of Vastey's name in *The Haitian Earth* (*Friends* 249). It is the black Pompey of *The Haitian Earth* who, during the last days of Christophe's rule, will wonder what the ultimate meaning of the Citadel can be for Haiti. Pompey suggests that the Citadel was built as a monument to France to help prove that Haiti was worthy of a king. Pompey says, ostensibly referring to Louis XIV, nicknamed the Sun King: "One king say to us he is the sun, and we niggers answers yes, and we was his shadows,/and the sun set, the King dead, and it was night again until the next King come, and we again was shadows. It wasn't for a king all this begin? I mean to say the King they kill in France?" (431). Still, the problem in *The Haitian Earth* rests with Christophe himself, who sought to become a king, and not with all of those merchants, politicians, and priests, colluding with world powers, who sought to prevent him from being one.

BARON DE VASTEY AS CHRISTOPHE'S SHADOW IN AIMÉ CÉSAIRE'S *LA TRAGÉDIE DU ROI CHRISTOPHE*

Errol Hill, the actor/director turned literary critic, who played Baron de Vastey in Walcott's *Henri Christophe*, argued that even though most of the twentieth-century dramas of the Haitian Revolution written by black playwrights criticized Haitian rulers, Césaire's Christophe had one loyal member of the populace. Césaire's Vastey, according to Hill, not only understood the Haitian king's efforts to use black labor as a form of Black Atlantic humanism but stood by him until the very end. Hill writes that in Césaire's *La Tragédie*, "Only Vastey, Christophe's private secretary, understands his ruler's obsession [with work]" (416).

In focusing primarily on two distinct episodes in Césaire's tragedy, involving two distinct notions of labor (slavery and work), I argue that this representation of Christophe's eventual downfall, which is figured to be the result of his own "obsession" with making his subjects perform hard labor—often read as forcing them into slavery—colludes with isolationist visions of Haiti, particularly in the Franco de Médina episode of the play. In so doing, I suggest that Césaire presents Vastey as the loyal, but burdened, shadow head of state. In pushing back against attempts to make any of these characters Césaire's "authorial double" (Bongie, *Friends*, 253 ftn180; Nesbitt, *Voicing Memory* 142), I am convinced that, in the end, it is Vastey, the character, and not Césaire, the author, who is the double of Christophe. After all, it is Vastey who is charged by the character called only "Deuxième Dame" with "carrying the burden of the Nation" (97).

Unlike Walcott's Vastey who feels remorse and preaches his complaints directly to Christophe at the end of *Henri Christophe*, Césaire's Vastey remains loyal to the king until the end. This loyalty amounts to upholding a vision of Haiti that jives with the goals of Black Atlantic humanism, much of which may have been culled from or influenced by Vastey's own writing. Césaire's Vastey echoes the real Vastey's spirited defenses of Christophe's monarchy in each of his publications: "What say the whites of France?" Césaire's Vastey asks, "That Pétion and Christophe are two weaklings. The French, don't you see, have no respect for republics. Napoléon has demonstrated that. And what does Haiti have? Not one, but two! Two republics, monsieur" (29). Vastey's answer to the ridicule he perceives as coming from abroad is to encourage Christophe to crown himself king: "The entire world is watching us," Vastey tells Christophe, "and people think that black men lack dignity! A king, a court, a kingdom, voilà, if we want to be shown respect, that is what we should show them" (29).

Part of the *real* Vastey's defense of monarchy entailed not only pointing out the problems in Pétion's decision to re-elect himself president without a vote (Vastey, *Essai* 297), but showing that a kingdom was better than an empire. In his *Essai*, Vastey pinpointed the problems with Dessalines's initial configuration of himself as "governor-general" in writing, "we had the feeling that we had not properly organized ourselves; the title of governor-general [for a head of state] was not at all appropriate" (46). Although Vastey believed that the "form of government" in Haiti had to be changed because, in his mind, a nation should not be ruled by a "governor-general," he apparently also strongly disagreed with Dessalines's desire to make himself an emperor after the fashion of Bonaparte. Vastey writes: "Thoughtlessness or rather force of habit had made us give the *Général en Chef de l'armée des indigènes* the title of *Governor-General*; the force of imitation compelled him to take the title of Emperor" (47). In the *Essai*, Vastey continues by explaining that since Bonaparte had an empire, Dessalines thought he needed one as well, a move which Vastey characterized as having "traded one excess for another" (47). Vastey's reading of Dessalines as a simple mimic man anticipates Hughes's presentation of the Haitian emperor as having problematically co-opted a European ruler's title. In the *Essai*, Vastey exclaimed, "Well then! we were far from the situation where we find ourselves now! If we had had at that time enough experience, wisdom, prudence, we would have founded a constitutional monarchy, and we would have created for ourselves useful institutions and a stable and regular government; how many ills and calamities would we have avoided!" (49). For Vastey, creating the kind of constitutional monarchy at the outset of Haitian independence that he had helped Christophe build, would have prevented Civil War because, in looking to England as his primary example, "one finds this institution [monarchy] in all of the most free people, the most civilized and the most enlightened on the earth" (*Essai* 155).

The secretary of Christophe was certainly one of the king's main defenders, but his defenses of monarchy, as we glimpsed in Chap. 3, did not rest solely on using the British monarchy to prove that such a form of governance could succeed in Haiti, as well. Vastey also concentrated on the racism that undergirded attempts to ridicule the fact that in Haiti there was a "crown on the head of a black man!" (*RP* 17):

> There you have what the French publicists, the journalists, the creators of Colonial Systems cannot digest; one would say to hear them, that a black king is a phenomenon that has never been seen in the world! Who will therefore reign over the blacks, if the blacks cannot be kings. Is royalty such a privilege that it belongs exclusively to the white color? (*RP* 17)

In Césaire's play Vastey similarly attempts to dispel the idea that there was anything exceptional about the creation of a monarchy by a black head of state in sardonically asking, "This black king, a fairy tale, is it not?" (32). Moreover, speaking of the nobles who were named after particular regions of Haiti, Césaire's Vastey used irony to point out the exceptionalism at work in French attempts to poke fun at Christophe's court: "The laughter of the French does not embarrass me!" Vastey states, "Marmelade, why not? Why not, Limonade? These are names that serve your appetite! Gastronomic wishes! After all, the French very well have their Duke of Liver and the Duke of Bouillon! Are these more appetizing?" (33).[18]

---

[18] Césaire likely arrived at this particular ironic statement from his familiarity with the writing of Victor Schoelcher who wrote in his *Colonies étrangères et Haïti* (1843), "having learned that [French] people were making fun of his princes of Marmelade and his dukes

One of Vastey's particular burdens in *La Tragédie*, as in Baron de Vastey's *real* life, was to defend Christophe's monarchy against its numerous racist detractors. The most clear example of how such defenses, when portrayed as the *raison d'être* for Christophe's kingdom, serve an isolationist reading of Haiti comes in Césaire's portrayal of the Franco de Médina episode. The *real* Agoustine Franco de Médina was one of the three French spies sent to the Caribbean in 1814 by the French government, along with Lavaysse and Dravermann, under the orders of the former colonist, turned minister of the navy, Pierre-Victor Malouet. The aim of the mission was to gather information about the two states of Haiti. The instructions given to the three spies by Malouet, on the order of the French King, direct them to interfere with Haiti's governance by encouraging Pétion to collude with France in returning Haiti to its status as a French colony. The larger goal of the mission, however, was to create conditions that would allow France to not only re-take its former colony but to re-establish slavery (see, Madiou 5: 260).

According to the interrogation of Franco de Médina performed by Christophe's government after they captured the spy, all three men embarked for Haiti around the 28th of June in 1814 (see Appendix C, Vastey, *An Essay*). They stopped at several different ports in the Caribbean before landing in Jamaica, where Lavaysse wrote to Pétion. After awaiting the latter's response, which he correctly anticipated would authorize him to enter the republic, Lavaysse proceeded on to Port-au-Prince with Dravermann while Franco de Médina entered Christophe's kingdom without authorization (Brière 68), where he was eventually captured, interrogated, and possibly executed.[19]

---

of Limonade (two districts of the island that he had made into fiefs), Christophe slyly said that he could completely understand how such a thing could cause laughter among those who had their own *Prince de Poix* (prince of Peas) and *Duc de Bouillon* (duke of Bouillon)" (2:151).

[19] In *Réflexions politiques* Vastey, who was intimately involved in the Franco de Médina affair, wrote that the French spy had not been executed by Christophe's government: "Franco Médina is still alive. For more than four years we have been keeping this spy as living proof of [Pétion's] loyalty to the French cabinet" (145). According to Jean Brière, Laffont de Labédat's 1815 account affirms Vastey's own (for more on this affair, see, Brière 68). Quevilly has read Vastey's assurance that Franco de Médina was still alive as sarcastic, citing Ardouin's claim that the French spy died in the royal prison (see, Quevilly 288; Ardouin, *Études* 8:112).

The character of Franco de Médina enters Césaire's play in Act II, scene 3, without any of this backstory. The scene begins with Vastey reading from a letter brought by Franco de Médina from France, addressed to "Monsieur le général Christophe, commandant la province nord de Saint-Domingue" (83). Christophe immediately takes umbrage that he is not recognized in the letter as the head of a state but only as a general. The king tells Franco de Médina, who appears here not as a spy, but merely as a messenger: "When one addresses me [...] one calls me 'Sire'...One says 'your Majesty...'" (84).[20] Christophe also explains that the letter's reference to "'*la question de Saint-Domingue*'" (84), effectively, makes slaves out of the people of his kingdom, including the nobles, since Saint-Domingue was the name Haiti held while under the yoke of colonial slavery. Christophe tells his court that the phrase "*la question de Saint-Domingue*" implies, therefore, that there is no Kingdom of Hayti, and consequently that the people of "Saint-Domingue" were merely rebels: "Do you hear that, you are rebelling slaves [...] you are *maroons*, and *precarious* is the situation of your king" (84–85, italics in original).

This is where the play becomes ideologically problematic since Franco de Médina is represented solely as the person sent to convey a letter from the king of France with the hopes of opening what is only described as a "transaction" with Christophe (85). Christophe threatens his captive in saying, "In truth, Monsieur, if you were not here in a civilized country and protected by diplomatic immunity..." (85). Christophe's incomplete threat, dampened only by the fact of ostensible "diplomatic immunity," is all but completed by Vastey who claims that "the envoy of the king of France, the agent of the king of France, as a native of the former Spanish side of Saint-Domingue, presently a Haitian province, has all the rights of a Haitian" (85). Césaire's historical revisionism here—the eastern

---

[20] These kinds of situations actually did occur, but with less dramatic effect. Vastey, for instance, used an article that was written in the *Gazette Royale d'Hayti*, the official publication of Henry Christophe's kingdom, to express his disdain over the actions of a U.S. American merchant ship from New York named the *Sidney Crispin*, under the captainship of Elesha Kenn. Vastey reprinted the article in his *Essai*, which stated that on October 17, 1816 Crispin, along with his crew, brought a letter from two French warships hovering off the coast of Cap-Henry to the Count of Marmelade, seeking to open negotiations with Christophe. Because the letter did not recognize the sovereignty of Christophe, addressing him as General Christophe rather than King Christophe, the Count naturally refused to transmit the letter (Vastey, *Essai*, 351–356).

part of the island, the present day Dominican Republic, was not part of Christophe's kingdom—allows Vastey to make the argument that the "agent of the King of France" can be dealt with as a Haitian, thereby, removing the latter's supposed "immunity." Christophe tells Vastey, to that end, "Parbleu! Merci, Vastey...Merci. I see that you you were born for understanding me, and for resolving the *essence of the Saint-Domingue question*" (86, italics in original).

Here, Christophe tasks Vastey with the burden of resolving the "Saint-Domingue question," which in Christophe's words, amounts to "making it known to France that, free in all rights and independent in fact, we will never renounce these advantages [....] never will we let anyone destroy the edifice that we have raised with our hands and cemented with our blood" (86). Eventually, Christophe does sentence the French emissary to certain death, pronouncing that "M. Franco de Médina will stand beside his coffin and will listen to his own funeral prayers" (87).[21]

---

[21] A detailed account of this actual mass is given in the official newspaper of the kingdom of Haiti, *La Gazette royale*, dated 20 November 1814. The *Gazette* reveals that after being briefed on the interrogation of Franco de Médina, Christophe, who was away from Sans Souci at the time of Franco de Médina's capture, "gave immediate orders that all the authorities of the kingdom should return to the capital in order to attend a *Te Deum* that would be sung to the All Mighty in order to praise the fact that he permitted us to discover and bring to light the criminal intentions of our implacable enemies" (1). This *Te Deum*, however, was apparently not a "messe de requiem" for Franco de Médina, as portrayed in Césaire's play. Instead, "the nave and the choir were hung for mourning, in allusion to the famous punishment of the execrable Donatien Rochambeau's [...] grand ball in Port-au-Prince [...]; this monster had all the rooms done up for mourning, and he announced to the women that they were going to attend the funerals of their husbands and their family members" (2). "Agoustine Franco, called Médina," the article continues, "was at this church service ordered by Christophe and "was displayed before the people, standing on a dock, his back leaning against a column." The account finishes by noting that Christophe's court and military simply scared *practically* to death the French spy: "*Agoustine Franco* could barely stand up on his legs; he staggered; he could not breathe; he prayed and consecrated his soul to all the Saints of heaven. The holiness of the place, the august aspect [...] the sight of this brilliant and numerous court, the crowd of richly decorated warriors that he had had the audacity to suspect of base infamy, in believing that they were capable of renouncing their rights, all of these circumstances together, assaulted the physical and moral faculties of Franco; he succumbed and fell to his knees when he heard the thunderous speech of M. le baron de Vastey: 'Friends! With these names of Slave and Master, nothing can stop the wrath that inflames you; the bell of freedom has sounded! ....Run to your weapons, to fire, to carnage, and to vengeance!' Hearing this appeal, Franco, imagining that thousands of bayonets were pointed at his chest, was seized with fear, he was not well; we were obliged to bring him some vinegar and a cordial in order to revive him after this necessary terror" (2). For more on this mass, see Vastey's *Essai* (217).

In effect, the way to let France know that Haitians were free was to kill someone presented in the play as a simple emissary. This portrayal makes it seem as if Christophe has literally shot the messenger, and that the Haitian state can *only* be supported by a form of violence against the French that is completely out of proportion to the threat. In other words, this violence is problematic because it is portrayed as excessive. Franco de Médina is represented here as an innocent envoy who merely implores, "Majesty, please understand me, I come here with an olive branch" (86), a claim that is not represented as ironic or disingenuous in the universe of the play.

An even larger problem with portraying Franco de Médina solely as an emissary sent to Haiti with a letter (mis)interpreted as seeking to reinstate slavery on the basis of one, single phrase—"*la question de Saint-Domingue*"—is that it makes the scene more of a comedy than a tragedy: first, when Christophe insists that Franco de Médina addresses him as "Sire" (84), and second, when Vastey continues to repeat that "M. Franco de Médina is a Haitian" (86). This claim comes off as empty in the play, especially since it is ultimately ignored by Christophe whose insistence on being addressed with a title of nobility, coupled with Vastey's ironic claim about the captive's "Haitian-ness," achieves a comedic effect that was precisely the opposite of what Césaire claimed to have intended. Césaire told Vergès, for instance, "*La Tragédie du roi Christophe* is not a comedy, it is a tragedy, a very real one, because it is our own. What does Christophe do? [...] he wants to imitate the king of France and surrounds himself with dukes, a marquis, a court. [...] These people take Europe as a model. Now, Europe makes terrible fun of them" (*Nègre* 57).

The trouble is that in the play Franco de Médina comes off as sincere and the only person mocking anyone appears to be Christophe, who playfully tells Franco de Médina after he finally addresses the king as "Majesty:" "Already, you are becoming Haitian" (84). Césaire stated that the real tragedy of Christophe was that "behind this decorum, behind this man," there were "profound questions about the meeting of civilizations" to be asked (*Nègre* 57). Although Césaire viewed as a tragedy that Christophe instituted a monarchy in an effort to prove Haiti's *civilization*, isn't the real tragedy the fact that the world powers tried to prevent him from governing in the fashion he chose?

The instructions discovered on the *real* Franco de Médina, as well as his actual interrogation, not only revealed that France sought to reconquer its former colony and reinstate slavery on the island of Hispaniola, but that it planned to do so by encouraging racial enmity between Christophe and Pétion. Malouet's instructions directly state that Pétion will be more amenable to a French take-over precisely because he was of mixed-race, and thus supposedly closer to whiteness than Christophe. Malouet writes,

> It is reasonable to suspect that Pétion and Borgella,[22] after being satisfied with having obtained personal favors for themselves and for a small number of their people […], will consent without difficulty to the fact that their caste, in acquiring almost the entirety of political rights, will remain still, in some respects, a little bit below the white caste; […] their caste will be more assured of dominating the free black caste, and […] of keeping the non-free blacks at the distance required to maintain them. So, [they] will allow a little bit of difference to subsist between them and the whites. (rpt in Madiou 5: 262)

Malouet plainly describes how and why he would reinstitute the same caste system that had ultimately led to colonial troubles in the first place. He also infers that convincing Pétion to help his agents, and ultimately, France, is the best method of conquering Christophe. Malouet instructed, "As far as we can presently tell from here, it seems that the most important thing is to come to an agreement with the party of Pétion, and that having been done, it will be easier to reduce that of Christophe to obedience without a great loss of blood" (rpt. in Madiou 5: 265).

What is missing, furthermore, from Césaire's portrayal is not only any discussion of Malouet and France's desire to use Pétion against Christophe but a representation of the patently genocidal quality of the instructions themselves. Resuming in bullet fashion what he desires the three spies to accomplish, Malouet states in instruction number 5, "Reduce to slavery, and return to their former owners, not only all the blacks who are currently laboring on the plantations, but bring back once again, as much as possible, those who freed themselves from this condition"; while instruction number six mandates, "Rid the island of

---

[22] Jérôme-Maximilien Borgella was a general in the Haitian army who fought in the war of independence. After the death of André Rigaud in 1811, he commanded the southwestern part of Haiti until joining with Pétion in 1812.

all the blacks whom it would be inappropriate to admit among the free and whom it would be dangerous to leave among those who are attached to the plantations" (rpt. in Madiou 5: 266). The eventual downfall of the *real* Christophe has to be seen within the context of a very *real* threat from France (as conveyed by Malouet's instructions) as opposed to the more chimerical one (as represented in Césaire's play). In reality, Franco de Médina's arrival in Haiti represented the threat from France to Christophe fully materialized and not merely symbolized.

Using his writing as a weapon to keep the French from re-taking Haiti was the *real* Baron de Vastey's largest intellectual and political burden. He devoted much of his energy to proving himself as a black writer and elevating Christophe's worth as a black king, thus insisting that Haiti could be and deserved to remain a black state. Vastey and Christophe's shared burden of carrying the black state during the Franco de Médina episode in Césaire's play strikes me as an overly isolationist reading, then, since it parodies Christophe's belief that France wanted to restore slavery to the colony. One of the play's greatest achievements, however, is how it makes Vastey visible, not merely as a "scribe," but as one whose intellectual contributions to the making of Haitian independence were no less meaningful than Christophe's own.

The *Ourika* episode is precisely what allows us to see Vastey slipping out of Christophe's shadow to help with the intellectual work of governing the state. After the Deuxième Dame tells Vastey that he alone is "carrying the burden of the Nation" (97), the Première Dame mentions "the romance of Ourika" (99). She subsequently explains that Ourika is "[t]he heroine of a novel that made all of Paris cry....It is the story of a little black girl raised in Europe in a rich white family, who suffers because of her color and dies from it" (100).[23] In a passage that revels with Black Atlantic humanism, Vastey responds by saying that Ourika's story makes him revere even more solidly Christophe's effort to uphold Haitian sovereignty: "I'm thinking of Christophe, Madame. Do you know why he works day and night?" Vastey asks. "Do you know these

---

[23] *Ourika* (1823) is a novel written by Claire de Duras about a black female child forcibly taken from Senegal to France to live with a white family. As Ourika ages, she comes to realize that the people in her social circle view her as ugly and unworthy because of her dark skin. When she falls in love with her adopted "mother's" son, but discovers that her love for him can never be reciprocated because of her skin color, she becomes despondent and ends up dying alone in a convent from despair.

wild fancies, as you say, this forced labor?...It is because from now on there will no longer in the world be a young black girl who is ashamed of her skin color and finds in her protector an obstacle to the realization of her heart" (100). Christophe's "obsession" with work to prove the worthiness of black people in *La Tragedie*, as in Walcott's *Henri Christophe*, reveals the resulting impotence of anti-colonial reversals. As Fanon has written, "you do not show proof of your nation from its culture [...] you substantiate its existence in the fight which the people wage" (223).

In the same way that Walcott's Christophe cannot understand that his mistake was in failing to "fight" with the "people," Césaire's Christophe, too, denies any responsibility for the alienation and isolation that results from his harsh labor policies. In one of the final scenes, Christophe states, "I tried to plant something in an ungrateful land" (152). A less isolationist reading would have had Christophe recognize and then curse his own desire to prove himself to European powers, and all the "conceptual coercion" that involves, rather than a portrayal of Christophe cursing and blaming the land of Haiti itself. Suggesting that there was something inherently problematic with the land on which Haiti sits is a time-worn tradition, one illustrated by Thomas Carlyle's horribly racist essay, "Occasional Discourse on the Nigger Question" (1849), in which Caryle refers to Haiti as "nothing but a tropical dog-kennel and pestiferous jungle."

The final image of Vastey in *La Tragédie*, where he is holding Christophe's dead body upright, insisting that he be interred that way (159), makes the Baron literally the double of king. As they walk along, it is Vastey who manipulates Christophe's arms and legs to move, and it is Vastey, who will have the final word in Césaire's play: "King on our shoulders, we drove you through the mountains, higher than the flood" (160).[24] Vastey has gone from carrying the metaphorical burden of Christophe's state to carrying the material burden of Christophe's body, which will be buried forever in this "ungrateful land."

---

[24] Both Miller and Césaire may have derived their portrayals of Vastey carrying the burden of Christophe's body from Vandercook who wrote that after the King's death, "the Queen, the two Princesses, and little fierce old Vastey left Sans Souci by a secret door and started up the long, dark trail that leads to Henry's Citadel. The dead King was a heavy load; double heavy for one old man, an old Negress, and two young girls, all heartbroken" (120).

PERFORMING VASTEY AS CRITIQUE OF HAITIAN SOVEREIGNTY

Before diving into *The Revolutionists* (1942) and how it uses Vastey to place the burden of carrying the legacy of Christophe's despotism on the shoulders of the Haitian people rather than in the Haitian ground, it is worth returning briefly to May Miller's one-act play, *Christophe's Daughters* (1935), which is ideologically connected to Césaire's version of the last days of Christophe. Vastey, described as "a small emaciated black man, dressed in the elaborate regalia of Christophe's court" (253), remains one of the only people in Miller's play, as in Césaire's, to remain loyal to the king until the end. This loyalty is important because Christophe's daughters make a point of blaming the Haitian people rather than any of Christophe's policies for the rebellion of his people against him. Améthiste, Christophe's oldest daughter tells her sister, Athénaire, that the *coup d'état* is "[b]ecause the politicians are corrupt and stir up rebellion. The mulattoes hate a black king. They call work slavery. The landlords hate justice, and the people, who themselves benefit by labor, are lazy. There is no hope for anything different. Our father, the King, works alone. He says that to be great is to be lonely; to be magnificent is to have men hate you" (245).[25]

If the burden of a monarch is to feel the hatred of his people, in Miller's play the burden of carrying Christophe's body is still Vastey's, or at least, for a time. The final scene of the play, after Christophe has committed suicide, shows Queen Marie-Louise (who initially wanted to desert her husband in order to join her lover, Claude), Vastey, and Améthiste "bearing the stretchers weighted down with Christophe's heavy body" (263). The burden of carrying the heavy legacy of his life, both materially and metaphorically, will ultimately be the Christophe family's alone in this earliest iteration of a dramatic Vastey. We are told that suddenly and subsequently, "Athénaire joins the procession, taking an end of the stretcher from the hand of Vastey" (264) and relieving him of his burden.

The final description of this scene and of the play portrays an implied incompatibility of monarchy with independence that drives against the real Vastey's claim that the method of government hardly mattered as

---

[25] Miller likely derived this portrayal from Vandercook's *Black Majesty*, where Christophe tells the character Duncan, "To be great [...] is to be lonely. To be magnificent is to have men hate you" (118).

long as "the government is wise, just, enlightened, and benevolent, and the governees have religion, virtues and good morals!" (*RM* 73). At the end of *Christophe's Daughters*, cries of "Down with the King! Long live Independence!" drown out the "half-choked sobs of Athénaire" (264). While the play labored to critique the laziness of the Haitian people, it is not clear what message we should derive at the end when the fall of a monarchy is equated with sustaining independence.

The Revolutionists (1942), in contrast to *Christophe's Daughters*, emphasizes the role of the Haitian people, not necessarily in Christophe's downfall, but rather in his rise. Rodman's play concentrates first, on the events that led to the kidnapping of Toussaint Louverture, then on the eventual assassination of Jean-Jacques Dessalines, and finally on the suicide of Henry Christophe. The guide to the Selden Rodman Papers, held by Yale University Library reveals that "[...] Rodman made a trip to Haiti as an intelligence officer in 1944, when his play *The Revolutionists* was produced by the Haitian government. The play was such a diplomatic success that shortly after the war the Bureau of Inter-American Affairs sponsored a second trip to Haiti, where he became co-director for the Haitian Centre d'Art (1949–1951)" (Guide). *The Revolutionists* may have come to the attention of the Haitian government through the play's translator, Dr. Camille Lhérisson, who was from Haiti herself and had translated Rodman's play into *Les Révolutionnaires* in 1942, where it was published by the Imprimerie de l'état.[26]

Even though both Césaire and Rodman allow the character Vastey the final word in their respective plays, their representations of Christophe's most important secretary could not be more different. While Césaire represents Vastey as having been loyal, even if burdened, until the end, Rodman's Vastey all but abandons Christophe in his greatest moment of need. The play even goes so far as to suggest that Vastey's abandonment may be regarded as responsible for Christophe's suicide. At one point, the desperate monarch implores, nay threatens, Vastey to remain by his side by shouting, "Vastey! You too?—I'll shoot you if you leave me" (190). Later in the same scene, after Vastey quits the palace, Christophe opines, "Vastey...infected with the same disease....And thinks I will

---

[26] Lhérisson had also served as Alain Locke's translator during the latter's stint as a Cultural Ambassador to Haiti from April 9-July 10, 1843 (Buck 181).

succumb to it!...And beg/The people's forgiveness!...Christophe on his knees!" (191).

We already know that Rodman did not intend to closely follow the historical record in his play, which probably accounts for the striking deviation that exists between his representation of a disloyal Vastey in contrast to Vandercook's depiction of Vastey as fatally loyal. Other deviations from the historical record persist in Rodman's portrayal. Vastey first appears in the play in Act II, scene 2, for example, as Christophe's orderly (93). Another part of the same scene directs our attention to Pauline Leclerc, who is described upon entering a room as "young, beautiful, and superbly attired; she is powdering her nose, but shrinks back, holding it, as she passes VASTEY at the door" (115). The implied reason for Pauline Leclerc's disdain is that Vastey appears in this play as a former slave, confirmed by a line in Act II, Scene 3, where Vastey states, "Leclerc has just decreed/The restoration here—we're slaves again" (142).

Regardless of the play's deviation from Rodman's own sources, *The Revolutionists* remains important for thinking about how performances of Vastey in dramas of the Haitian Revolution and Haitian independence become a vehicle for criticizing Haitian leadership. If Vastey emerged out of Christophe's shadow to become his double in Césaire's *La Tragédie*, in *The Revolutionists* Vastey is Christophe's most immediate foil. Vastey's role in this play appears to be almost solely to criticize and point out the monarch's mistakes, and in great contradistinction to Walcott's *The Haitian Earth*, indict the Haitian people far less ambiguously.

In Rodman's depiction, Vastey is initially presented as being extremely loyal to Christophe, even encouraging him to burn down Cap Français (106), and later, to crown himself king (159). By the end of the play, however, Vastey is Christophe's strongest critic. Beginning in Act III, Scene 2, fissures already begin appearing in Christophe's court. Richard is presented as conspiring, along with a number of others, including Prévost and Dupuy, to overthrow the king (166). Vastey is not among these conspirators, who complain, "We are slaves/In everything but name again..." (168). Impending defection, at any rate, is not the only problem in Christophe's kingdom. There is also a certain and palpable sense of disorder, as well as disaffection. Dupuy, for example, is so resigned that he basically infers that the only freedom he has is the freedom to drink alcohol (170). Christophe's discovery of Dupuy's drunkenness provides Vastey with his first real opportunity to voice his criticism of the monarch. In an earlier scene, in which Christophe appears to be colluding with General Leclerc to get rid of Louverture, Vastey tells Christophe, "You play a dangerous game" (120), and later Vastey is revealed in the stage directions to be "*shaking his head*" behind Christophe's back in disagreement (120). After Christophe tells Dupuy, "your duties and your rank/Are at an end!" (174), essentially, banishing him from the kingdom, Vastey criticizes Christophe more directly. "If you will permit me, Your Majesty," Vastey tells the king, "Dupuy is loyal; the garrison at Hinche/Is our most dangerous and lonely outpost./You would not send another friend to Pétion–?" (174).

The issue here is that while Dupuy, Richard, and the others' objections to Christophe's method of governance are portrayed as reasonable, their behaviors are not. The nobles, as equally as the soldiers, of Christophe's kingdom are portrayed as drunk, lazy people who sleep on the job. And Richard is once again represented as being animated to conspire against Christophe because of his own class prejudices rather than because of any desire to politically organize with the goal of ridding Haiti of someone he believed to have instituted a second slavery. Act III, Scene 2 shows Richard and the other conspirators complaining about Queen Marie Louise, "that servant girl—we have to bow to" (166). Christophe's labor policies are portrayed as failing to inspire anything other than the very laziness and prejudices he abhors.

Rodman's Christophe also alienates his foreign supporters, namely, Dr. Stuart, who tells Christophe to remember to abide by the law, "[a] little thing [...] that men must wear" (176). This Christophe cannot handle the criticism, which exposes the play's condemnation of the relationship between Haitian independence and black uplift. Christophe seeks to use his position of power to prove the dignity of blackness, revealing once again the paradoxical desire to prove one's humanity through violence. He tells Dr. Stuart and Sir Home Popham, Admiral of the British West Indies fleet, "You think we are undignified? You make fun/Of my efforts to give the Black man confidence? Very well. You are like the French. You will be taught/The hard way—" (177). Christophe's threat of punishing any person in his kingdom whom he perceives to be disloyal can only be mitigated for a moment by Vastey, who is portrayed as the only reasonable person in this kingdom. Once again, using the voice of logic, Vastey states, "Sire, we are alone. It is getting late. Everyone turns against you. I am afraid—" (177). While they are alone in the room at this point, Vastey's warning does double duty, for, they are alone politically as well.

What actually turns Vastey against Christophe though is the senseless violence that the baron perceives the monarch to be using against his own people. Once Christophe finds his gunner asleep on the job, Christophe orders his death: "We'll teach all Haiti this time that to sleep/In working hours, is to sleep with Death," Christophe states, "Command the gunner, Vastey, to open fire/On that hut" (179). This action interminably shocks Vastey who cries out, "Your majesty!" (179). Rodman's Christophe eventually suffers a debilitating stroke but this does not lessen his desire to despotically control the people of Haiti. The stroke does, in this depiction, augment Vastey's sense that he can now more openly and directly criticize the monarch.

Christophe's neurological illness represents the turning point in the play. Vastey asks him if he simply means to obliterate every person in the kingdom for the most insignificant slights. With more than a touch of the pathos of poetry, Vastey asks his leader what is next: "Fire on the people? As well/Fire on the forests for absorbing sunlight,/Or on the sea for being salt! We must/Admit our errors, and start fresh from there" (187). Like Walcott's Vastey, Rodman's iteration of the character teems with remorse. Vastey seems willing to admit his mistakes in the hopes that something of the kingdom can be salvaged. Rodman's Christophe, although entirely megalomaniacal, is actually willing to forgo ruling Haiti, as long as he believes that his memory will live on in the Citadel. He tells Vastey, "Who will remember Toussaint's meager vision,/His woman's-kindness or his misplaced trust?/This fort will stand when everything that's human/On all this planet is reduced to dust!" (188).

The Citadel once again becomes a monument to every mistake made by Christophe instead of the kind of monument to black humanity that Christophe sought. Vastey's statement to that effect presents a fascinating deconstruction of the relationship of historical monuments to the labor that produced them. Vastey warns Christophe: "The Cross is gone: the Pyramids remain./I *hate* this Citadel and all it stands for!/And I tell you, Henry, Vastey, too, is leaving!" (188). A true martyr needs no monument, according to Vastey, who makes the utmost distinction between the Haitian king and Christ the King. Vastey implies that the making of the Pyramids, often understood in the popular imagination to have been constructed using slave labor, are not remembered for any particular

individual who commanded their construction. In contrast, Christ's cross
is gone, but Christ himself is remembered by all. Rodman's equation of
the construction of the Citadel with the construction of the Pyramids,
squares with Walcott's own feeling that both were difficult monuments
to reconcile with the kind of labor used to build them. Walcott, in fact,
made precisely this comparison between the Pyramids and the Citadel in
What the Twilight Says in writing, "There was only one noble ruin in the
archipelago: Christophe's massive citadel at La Ferrière[…] It was the
summit of the slave's emergence from bondage. Even if the slave had
surrendered one Egyptian darkness for another" (13).

Rodman's Vastey is much more critical of the Citadel than even
Walcott's. After learning that "[t]he State's Treasure's gone" (190), having been hidden away in Europe for Christophe's own family, Vastey
exclaims, "Good God! Was it *this* we toiled for?/Was it for this—to make
your family rich–/That Haiti was delivered out of slavery,/And then
subjected to the sacrifices/Of your colossal ego?—I was blind!/This is
the end: I will unlock the gates;/Answer to the people! They may be
more kind" (190). Vastey does not merely abandon Christophe's government in this portrayal, he abandons Christophe's life by allowing
rebel citizens to enter the palace.

Vastey's disloyalty, in any event, does not ultimately result in a critique
of Christophe alone. The King turns to his only remaining soldier and
tells him, "My friend,/you are the stuff that empires are made of,/But
there were too few of us….You will go now/And lead the rabble to this
platform" (191). This wistfully populist moment of affection for a simple soldier is completely shattered by Vastey who turns toward the mob,
pronouncing a painful soliloquy about Christophe:

> I loved him once. I still love this about him:
> He built to give his race and people pride
> Instead of waging wars of conquest….Cleaner
> His rejection of escape! Better that he died
> This way, than mourning on a St. Helena….
> Yielding to passionate impulse is not freedom. (192)

At the end of the soliloquy Vastey addresses a Haitian peasant and
nearby soldier, remonstrating: "But you!—his retribution is not yours!
Are those who accept the tyrant fit for freedom? Your apathy involves
you in his guilt" (192). This statement about the "apathy" and

"guilt" of the people being responsible for the "tyrant"—since they are portrayed here as having tolerated his violent rule— is apparently directed toward the "peasant" as well, who replies to Vastey, "What could we do?" (192). Vastey eventually indicts both the "peasant" and the soldier in stating, "Have your backs been bent/From crawling like the serpent?/Are your hands/Atrophied in the position of the salute?" (193). The soldier then replies, "Our will to rule is dead;/we must find another master!" (193). Vastey, who gets the final word once again, utterly places the blame for Christophe's tyranny squarely on the heads of the people the king ruled when he laments, "Then prepare/For years of violence; chaos lies ahead" (193). At the end of the day, Rodman's play is the most pessimistic of them all, presenting a Haiti and Haitians who do not want to be free—they seek "another master"—and who are incapable of taking responsibility for the governance of their country.

Before turning to the ways that Philoctète's play provides a more relational representation of the downfall of Christophe while still using Vastey as the primary vehicle for a critique of despotic displays of power, I will end this chapter with a brief commentary on Dan Hammerman's play. Hammerman's *Henri Christophe*, although never published, was produced by the American Negro Theatre in New York City in 1945.[27] Corbould tells us that

> well into the 1940s, the American Negro Theatre (ANT) finished its hit season with a play titled *Henri Christophe*. Though the play was panned for being overly 'talkative', one writer in the *New York Times* conceded nevertheless that 'the story of the King of Haiti is always legitimate, and with its present-day applications no one has a better right to tell it than a Negro theatre'. As the play closed with the Broadway producer choosing not to exercise his option to take it downtown from the 135th Street Library, the theater where it is was playing, another *Times* reporter noted of the ANT that 'the hardy experimentalists acknowledge that the Dan Hammerman play did not quite ring the bell, [however] the group felt that the significance of the theme justified its presentation. (qtd. in 280)

---

[27] The American Negro Theater was created in New York City in 1940 by Abram Hill and Frederick O'Neal, two actors from Harlem. The ANT was a part of the Federal Theatre Project begun in Harlem and was most active from 1940–1955.

Although Vastey plays a minor role in this play, Hammerman's attempt to dramatize the life of Vastey, alongside that of Christophe, is worth meditating on because of a few small, but significant details of the casting legend. The opening page of Hammerman's never published manuscript, *Henri Christophe*,[28] tells us that "[t]he entire play takes place in and around the city of Cap François in Haiti during the years 1791 to 1820" (n.p.). Under the heading, "Cast:" we learn that "[t]here are 22 characters: 14 colored and 8 whites" (n.p.). Under the heading "Some Character Descriptions:" "Henri Christophe" is described as "a powerful colored man, well over 6 feet, age 24 when the play begins, over 50 when it ends. His features are sharp, good looking, and extraordinarily striking....He is ambitious, shrewd, and considering that he never had any schooling his intelligence is far above average" (n.p.). Vastey is described as "Secretary to Christophe and very scholarly. Sincerely devoted to him. A small, frail mulatto man of 30, with a great understanding of human nature" (n.p.). This description of Vastey starkly contrasts with that of Dessalines who is described as: "A short, very ugly, square man of 35. Has a fanatical hatred for the white man. Cruel and ambitious" (n.p.). In concert with continuous attempts to romanticize the character of Louverture, the general is naturally presented as a "Short, dignified-looking Negro of about 50, with grey hair. Admired by all for his kindness, for his wisdom, and for his zeal to set San Domingue free" (n.p.).

It seems telling to me that the only other descriptions are of Queen Marie Louise—Christophe's wife—and a "beautiful mulatto girl of 16," Clodomire, whom we learn "is torn between her love for a white French officer and Christophe's cause for freedom" (n.p.). Richard, Lebrun, Dupuy, Leclerc, Boukman, and the 17 other characters who also appear in the casting legend, do not get these lengthy descriptions. For example, Leclerc is simply described as "a French general," Richard is "a faithless follower of Christophe," and Jean François and Biassou are merely listed as "follower[s] of Boukmann."

The idea that Vastey had a "great understanding of human nature," as described in the casting legend, allows him to simultaneously offer counsel and critique to an ultimately doomed Christophe. At times,

---

[28]The play is held by Rare Manuscript Division at the Schomburg Center of the New York Public Library.

Vastey's function appears to be to provide the soundbite. He tells Richard after Christophe has narrowly missed being stabbed by either Boukmann or Jean-François, "faith in an ideal has eternal strength like a mountain. It cannot be shattered" (2-1-1). At another point, Vastey says to Richard, "Fidelity comes from deeds, not words" (3-1-8). These pithy remonstrances against Richard's impending conspiracy allow Christophe to offer him praise: "Vastey, you never speak of your loyalty, yet I have more faith in yours than all who constantly assure me of it" (2-1-8). Even though Vastey warns Christophe of the impending rebellion against him (3-1-12), the Haitian monarch is presented much more triumphantly at the end of this play. Christophe tells a character named Maurice that his downfall has more to do with metaphysics than logic: "I don't know," he reflects, "maybe it's because a man has no right being a king in the first place. Maybe there's no such job as a king but only a well laid trap to punish a too ambitious soul. Maybe a throne is a precipice from which to fling an aspiring fool" (3-2-17). Though the blame here is all Christophe's, even if the damning fate of monarchies is written in the cosmos, it is the Haitian monarch, rather than Vastey (who does does not even appear in the final scene), who gets the last word in Hammerman's play. "How many great men ended their days still seated on their throne?" Christophe boasts, "How many chose their own time to go? Napoleon? Caesar? But Henri Christophe will be king to the end" (3-2-18).

Jeremy Glick has recently described twentieth-century theatrical representations of the Haitian Revolution as a "springboard for thinking about the problem of leaders and masses in processes of revolutionary overhaul—the intersection of stagecraft with statecraft" (3). In the end, in all of these performances "stagecraft" and "statecraft" collide to help us think about the semantics of naming with respect to ruling. The major complaint of Walcott, Césaire, as equally as Hammerman, Rodman, and Miller, appears to be that Christophe called himself a king. Perhaps, Christophe's creation of a kingdom rather than a republic accounts for the overwhelming desire to portray his life over that of Pétion's in the theater of Haitian independence. Would Christophe have been so *interesting*, and would Christophe have been considered so despotic (and Vastey, by extension), if he had merely called himself a president like Pétion? In many ways, Hammerman's Christophe fails not because of a king's poor leadership, or because of his lack of connection to the "masses" he rules, but because a king is destined to fail in a postcolonial world. The only way for Christophe to avoid the kingly fate that is written for him in the cosmos, is to take his own life, and therefore to avoid the fate of regicide when he "choose[s] [his] own time to go."

Ultimately, what appears to be under critique in these pieces from the theater of Haitian independence is not merely the vindicationist king, but also the vindicationist humanism marked by Baron de Vastey's writings. Although, it is unclear what level of engagement or familiarity each of these playwrights may have had with Vastey's works, his quest to produce black people as subjects appears to be under siege. If Christophe can be seen as having tried to create a sovereign black state in order to defend blackness itself, Vastey tried to write both the Haitian state and blackness into existence in world that constantly rejected both. Even if we see the merits in being against the energy expended in vindicationism and believe it could be better spent elsewhere, we must take seriously a world-view in which the most pressing concern of black writers, and the only sovereign black state of the New World, was to defend not only their right to be free but their right to simply *be*.

EPILOGUE: COLONIALISM AFTER SOVEREIGNTY: THE COLONIAL RELATION IN RENÉ PHILOCTÈTE'S *MONSIEUR DE VASTEY* (1975)

> *C'est un penseur, Monsieur de Vastey!... Un guerrier, Monsieur de Vastey!*
> *Un héros même, Monsieur le baron de Vastey!*
> —René Philoctète, *Monsieur de Vastey*

If the Haiti of Walcott, Miller, Césaire, Hammerman, and Rodman, is a Haiti isolated by its own leaders, Philoctète's *Monsieur de Vastey* shows a country highly connected to and controlled by its formal colonial occupier, France, as well as by other regional powers with interests in Haiti, including the United States and Great Britain. Although Philoctète portrays these countries as manifestly *interested* in the country, his depiction of the essential connectedness of Haiti to the rest of the world does not revel in blame.

The play embraces a central understanding of the colonial relation as necessarily global, enabling its author to simultaneously critique both Haitian political leaders and the world powers that circumscribed their abilities to effectively lead the country. Philoctète shows that one can engage in this kind of analysis without asserting one definitive cause for Haiti's ongoing political woes. He paints Haiti's dire political and economic problems as directly connected to an amorphous form of neo-colonialism without either viewing Haitian rulers as mere bystanders in

© The Editor(s) (if applicable) and The Author(s) 2017   183
M.L. Daut, *Baron de Vastey and the Origins of Black Atlantic Humanism*,
The New Urban Atlantic, DOI 10.1057/978-1-137-47067-6

their own destruction or scapegoating the Haitian people. *Monsieur de Vastey*, thus, achieves a more relational critique of the effect of global capital world power on Haiti, one that demonstrates, as in the *real* Baron de Vastey's words, "Our internal problems derive, therefore, from both exterior and interior political intrigues" (*RP* 66).

Although Philoctoète did not write political essays or involve himself overtly in Haitian politics, he acknowledged that his theatrical works were influenced by the inherently political literary philosophies of Bertolt Brecht. Brecht, a famous playwright most well known for *Mother Courage and Her Children* (1939) and the collaboratively written *Three Penny Opera* (1928), believed that the theatre should not cause spectators to become lost in fantasy to the point of forgetting reality. Instead, he argued that staged dramas should compel audience members to reflect and act on the political struggles of the present. In his essay, "The Epic Theatre and its Difficulties" (1927), Brecht wrote: "The essential point of the epic theatre is perhaps that it appeals less to the feelings than to the spectator's reason. Instead of sharing an experience the spectator must come to grips with things" (129).

Philoctète told an interviewer in 1992: "My best play is, in my opinion, *Monsieur de Vaté* [*Vastey*].[1] I write a Brechtian kind of theater. My plays might appear as historical but, rather than historical, my theater is in fact political, and it announced the fall of Duvalier" (62).[2] Philoctète here suggests that *Monsieur de Vastey* is not solely a play about a historical moment involving Baron de Vastey nor is it a play only about the anguished downfall of Henry Christophe, but rather it is a play about the Haiti of Philoctète's era, one tyrannized by the regime, first, of François Duvalier (1907–1971), and then of his son, Jean-Claude Duvalier (1951–2014). The rising up of the people against Christophe in the play, thus, foretells the rising up of the Haitian people against Baby Doc Duvalier in February 1986, eleven years after the publication and first staging of *Monsieur de Vastey*.

The tyranny of the Duvaliers, like the *coup d'état* against Baby Doc, was not created in a vacuum, something recognized in Philoctète's play

---

[1] The unnamed transcriber of the interview spells Vastey's name phonetically. The "s" is ordinarily silent.

[2] Philoctète was the author of three other plays, *Rose morte* (1962), *Boukman, ou le rejeté des enfers* (1963), and *Escargots* (1965).

if it is to be read as an allegory for *dechoukaj*.[3] As Christophe's downfall becomes imminent, Philoctète's Monsieur de Vastey notes: "And everyone wants at least a little bit, even the smallest wing [...] they will hide their policies with seemingly innocent phrases: *la francophilie*, for example. Or even better: French for everyone! Chinese therapy! Americanness! Germanness! And in a distant era, we will even come to know Canadianness. Like Thrombosis, Cirrhosis, Tuberculosis, Arteriosclerosis, Avitaminosis. The entire clinic, yes! And the therapy, naturally....Then the death...the dividing up, *le repartimento*..." (64). This is a trenchant critique of a new form of colonialism that infects a country like a disease that only further colonial actions, disguised in the vocabulary of "aid," can quarantine, treat, and heal, after quartering and killing the patient, of course. Quartering Haiti was apparently exactly what the neocolonial doctor had ordered. Philoctète's Vastey says that the world powers are all ready to pounce on Haiti and each will settle for just "a tiny little thigh... or once again the neck... or the feet....the throat...the guts" (64).

Centering his focus on Baron de Vastey, rather than on the more well-known figures of Christophe and Dessalines, may be what allows Philoctète to offer a much less isolationist account of the pitfalls of political leadership in a postcolonial (read: neocolonial) world. Vastey's appearance in the starring and title role of the play upsets the aesthetic and political logic of the theater of Haitian independence as the history of so many "strong black men" who led the masses into freedom since Vastey could not have been considered either a leader or a part of the larger masses of enslaved and formerly enslaved Africans, who together helped to achieve Haitian independence. Instead, Philoctète's rendition of a sovereign, independent Haiti centers on Baron de Vastey's attempt to preserve the Haitian monarchy amidst both internal and external threats. This artfully complicates the idea that the theater

---

[3] The ousting of Jean-Claude Duvalier (called Baby Doc) by the Haitian people was called *dechoukaj*, which, in the words of Laënnec Hurbon, "was not merely the cleaning up or eradication of the *macoute* network, the nighttime eye of the terror infiltrating every cranny of this society. It was above all the expression of a desire to rebuild the nation on a foundation radically different from that of despotism" (*Comprendre Haïti* 8). Explaining the more socio-linguistic origins of the term *dechoukaj* itself, Amy Wilentz writes, "'Dechoukaj,' like many other Haitian political slogans, is a word that comes straight out of Haiti's farm culture. It means to uproot a tree, to pull it out of the ground, roots and all, so that it will never grow back, and you do it when you are clearing a field to plant" (53).

of Haitian independence necessarily involved dramatizing the contest not only between the French military and Dessalines's *armée indigène* but also the split between the people, usually described as enslaved Africans, and those who led them.

Monsieur de Vastey neither attempts to narrate the overthrow of Henry Christophe *through* the people nor to tell the history of Haitian independence with "a narrative of emancipation in which black agency and universal intent were central" (Kaisary 2). Instead, Vastey is painted in Philoctète's play as a "thinker," and a humanist (the British Consul calls him "an intellectual, above all" [94]), who is deeply worried about the meaning of civil unrest for Haiti, not solely because of his loyalty to Christophe, but also because of the future implications of a *coup d'état*, especially one encouraged and supported by foreign powers. There is a cyclical analysis involved in Philoctète's Vastey-centered version of early Haiti's history that allows us to focus on the ideological meanings we might derive from this form of staging Haiti's sovereignty.

In contrast to the plays of Haitian independence under examination in Chapter Four, Philoctète's *Monsieur de Vastey*, performs a reading of Vastey's writing, not merely to presage the downfall of Duvalier (as Philoctète alluded to in the abovementioned interview), but to critique the role of what Brenda Gayle Plummer (1988) has called "the great powers" in setting the stage for continuous political unrest in Haiti. This relational understanding of Haitian sovereignty is itself a new narrative in certain ways. Haitian historical analysis tends to be dominated by the concept of "blame," whether that blame is directed toward "the West" or toward the Haitian people themselves. Philoctète's tale serves neither of these narratives. On the contrary, the play probes the essential interconnectedness of people and their worlds to produce a more humanist vision for Haiti that is hopeful, even if the source of that hope seems unreasonable, misdirected, or unclear. It is Philoctète's embrace of the uncertainty of the future, a sense of the opacity of political as well as personal life, that makes *Monsieur de Vastey* the most compelling and black humanist drama in the twentieth-century theater of Haitian independence.

*

Few studies exist of the oeuvre of René Philoctète, none of whose works were printed in their entirety beyond Haiti until 2003, when his novel *Le Peuple des terres mêlées* (1989) was translated into Spanish as

Perejil by Mireia Porta (Glover 23).[4] Even though Philoctète's works may not have circulated very far beyond the borders of his country during his own life (in contrast to the works of Césaire, Rodman, and Walcott), it is his play, *Monsieur de Vastey*, which properly puts the downfall of Henry Christophe into relational, comparative perspective, both historically and politically.

Even its performance history requires comparative analysis. Judging by the first review of *Monsieur de Vastey*, authored by Dany Laferrière in March 1975 for the Haitian newspaper, *Le Petit samedi soir*, Philoctète's play premiered sometime in the spring of that year. A subsequent review, also published in *Le Petit samedi soir* by Gérard Résil in May 1975, indicates that the play had simultaneously been both published and performed since the author begins by acknowledging, "Éditions Fardin has just published 'Monsieur de Vastey'" (12).[5] Additional reviews of the play, published in Port-au-Prince later that same year by the Haitian novelist Jean-Claude Fignolé (*Le Nouvelliste* 27 November 1975), Radio Haïti Inter's Michèle Montas (*Le Nouvelliste* 1 December 1975), and author Roger Gaillard (*Le Nouveau monde* 27–28 December 1975) suggest that it may have continued to be performed throughout 1975. By December, the play which Laferrière likened to the works of Bertolt Brecht and Jean Genet,[6] but called a "difficult read" (15), had crossed the Atlantic, where it would be performed on the evening of 6 December 1975 at Barnard College by Le Théâtre National d'Haïti.

A review of the New York performance, published on 4 January 1976 in the journal, *Lakansiel*, which means rainbow in Haitian Kreyòl,

---

[4] In 2005, the novel, which centers on the 1937 border conflict between the Dominican Republic and Haiti that resulted in the massacre of somewhere in the realm of 10,000–12,000 Haitians, went on to be translated into English by Linda Coverdale with the title of *Massacre River*. It was published in New York by New Directions Press with a preface by Edwidge Danticat, whose own novel, *The Farming of Bones* (1998), takes up the topic as well, and an introduction from the famed Haitian writer, Lyonel Trouillot.

[5] The play must have appeared in print around the same time or shortly after it was actually performed since Laferrière refers to having seen the play and to have read an advanced copy of the book (15).

[6] Genet (1910–1986) was a famous French poet, playwright, and novelist. He was a well-known figure in the avant-garde theater as well as in the theater of the absurd. Résil also compared *Monsieur de Vastey* to the kinds of plays published by Brecht, but he added that there was a bit of the "poetics of the present that recalls T.S. Eliot" (12).

called *Monsieur de Vastey* "words sliced on a historic background," observing that "the piece takes place during the era of Christophe." "But the past is not an escape" ("Monsieur de Vastey" 40), the reviewers write,[7] "From the political theater, hard, cruel in its reduced décor. M. de Vastey is the future" (41). The point expressed in *Lakansiel* that *Monsieur de Vastey* was as equally about the historical events that led to the suicide of Henry Christophe, as about the political events of their own day, was also shared by Laferrière, who wrote with irony that "René Philoctète makes use of history only as as an embellishment" (15). Of course, Philoctète, as we observed earlier in this chapter, was well aware that the historical setting of his play was one that had as much resonance with the present as with the past and the future.

Although, Philoctète did not consider himself a politician, a political theorist, or a literary critic (he did not write at length about any of his own works, in the vein of Glissant, Lamming, James, Césaire, or Walcott), in the earlier mentioned 1992 interview, his description of the reasons that he gave the title *Ces îles qui marchent* to his 1963 collection of poems, amounts to a concept of human futurity that approaches Glissant's theory of relation: "As I was coming from Canada, our plane flew over the islands," Philoctète said:

> The plane was flying, and I looked down and, by some kind of optical illusion, I saw Cuba running. We flew over Jamaica, and I saw Jamaica going, walking, as it were. That was a direct impact. The emotional, almost political, impact is the vision of the poets of these places marching toward freedom, development, humanism—in fact, moving away from the exploitation and obscurantism, promising a bright future. So these islands were moving physically as I saw them from the plane, and also politically, because I predict that they will change from their status quo. Martinique and Guadeloupe, for example, will gain their independence from the French. I remember predicting, at the time, Jamaica's independence and Haiti's liberation from dictatorship, and both events took place, even

---

[7] I refer to reviewers in the plural because the review was signed with the names Michel Amer, Michel Fils, Lakol Jules Lavanture, Cauvin L. Paul, L. Raymond, Henriette St-Victor, and Karl Toulanmanche (41). The review also lists the actors of this performance as Madeleine Gardiner, Fayolle Jean, Fritz Valescot, François Latour, Lys Marra Fontaine, Yves Pierre, Renaud Cadet, Richard Brisson, Max Oswald Beauboeuf, Jean-Claude Exulien, Sophie Mouteaud, Richard Coles, Serge François, Michael Brudent, and Guy Plantin.

though Jamaica is still part of the Commonwealth. This is why I called that book *Ces îles qui marchent*. (625)

Philoctète's explanation revels, at once, in a visionary will to sovereignty for the other islands of the Caribbean, seeing them not in isolation from one another but in "Total Relation," a concept articulated in the more well-known theoretical writings of Glissant.

In his *Poetics of Relation*, originally published in French in 1990, Glissant explained that the French word *relation* cannot correspond to the English word "relationship" (27) since "when we speak of a poetics of Relation, we no longer need to add: relation between what and what." In other words, "the consciousness of Relation is total," Glissant writes, "focusing upon the realizable totality of the world" (27). Glissant states, in fact, that the Caribbean is "one of the places in the world where Relation presents itself most visibly" (*Poetics* 33).

Glissant's use of the word "realizable" touches upon the cornerstone of his vision for a more relational reading of the Caribbean. He asserts that although the total relation of the Caribbean islands already exists and in many respects can be acknowledged as always having existed, it has not yet been fully *realized*. In *Caribbean Discourse*, Glissant wrote, to that end: "What is the Caribbean in fact? A multiple series of relationships. We all feel it, we express it in all kinds of hidden or twisted ways, or we fiercely deny it" (139). Although the Caribbean archipelago seemed a natural metaphor for such *relation*, for Glissant the material and political realities on the ground for these islands meant that they had been unnaturally separated from one another, not only by geography and imposed colonial languages, but by decolonization itself. "Most of the nations that gained freedom from colonization," he argues, "have tended to form around an idea of power—the totalitarian drive of a single, unique root—rather than around a fundamental relationship with the Other" (14). Glissant goes on to theorize that poetics rather than politics might hold the key to maintaining and restoring a fundamental ecology of relation in the Caribbean. He writes, "in literature, just like everywhere else in the world, one of the full-senses of modernity is provided henceforth by the action of human cultures identifying one another for their mutual transformation" (24).

Philoctète, too, appeared to believe in the transformative power of poetry, in particular, to restore, create, and forge the kind of "freedom, development, humanism" that he spoke of in the interview. He once said, "I want to be the poet of the streets, of yards, and of fields; I would like for all the poems of Haiti and of the world to become so popular that they end up flying from lip to lip like gentle butterflies announcing the arrival of a new season filled with flowers, fruit, and kisses" (qtd. in Wattara 85, my translation). According to Mamadou Wattara, such a humanism distinctly reveals the reason that Philoctète penned *Le Peuple des terres mêlées*, his novel about Dominican dictator Rafael Trujillo's 1937 slaughter of thousands of Haitians along the border of Haiti and the Dominican Republic. Wattara writes, "This authorial admission testifies to Philoctète's poetic intent to inscribe, if not to re-inscribe, the artistic and literary influence of Haiti in a global world. But to start, he had to reinvent a new imaginary of the borders of the island of Hispaniola" (85).

In concert with this idea of restoring a "new imaginary," Philoctète revealed that his goal with the novel was to achieve a kind of "reworlding" for Haiti, to use John Muthyala's term. Muthyala writes that in reworlding, "[t]he task [...] is not just to discover what ideas of America, what different dreams of the New World, what kinds of desperate negotiations writers and texts in non-English languages articulate in attempting to give shape and meaning to America. It is also to study how non-English texts can emerge as American literary works of art through acts of ideological manipulation that elide their multiple allegiances to conflicting intellectual and aesthetic traditions" (16). This idea of "reworlding" seems apt for discussing Philoctète's novel because one of the explicit imperatives of Muthyala's theory is for the reader to gain a "border consciousness" or "the trans-border processes of social and cultural exchange that link the U.S. Southwest to Latin America and the Caribbean as the border-landers search for what Lois P. Zamora calls a 'usable past'" (17). Philoctète's "reworlding" had to begin at the origins of the conquest of the Americas and with the island of Hispaniola because Haiti's imagined reconciliation with the Dominican Republic represented for Philoctète a first move toward the realization of the new kind of "border consciousness" or *relation* called for in the theory of "reworlding." Philoctète said that *Le Peuple des terres mêlées*, the title of which can be literally translated as "the people of the blended lands,"

> is a novel about the Dominican and the Haitian peoples; it calls for a harmony between the two because, whether we want it or not, the dissension and the hatred between those two peoples are, for me, but an accident of

history. History has stupidly, ridiculously, divided those two peoples. [...] These two peoples, who had violent disputes about their government, are in fact only one people. These are two peoples who on the borders speak the same language, which is neither French nor Spanish, but what I would call the border language -a Dominican at the border speaking to a Haitian learns Creole words, just as the Haitian learns Spanish words. (Interview 624)

Philoctète's desire to use history for poetry and to make poetry out of history to remove the unnatural borders among the islands of the Caribbean not only strikes me as relational poetics, but as a beautifully optimistic and refreshingly "new narrative of Haiti" (see, Ulysse 2015). Recall that Philoctète's aerial prophecy from the sky imagined a sovereign future for not only Jamaica, but also for the French departments of Martinique and Guadeloupe. This hope of sovereignty for Haiti's island neighbors stands in stark contrast to the wholly pessimistic and negatively charged ideas about Haiti expressed by Césaire and Walcott.

There is something decidedly non-threatening and non-competitive about Philoctète's wish for Martinique to follow Haiti and gain its independence and this hope lies in stark contrast to Césaire's criticisms of Haitian post-revolutionary society. Figueroa states that writers like Césaire may express harsh opinions about Haiti because although they "write about Haiti, and what they write certainly sheds light on the Haitian Revolution, [...] they also, and mainly, write about what the revolution says about their own societies. Thus Césaire, who regards Haiti as the country 'where negritude rose for the first time,' also looks at it as a cautionary tale, as an example of what to avoid, as a road better not taken. Haiti has become an illustration of all that can go wrong and that has gone wrong with the Caribbean..." (23).

Haiti continues to be *used* to diffuse fears that the costs of liberty and sovereignty in a neo-colonial world may be too much to bear. The perhaps unwitting process by which Caribbean authors have isolated Haiti by using the country as a warning, recalls Farmer's observation that even though "Haiti became the outcast of the international community [...] and some have confused this status with economic and political isolation, a pariah nation may have many *uses*" (*The Uses* 67). Among them, Farmer suggests: "It may be a source of raw materials and tropical produce, much as a colony; it may serve as a market for goods; it may serve as a cautionary tale. For the French, the uses of Haiti included all of these" (*The Uses* 67). Philoctète's relational reading of

Haiti's revolutionary history in *Monsieur de Vastey* represents an important pushback against those who in J. Michael Dash's words, "cynically exploit [the Haitian Revolution], as many inside and outside of Haiti have done, by turning the bicentenary into a tragic farce" ("Theater of the Haitian Revolution" 22).

Philoctète's reflections on crafting a poetics of humanism can help us to understand how *Monsieur de Vastey* offers not only a highly original take on the events of October 1820 that resulted in a regime change for Haiti, but a relational critique of Haitian politics that ultimately exposed Haiti's often opaque connections to the rest of the world. *Monsieur de Vastey*'s opacity approaches the theater of the absurd, à la Samuel Beckett or Eugène Ionesco (particularly, in the realm of dialogue), even though Philoctète rejected the idea that his writing was related to "Camus' notion of the absurd" (Interview 624). Nonetheless, a certain sense of absurdity surges through Act I, appropriately titled, "Fiasco," which opens in the home of Baron de Vastey, where his servants are setting the table for a dinner party. This dinner party represents the ultimate *diner de cons* because it will be attended by no one, even though Vastey's maid, Clémence, notes threateningly, "That is the worst thing! To refuse the invitation of the Baron de Vastey!" (2). The servants, who understand that no one will come to dinner, as these are the final days of Christophe and the monarch has few friends left in the kingdom, simulate serving the meal to the invited guests anyway. When a dejected Vastey enters the scene, he too begins to realize that his guests will never arrive and starts pretending that he is dining with the invited guests, speaking to them, and passing them dinner dishes, while the servants look on in stunned silence.

The whole "fiasco" is like a performance of royalty, begging the spectators to ask what the meaning of this dinner for no one can be? The stage descriptions, in Brechtian fashion, often direct the characters to stare out at and directly speak to the audience. This squares with Philoctète's own thoughts on Haitian theater as a theater of participation: "Our theater is a theater in which the spectator participates fully. The spectators enter the sacred, and sometimes they take so much part of what is happening on the stage that they share the pathos with the actors and are in the same crises as them" (Interview 625–626). The viewer can also share in the sense that life is one big performance, as the characters repeatedly ask one another what role they are playing, for example, that of soldier (45, 46), or priest (66).

The real crises of the play begins when one of Vastey's dinner guests finally does show up, albeit extremely late. Colonel Johnsburry, the British Consul, arrives at Vastey's home just after the baron has finished explaining to his other, non-existent guests that the construction of the Citadel was done in the name of the people: Vastey even exclaims, "Chère Citadelle!" (28). When the Colonel arrives, nevertheless, Vastey tells him, "I heard the drums" (32), the universal sign of revolution and rebellion in nearly all plays about Haiti. Johnsburry tries to coyly ease Vastey's fears by telling him that England will remain loyal to Christophe as long as their monetary interests compel them to do so. Johnsburry says to Vastey, "Commerce is the backbone of my country" (32). This scene sets us up to understand that the biggest threat to Christophe comes not from the people living in his kingdom, or even from Boyer's republic, but from the many outsiders the king has allowed into his inner circle, such as the character of L'Archevêque from France. L'Archevêque tells Vastey in no uncertain terms that "the clergy is on the side of the winner" (81).

Vastey's meeting with L'Archevêque reveals just how much monetary, and therefore, neocolonial control England has over Christophe's Haiti in the play. Vastey tells L'Archevêque, "Everything in the Kingdom of the North is 'made in England'" (61). Vastey subsequently goes on to provide a long list detailing that nearly every consumer good in northern Haiti has been made in England, including "the currency of the kingdom of Sans-Souci" (61). This compilation highlights the unevenness of trade and food dependencies that is a hallmark of neocolonialism. L'Archevêque tells Vastey: "Even your Majesty is 'made in England'" (61). Vastey responds to L'Archevêque by remarking: "The only thing that remains is for the Constitution of the Kingdom of the North to be marked with the seal of His British Majesty" (62). In a compelling indictment of modern colonialism, Philoctète's Vastey, like the historical Baron de Vastey, turns to the audience and states: "Nevertheless, the colonial system has been unveiled for a long time. (To the Public.) These people here are looking for another form of colonization. They will find it" (64). The form of colonialism that the foreigners surrounding Christophe will ultimately use "will be legal colonization," in Monsieur de Vastey's words (65).

Evoking *Le Système colonial dévoilé* allows Philoctète to use the writings of Baron de Vastey to critique the forms of neo-colonialism—religious interventions, food dependencies, trade embargoes, debt, etc.— that have continued to plague Haiti to this day. Such a portrayal draws a line from colonialism to sovereignty in the Caribbean that is both static and dynamic—the form may have changed, but the outcome remains the same: global capitalist domination. Even the Catholic Church, represented by L'Archevêque, rejects Christophe because the monarch will not do its bidding. Vastey acknowledges as much when he tells the French priest that the Church is turning its back on Christophe because "the musicians here poorly play the music of the Administration" (66).

It is not surprising that a critique of the neo-colonial system that was developed immediately after Haitian independence is offered in a play named after Baron de Vastey. Reading the entirety of Vastey's writing enables us to understand how Haiti was mired in a global capitalist world-system that attempted to alienate Haitian leaders from the other world powers with the goal of forcing the failure of the state. One of Vastey's first publications foreshadows the effects of these attempts when, responding to the former colonist Pierre-Victor Malouet's appeal for Europeans to create "a confederation of their interests" against Haitians, "their natural enemies" (qtd. in Vastey, *Notes* 8), Vastey writes:

> Why are are you calling for the creation of a confederation of powerful European states to work against the Haitian people? What interests would these other powers have in allying themselves with you?...What would be the benefit of them helping you in this unjust enterprise?...Why would we be their natural enemies? Have we ever tried to invade their territories? Have we ever troubled the peace or the happiness of our neighbors by ransacking their capitals? Have we ever involved ourselves directly or indirectly in their domestic or foreign policies? (9–10)

Malouet's call for a European confederation based on whiteness—he wrote that this European confederation could help France to re-establish "the preponderance of our color" in Saint-Domingue (qtd. in Vastey, *Notes* 8; original in Malouet 33)—purveys the essence of neo-colonialism: the creation of interstate alliances that not only exclude, but deliberately undermine weaker states. Considering that Haiti was the first former colony of the Caribbean to achieve sovereignty, Michel-Rolph Trouillot's words have never rung more true: Haiti "represents the longest neocolonial experiment in the history of the West" ("Odd" 6).

Laferrière picked up this very sentiment from Philoctète's play when he wrote of the proliferation of conspirators in *Monsieur de Vastey*, "behind all of this carefree riffraff [...] there is Europe-the

United States, France, Canada, who with their full claws out pre-
pare to..." Laferrière never finishes the thought because, as his next
sentence reveals, he can't finish it since "the sword of Damocles has
not yet been returned to its sheath" (15). The *Lakansiel* review is
even more direct in its recognition of Philoctète's ardent critique of
Haiti's postcolonial past in service of representing the disastrous consequences of Haiti's neo-colonial present: "The past rises up in our
throats," the reviewers write, "Everything is denounced. Necolonialism
with its Institutes and Institutions. Yankee capitalist America. The
Machiavellian Church" (40).

A chaotic rendering of the Haitian social landscape is what results
from such international interference. Philoctète's Vastey tells the British
Consul at one point, "I have every reason to believe that in this country, the day will come when children will denounce their own parents for
some government job. When mothers will sleep with their sons. When
we will say hello to one another by way of a *fuck you*" (31). A social
world where the meanings of everyday life—the roles of parents and children, mothers and sons, citizen and citizen—suddenly become inordi-
nately meaningless, or at least, deeply inverted, troubles Vastey because
as he queries: "After everything, who knows what the end will be?" (58).
Later, he states, "we are afraid of the end which will deliver us from fear"
(80). Philoctète's play shows that the form of colonialism on display has
no easy end because it is practically invisible and almost impossible to
eradicate. Indeed, the Archêveque says at one point that he will "work
alone" to disrupt political life in Haiti, "in the shadows" (96).

Philoctète's representation of the foreigners surrounding Christophe,
such as Dr. Stewart, the British Consul, and the Archevêque, greatly contrasts with the role given to these characters by other playwrights within
the theater of Haitian independence. *Monsieur de Vastey* is the only
one in this corpus of Vastey representations that inserts characters from
France and England into the play not so that they can offer the voice of
reason or play the victim to Dessalines or Christophe's implied treach-
ery. These figures instead symbolize the bare fact that the world powers
they represent actually conspired to encourage internecine strife in Haiti.
Foreigners are no longer portrayed as those against whom Christophe
and Vastey conspire, as in Césaire and Walcott's plays, but are themselves
represented as the conspirators.

The conspiracy of England and France against Haiti develops most
fully when L'Archevêque momentarily convinces Vastey to defect from

the side of Christophe, promising the baron that "[t]his is merely a simple change of dignity. You are not playing at anything, no abandonment, no duplicity. It's for stability, my dear baron!" L'Archeveque subsequently urges Vastey, "Be a calculating man. A man of numbers. Win the party of the moment, the party of the times, the party in style. After royal groveling, republican groveling. Wind of the north, wind of the South, we turn with the wind" (81). Yet not long after this scene, the priest and the British Consul collude in a plot to get rid of Vastey. L'Archevêque tells the Consul: "Mr. de Vastey is a patriot; he is dangerous" (94).

The subsequent stage directions are deep and disturbing even in all of their poetic mastery. The reader is told that what follows is a "(Mute sene between the Archevêque and the Consul whereby they simulate an assassination; a kind of *ballet macabre*)" (95). Such a "ballet of murder" to use the Consul's words, is preceded by the Consul's characterization of Vastey as a part of a "terrible race!" (94), making Vastey's death the work of not only foreign political intrigues, but external, rather than internal racism. The Archevêque details his own participation in such interference when he admits that he will wage a silent war against Haiti, "The cold war!" in order to pit "Everyone against everyone!" (96).

Philoctète's wholly divergent portrayal of the reason that Vastey's body was found in a ditch shortly after Christophe's death turns the documentation of the *real* Baron de Vastey's death into its own "ballet macabre" for black Atlantic humanism. Vastey's was a real murder that the British abolitionist William Wilberforce had sought to prevent in pleading with Boyer for Vastey's life after news of the death of Christophe had reached Europe. Wilberforce urged "mercy" for Vastey on the grounds of Black Atlantic humanism in stating:

> I am utterly ignorant of the crimes of which M. de Vastey may have been guilty; and therefore it is not for me to presume to form any opinion on the punishment to be inflicted upon him. But it cannot be wrong, nor can it, I trust, be in any degree likely to offend, if taking, as I must ever do, a deep interest in all that concerns the character and fortunes of all the descendants of the African race, I feel desirous of enforcing on you the important truth, that the eyes of all the civilised world are anxiously directed towards you; and that the course which the Haytians shall pursue in their present circumstances, may tend to powerfully gladden or to

depress the hearts of those who, like myself, have long been their partisans and their advocates. Often it has been confidently affirmed by those who would support the old prejudices [...] that one of the proofs of [African] inferiority was the violence and cruelty with which they have been disposed to act towards each other.

"An occasion has lately arisen among you," Wilberforce continues, "for verifying or refuting the charge of which I have been speaking [...] by letting the principles of your proceedings be manifest to the world" and allowing "even guilty men" the "benefit of a fair and impartial trial" (rpt. in Griggs and Prator 393). Wilberforce was worried that condemning and executing Vastey without putting on the spectacle of a trial for a world audience, would convince and confirm for the "civilised world" that Haitians were not civilized. In Philoctète's play there is immediate irony to the idea that Haitians could be the ones considered to be barbaric. We learn that the the barbarity of seeking to kill Vastey without a trial, "[i]n the name of civilization!" in the Consul's words, and "[i]n the name of fraternity between peoples" (96), in the Archevêque's sentiment, is all on the side of the French and the British, with the United States ready to pounce on Haiti (and Vastey) in the background.

In an earlier scene the Consul had remarked that getting rid of Vastey would help to keep the United States from taking over Haiti, to the detriment of its commerce with England and France (89–92): "the United States is young and voracious," the Consul states, "Already, it covets Puerto-Rico, Cuba, Panama. Its politics will soon be perfected...and will soon surpass our own. The world will be Yankee Capitalist" (93). This statement recalls Césaire's sense of "American domination" as "the only domination from which one never recovers [....] from which one never recovers unscarred" (77). It also strikingly resembles the Haitian poet Pierre Faubert's poetics of the United States's imperial designs. In his 1856 poem, "Aux Haïtiens," Faubert wrote, alluding to the U.S., "Hatred, dissension, and this rapacious vulture/Hovering over your skies already/To further perpetuate the ills of your race/Prepares to swoop down on Cuba" (145).

While U.S. capitalism as the dominant neo-colonial power is undoubtedly under critique in *Monsieur de Vastey*, Haitian political leaders do not escape their fair share of criticism. If Boyer appears to escape judgment (and even representation) in many of the other plays of the Haitian Revolution discussed here, this is not the case in Philoctète's play (101).

We learn that under Boyer, declared by one of his own magistrates to be above the law (103), the monarchy will continue merely under the guise of a republic.

It would be easy to read a critique of the Duvalier regime as well into this portrayal of Boyer as simply seeking to continue despotic leadership in another name. There is sadness in the truth of Baron de Vastey's poignant expression that even he is fearful since in Haiti, "We are mister everyone who is afraid" (80). This statement calls forth the arresting image of not only the terror instituted by Duvalier's henchmen, the *tonton makouts*, but the general "*ensekirite*" experienced by all Haitians during and after every *coup*. "The sense of risk and vulnerability" in Haiti, writes anthropologist Erica Caple James, "crosse[s] racial, class, and gender boundaries" (8).

In the end, Philoctète's *Monsieur de Vastey* shows both the internal and external powers at work who made of colonialism, a form of geopolitical terror, "[a]n infernal vicious circle," in the character Antonin's deceptively simple words; or in the character Isidore's sage metaphor, "[t]he carousel of the history of peoples and their leaders;" or in Normil's sad statement, "the ladder that, without any steps, loses its chance at the sky" (118). Perhaps, it is more fitting to leave this analysis of *Monsieur de Vastey* and *Baron de Vastey and the Origins of Black Atlantic Humanism* with Philoctète's Vastey's own enigmatic words, uttered to a single, remaining portrait of Henry Christophe hanging in the baron's house, "We do not want you to build this people..." (66).

*

Any reading of a text is an effort to center it with respect to theory, aesthetics, history, biography, or genre, which requires focusing on some elements while leaving out others. The multiply centered reading of Vastey's writing offered here, like the multiple sites of Vastey's epistemology, is by no means free of these constraints. By focusing almost completely on what we can glean about the relationship of decolonization and sovereignty in Haiti to Black Atlantic humanism by reading the works of Vastey, I have offered my own portrait of the intellectual that praises Vastey for being populist and resistant but has very little to conclude about the proliferation of descriptions by nineteenth-century observers of Vastey's role in the brutality of the Christophe regime. By continuing to focus attention away from the dominant idea of Vastey as a propagandist for a brutal regime or a mere ideologue (and thus as potentially the discursive, and physical, arm of state violence against the Haitian people themselves), what I hope is to open up a conversation about the "other" Vastey that we might be able to discover through his writings. In other words, the Vastey I hope I have unveiled is the one whom we read rather than dismiss, and whose complicated humanism we contemplate rather than condemn.

Considering Vastey both *in* and *against* the Euro-American historical traditions that he addresses, we can begin to see the theoretical connections of his work to the many later nineteenth- and early-twentieth-century writers more immediately associated with the genesis of Afro-diasporic thought. Vastey was both a crucial point of reference in the nineteenth-century transatlantic abolitionist movement as well as an important critical antecedent for many of those whom scholar Paul Gilroy has identified as a part of a "Black Atlantic" modern consciousness. These points of reference, which have included Walcott and Césaire; Grégoire and Clarkson; and McCune Smith and Du Bois, place Vastey, and the writings of early post-independence Haiti, at the origins of a global, philosophical, political, and intellectual tradition of Black Atlantic humanism.

Dakar, August 5, 2016

BIBLIOGRAPHY

Acte de Baptême, Jean Louis Vastey, 29 March 1788, Paroisse de Plaisance, Saint-Domingue (Haiti). Original in possession of État-Civil de Saint-Domingue. Archives Nationales d'Outre-Mer, Aix-en-Provence, France.

Acte de Mariage, Jean Valentin Vastey and Élisabeth Dumas, 3 July 1777, Paroisse de Plaisance, Saint-Domingue (Haiti). Original in possession of État-Civil de Saint-Domingue. Archives Nationales d'Outre-Mer, Aix-en-Provence, France. 85MIOM/66FR ANOMIDPPC2424.

Adams, John. "Defence [sic] of the Constitutions of the Governments of the United States." 1787. http://press-pubs.uchicago.edu/founders/documents/v1ch11s10.html. Accessed 10 June 2016.

Adorno, Theodor. "Commitment." *Aesthetics and Politics: The Key Texts of the Classic Debate Within German Marxism*. Ed. Theodor Adorno, Ernst Bloch, et al. Tr. Ronald Taylor. London: Verso, 1980. Print.

"AFRICA. Extract from Baron De Vastey," *Freedom's Journal*. February 7, 1829. Print.

"AFRICA. Extracts from Baron De Vastey." *Freedom's Journal*. February 14, 1829. Print.

Agamben, Giorgio. *Homo Sacer: Sovereign Power and Bare Life*. Stanford: Stanford University Press, 1998. Print.

Aljoe, Nicole. *Creole Testimonies: Slave Narratives from the British West Indies, 1709–1838*. Palgrave Macmillan, 2012. Print.

Allewaert, Monique. *Ariel's Ecology: Plantations, Personhood, and Colonialism in the American Tropics*. Minneapolis: U of Minnesota P, 2013. Print.

Almanach Royal d'Hayti pour l'année bissextile 1814, Onzième de l'indépendance, et la troisième du règne de sa majesté, présenté au roi, par P. Roux. Cap-Henry: P. Roux, 1814. Print.

© The Editor(s) (if applicable) and The Author(s) 2017   201
M.L. Daut, *Baron de Vastey and the Origins of Black Atlantic Humanism*, The New Urban Atlantic, DOI 10.1057/978-1-137-47067-6

Almanach Royal d'Hayti pour l'année bissextile 1815, Douzième de l'indépendance, et la quatrième du règne de sa majesté, présenté au roi, par P. Roux. Cap-Henry: P. Roux, 1815. Print.

Almanach Royal d'Hayti pour l'année bissextile 1816, Treizième de l'indépendance, et la cinquième du règne de sa majesté, présenté au roi, par P. Roux. Cap-Henry: P. Roux, 1816. Print.

Almanach Royal d'Hayti pour l'année bissextile 1820, Dix-septième de l'indépendance, et la neuvième du règne de sa majesté, présenté au roi, par Buon. Sans-Souci: Imprimerie Royale, 1820. Print.

Anaïde et Alcidore. Advertisement. *Journal typographique et bibliographique, publié Par P. Roux.* Paris: Chez L'Editeur, 1801. Print.

Anaïde et Alcidore. Advertisement. *La France révolutionnaire et impériale: annales de bibliographie méthodique. . .* 5 (1938). Print.

Anderson, Benedict. *Imagined Communities: Reflections on the Origin and Spread of Nationalism.* London: Verso, 1999.

"Anecdote of Naimbana." *The Anti-Slavery Record* 1.11 (Nov. 1835): 129. Print.

Aravamudan, Srinivas. *Tropicopolitans: Colonialism and Agency, 1688–1804.* Durham: Duke UP, 1999. Print.

Ardouin, Beaubrun. *Études sur l'histoire d'Haïti, 11 tomes réunis en 3 volumes.* Vol. 6. Port-au-Prince: Éditions Fardin, 2004. Print.

———. *Études sur l'histoire d'Haïti; suivies de la vie du général J.-M. Borgella,* 11 vols. Paris: Dezobry et E. Magdeleine, 1853–60. Print.

"Article III." *Edinburgh Review.* 1806. Print.

"Article V—Reflexions sur une Lettre de Mezeres [sic], Ex-Colon français, addressee à M.J.C.L. Sismonde de Sismondi, etc." *The Analectic Magazine* 9 May 1817: 403. Print.

"Article VI.," *Monthly Repository of Theology and General Literature* 14 (1819): 329. Print.

Bacon, Jacqueline. *Freedom's Journal: The First African American Newspaper.* New York: Lexington, 2007. Print.

Bakhtin, M.M. *The Dialogic Imagination.* Trans. Caryl Emerson and Michael Holquist. Ed. Michael Holquist. Austin: U of Texas P, 1981. Print.

"Baron De Vastey; Whites; Blacks; Hayti; Land." *Essex Register* 18.43, 27 May 1818: 2. Print.

Barthes, Roland. *On Racine.* Berkeley: University of California Press, 1992.

Baudry de Lozières, Louis Narcisse, *Précis pour le Sieur Pierre Dumas, habitant à la Marmelade, appelant de sentence de la sénéchaussée du Cap, rendue le 13 mars dernier; contre le Sieur Jean-Baptiste Auspice Dugaric Duzech, ci-devant Capitaine de mulâtres grenadiers-volontaires de Saint-Domingue, & la dame son épouse, se disant aux droits par transport d'un Sieur Jean-Claude Michaut, intimés; et le Sieur Michaut, en son nom personnel.* Port-au-Prince: L'Imprimerie Mozard, 1788.

Bauer, Ralph. "Hemispheric Studies." *PMLA* 124.1 (Jan. 2009): 234–50. Print.

Bay, Mia. *The White Image in the Black Mind: African-American Ideas about White People, 1830–1925.* Oxford: Oxford University Press, 2000.

Beecher, Jonathan. *Charles Fourier: The Visionary and His World.* Berkeley: U of California P, 1990. Print.

Bell, Madison Smartt. *Toussaint Louverture: A Biography.* New York: Vintage Books, 2008. Print.

Bellegarde-Smith, Patrick. *Haiti: The Breached Citadel.* Boulder: Westview Press, 1990. Print.

———. "Overview of Haitian Foreign Policy and Relations: A Schematic Analysis." *Haiti: Today and Tomorrow: An Interdisciplinary Study.* Ed. Charles Foster and Albert Valdman. Lanham: UP of America, 1984. 265–81. Print.

Belohlavek, John M. *Broken Glass: Caleb Cushing and the Shattering of the Union.* Kent, OH: Kent State University Press, 2005. Print.

Benot, Yves. "Grégoire contre Christophe: un manuscrit inédit." *Revue française d'histoire d'outre-mer.* 87.328–329 (2000): 143–48. Print.

Bentham, Jeremy. *Canada: Emancipate Your Colonies!* London: E. Wilson, 1838. Print.

Bergeaud, Émeric. *Stella.* Paris: E. Dentu, 1859.

Bernasconi, Robert. "A Haitian In Paris: Anténor Firmin as philosopher against racism." *Patterns of Prejudice* 42. 4–5 (2008): 365–383. Print.

Berrou, Raphaël, and Pradel Pompilus. *Histoire de la littérature haïtienne illustrée par les textes.* Vol. 1. Port-au-Prince: Éditions Caraïbes, 1975. Print.

Beverley, John. "The Margins at the Center: On Testimono" (Testimonial Narrative). *MFS: Modern Fiction Studies* 35.1 (Spring 1989): 11–28. Print.

Blanchelande, Philibert François Rouxel de. "Proclamation." *Supplément au numéro 91 de La Feuille du jour* (31 March 1792). Print.

Blane, William Newnham. *Travels through the United States and Canada.* London: Baldwin and Company, 1828. Print.

Boisrond-Tonnerre, Louis Félix. *Mémoires pour servir à l'histoire d'Haïti.* À Dessalines, Haiti: De l'imprimerie centrale du gouvernement. 1804. Print.

Bongie, Chris. "'Monotonies of History': Baron de Vastey and the Mulatto Legend of Derek Walcott's *Haitian Trilogy.*" *Yale French Studies: The Haiti Issue: 1804 and Nineteenth-Century French Studies* 107 (2005): 70–107. Print.

———. *Friends and Enemies: The Scribal Politics of Post/Colonial Literature.* Liverpool: Liverpool UP, 2008. Print.

———. "The Cry of History: Juste Chanlatte and the Unsettling (Presence) of Race in Early Haitian Literature." *MLN* 130.4 (2015): 807–835. Print.

———. *The Colonial System Unveiled.* Ed. and Tr. Chris Bongie. Liverpool: Liverpool UP, 2015. Print.

Bonilla, Yarimar. *Non-Sovereign Futures: French Caribbean Politics in the Wake of Disenchantment.* Chicago: U. of Chicago Press, 2015. Print.

"Boston: Friday Morning, Sept. 15." *Boston Daily Advertiser* (15 Sept 1815): 2. Print.

"Boston: Friday Morning, Sept. 15." *Enquirer.* 6 July 1816. Print.

Botelho, Keith M. "'Look on this picture, and on this': Framing Shakespeare in William Wells Brown's 'The Escape'". *Comparative Drama* 39.2 (2005): 187–212.

Boulle, Pierre H. "In Defense of Slavery: Eighteenth-Century Opposition to Abolition and the Origins of a Racist Ideology in France." *History from Below: Studies in Popular Protest and Popular Ideology.* Ed. Frederick Krantz. Oxford: Basil Blackwell, 1988: 219–46. Print.

Braziel, Jana Evans. "Haiti, Guantánomo, and the 'One Indispensable Nation': U.S. Imperialism, 'Apparent States,' and Post-colonial Problematics of Sovereignty." *Cultural Critique* 64 (Fall 2006): 127–60. Print.

Brecht, Bertolt. "The Epic Theatre and its Difficulties." Ed. and Tr. J. Willet. *Brecht on Theatre: The Development of an Aesthetic.* London: Methuen, 1974. Print.

Brickhouse, Anna. *Transamerican Literary Relations and the Nineteenth-Century Public Sphere.* Cambridge: Cambridge UP, 2004. Print.

Brière, Jean-François. "Du Sénégal aux Antilles: Gaspard-Théodore Mollien en Haïti, 1825–1831." *French Colonial History* 8 (2007): 71–79. Print.

——. *Haïti et la France, 1804–1848: Le rêve brisé.* Paris: Éditions Karthala, 2008.

Brooks, Linda Marie. "*Testimonio*'s Poetics of Performance." *Comparative Literature Studies* 42.2 (2005): 181–222.

Brown, Gordon S. *Toussaint's Clause: The Founding Fathers and the Haitian Revolution.* Oxford: U of Mississippi P, 2005. Print.

Brown, Vincent. *The Reaper's Garden: Death and Power in the World of Atlantic Slavery.* Cambridge, MA: Harvard University Press, 2008. Print.

Brown, William Wells. "A Lecture delivered before the Female Anti-Slavery Society of Salem." Ed. Ezra Greenspan. *William Wells Brown: A Reader.* Athens: University of Georgia Press, 2008: 107–29.

——. *The Black Man, His Antecedents, His Genius, and His Achievements.* New York: Thomas Hamilton, 1863. Print.

——. *Clotel; or the President's Daughter.* Ed. Robert Levine. Boston: Bedford/St. Martin's, 2000. Print.

Buck, Christopher. *Alain Locke: Faith and Philosophy.* Los Angeles: Kalimat Press, 2005. Print.

Buck-Morss. *Hegel, Haiti, and Univeral History.* Pittsburgh: U of Pittsburgh P, 2009. Print.

Buffon, Georges Louis Leclerc, Comte de. *De l'Homme.* Ed. Michèle Duchet. Paris: Bibliothèque d'Anthropologie François Maspero, 1971. Print.

———. *Histoire naturelle générale et particuliére, avec la description du cabinet du roy.* http://www.buffon.cnrs.fr/?lang= Web. Accessed 10 August 2015.

Candler, John. *Brief Notices of Hayti.* London: T. Ward and Co., 1842. Print.

"Carl Ritter's *Researches in the Island of Hayti.*" *The Foreign Quarterly Review* 20 (no. 39, October 1837): 73–97.

Carlyle, Thomas. "Occasional Discourse on the Nigger Question." *The Collected Works of Thomas Carlyle.* Vol. 13. London: Chapman and Hall, 1864. 1–28. Print.

Carretta, Vincent. "Introduction." *Unchained Voices: An Anthology of Black Authors in the English-Speaking World of the Eighteenth Century.* Ed. Vincent Carretta. Kentucky, 1996. 1–16.

———. *Equiano, the African: Biography of a Self-Made Man.* Atlanta: University of Georgia, Press, 2005.

"Carte de sûreté," Pompé[e] Vastey, 1794. Archives Nationales de la France. F7/4803.

"Cartes de sûreté des Normands à Paris." Association Parisienne de Généalogie Normande. http://www.apgn.org/cartes.htm. Web. Accessed 3 Oct. 2011.

Castera, Justin Emmanuel. *Bref coup d'oeil sur les origines de la presse haïtienne.* Port-au- Prince, Haiti: Imprimerie Henri Deschamps, 1986. Print.

Césaire, Aimé. *Discourse on Colonialism.* Trans. Joan Pinkham. 1972. New York: Monthly Review P, 2000. Print.

———. *La Tragédie du roi Christophe.* Paris: Présence Africaine, 1963. Print.

———. *Cahier d'un retour au pays natal.* Paris: Présence Africaine, 1983. Print.

Chan, Melissa. "Rudy Giuliani Says 'Black Lives Matter' Is 'Inherently Racist'." *Time Magazine.* 10 July 2016. http://time.com/4400259/rudy-giuliani-black-lives-matter/. Web. Accessed 20 July 2016.

Chanlatte, Juste. *Le Cri de la nature, ou, Hommage haytien au très-vénérable abbé H. Grégoire, auteur d'un ouvrage nouveau, intitulé De la littérature des Nègres, ou, Recherches sur leurs facultés individuelles, leurs qualités morales et leur littérature; suivies de notices sur la vie et les ouvrages des Négres qui se sont distingués dans les sciences, les lettres et les arts.* Cap-Haïtien: P. Roux, 1810. Print.

Cheesman, Clive. Ed. *The Armorial of Haiti: Symbols of Nobility in the Reign of Henry Christophe.* London: College of Arms, 2007. Print.

Christophe, Henry. *Manifeste du Roi.* Cap-Henry: P. Roux, 1814. Print.

———. Letter to the editor. *The Republican Watch-Tower* 28 July 1809. Print.

"Civilisation—Réflexions politiques sur quelques ouvrages et Journaux français concernant Hayti, par le Baron de Vastey, Secrétaire du Roi, Chevalier de l'ordre royal et militaire de Saint-Henry, Précepteur de Son Altesse Royale Monseigneur le Prince Royal d'Hayti, etc. À Sans-Souci, de l'Imprimerie royale, année 1817, quatorzième de l'indépendance" *Bibliothèque universelle des sciences, belles-lettres, et arts.* Genève: Imprimerie de la Bibliothèque universelle, 1819. Print.

Clavin, Matthew J. "Race, Rebellion, and the Gothic: Inventing the Haitian Revolution". *Early American Studies* 5.1 (2007): 1–29. Print.

———. *Toussaint Louverture and the American Civil War: The Promise and Peril of a Second Haitian Revolution.* Philadelphia: U of Pennsylvania P, 2010. Print.

Cohen, Laura and Jordan Stein. *Early African American Print Culture.* Philadelphia: U. of Pennsylvania Press, 2012. Print.

Cole, Hubert. *Christophe: King of Haiti.* London: Eyre & Spottiswoode, 1967. Print.

Colombel, Noël. *Examen d'un pamphlet, ayant pour titre: Essai sur les causes de la révolution et des guerres civiles d'Haïti.* Port-au-Prince, 1819. Print.

———. *Réflexions sur quelques faits relatifs à notre existence politique.* Port-au-Prince: De l'imprimerie du gouvernement, 1815. Print.

Colwill, Elizabeth. "Sex, Savagery, and Slavery in the Shaping of the French Body Politic." *From the Royal to the Republican Body: Incorporating the Political in Seventeenth and Eighteenth-Century France.* Eds. Sara E. Melzer and Kathryn Norberg. Berkeley: U of Calif. Press, 1998. 199-224. Print.

"Constitution of 1801." http://thelouvertureproject.org/index.php?title=Haitian_Constitution_of_1801_%28English%29. Web. Accessed 4 November 2015.

"Constitution of 1805." http://mjp.univ-perp.fr/constit/ht1805.htm Web. Accessed 12 December 2015.

"Constitution of 1807." http://mjp.univ-perp.fr/constit/ht1807.htm. Web. Accessed 14 February 2016. Print.

Cook, Mercer. *An Introduction to Haiti.* Washington, DC: Dept. of Cultural Affairs, Pan American Union, 1951. Print.

———. *Education in Haiti.* Washington, D.C.: Federal Security Agency, Office of Education, 1948. Print.

Cooper, Frederick. *Colonialism in Question: Theory, Knowledge, History.* Berkeley: University of California Press, 2005. Print.

Corbould, Clare. "At the Feet of Dessalines: Performing Haiti's Revolution during the New Negro Renaissance." *Beyond Blackface: African Amerians and the Creation of American Popular Culture.* Ed. W. Fitzhugh Brundage. Chapel Hill, NC: University of North Carolina Press, 2011. 249–88. Print.

Cordié, Carlo. "Il barone Pompée-Valentin de Vastey e l'indipendenza di Haiti (a proposito d'una recensione 'inedita' del Sismondi, scritta per il 'Conciliatore'". *Annali della scuola normale superiore di Pisa.* 2nd series. 26 (1957): 250–66. Print.

Cugoano, Ottobah, *Thoughts and Sentiments on the Evil and Wicked Traffic of the Human Species.* London, 1787. https://books.google.com/books?id=BkUS AQAAMAAJ&pg=PA112&lpg=PA112&dq=Is+it+not+strange+to+think,+t hat+they+who+ought+to+be+considered+as+the+most+learned+and+civilized +people+in+the+world,+that+they+should+carry+on+%E2%80%9D&source= bl&ots=r_or1kkrn7&sig=hfF7Zd7rB0Zad6Iwi8HACrPihx8&hl=en&sa=X &ved=0ahUKEwjJhcSclNXOAhWC2R4KHavJBXMQ6AEIMzAF#v=onepa ge&q&f=false. Web. Accessed 22 August 2016.

Curran, Andrew S. *The Anatomy of Blackness: Science and Slavery in an Age of Enlightenment*. Baltimore: Johns Hopkins University Press, 2011. Print.

Cushing, Caleb. "Article VI—Reflexions Politiques sur quelques Ouvrages et Journaux Français." *The North American Review and Miscellaneous Journals* 3.1, Jan. 1821: 112–34. Print.

Cushing, William. Ed. *Index to the North American Review*. Cambridge, MA: Press of John William and Son, 1878. Print.

Dain, Bruce. *A Hideous Monster of the Mind: American Race Theory and the Early Republic*. Cambridge: Harvard UP, 2002. Print.

Dalby, Jonathan. *Crime and Punishment in Jamaica: A Quantitative Analysis of the Assize Court Records, 1756–1856*. Social History Project, Department of History. University of the West Indies, 2000. Print.

Dash, J. Michael. *Culture and Customs of Haiti*. Westport, CT: Greenwood, 2001. Print.

———. *Literature and Ideology in Haiti, 1915–1961*. Palgrave Macmillan, 1981. Print.

———. "Nineteenth-Century Haiti and the Archipelago of the Americas: Anténor Firmin's Letters from St. Thomas." *Research in African Literatures* 35.2 (2004): 44–53. Print.

———. *Haiti and the United States: National Stereotypes and the Literary Imagination*. New York: St. Martin's Press, 1988. Print.

———. "Marvellous Realism: The Way Out of Negritude." *Caribbean Studies* 13.4 (Jan. 1973): 57–70. Print.

———. "Haïti Chimère: Revolutionary Universalism and its Caribbean Context." *Reinterpreting the Haitian Revolution and its Cultural Aftershocks*. Ed. Martin Munro and Elizabeth Walcott-Hackshaw. Mona, Jamaica: U of West Indies P, 2006. 9–37. Print.

———. "Before and Beyond Négritude." *A History of Literature in the Caribbean*. Eds. A. James Arnold, Julio Rodriguez-Luis and J. Michael Dash. Vol. 1. Philadelphia: John Benjamins, 1994. 529–46. Print.

———. "The Theater of the Haitian Revolution/The Haitian Revolution as Theater." *Small Axe* 9.2 (2005): 16–23. Print.

Daut, Marlene L. "Un-Silencing the Past: Boisrond-Tonnerre, Vastey, and the Re-Writing of the Haitian Revolution, 1804–1817." *South Atlantic Review* 74.1 (2009): 35–64. Print.

———. "The 'Alpha and Omega' of Haitian Literature: Baron de Vastey and the U.S. Audience of Haitian Political Writing." *Comparative Literature* 64.1 (2012): 49–72.

———. "From Classical French Poet to Militant Haitian Statesman: The Early Years and Poetry of the Baron de Vastey." *Research in African Literatures* 43.1 (2012): 35–57. Print.

———. *Tropics of Haiti: Race and the Literary History of the Haitian Revolution in the Atlantic World, 1789–1865*. Liverpool: Liverpool UP, 2015. Print.

————. "Monstrous Testimony: Baron de Vastey and the Politics of Black Memory." *The Colonial System Unveiled*. Ed. Chris Bongie. Liverpool: Liverpool UP, 2014. 173–210. Print.

————. "The 'Alpha and Omega' of Haitian Literature: Baron de Vastey and the U.S. Press," *The Haitian Revolution and the Early U.S.: Histories, Textualities, Geographies*. Eds. Elizabeth Maddock Dillon and Michael Drexler. University of Pennsylvania Press, 2017. 287–213. Print.

Davies, Carol Boyce. "Beyond Uni-Centricity: Transcultural Black Presences." *Research in African Literatures* 30.2 (1999): 96–109. Print.

Davis, David Brion. *Inhuman Bondage: The Rise and Fall of Slavery in the New World*. Oxford: Oxford University Press, 2006. Print.

Dayan, Joan. *Haiti, History, and the Gods*. Berkeley: University of California Press, 1995. Print.

Declaration of the Rights of Man and the Citizen. http://avalon.law.yale.edu/18th_century/rightsof.asp. Accessed 11 November 2015.

Descourtilz, Étienne. *Voyages d'un naturaliste en Haïti*. Paris: Dufart, père, 1809. Print.

Desormeaux, Daniel. "The First of the (Black) Memorialists: Toussaint L'Ouverture." *Yale Nineteenth-Century French Studies: The Haiti Issue* 107 (Spring 2005): 131–46. Print.

————. *Mémoires du général Toussaint Louverture*. Paris: Classiques Garnier, 2011. Print.

Desquiron, Jean. *Haïti à la une: une anthologie de la presse haïtienne de 1724 à 1934*. 6 Vols. Port-au-Prince, Haiti: Imprimeur II, 1993.

Dessalines, Jean-Jacques. "Proclamation à la Nation." http://www.haitilibre.com/article-2019-haiti-societe-nous-vous-souhaitons-une-bonne-fete-de-l-independance.html. Web. Accessed 16 Oct 2011.

Dessarts, N.-L.-M. *La Cruche d' Hypocrène*. Advertisement. *Les Siècles Littéraires de la France ou Nouveau dictionnaire historique, critique, et bibliographique* 6 (1801): 327. Print.

D'I***, C. *Anaïde et Alcidore*. Advertisement. *Bibliographie des ouvrages relatifs à l'amour, aux femmes, au mariage, etc.* 3 (1871): 233. Print.

Diawara, Manthia. "Englishness and Blackness: Cricket as Discourse on Colonialism". http://www.blackculturalstudies.net/m_diawara/callaloo.html. Web. Accessed 1 May 2016.

————. "One World in Relation: Édouard Glissant in Conversation with Manthia Diawara." *Journal of Contemporary African Art* 28 (Spring 2011): 4–19. Print.

Dickens, Charles. *Dickens's Dictionary of Paris: An Unconventional Handbook*. London: Macmillan, 1882. Print.

Dixon, Chris. *African America and Haiti: Emigration and Black Nationalism in the Nineteenth Century*. Westport: Greenwood Press, 2000. Print.

Dize, Nathan, Abby Broughton et al. *A Colony in Crisis: The Saint-Domingue Grain Shortage of 1789*. https://colonyincrisis.lib.umd.edu/. Web. Accessed 10 June 2016.

Douglass, Frederick. *Narrative of the Life of Frederick Douglass, an American Slave*. Cambridge: Belknap Press, 1960. Print.

———. "What to a Slave is the Fourth of July?" http://rbscp.lib.rochester.edu/2945. Web.Accessed 24 May 2016.

Drexler, Michael. "Haiti, Modernity, and U.S. Identities." *Early American Literature* 43. 2 (2008): 453–465. Print.

Drouin de Bercy, L. M. C. A. *De Saint-Domingue, de ses guerres, de ses révolutions, de ses ressources*. Paris: Chocquet, 1814.

Du Bois, W.E.B. *W.E.B. Du Bois: Writings: The Suppression of the African Slave-Trade, The Souls of Black Folk, Dusk of Dawn, Essays and Articles*. New York, NY: Library of America, 1986. Print.

———. Ed. *A Select Bibliography of the Negro American: A Compilation Made Under the Direction of Atlanta University*. Atlanta: The Atlanta University Press, 1905. Print.

Dubois, Laurent and Julius Scott. Eds. *Origins of the Black Atlantic*. New York: Routledge, 2009. Print.

Dubois, Laurent. *Avengers of the New World: The Story of the Haitian Revolution*. Cambridge: Harvard UP, 2004. Print.

———. *Haiti: The Aftershocks of History*. New York: Metropolitan Books, 2012. Print.

Duchet, Michèle. *Anthropologie et histoire au siècle des lumières: Buffon, Voltaire, Helvétius, Diderot*. Paris: Bibliothèque d'Anthropologie François Maspero, 1971. Print.

Ducrest, George. *Mémoires sur l'impératrice Josephine, ses contemporains, la cour de Navarre et de Malmaison*. Vol. 3. Paris : Ladvocat, 1828. Print.

Dumesle, Hérard. *Voyage dans le nord d'Hayti, ou, Révélations des lieux et des monuments Historiques*. Aux Cayes: De L'Imprimerie du Gouvernement, 1824. Print.

Dun, James Alexander. *Dangerous Neighbors: Making the Haitian Revolution in Early America*. Philadelphia: University of Pennsylvania Press, 2016. Print.

Durand, Oswald. "Tournée Littéraire et Sociale." *Haïti Littéraire et Sociale* 20 Sept. 1905: 404. Print.

Duras, Claire de. *Ourika*. Tr. John Fowles. New York: MLA, 1994. Print.

During, Simon. "Literature—Nationalism's Other? The Case for Revision." *Nation and Narration*. Ed. Homi K. Bhabha. London:Routlege, 1990. Print.

Edwards, Bryan. *The History Civil and Commercial, of the British Colonies in the West Indies: To which is Added, an Historical Survey of the French Colony in the Island of St. Domingo*. Edinburgh: Crosby and Letterman, 1798. Print.

Edwards, Phyllis I. "Sir Joseph Banks and the Botany of Captain Cook's Three Voyages of Exploration." Utah: Brigham Young University, 1978. Print.

Egerton, George. "Politics and Autobiography: Political Memoir as Polygenre." *Biography: An Interdisciplinary Quarterly* 15.3 (1992): 221–42. Print.

———. *Political Memoir: Essays on the Politics of Memory*. Psychology Press, 1994. Print.

Emmer, Pieter. "'A Spirit of Independence' or Lack of Education for the Market? Freedman and Asian Indentured Labourers in the Post-Emancipation Caribbean, 1834–1917." *After Slavery: Emancipation and its Discontents*. Ed. H. Temperly. London, 2000. 150–168. Print.

Ersch, Jean Samuel. *Supplément à la France litéraire* (sic) *de 1771–1796*. Hambourg: Bibliothécaire de L'Université de Jena, 1800. Print.

———. *Second supplément à la France Litéraire* (sic) *depuis 1771*. Hambourg: Chez H. G. Hoffmann, 1806. Print.

"Étienne Vigée." *Revue encyclopédique ou analyse raisonnée des productions les plus remarquables dans la littérature, les sciences et les arts* 7 (1820): 291. Print.

Equiano, Olaudah. *The Interesting Narrative and Other Writings*. New York: Penguin Classics, 2003. Print.

Esterquest, Ralph T. "L'Imprimerie Royale d'Hayti (1817–1819). A Little Known Royal Press of the Western Hemisphere." *The Papers of the Bibliographical Society of America* 34 (January 1940): 171–84. Print.

Ewcorstart, John K. "The Negro—not a distinct species." *Medical and Surgical Reporter* II (1858): 272.

"Extracts from the Baron De Vastey's work in answer to the ex-colonist Mazeres and others." *Freedom's Journal*. December 12, 1828. Print.

Eze, Emmanuel Chukwudi. Ed. *Race and the Enlightenment: A Reader*. Malden, MA: Blackwell Publishing, 1997. Print.

Fanini, J. C. *I Am within the Crowd*. Lincoln, NE: Writers Club P, 2002. Print.

Fanning, Sara. "The Roots of Early Black Nationalism: Northern African Americans' Invocations of Haiti in the Early Nineteenth Century." *Slavery & Abolition* 28.1 (2007): 61–85. Print.

Fanon, Frantz. *The Wretched of the Earth*. Tr. Constance Farrington. 1963. New York: Grove, 1968. Print.

———. *Black Skin, White Masks*. Tr. Charles L. Markmann. New York: Grove Press 1967. Print.

Fanuzzi, Robert. "Taste, Manners, and Miscegenation: French Racial Politics in the U.S." *American Literary History* 19.3 (2007): 573–602. Print.

Fardin, Dieudonné. *Histoire de la littérature haïtienne*. Port-au-Prince: Éditions Fardin, 1967. Print.

Farmer, Paul. *The Uses of Haiti*. Monroe, ME: Common Courage, 1994. Print.

———. *Aids and Accusation: The Geography of Blame*. Berkeley: U of California P, 1993. Print.

Faron, Olivier and Cyril Grange. "Un recensement parisien sous la Révolution. L'exemple des cartes de sûreté de 1793." *Mélanges de l'Ecole française de Rome, Italie et la Méditerranée* 111.2 (1999): 795–826. Print.

Faubert, Pierre. *Ogé; ou le préjugé de couleur.* Paris: Librairie de C. Maillet-Schmitz, 1856. Print.

———. "Aux Haïtiens." *Ogé; ou le préjugé de couleur.* Paris: Librairie de C. Maillet-Schmitz, 1856. Print.

Ferguson, Moira. Ed. *Nine Black Women: An Anthology of Nineteenth-Century Writers from the United States, Canada, Bermuda and the Caribbean.* London: Routledge, 1997. Print.

Festa, Lynn. *Sentimental Figures of Empire in Eighteenth-Century Britain and France.* Baltimore: Johns Hopkins University Press, 2006.

Fick, Carolyn. *The Making of Haiti: The Saint-Domingue Revolution from Below.* Knoxville: University of Tennessee Press, 1990. Print.

Fignolé, Jean-Claude. "Pour présenter Monsieur de Vastey, de René Philoctète" *Le Nouvelliste* (27 November 1975). Print.

Figueroa, Victor. *Prophetic Visions of the Past: Pan-Caribbean Representations of the Haitian Revolution.* Columbus, OH: The Ohio State University Press, 2015. Print.

Findlay, George Gillanders, and William West Holdsworth. *The History of the Wesleyan Methodist Missionary Society.* Vol. 2. London: The Epworth Press, 1921. Print.

Firmin, Anténor. *De L'Égalité des races humaines: anthropologie positive.* Paris: Librairie Cotillon, 1885. Print.

Fischer, Sibylle. *Modernity Disavowed: Haiti and the Cultures of Slavery in the Age of Revolution.* Durham: Duke UP, 2004. Print.

———. "Haiti: Fantasies of Bare Life." *Small Axe* 11.2 (2007): 1–15. Print.

Fleischer, Guillaume. *Annuaire de la Librairie, première année.* Paris: Chez Levrault frères, 1802. Print.

Franklin, James. *The Present State of Hayti.* London: John Murray, 1828. Print.

Frieze, Henry S. and Walter Denison. *Virgil's Aenid.* London: American Book Company, 1902. Print.

"From a Late English Paper." *City of Washington Gazette* 3.165, 21 May 1818: 2. Print.

"From the Catskill Recorder: Revolutionary Incidents. St. Domingo." *Rhode Island American* 13 Feb. 1821. Print.

Frossard, Benjamin Sigismund. *La Cause des esclaves nègres et des habitans de la Guinée, portée au Tribunal de la Justice, de la Réligion, de la Politique* [...] 2 vols. Lyon: Imprimerie d'Aimé de la Roche, 1789.

Fuss, Diana. "Corpse Poem." *Critical Inquiry* 30.1 (Autumn 2003): 1–30. Print.

Gaffield, Julia. *Haitian Connections in the Atlantic World: Recognition after Revolution.* Chapel Hil, NC: U. of North Carolina Press, 2015. Print.

Gaillard, Roger. "Monsieur de Vastey et la canaille" *Le Nouveau Monde* (27–28 December 1975). Print.

Garran de Coulon, Jean-Philippe. *Rapport sur les troubles de Saint-Domingue.* 4 vols. Paris: Imprimerie nationale, 1797–1799. Print.

Garraway, Doris L. "Empire of Freedom, Kingdom of Civilization: Henry Christophe, the Baron de Vastey, and the Paradoxes of Universalism in Postrevolutionary Haiti." *Small Axe* 39 (2012): 1–21. Print.

———. "Introduction." *Tree of Liberty: Cultural Legacies of the Haitian Revolution in the Atlantic World.* Ed. Doris L. Garraway. Charlottesville: U of Virginia P, 2008. 1–17. Print.

———. "Abolition, Sentiment, and the Problem of Agency in *Le système colonial dévoilé.*" *The Colonial System Unveiled.* Ed. Chris Bongie. Liverpool: Liverpool University Press. 211–246. Print.

———. "Print, Publics, and the Scene of Universal Equality in the Kingdom of Henry Christophe." *L'Esprit Créateur* 56.1 (Spring 2016): 82–100. Print.

Garrigus, John D. *Before Haiti: Race and Citizenship in French Saint-Domingue.* New York: Palgrave Macmillan, 2006. Print.

Gastine, Civique de. *Histoire de la république d'Haïti ou Saint-Domingue, l'esclavage et les Colons.* Paris: Chez Plancher, 1819. Print.

Gates Jr., Henry Louis. *Pioneers of the Black Atlantic: Five Slave Narratives, 1772–1815.* Washington, D.C.: Basic Civitas Books, 1998. Print.

Geggus, David. "The Naming of Haiti." *NWIG: New West Indian Guide* 71.1/2 (1997): 43–68. Print.

———. "The Caradeux and Colonial Memory." *The Impact of the Haitian Revolution in the Atlantic World.* Ed. David Geggus. Columbia: University of South Carolina Press, 2001: 231–46. Print.

———. *Haitian Revolutionary Studies.* Bloomington: Indiana UP, 2002. Print.

———. "Haiti's Declaration of Independence." *The Haitian Declaration of Independence: Creation, Context, and Legacy.* Ed. Julia Gaffield. Charlottesville, VA: U of Virginia Press, 2016. 25–41. Print.

Gilmore, Paul. *The Genuine Article: Race, Mass Culture, and American Literary Manhood.* Durham, NC: Duke University Press, 2001. Print.

Girard, Philippe. "The Ugly Duckling: The French Navy and the Saint-Domingue Expedition, 1801–1803." *International Journal of Naval History* 7.3 (2008). http://www.ijnhonline.org/wp-content/uploads/2012/01/Giraud.pdf. Web. Accessed 10 May 2014.

Glick, Jeremy. *The Black Radical Tragic: Performance, Aesthetics, and the Unfinished Haitian Revolution.* New York: New York University Press, 2016. Print.

Glick-Schiller, Nina, and Georges Fouron. *Georges Woke Up Laughing: Long Distance Nationalism and the Apparent State.* Durham: Duke UP, 2001. Print.

Glissant, Édouard. *Introduction à une poétique du divers.* Paris: Gallimard, 1996. Print.

———. *Monsieur Toussaint.* Tr. J. Michael Dash. Three Continets Press, 2005.

———. *Caribbean Discourse: Selected Essays.* Tr. J.Michael Dash. Charlottesville: UP of Virginia, 1989. Print.

———. *Poetics of Relation.* Tr. Betsy Wing. Ann Arbor: U of Michigan P, 1997. Print.

———. *Philosophie de la relation: poésie en étendue.* Paris: Gallimard, 2009. Print.

Gilroy, Paul. *The Black Atlantic: Modernity and Double Consciousness.* Cambridge, MA: Harvard UP, 1993. Print.

Glover, Kaiama. *Haiti Unbound: A Spiralist Challenge to the Postcolonial Canon.* Liverpool: Liverpool University Press, 2010. Print.

Goddu, Theresa. *Gothic America.* New York: Columbia University Press, 1997. Print.

Goudie, Sean. *Creole America: The West Indies and the Formation of Literature and Culture in the New Republic.* Philadelphia: U of Pennsylvania P, 2006. Print.

Goujard, Philippe. "L'homme de masses sans les masses, ou Le déchristianisateur malheureux." *Annales historiques de la Révolution française* 264 (1986): 160–80. Print.

Graeme, Bruce. *Drums of Destiny.* New York: G.P. Putnam's Sons, 1947. Print.

Grégoire, Henri (abbé de). *De la noblesse de la peau.* 1820. Paris: J. Millon, 1996. Print.

———. *De la littérature des Nègres, ou Recherches sur leurs facultés intellectuelles, leurs qualités morales et leur littérature.* Paris: Chez Maradan, 1808. Print.

———. *De la traite de l'esclavage des Noirs et des Blancs.* Paris: Adrien Égron, 1815. Print.

———. "Observations sur la constitution du Nord d'Haïti et sur les opinions qu'on s'est formées en France de ce gouvernement." *Revue française d'histoire d'outre mer* 87.328–329 (2000): 149–52. Print.

———. *Mémoire en faveur des gens de couleur ou sang-mêlés de St.-Domingue,* Paris: Belin, 1789. Print.

———. *An Inquiry Concerning the Intellectual and Moral Faculties and Literatures of Negro.* Tr. D.B. Warden. Brooklyn, NY: Thomas Kirk, 1810. Print.

Griggs, Earl Leslie, and Clifford H. Prator. *Henri Christophe and Thomas Clarkson: A Correspondence.* New York; Greenwood, 1968. Print.

Gronniosaw, Ukawsaw. *A Narrative of the Most Remarkable Particulars in the Life of James Albert Ukawsaw Gronniosaw, an African Prince, as Related by Himself.* Bath: W. Gye, 1772. Print.

Gros. *Isle de Saint-Domingue, province du Nord. Précis historique; qui expose dans le plus grand jour les manoeuvres contre révolutionnaires employées contre St.

Domingue; qui désigne et fait connoître les principaux Agents de tous les massacres, incendies, vols et dévastations qui s'y sont commis. Paris, 1793. Print.

Guide to the Selden Rodman Papers. Yale University Library. http://drs.library.yale.edu/HLTransformer/HLTransServlet?stylename=yul.ead2002.xhtml.xsl&pid=mssa:ms.0871&clear-stylesheetcache=yes. Accessed 6 January 2016. Web.

Hager, Christopher. *Word by Word: Emancipation and the Act of Writing.* Cambridge: Harvard UP, 2013. Print.

Hall, Stephen G. *A Faithful Account of the Race: African American Historical Writing in Nineteenth-Century America.* Chapel Hill: U. of North Carolina P, 2009. Print.

Hamilton, William. "To Joseph Banks." Banks Correspondence. British National Museum. 160–62. 1819. Unpublished Manuscript.

———. "Vines within the Tropics." *The Gardener's Magazine and Register of Rural and Domestic Improvement.* Ed. John Claudious Loudon. Vol. 5. (July 1829): 98–100. Print.

———. Application for Doctor Radcliffe's Traveling Fellowship. Kew Botanical Library and Archives. Director's Correspondence. Vol. 5. English Letters H.-L. 1832–35. Unpublished Manuscript.

———. *Memoir on the Cultivation of Wheat within the Tropics.* Plymouth, England: Henry H. Heydon, 1840. Print.

Hammerman, Dan. *Henri Christophe.* Manuscript held by New York Public Library. Mss 1984-011

Hanchard, Michael. "Black Memory vs. State Memory: Notes Toward a Method." *Small Axe* 26 (June 2008): 45–62. Print.

Hartman, Geoffrey. "On Traumatic Knowledge and Literary Study." *New Literary History* 26.3 (1995): 537–63. Print.

Harvey, William Woodis. *Sketches of Hayti: From the Expulsion of the French to the Death of Christophe.* London: Christophe. L. B. Seely and Son, 1827. Print.

"Hayti." *Liverpool Mercury* (5 May 1818). Print.

Hector, Michel. "Une autre voie de construction de l'État-nation: L'expérience christophienne (1806-1820)." M. Hector and Laënnec Hurbon. Eds. *Genèse de l'État haïtien (1804–1859).* Paris: Éditions de la Maison des sciences de l'homme, 2009. 243–72. Print.

Heinl, Nancy and Robert. *Written in Blood: The Story of the Haitian People, 1592–1995.* Lanham, MD: UP of America, 1996. Print.

Heuer, Jennifer. "The One-Drop Rule in Reverse? Interracial Marriages in Napoleonic and Restoration France." *Law and History Review* 27.3 (2009): 515-548. Print.

Hickey, Donald. "America's Response to Slave Revolts in Haiti." *JER* 2 (1982): 361–79. Print.

Hill, Errol. "The Revolutionary Tradition in Black Drama." *Theatre Journal* 38.4 (1986): 408–26. Print.

Hinks, Peter. *To Awaken My Afflicted Brethren: David Walker and the Problem of Antebellum Resistance.* University Park, PA: The Pennsylvania State UP, 2007. Print.

"History of Hayti" *Boston Commercial Gazette* 62.43, 31 Oct. 1822: 1. Print.

"History, Literature, and Present State of Hayti." *The British Review, and London Critical Journal* 15 (March 1820): 45–78. Print.

Hodgson, Kate. "'Internal Harmony, Peace to the Outside World': Imagining Community in Nineteenth-Century Haiti." *Paragraph* 37.2 (June 2014): 178–92. Print.

Hoffmann, Léon François. "Lamartine, Michelet, et les Haïtiens." Web. http://webcache.googleusercontent.com/search?q=cache:NSUNn8Q9OCUJ:class iques.uqac.ca/contemporains/hoffmann_leon_francois/lamartine_michelet_haitiens/lamartine.html+&cd=2&hl=en&ct=clnk&gl=us. 1985. Accessed 10 March 2015.

Hook, Theodore Edward. *Precepts and Practice.* London, Ward and Lock, 1857. Print.

Hopkirk, John Glassford. *An Account of the Insurrection in St Domingo, Begun in August 1791: Taken from Authentic Sources.* London: T. Cadell, 1833. Print.

Howard, Richard A. et al. "WILLIAM HAMILTON (1783–1856) AND THE PRODROMUS PLANTARUM INDIAE OCCIDENTALIS (1825).'" Web. http://biostor.org/reference/61820.text. Accessed 10 March 2014.

Hughes, Langston. "The Emperor Dessalines." *The Collected Works of Langston Hughes: The Plays to 1942.* Vol. 5. Eds. Leslie Catherine Sanders and Nancy Johnston. Columbia, MO: University of Missouri Press, 2002. 278–32. Print.

Hugo, Victor. *Bug-Jargal/Victor Hugo and Tamango/Prosper Mérimée: Histoires d'esclaves révoltés.* 1826. Ed. Gérard Gengembre. Paris: Pocket Classiques, 2004. Print.

Hulme, Peter. *Colonial Encounters: Europe and the Native Caribbean, 1492–1797.* London: Methuen, 1986. Print

Hume, David. *Essays on Treatises and Several Subjects.* Vol 1. 2nd Edition. London: A. Millar, 1760. Print.

Hunt, Alfred N. *Haiti's Influence on Antebellum America: Slumbering Volcano in the Caribbean.* Baton Rouge: Louisana State UP, 1988. Print.

Hurbon, Laënnec. *Comprendre Haïti: Essai sur l'État, la nation, la culture.* Paris: Karthala, 1987. Print.

Hutton, Clinton A. *The Logic and Historic Significance of the Haitian Revolution and the Cosmological Roots of Haitian Freedom.* Kingston, Jamaica: Arawak, 2005. Print.

Iannini, Christopher. *Fatal Revolutions: Natural History, West Indian Slavery, and the Routes of American Literature.* Chapel Hill: University of North Carolina Press, 2012. Print.

Irail, Simon Augustin. *Querelles littéraires, ou Mémoires pour servir à l'histoire des Révolutions de la république des lettres, depuis Homère jusqu'à nos jours.* Paris: Chez Durand, 1761. Print.

Jacobs, Harriet Ann. *Incidents in the Life of a Slave Girl.* New York: Signet Classics, 2000. Print.

James, C.L.R. *The Black Jacobins: Toussaint L'Ouverture and the San Domingo Revolution.* New York: Vintage Books. 1963, 1989. Print.

————. *Toussaint Louverture: The Story of the Only Successful Slave Revolt in History; A Play in Three Acts.* Ed. Christian Høgsbjerg. Durham, NC: Duke UP, 2012. Print.

James, Erica Caple. *Democratic Insecurities: Violence, Trauma, and Intervention in Haiti.* Berkeley: University of California Press, 2010. Print.

Jenson, Deborah. "Before Malcom X, Dessalines: A 'French' Tradition of Black Atlantic Radicalism." *International Journal of Francophone Studies* 10.3 (2007): 329–44. Print.

————. "From the Kidnappings of the Louvertures to the Alleged Kidnapping of Aristide: Legacies of Slavery in the Post/Colonial World." *Yale French Studies* 107 (2005): 162–86. Print.

————. *Beyond the Slave Narrative: Politics, Sex, and Manuscripts in the Haitian Revolution.* Liverpool: Liverpool University Press, 2011. Print.

————. "Toussaint Louverture, Spin Doctor? Launching the Haitian Revolution in the French media." *Tree of Liberty: Cultural Legacies of the Haitian Revolution in the Atlantic World.* Ed. Doris L. Garraway. Charlottesville, VA: U of Virgina P, 2008. 41–62. Print.

Jefferson, Thomas. *Notes on the State of Virginia.* Ed. William Peden. Chapel Hill: University of North Carolina Press, 1982.

Jonassaint, Jean. "Pour un projet de sauvegarde et d'édition critique d'oeuvres haïtiennes." *Littératures au Sud.* Ed. Marc Cheymol. Paris: Éditions des archives contemporaines, 2009. 197–207. Print.

Kadish, Doris and Deborah Jenson. Eds. *Poetry of Haitian Independence.* Tr. Norman Shapiro. New Haven, Yale UP, 2015. Print.

Kadish, Doris. "The Black Terror: Women's Responses to Slave Revolts in Haiti." *The French Review* 68.4 (March 1995): 668–80. Print.

Kaisary, Philip. *The Haitian Revolution in the Literary Imagination: Radical Horizons, Conservative Constraints.* Charlottesville, VA: U. of Virginia Press, 2014. Print.

Kant, Immanuel. *Observations on the Feeling of the Beautiful and the Sublime.* Tr. John T. Goldthwait. Berkeley: U. of California Press, 1960. Print.

Kazanjian, David. *The Brink of Freedom: Improvising Life in the Nineteenth-Century Atlantic World.* Durham, NC: Duke University Press, 2016. Print.

Kim, Julie Chun. "John Tyley and Botanical Illustration in the Eighteenth-Century Caribbean and Atlantic Worlds." London and the Americas Special Conference. Society for Early Americanists. 17 July 2014.

Krantz, Frederick. Ed. *History from Below: Studies in Popular Protest and Popular Ideology.* Oxford: Basil Blackwell, 1988. Print.

Krise, Thomas. Ed. *Caribbeana: An Anthology of English Literature of the West Indies, 1657–1777.* Chicago: U. of Chicago P., 1999. Print.

Kristeva, Julia. *Powers of Horror: An Essay on Abjection.* New York: Columbia University Press, 1982. Print.

L'Intermédiare des chercheurs et curieux. 34 (10 July 1896). Print.

L'Olivier de la paix. Cap-Henry: P. Roux, imprimerie du roi, 1815. Print.

Lachèvre, Frédéric. *Bibliographie sommaire de L'Almanach des Muses (1765–1833).* Paris: L. Giraud-Badin, 1928. Print.

Laferrière, Dany. "Monsieur de Vastey, de René Philoctète" *Le Petit Samedi soir* 3.88 (8–14 March 1975): 15. Print.

Lallié, Alfred. *Les noyades de Nantes.* Nantes: Imprimerie Vincent Forest et Émile Grimaud, 1878, 1879. Print.

Lamming, Georges. *The Pleasures of Exile.* Ann Arbor, U of Mich. P, 1991. Print.

"Last Days of Christophe, The." *Littell's Living Age* 48. 618 (29 March 1856): 799–804. Print

Lawless, Robert. *Haiti's Bad Press.* Rochester: Schenkman Books, 1992. Print.

Lavaysse, Jean-François Dauxion. *A Statistical, Commercial, and Political Description of Venezuela, Trinidad, Margarita, and Tobago.* London: G. & W. B. Whittaker, 1820. Print.

le Borgne de Boigne, Claude Pierre Joseph. *Nouveau système de colonisation.* Paris: Dondy Dupré, 1817. Print.

Leconte, Vergniaud. *Henri Christophe dans l'histoire d'Haïti.* Paris: Éditions Berger-Levrault, 1931. Print.

"Letter Concerning Hayti." *Blackwood's Edinburgh Magazine* 4 (1819): 130. Print.

Leyburn, James. *The Haitian People.* New Haven: Yale UP, 1966. Print.

Lindsay, Lisa A. and John Wood Sweet. Introduction. *Biography and the Black Atlantic.* Eds. Lisa A Lindsay and John Wood Sweet. Philadelphia. U. of Pennsylvania Press, 2014. 1–18. Print.

Locke, Alain. *The New Negro.* New York: Simon and Schuster, 1997. Print.

Logan, Rayford W. *The Diplomatic Relations of the United States with Haiti, 1776–1891.* Chapel Hill: U of North Carolina P, 1941. Print.

———. "Education in Haiti." *Journal of Negro History* 15 (October 1930): 401–60. Print.

Louverture, François Dominque Toussaint. *Mémoires du Général Toussaint-L'Ouverture, écrits par lui-même.* Ed. Joseph Saint-Rémy. Paris: Pagnerre, 1853. Print.

La Cruche d'Hypocrène. Advertisement. *Journal Général de la Littérature de France, troisième année.* Paris: Chez Truetel et Würtz, 1800. Print.

Lechevalier, A. *Le Pays de Caux.* Advertisement. *Bibliographie Méthodique de L'Arrondissement du Havre.* Le Havre, France: Imprimerie H. Micaux, 1901. Print.

Lemaistre, John Gustavus. *A Rough Sketch of Modern Paris*. London: J. Johnson, 1803. Print.

Le Pays de Caux. Advertisement. *Manuel du bibliographie Normand*. Paris, 1801. Print.

Le Peuple de la République d'Hayti à Messieurs Vastey & Limonade. Port-au-Prince: De L'Imprimerie du gouvernement, 1815. Print.

Lewis, R. B. *Light and Truth, Collected from the Bible and Ancient and Modern History, Containing the Universal History of the Colored and the Indian Race from the Creation of the World to the Present Time*. Boston: Benjam F. Roberts, 1844. Print.

Lewis, Gordon K. 1983: *Main Currents in Caribbean Thought: The Historical Evolution of Caribbean Society in Its Ideological Aspects, 1492–1900*. Baltimore: Johns Hopkins University Press, 1983. Print.

Lois et actes sous le règne de Jean-Jacques Dessalines. Port-au-Prince: Éditions Presses Nationales d'Haïti, 2006. Print.

Lubin, Maurice A. "In memoriam: Dr Mercer Cook." *Présence Africaine* 144 (4):156. Print.

Mackenzie, Charles. *Notes on Haiti, Made During a Residence in that Republic*. 2 vols. London: Henry Colburn and Richard Bentley, 1830. Print.

Madiou, Thomas. *Histoire d'Haïti, Tome I, 1492–1799*. Port-au-Prince: Éditions Deschamps, 1989. Print.

———. *Histoire d'Haïti, Tome III, 1803–1807*. Port-au-Prince: Éditions Deschamps, 1989. Print.

———. *Histoire d'Haïti, Tome VII, 1827–1843*. Port-au-Prince: Éditions Deschamps, 1989. Print.

Maffly-Kipp, Laurie F. *Setting Down the Sacred Past: African-American Race Histories*. Cambridge, MA: Harvard UP, 2010. Print.

Mahul, Alphonse Jacques. *Annuaire nécrologique* 2 (1821): 322. Print.

Mariátegui, José Carlos. *Jose Carlos Mariátegui: An Anthology*. Eds. Harry E. Vanden and Marc Becker. New York: Monthly Review Press, 2011. Print.

Malouet, Pierre-Victor. *Collection de mémoires sur les colonies et particulièrement sur Saint-Domingue*. Vol. 4. Paris: Baudouin, 1802. Print.

Marrant, John. *A Narrative of the Lord's Wonderful Dealings with John Marrant, a Black*. London: Gilbert and Plummer. 1785. Print.

Marx, Karl. "Estranged Labor." *The Political Theory Reader*. Ed. Paul Schumaker. Walden, MA: Wiley Blackwell, 2010. 137–40. Print.

Martineau, Harriet. *The Hour and the Man, a Romance*. 2 vols. London: Edward Moxon, 1841. Print.

Matthewson, Tim. "Jefferson and the Non-Recognition of Haiti." *American Philosophical Society* 140 (1996): 22–48. Print.

May, Gita. *Élisabeth Vigée Le Brun: The Odyssey of an Artist in an Age of Revolution*. New Haven, CT: Yale UP, 2005. Print.

Mazères, colon. *De L'Utilité des colonies, des causes intérieures de la perte de Saint Domingue et des moyens d'en recouvrer la possession.* Paris: Renard, 1814. Print.

Mazrui, Ali Al'Amin. *Power, Politics, and the African Condition.* Africa World Press Books, 2004. Print.

McClellan, James E. *Colonialism and Science: Saint Domingue in the Old Regime.* Baltimore: Johns Hopkins University Press, 1992. Print.

McCune Smith, James. *A Lecture of the Haytian Revolution with a Sketch of the Character of Toussaint L'Ouverture.* New York: Daniel Fanshaw, 1841. Print.

Métral, Antoine. "De la littérature haïtienne." *Revue encyclopédique* (1819): 1:524-37. Print.

———. "De la littérature haïtienne." *Revue encyclopédique* (1819): 3: 132–349. Print.

Miller, Christopher. *The French Atlantic Triangle: Literature and Culture of the Slave Trade.* Durham: Duke UP, 2008. Print.

Miller, May. "Christophe's Daughters." *Negro History in Thirteen Plays.* Eds. May Miller and Richard Willis. Associated Publishers, 1935. 251–64. Print.

Milscent, Jules Solime. "Considérations sur l'île d'Haïti, par J.S. Milscent, Haïtien." *L'Abeille Haytienne.* (1 August 1817): 5–9. Print.

———. "Des Devoirs du journaliste." *L'Abeille Haytienne: journal politique et littéraire.* Port-au-Prince. (January 1818): 11–12. Print.

———. "Intérieur." *L'Abeille Haytienne: journal politique et littéraire* (16 August 2017). Print.

———. "Suite des Considérations sur L'Ile d'Haïti." *L'Abeille Haytienne: journal politique et littéraire* (16 September 2017): 3–5. Print.

Mintz, Sidney. Foreword. *The Haitian People.* New Haven: Yale UP, 1966. Print.

"Miscellaneous and Literary Intelligence." *North American Review* 1.1, May 1815: 126–40. Print.

Mollien, Gaspard Théodore. *Haïti ou Saint-Domingue.* Ed. Francis Arzalier. 2 vols. Paris: L'Harmattan, 2006. Print.

"Monsieur de Vastey, de René Philoctète." *Lakansièl* (4 January 1976): 40. Print.

Montas, Michèle. "Un balançoire dans son coeur." *Le Nouvelliste* (1 December 1975). Print.

Montesquieu, Charles le Secondat (baron de). *The Spirit of the Laws.* Tr. Thomas Nugent. London: J. Noures and P. Vaillant, 1900. Print.

Moreau de Saint-Méry, Médéric-Louis-Élie. *Description topographique, physique, civile, politique et historique de la partie française de l'isle Saint-Domingue. Avec des observations générales sur sa population, sur le caractère & les moeurs de ses divers habitans; sur son climat, sa culture… accompagnées des détails les plus propres à faire connaître l'état de cette colonie à l'époque du 18 Octobre 1789; et d'une nouvelle carte de la totalité de l'isle. Par M. L. E. Moreau de Saint-Méry.* Philadelphia: Chez L'Auteur, 1797. Print.

Morgan, Philip D. *Slave Counterpoint: Black Culture in the Eighteenth-Century Chesapeake and Lowcountry.* Chapel Hill: University of North Carolina Press, 1998. Print.

Moten, Fred. "Democracy." *Keywords for American Cultural Studies.* Eds. Glenn Hendler and Bruce Burgett. New York: New York UP, 2007. Print.

Muthayala, John. *Reworlding America: Myth, History, and Narrative.* Columbus, OH: The Ohio State University Press, 2006. Print.

Nesbitt, Nick. "The Idea of 1804." *The Haiti Issue: 1804 and Nineteenth-Century French Studies. Yale French Studies* 107 (2005): 6–38. Print.

———. "Afterword." *The Colonial System Unveiled.* Ed. Chris Bongie. Liverpool: Liverpool University Press, 2014. 285–300. Print.

———. *Voicing Memory: History and Subjectivity in French Caribbean Literature.* Charlottesville, VA: University of Virginia Press, 2003. Print.

———. *Universal Emancipation: The Haitian Revolution and the Radical Enlightenment.* Charlottesville: University of Virginia Press, 2008.

———. *Caribbean Critique: Antillean Critical Theory from Toussaint to Glissant.* Liverpool: Liverpool UP, 2013. Print.

Nicholls, David G. *From Dessalines to Duvalier: Race, Colour and National Independence in Haiti.* Cambridge: Cambridge UP, 1979. Print.

———. "Pompée Valentin Vastey: Royalist and Revolutionary." *Revista de Historia de América* 109 (Jan–Jun 1990): 129–43. Print.

Nkrumah, Kwame. "Neo-Colonialism, the Last Stage of Imperialism." https://www.marxists.org/subject/africa/nkrumah/neo-colonialism/introduction.htm. Web. Accessed 10 May 2016.

Noël, François, and M. L. J. Carpentier. *Philologie française ou Dictionnaire étymologique critique, historique, anecdotique, littéraire, etc.* Paris: Le Normant Père, 1831. Print.

"*North American Review, The.*" *The Literary Gazette; or Journal of Criticism, Science, and the Arts* 1.7 (17 February 1821): 100-05. Print.

Nwankwo, Ifeoma Kiddoe. *Black Cosmopolitanism: Racial Consciousness and Transnational Identity in the Nineteenth-Century Americas.* Philadelphia, U. of Pennsylvania Press, 2005. Print.

O'Brien, Colleen. "Paternal Solicitude and Haitian Emigration: The First American Occupation?" *South Central Review.* 30.1 (Spring 2013): 32–54. Print.

Ong, Aiwha. *Flexible Citizenship: The Cultural Logics of Transnationality.* Durham, NC: Duke University Press, 1999. Print.

"Original and Interesting State Papers." *Liverpool Mercury* (3 April 1818). Print.

"Pagine inedite del 'Conciliatore'." *Museo del Risorgimento Nazionale.* Eds. Marcello Visconte Di Modrone. Milano, 1930. Print.

Pagliai, Letizia. *Sismondiana.* Polistampa, 2005. Print.

Peabody, Sue. *"There are no slaves in France': The Political Culture of Race and Slavery in the Ancien Régime.* Oxford: Oxford UP, 1996. Print.

———. "Négresse, Mulâtresse, Citoyenne: Gender and Emancipation in the French Caribbean 1650–1848." *Gender and Slave Emancipation in the Atlantic World*. Eds. Pamela Scully and Diana Paton. Durham: U. of North Carolina P, 2005. Print.

Parry, Benita. *Postcolonial Studies: A Materialist Critique*. London: Routledge, 2004. Print.

"Past and Present State of Hayti." *The Quarterly Review* 21.42 (April 1819): 430–60. Print.

Patterson, Orlando. *Slavery and Social Death: A Comparative Study*. Cambridge: Harvard UP, 1982. Print.

Perkins, Kathy A. Ed. *Black Female Playwrights: An Anthology of Plays Before 1850*. Bloomington, IN: Indiana UP, 1990. Print.

Phillips, Wendell. "Toussaint L'Ouverture." Ed. W. Phillips. *Speeches, Lectures, and Letters*. Boston: Lee and Shepard, 1884. 468–94. Print.

Philoctète, René. *Monsieur de Vastey*. Port-au-Prince: Éditions Fardin, 1975. Print.

———. Interview. *Callaloo* 15.3 (Summer 1992): 623–27. Print.

Plon-Nourrit. *Le Marquis de Bièvre, sa vie, ses calembours, ses comédies, 1747–1789*. 2 ed. Paris: Librairie Plon, 1910. Print.

Plummer, Brenda Gayle. *Haiti and the Great Powers, 1902–1915*. Baton Rouge: Louisiana State UP, 1988. Print.

Popkin, Jeremy. "Facing Racial Revolution: Captivity Narratives and Identity during the Saint-Domingue Insurrection." *Eighteenth-Century Studies* 36: 4 (2003). 511–33. Print.

Potkay, Adam. "Introduction". *Black Atlantic Writers of the Eighteenth Century: Living the New Exodus in England and the Americas*. Eds. A. Potkay and Sandra Burr. New York: St. Martin's Press, 1995. 1–22. Print.

Price-Mars, Jean. *So Spoke the Uncle*. Tr. Magadaline W. Shannon. Washington, D.C.: Three Continents Press, 1983. Print.

Quérard, Joseph-Marie. "Vastey (le baron Pompée Valentin de)." *La France Littéraire ou Dictionnaire bibliographique* 10 (1839): 65. Paris: Chez Firmin Didot Frères. Print.

Quevilly, Laurent. "Le fils de Jumiègois devenu bras droit d'un roi." Web. http://jumieges.free.fr/vastey.html. Accessed 10 March 2013.

———. Le *Baron de Vastey*. Books on Demand, 2014. Print.

Racine, Karen. "Imported Englishness: Henri Christophe's Education Programme in Haiti, 1806–1820." *Imported Modernity in Postcolonial State Formation: The Appropriation of Political, Educational, and Cultural Models in Nineteenth-Century Latin America*. Eds. Eugenia Roldán Vera and Marcelo Caruso. Frankfurt Am Main: Peter Lang, 2007. 205–30. Print.

Ragueneau de la Chainaye, Armand Henri. *Brunetiana: Recueil dédié à Jocrisse*. 15 ed. Paris, Mme Cavanagh, 1806. Print.

Raimond, Julien. *Mémoire sur les causes des troubles et des désastres de la colonie de Saint-Domingue.* Paris: Imprimerie du Cercle Royale, 1793. Print.

———. *Observations sur l'origine et les progrès du préjugé des colons blancs contre les hommes de couleur.* Paris: Belin, 1791. Print.

———. *Réponse aux considérations de M. Moreau, dit Saint-Méry, député à l'Assemblée nationale, sur les colonies, par M. Raymond.* Paris: Imprimerie du patriote français, 1791. Print.

———. *Réflexions sur les véritables causes des troubles et des désastres de nos colonies, notamment sur ceux de Saint-Domingue; avec les moyens à employer pour préserver cette colonie d'une ruine totale.* Paris: Imprimerie des patriotes, 1793. Print.

———. *Lettres de J. Raimond, à ses frères les hommes de couleur. En comparaison des originaux de sa correspondance, avec les extraits perfides qu'en ont fait MM. Page et Bruelly, dans un libelle intitulé: Developpement des causes, des troubles, et des désastres des Colonies françaises.* Paris: Imprimerie du cercle social, 1794. Print.

Rainsford, Marcus. *An Historical Account of the Black Empire of Hayti: Comprehending a View of the Principal Transactions in the Revolution of Saint Domingo; with its Ancient and Modern State.* London: Albion Press, 1805. Print.

Ramage, Craufurd Tait. *Beautiful Thoughts from French and Italian Authors.* 2nd ed. Liverpool: Edward Howell, 1875. Print.

Ramsey, Kate. *The Spirits and the Law: Vodou and Power in Haiti.* Chicago: University Press of Chicago, 2011. Print.

Raynal, Abbé Guillaume-Thomas. *Histoire philosophique et politique des établissemens et du commerce des Européens dans les deux Indes.* 3rd ed. 10 vols. Geneva: Jean-Leonard Pellet, 1780–84. Print.

Redpath, James. *Toussaint L'Ouverture: A Biography and Autobiography.* Ed. James Redpath. Boston: James Redpath, 1863. Print.

———. *Echoes of Harper's Ferry.* Boston: Thayer and Eldridge, 1860. Print.

Regaldo, M. *Un milieu intellectuel: la décade philosophiquee.* 5 vols. Lille: Atelier de Reproduction des thèses, 1976. Print.

Reinhardt, Catherine A. *Claims to Memory: Beyond Slavery and Emancipation in the French Caribbean.* New York: Berghan Books, 2006. Print.

"Researches in Hayti." *The Museum of Foreign Literature, Science, and Art* 32 (March 1838): 333. Print.

Résil, Gérard, "Monsieur de Vastey, de René Philoctète" *Le Petit samedi soir* 3.95 (3–9 May 1975): 12 and 21. Print.

"Review of New Books." *The Literary Gazette; or Journal of Criticism, Science, and the Arts.* 17 Feb 1821. Print.

"Review of New Books." *The Literary Gazette and Journal of Belles Lettres, Arts, Sciences.* 12 December 1818: 790. Print.

Rev. of Vastey (Pompée Valentin). *Les Ombres; ou les vivans qui sont mort, Almanach pour l'an X*. Paris: L'imprimerie de la Rue Cassette, 1801. 146. Print.

Rev. of *La Cruche d'Hippocrène*. *Almanach des Muses pour l'an IX de la République Française*. Paris: Chez Louis, 1801. Print.

Ribbe, Claude M. *Le Crime de Napoléon*. Édition Privé, 2005. Print.

Rigaud, André. *Mémoire du Général de Brigade André Rigaud, en Réfutation des écrits Calomnieux contre les citoyens de couleur de Saint-Domingue*. Aux Cayes: L'Imprimerie de LeMéry, 1797. Print.

Rodman, Selden. *The Revolutionists, a Tragedy in Three Acts*. New York: Duell, Sloan, & Pierce, 1942. Print.

———. *Les Révolutionnaires*. Tr. Camille Lhérisson. Port-au-Prince, Haïti: Imprimerie de l'état, 1942. Print.

Rodriguez, Junius P. "African Institution." *Encyclopedia of Emancipation and Abolition in the Transatlantic World*. Ed. Junius Rodriguez. New York: Routledge, 2015. 12–14. Print.

Romain, C. *Le district de Cany pendant la Révolution*. Yvetot: Imprimerie A. Bretteville, July 1899. Print.

Romain Jean-Baptiste, *Noms de lieux d'époque coloniale en Haïti: essai sur la toponymie du nord à l'usage des étudiants*. Port-au-Prince: Imprimerie du gouvernement, 1960. Print.

Roumain, Jacques. *Masters of the Dew*. Tr. Langston Hughes and Mercer Cook. Heineman, 1978. Print.

Routledge Dictionary of Cultural References in Modern French. Ed. Michael Mould. London: Routledge, 2011. Print.

"Royalty." *Niles Weekly Register* 11. 271, 9 Nov. 1816: 168. Print.

Rudé, George and Frederick Krantz. Eds. *History from Below: Studies in Popular Protest and Popular Ideology in Honour of George Rudé*. Montréal: Concordia University, 1985. Print.

"Rue de Richelieu: Villes et Monuments." *Imago Mundi Dictionnaire*. Web. http://www.cosmovisions.com/monuParisRueRichelieu.htm. Accessed 1 December 2009.

Sabin, Joseph. *Bibliotheca Americana: A dictionary of books relating to America from its discovery to the present* time. Vol 5. New York: J. Sabin & Sons, 1873. Print.

Saillant, John. "'Wipe away All Tears from Their Eyes': John Marrant's Theology in the Black Atlantic, 1785–1808." *Journal of Millenial Studies*. 1.2. http://www.mille.org/publications/winter98/saillant.PDF. Web. Accessed 12 January 2017.

Saint-Aubin, Arthur F. "Editing Toussaint Louverture's Memoir: A Profile in Black" *Journal of Haitian Studies* 17.1 (Spring 2011).

Saint-Rémy, Joseph. Ed. *Mémoire pour servir à l'histoire d'Haïti*. Louis-Félix Boisrond-Tonnerre. Port-au-Prince, 1851. Print.

———. *Pétion et Haïti, étude monographique et historique.* Vol. 4. Paris: Auguste Durand, 1857. Print.

Sanchez, Romy. "Enjeux politiques d'une circulation américaine des savoirs: la bibliothèque abolitionniste de Jorge Davidson." *Les savoirs-mondes: mobilité et circulation des savoirs depuis le moyen age.* Rennes: Presses Universitaires de Rennes, 2015. 461–74. Print.

Sancho, Ignatius. *Letters of the Late Ignatius Sancho, An African. In Two Volumes. To Which Are Prefixed, Memoirs of His Life.* 2 vols. London: Printed by J. Nichols, 1782. Print.

Sansay, Leonora. *Secret History, or the Horrors of Santo Domingo and Laura.* Ed. Michael Drexler. Ontario, Canada: Broadview Editions, 2007. Print.

Sartre, Jean Paul. *Colonialism and Neocolonialism.* Trans. Azzedine Haddour, Steve Brewer, and Terry McWilliams. New York: Routledge, 2001. Print.

Saunders, Prince. *Haytian Papers: A Collection of the Very Interesting Proclamations, and Other Official Documents; together with Some Account of the Rise, Progress, and Present State of the Kingdom of Hayti.* London: W. Reed, 1816. Print.

———. *A Memoir Presented to the American Convention for Promoting the Abolition of Slavery, And Improving the Condition of the African Race, December 11th, 1818.* Philadelphia: Dennis Heartt, 1818. Print.

Schade, Louis. *A Book for the "impending Crisis"! Appeal to the Common Sense and Patriotism of the People of the United States. "Helperism" Annihilated! The "irrepressible Conflict" and Its Consequences!.* Washington, D.C.: Little, Brown, and Company, 1860. Print.

Schiebinger, Londa. *Plants and Empire: Colonial Bioprospecting in the Atlantic World.* Cambridge, MA: Harvard UP, 2007. Print.

Schoelcher, Victor. *Colonies étrangères et Haïti: résultats de l'émancipation anglaise.* Paris: Pagnerre, 1843. Print.

———. *Vie de Toussaint Louverture.* Paris: Éditions Karthala, 1982. Print.

Schomburg, Arthur. "The Negro Digs up His Past." http://hisblkamerica2012. voices.wooster.edu/files/2012/01/Arthur-Schomburg-The-Negro-Digs-Up-His-Past.pdf. Web. Accessed 15 May 2016.

Schuller, Karin. "From Liberalism to Racism: German Historians, Journalists, and the Haitian Revolution From the Late Eighteenth to the Early Twentieth Centuries." *The Impact of the Haitian Revolution in the Atlantic World.* Ed. David Patrick Geggus. Columbia, SC: U of South Carolina P, 2001. 23–43. Print.

Scott, David. *Conscripts of Modernity: The Tragedy of Colonial Enlightenment.* Durham: Duke UP, 2004. Print.

Scott, Joan Wallach. "The Evidence of Experience." *The Historic Turn in the Human Sciences.* Ed. Terence J. McDonald. Ann Arbor: U of Michigan P, 1996. 379–406. Print.

Sepinwall, Alyssa Goldstein. "Exporting the Revolution: Grégoire, Haiti and the Colonial Laboratory, 1815–1827." *The Abbé Grégoire and His World*. Eds. Richard Popkin and Jeremy H. Popkin. Boston: Kluwer Academic, 2000. Print.

———. *The Abbé Grégoire and the French Revolution: The Making of Modern Universalism*. Berekely: U of California P, 2005. Print.

Sharp, Granville. *A Representation of the Injustice and Dangerous Tendency of Tolerating Slavery, or of Admitting the Least Claim of Private Property in the Persons of Men, in England*. London, Benjamin White, 1769. Print.

Sheller, Mimi. " 'The Haytian Fear': Racial Projects and Competing Reactions to the First Black Republic." *Politics and Society* 6 (1999): 283–303. Print.

Sidbury, James. "Saint Domingue in Virginia: Ideology, Local Meanings, and Resistance to Slavery, 1790–1800." *The Journal of Southern History* 63.3 (1997): 531–52. Print.

Smith, Faith. *Creole Recitations: John Jacob Thomas and Colonial Formation in the Late Nineteenth-Century Caribbean*. Charlottesville, VA: U. of Virginia Press, 2002. Print.

Stanley, Amy Dru. *From Bondage to Contract: Wage Labor, Marriage, and the Market in the Age of Slave Emancipation*. Cambridge: Cambridge University Press, 1998. Print.

"'State of Hayti.' Rev. of 'La [sic] Système colonial dévoilé'—Par le Baron de Vastey." *The Port-Folio* 7.4 (April 1819): 315. Print.

Stoll, David. *Rigoberta Menchù and the Story of All Poor Guatemalans*. Boulder, CO: Westview Press, 1999. Print.

"Strafford Indictment." *Middlesex Assizes Register, 1804–1819*. Manuscript held by Jamaica National Archives. February 1817. 1A/7/4/3, Pleas of the Crown, Middlesex.

Tardieu, Patrick D. "P. Roux et Leméry: Imprimeurs de Saint-Domingue à Haïti." *Revue de la société haïtienne d'histoire et de géographie* 218 (July–September 2004): 1–30. Print.

Thatcher, B.B. *Memoir of Phillis Wheatley, A Native African and a Slave*. Boston: Geo W. Light, 1834. Print.

"The Annual Report of the Library Company of Philadelphia for the Year 1971." Philadelphia: The Library Company of Philadelphia, 1972, 52. Print.

"The Namesakes." *Baltimore Patriot* 5.117 (19 May 1815) 2. Print.

Thomasson, Fredrik. "Sweden and Haiti 1791–1831." Shaking Up the World? Global Effects of Haitian Tremors: 1791, 2010. Symposium, University of Aarhus, Denmark. August 10–12, 2017.

Thwaites, Elizabeth Hart. "Letter to a Friend." *Nine Black Women: An Anthology of Nineteenth-Century Writers from the United States, Canada, Bermuda and the Caribbean*. Ed. Moira Ferguson. London: Routledge, 1997. Print. 18–21.

"*Toussaint L'Ouverture: a Biography and Autobiography.*" Review. *The North American Review.* 98. 202 (1864): 595–602. Print.

"Translated for the Boston Palladium, Cape Henry (Hayti) Aug. 20." *Daily National Intelligencer* [sic] 4.118, 16 Oct. 1816: 2. Print.

Trinkle, Dennis A. *The Napoleonic Press: The Public Sphere and Oppositionary Journalism.* Lewiston, NY: Edwin Mellen P, 2002. Print.

Trouillot, Hénock. "Le gouvernement du roi Henri Christophe." *Revue de la société Haïtienne d'histoire de géographie et de géologie* 35. 116 (October–December 1972): 1–145.

———. *Les Origines sociales de la littérature haïtienne.* Port-au-Prince, Impr. N.A. Théodore, 1962.

Trouillot, Michel-Rolph. "The Odd and the Ordinary." *Cimarrón* 2.3 (1990): 3–12. Print.

———. *Silencing the Past: Power and the Production of History.* Boston: Beacon Press, 1995. Print.

Turner, Richard Brent. "Islam in the African-American Experience." *The Black Studies Reader.* Eds. Jacqueline Bobo, Cynthia Hudley, and Claudine Michel. London: Routledge, 2004. 445–71. Print.

Twa, Lindsey J. "Jean-Jacques Dessalines: Demon, Demigod, and Everything in Between." *Romantic Circles.* https://www.rc.umd.edu/praxis/circulations/HTML/praxis.2011.twa.html. Web. Accessed 10 April 2016.

Tyson, George F. *Toussaint L'Ouverture.* New York: Prentice Hall, 1975. Print.

Ulysee, Gina. *Why Haiti Needs New Narratives: A Post-Quake Chronicle.* Middletown, CT: Wesleyan UP, 2015. Print.

Vandercook, John W. *Black Majesty: The Life of Christophe King of Haiti.* New York: Harper and Brothers, 1928. Print.

Vastey, Pompée Valentin de. "Derniers Adieux." *La Mouche, journal des grâces.* 1799.

———."Épigramme" (3). *Journal des Arts, de Littérature et de Commerce.* 1807. Print.

———. "Épître à Monsieur Syntaxe, satire." *La Décade Philosophique.* 1802.

———. "FRAGMENT d'un poëme sur le pays de Caux." *La Décade Philosophique.* 1801. 556. Print.

———."L'Aurore du Siècle—Satire." *Journal des Arts, de Littérature, et de Commerce.* 18 May 1809: 137. Print.

———. "La Guerre et L'Amour." *La Mouche, journal des grâces* 1799. Print.

———."Le Monde Primitif—Allégorie." *Journal des Arts, de Littérature, et de Commerce* 22 July 1809: 10–12. Print.

———."Les Cauchoises, fragment d'un *Poëme sur le Pays de Caux.*" *La Décade Philosophique, Littéraire, et Politique* 3 Jan. 1801: 42–43. Print.

———. "Les Soupçons." *Journal des Arts, de Littérature et de Commerce* 20 Mar. 1809: 154. Print.

———."L'Explication–Elégie" *Journal des Arts, de Science*. 17 and 19 June 1809: 382–83. Print.

———. "L'Origine des procès en Normandie." *La Mouche, journal des grâces*. 1799. Print.

———. "Satire (1)." *Journal des Arts, de Littérature et de Commerce*. 14 Mar. 1809: 102-07. Print.

———. "Satire (2)." *Journal des Arts, de Littérature et de Commerce*. 26 Apr. 1809: 444–45. Print.

Vastey, Baron de. *Essai sur les causes de la révolution et des guerres civiles d'Hayti, faisant suite au Réflexions politiques sur quelques ouvrages et journaux français concernant Hayti*. Sans-Souci, Haïti: L'Imprimerie Royale, 1819. Print.

———. *Le Cri de la patrie*. Cap-Henry: Chez P. Roux, 1815. Print.

———. *Le Cri de la conscience*. Cap-Henry, Chez P. Roux, 1815. Print.

———. *Le Système coloniale dévoilé*. Cap-Henry: P. Roux Imprimerie du Roi, 1814. Print.

———. *Notes à M. le Baron V.P. de Malouet*. Cap-Henry: Chez P. Roux, 1814. Print.

———. *À Mes Concitoyens*. Cap-Henry: P. Roux, imprimeur du Roi, 1815. Print

———. *Réflexions adressées aux Haytiens de partie de l'Ouest et du Sud, sur l'horrible assassinat du Général Delvare, commis au Port-au-Prince, dans la nuit du 25 Décembre 1815, par les ordres de Pétion*. Cap-Henry: P. Roux, 1816. Print.

———. *Communication officielle de trois lettres de Catineau Laroche: ex-colon, agent de Pétion; imprimées et publiées par ordre du gouvernement*. Cap-Henry: P. Roux, imprimeur du Roi, 1816. Print.

———. *Translation of an Official Communication From The Government of Hayti, Dated 29 February 1816*. Tr. Marcus Rainsford. Bristol: John Evans Company, 1816. Print.

———. *Réflexions politiques sur quelques ouvrages et journaux français concernant Hayti*. Cap-Henry: Chez P. Roux, 1817. Print.

———. *Réflexions sur une lettre de Mazères, ex-colon français, . . . sur les noirs et les blancs, la civilisation de l'Afrique, le Royaume d'Hayti, etc*. Sans Souci: L'Imprimerie Royale, 1816. Print.

———. *Reflexions on the Blacks and Whites: Remarks upon a Letter Addressed by M. Mazères, a French Ex-Colonist, to J.C.L. Sismonde de Sismondi ...* [Tr. William Hamilton]. London : J. Hatchard, 1817. Print.

———. *Relation de la fête de la Reine S. M. D'Hayti*. Cap-Henry: Chez P. Roux, 1816. Print.

———. *Political Remarks on some French Works and Newspapers, concerning Hayti*. [Tr. William Hamilton]. Sans Souci: King's Printing Office, 1818. Print.

———. *De Negerstaat van Hayti of Sint Domingo, geschetst in zijne geschiedenis en in zijnen tegenwoordigen toestand; naar het Engelsche der QUARTERLY REVIEW, en naar het Fransche geschrift des Negers, Baron de Vastey, Minister des gewezen Konings Christophe (Henri I)*. Amsterdam: G. A. Diederichsen en Zoon, 1821. Print.

———. *An Essay on the Causes of the Revolution and Civil Wars of Hayti: Being a Sequel to the Political remarks upon Certain French Publications and Journals Concerning Hayti*. [Tr. William Hamilton]. Exeter: Western Luminary Office, 1823. Print.

"Vastey, P. J. V. of Bacqueville." *The Repertory of Arts, Manufactures, and Agriculture*. London: Repertory Office, Hatton Garden, 1821. 127. Print.

Vaval, Duraciné. *Histoire de la littérature haïtienne, ou 'L'âme noire.'* Port-au-Prince: Auguste. A. Heraux, 1933. Print.

Vergès, Françoise. *Nègre je suis, nègre je resterai: Aimé Césaire entretiens avec Françoise Vergès*. Paris: Albin Michel, 2005. Print.

Vigée, Jean-Baptiste Etienne. "À Pompée Valentin Vastey." *Almanach des Muses pour L'an XI*. Paris: Chez Louis, 1803. 64. Print.

———. "Représaille" (sic). *Almanach des Muses ou choix de poésies fugitives de 1808*. Paris: Chez Louis, 1808. 251. Print.

Voltaire, François Marie Arouet de. *Essais sur les mœurs*. Web. http://www.voltaire-integral.com/Html/11/04INT_10.html#i2. Web. Accessed 10 February 2015.

Walcott, Derek. *The Haitian Trilogy: Henri Christophe, Drums and Colours, and The Haytian Earth*. New York: Farrar, Straus, and Giroux, 2002. Print.

———. *What the Twilight Says: Essays*. New York: Farrar, Strauss, and Giroux, 1998. Print.

Wallerstein, Immanuel. "The Caribbean and the World System." *Caribbean Dialogue*. 8.3 (2002): 15–30. Print.

Walsh, John Patrick. "Toussaint Louverture at a Crossroads: The 'Mémoire' of the 'First Soldier of the Republic of Saint-Domingue'." *Journal of Haitian Studies* 17.1 (Spring 2011): 88–105. Print.

———. *Free and French in the Caribbean: Toussaint Louverture, Aimé Césaire and Narratives of Loyal Opposition*. Bloomington, IN: Indiana UP, 2013. Print.

Wattara, Mamadou. "*Le peuple des terres mêlées* de René Philoctète: Au-délà de la spirale." *Antillanité, créolité, littérature-monde*. Eds. Isabelle Constant, Kahiudi C. Mabana et al. Newcastle upon Tyne: Cambridge Scholars Publishing, 2013. 83–96. Print.

Weekly Recorder. July 10, 1816. Print.

Weheliye, Alexander. *Habeas Viscus: Racializing Assemblages, Biopolitics, and Black Feminist Theories of the Human*. Durham, NC: Duke Unviersity Press, 2014. Print.

Wheatley, Phillis. *The Collected Works of Phillis Wheatley*. Ed. John Shields. New York, Oxford University Press, 1988. Print.

Whipple, Charles K. "Falsehood in Support of Slavery (From the Boston Atlas and Daily Bee)." *Liberator, published as the Liberator* 30.3, 20 Jan 1860: 10. Print.

Whipple, Charles K. "Falsehood in Support of Slavery (From the Boston Atlas and Daily Bee)." *Harper's Weekly*, September 28, 1861. Print.

White, Ashli. "The Limits of Fear: The Saint Dominguan Challenge to Slave Trade Abolition in the United States." *Early American Studies: An Interdisciplinary Journal* 2.2 (2004): 362–97. Print.

———. *Encountering Revolution: Haiti and the Making of the Early Republic.* Baltimore: The Johns Hopkins UP, 2010. Print.

Wigmoore, Francis. "Nineteenth- and Early-Twentieth-Century Perspectives on Women in the Discourses of Radical Black Caribbean Men." *Small Axe* 13 (2003): 116–39. Print.

Wilberforce, William. *The Correspondence of William Wilberforce.* Eds. Samuel Wilberforce and Robert Isaac Wilberforce. Vol. 1. Philadelphia: Henry Perkins, 1841. Print.

Wilentz, Amy. *The Rainy Season: Haiti since Duvalier.* New York: Simon & Schuster, 1990. Print.

Williams-Wynn, Frances. *Diaries of a Lady of Quality from 1797–1844.* Ed. A. Hayward. 2 ed. London: Longman, Green, Longman, Roberts, and Green, 1864. Print

Wirzbicki, Peter. "'The Light of Knowledge Follows the Impulse of Revolutions': Prince Saunders, Baron de Vastey and the Haitian Influence on Antebellum Black Ideas of Elevation and Education." *Slavery & Abolition* 36.2 (2015) 275–97. Print.

Wood, Marcus. *Blind Memory: Visual Representations of Slavery in England and America.* London: Routledge, 2000. Print.

———. *Slavery, Empathy, and Pornography.* Oxford: Oxford University Press, 2002. Print.

Wright, John. *Refutation of the sophisms, gross misrepresentations, and erroneous quotations contained in 'An American's' 'Letter to the Edinburgh reviewers.'* Washington, D.C.: Printed for the Author, 1820. Print.

Young, Robert. *Colonial Desire: Hybridity in Theory, Culture, and Race.* New York: Routledge, 1995. Print.

Youngquist, Paul and Grégory Pierrot. Introduction. *An Historical Account of the Black Empire of Hayti.* Eds. Paul Youngquist and Grégory Pierrot. Durham: Duke UP, 2013. Print.

Yúdice, George. 1991: "*Testimonio* and Postmodernism." *Latin American Perspectives* 18.3: 15–31. Print.

Ziarek, Ewa. "Bare Life." *Impasses of the Post-Global: Theory in the Era of Climate Change.* Ed. Henry Sussman. Vol. 2. Web. 15 November 2015. http://quod.lib.umich.edu/o/ohp/10803281.0001.001/1:11/--impasses-of-the-post-global-theory-in-the-era-of-climate?rgn=div1;view=fulltext.

Zuckerman, Michael. "The Power of Blackness: Thomas Jefferson and Revolution in Saint-Domingue." *Almost Chosen People: Oblique Biographies in the American Grain.* Ed. Conor Cruise O'Brien. Berkeley: U of California P, 1993. 280–93. Print.

Author Index

A

Adams, John, 98
Adorno, Theodor, 126
Agamben, Giorgio
  Bare life, 130
Aljoe, Nicole, 22, 124
Alleweart, Monique, 111
Anderson, Benedict, 124
Aravamudan, Srinivas, 115
Ardouin, Beaubrun, 7, 50, 58, 59, 165

B

Banks, Joseph, 75, 80, 82, 83, 96
Barthes, Roland, 155
Bauer, Ralph, 95
Beard, John Relly, 93
Beckett, Samuel, 192
Benezet, Anthony, xx
Benot, Yves, 106
Bercy, Drouin de, 23, 132
Bergeaud, Émeric, 118
Bernardin de Saint-Pierre, xx
Beverley, John, 24, 114, 116, 118, 120

Biassou, Georges (Jean), 179
Birt, Jabez Sheen, 56
Bland, Sandra, xxxix
Boileau, 46
Boisrond-Tonnerre, Louis-Félix, 14, 15, 21, 45, 118
Bonaparte, Napoleon, 12, 15, 163
Bongie, Chris, 41, 60, 149
Bonilla, Yarimar, 25
Borgella, Jérôme Maximilien, 50, 169
Botelho, Keith M., 128
Boukman, 179, 184
Boyer, Jean-Pierre, 19, 32, 47, 50, 138, 149, 193, 196, 197
Braziel, Jana Evans, xxvii
Brecht, Bertolt, 184, 187
Brelle, Corneille, 159
Brickhouse, Anna, 94
Brière, Jean-Francois, 40, 165
Brooks, Linda, 116
Brown, William Wells, 9, 128
Brunet, 40
Buck-Morss, Susan, xxv
Buffon, Georges-Louis Leclerc (comte de), 92
Buon, 40

© The Editor(s) (if applicable) and The Author(s) 2017
M.L. Daut, *Baron de Vastey and the Origins of Black Atlantic Humanism*,
The New Urban Atlantic, DOI 10.1057/978-1-137-47067-6

C

Camus, Albert, 192
Candler, John, 56
Carlyle, Thomas, 171
Carrier, Jean-Baptiste, 32, 47–49
Casimir, Jean, 59
Césaire, Aimé, 135
Chanlatte, Juste (Comte de Rosiers), 19
Cheesman, Clive, 20
Christophe, Henry (King), 18, 19, 31, 40, 50, 58, 63, 80, 81, 90, 100, 135, 138, 153, 173, 184, 186–188, 198
Christophe, Mary Louise (Queen), 172, 175, 179
Claparède, 41
Clavin, Matthew, 111, 112, 127
Cohen, Lara, 113
Colombel, Noël, 19, 23, 32, 46–50, 52–57, 60, 62, 149
Colonist Gros, 7
Cook, Mercer, 146
Cooper, Frederick, 130
Corbould, Clare, 141
Cotin, 37
Coverdale, Linda, 187
Cugoano, Ottobah, 3, 17
Curtis, Lesley, viii
Cushing, Caleb, 68, 88, 89

D

Dain, Bruce, xviii
Dalby, Jonathan, 65
Dash, J. Michael, xxviii, 138, 192
Davidson, Jorge, 64
Dayan, Colin (Joan), 131
de Blanchelande, François, 7, 8
De Cockburne Family, 121, 122
De Lille, Jacques, 158
de Limonade, Comte (Julien Prévost), 50, 82

Delorme, Demesvar, 129
Delvare, General, 19
Desormeaux, Daniel, 13
Dessalines, Jean-Jacques
    armée indigène, 11
Diawara, Manthia, 107
Dillon, Elizabeth Maddock, viii
Dixon, Chris, 112
Douglass, Frederick
    Narrative of the Life, xxxi
    "What to a Slave is the 4th of July?, xxxii
Dravermann, 50, 51, 54, 165
Drexler, Michael, 111
Dubois, Laurent, 8, 142
Du Bois, W.E.B., xvii, xxviii, 145, 146, 199
Dubois, William, 141
Dumesle, Hérard, 59
Dupré, Antoine, xxiv
Dupuy, Baron, 19, 57, 58, 75, 174, 175, 179
Duras, Claire de
    Ourika, 170
During, Simon, 95
Duvalier, François, 184
Duvalier, Jean-Claude, 184, 185

E

Easton, William Edgar, 147
Edwards, Bryan, 121
Egerton, George, 13
Equiano, Olaudah, 17, 23, 69
Esterquest, Ralph T., 28, 40, 59
Ewcorstart, John K., 68

F

Fanning, Sara, 112
Fanon, Frantz, 109
Fanuzzi, Robert, 92, 95
Fardin, Dieudonné, 187

Farmer, Paul, 94, 139
Faubert, Pierre, 197
Festa, Lynn, 118
Figueroa, Victor, 136, 152
Firmin, Anténor, xxxv
Fischer, Sibylle, 95
Foucault, Michel, 49
Fouron, Georges, xxvii
Franklin, Benjamin, 88
Franklin, James, 28, 56
Frossard, Benjamin, 121
Fuss, Diana, 125, 131

G
Gaffield, Julia, 100
Gaillard, Roger, 187
Galbaud, General, 154
Garraway, Doris, 59, 66
Garrigus, John, 10
Geggus, David, 60, 104
Gilmore, Paul, 128
Gilroy, Paul, 2, 199
Glick, Jeremy, 180
Glick-Schiller, Nina, xxvii
Glissant, Édouard, 107, 109, 140,
    188, 189
Glover, Kaiama, 136
Goddu, Theresa, 117
Goujard, Philippe, 48, 49
Graeme, Bruce, 145
Grégoire, Henri (Abbé de), xx, 3, 17,
    21, 38, 69, 92–94, 97, 101–103,
    105, 106, 108, 123, 150, 151,
    199
Griggs, Earl Leslie, 28, 95, 197
Gronniosaw, Ukawsaw, 23

H
Hegel, Georg Wilhem Friedrich,
    xxv
Hager, Christopher, xxxiv

Hamilton, William (W.H.M.B), 68,
    70–75
Hammerman, Dan, 25, 137–140,
    178–180, 183
Harris, Helen Webb, 141
Hartman, Geoffrey, 126
Harvey, William Woodis, 28, 41, 55,
    56, 59
Hayward, Abraham, 28
Henrion, Charles, 40
Heuer, Jennifer, 102
Hill, Errol, 141, 162
Hoagland, Sarah, 161
Hodgson, Kate, 152
Hoffmann, Léon-François, 102
Hughes, Langston, 140, 146,
    149–151, 163
Hugo, Victor, 103
Hulme, Peter, 71
Hume, David, xix
Hunt, Alfred, 112

I
Ionesco, Eugène, 192

J
Jacobs, Harriet, 117
Jacquelin, André, 41
James, C.L.R., 140, 153
James, Erica Caple, 198
Jean-François, 180
Jeannot, 7
Jefferson, Thomas, 17, 98
Jenson, Deborah, 16, 104, 142

K
Kadish, Doris, 102
Kaisary, Philip, 144
Kazanjian, David, xxxv
Kristeva, Julia, 131

L

Lachèvre, Frédéric, 37
Laferrière, Dany, 187, 188, 194
Lamming, George, 149, 188
Lavaysse, Dauxion, 50, 54, 165
Laveaux, Étienne, 153
Leborgne de Boigne, Claude Pierre
  Joseph, 102
Leclerc, Charles Victoire Emmanuel
  (General), 12, 153, 175
Leclerc, Pauline, 174
Leyburn, James, 100, 154
Lhérisson, Camille, 173
Lindsay, Lisa, xxi, xxxiv
Locke, Alain, 145, 146, 173
Logan, Rayford W., 98, 146
Louis XIV, 10, 162
Louverture, Toussaint, 12, 15–17, 29,
  40, 70, 104, 140–142, 144, 152,
  173, 175, 179

M

Macaulay, Zachary, 21, 72, 102
Mackenzie, Charles, 56
Madiou, Thomas, 58, 59, 70, 165,
  169
Malouet, Pierre Victor, 4, 21, 33, 165,
  194
Marrant, John, xviii, xxii
Martineau, Harriet, 141
Marx, Karl, 78
Matheus, John, 140
Mazères, 3, 4, 21–23, 28, 29, 40, 59,
  65–71, 77, 85, 96, 99, 157
McClellan, James, 71
McCune Smith, James, 28, 31, 38,
  199
Médina, Franco Augustine, 50, 165,
  167
Métral, Antoine, 68, 101–106, 108,
  109

Michelet, Jules, 124, 125
Miller, Christopher, 1, 138, 139
Miller, May, 24, 137, 141, 145, 172
Milscent, Jules Solime, 19, 52, 54, 55
Mintz, Sidney, 100
Mollien, Gaspard, 45, 57
Montas, Michèle, 187
Montesquieu, 9, 99
Moreau de Saint-Méry, M.L.E., 5, 123
Morgan, Philip D., 130
Morrison, Toni, 131
Moten, Fred, 96
Muthyala, John, 190

N

Nesbitt, Nick, 59, 95, 152
Nicholls, David, 60, 107, 149
Nkrumah, Kwame, 137

O

Ogé, Vincent, 11

P

Paine, Thomas, xx
Patterson, Orlando
  social death, 130
Phillips, Wendell, 123
Philoctète, René, 25, 136, 178,
  183–192
Plummer, Brenda Gayle, 186
Popham, Sir Home, 175
Porta, Mireia, 187
Popkin, Jeremy, 8
Prator, Clifford H., 28, 95, 197

Q

Quevilly, Laurent, 28, 29, 34, 35, 45,
  46, 49, 59, 120, 144, 145, 165

R

Racine, Karen, 21
Ragueneau de la Chainaye, Alexandre-
    Louis, 40
Raimond, Julien, 5–8, 10, 11, 13, 16,
    17, 69, 143
Rainsford, Marcus, xvi, 122
Ramsey, Kate, 132
Raynal, Guillaume-Thomas (abbé de),
    xix, 119, 123
Redpath, James, 122
Reinhardt, Catherine, xix, xxiv, 1, 22
Résil, Gérard, 187
Ribbe, Claude M., 11, 71
Rigaud, André, 6, 7, 11, 13, 16–18,
    169
Rochambeau, Donatien-Marie-Joseph
    de Vimeur, vicomte de (General),
    11, 104
Rodman, Selden, 25, 27, 137–139,
    141, 151–154, 173–178, 180,
    183, 187
Rodriguez, Junius P., 72
Roumain, Jacques, 146
Rousseau, Jean-Jacques, 9, 101, 158
Roux, P., 39, 40
Rudé, George, 122
Rudy Giuliani, xxxix

S

Saint-Rémy, Joseph, 12, 54, 58, 59
Sanchez, Romy, 64
Sancho, Ignatius, 17, 23, 69
Sansay, Leonora, 116, 117
Sartre, Jean-Paul, xxviii
Saunders, Prince, 21, 81–83, 96
Scarry, Elaine, 125
Schiebinger, Londa, 71
Schoelcher, Victor, 70, 164
Schomburg, Arthur, 146, 179
Schuller, Karin, xv
Scott, Joan, 13

Senghor, Léopold Sedar, xxxiii
Sepinwall, Alyssa Goldstein, xxix, 92,
    106
Sharp, Granville, xx
Sheller, Mimi, 111, 112
Smith, Faith, xxxiv
Spinoza, Baruch, xxv
Spivak, Gayatri, 73, 128
Stanley, Amy Dru, 118
Stein, Jordan, xxxv, 113
Stoddard, Lorthrop, 153
Stoll, David, 116
Strafford, Thomas, 63–67, 70, 77, 80,
    81, 85, 87
Sweet, John Wood, xxi, xxxiv

T

Tardieu, Patrick, xxiii, 40
Thatcher, B.B., 64
Thomas, John Jacob, xxxiv
Thwaites, Elizabeth Hart, 128
Trouillot, Hénock, 8, 38
Trouillot, Lyonel, 187
Trouillot, Michel-Rolph, 142, 194
Trujillo, Rafael, 190
Turner, Richard Brent, 130
Twa, Lindsey, 150

U

Ulysse, Gina, 191

V

Vandercook, John, 31, 154, 171
Vastey, Jacques Valentin Pompée, 41
Vastey, Pierre Jean-Valentin, 35, 49,
    144
Vastey, Baron de (Jean Louis de), 1,
    2, 4, 5, 17, 19, 20, 22–27, 29,
    32, 34–36, 38–41, 45, 46, 48,
    49, 58, 60, 64–67, 70–72, 74,

76, 77, 83–85, 90, 97, 102, 105,
    111–113, 120, 121, 133, 137,
    138, 141, 144, 146, 149, 154,
    156, 157, 162, 165, 167, 170,
    181, 184, 185, 192–194, 196,
    198
Vaval, Duraciné, 27
Venault de Charmilly, Peter Francis,
    120
Vergès, Françoise, 135, 168
Vernet, André, 20, 45
Virgil, 123
Voltaire, François-Marie Arouet, 158

W
Walcott, Derek, 25, 135–140, 147–
    149, 155, 158, 159, 161, 177,
    180, 183, 187, 188, 191, 199
Walker, David, xxviii

Walsh, John Patrick, 136
Washington, George, 88
Wheatley, Phillis, 17, 23, 64, 68, 69
Wilentz, Amy, 185
Williams-Wynn, Frances, 28
Willis, Richard, 141, 147
Wimpffen, Baron de, 123
Wood, Marcus, 118, 123, 131
Woodson, Carter G., 146, 147
Wright, John, xvi

Y
Yúdice, George, 115

Z
Zamora, Lois P., 190
Ziarek, Ewa, 130
Zuckerman, Michael, 98

Subject Index

A

Abolitionist movement
  Clarkson, Thomas, 28, 60, 80
  Douglass, Frederick, xxxi
  France, 102
  Garrison, William Lloyd, 121
  Great Britain, 102
  Hamilton, William, 68, 71–75
  Haiti, vii, 3, 103
  Jamaica, 191
  transatlantic, 55
  U.S., 9, 24
  Wilberforce, William, 80
Abortion, 131
Affranchis (free people of color), 143
African American literature, xxv, xxv
Age of Revolutions, 4, 16
Alienation (natal), 157
Almanach Royal d'Hayti, 64, 75
Antillanité, 136

B

Bare life, 130
Black Lives Matter, 16
Botany, 74

Bourbon restoration, 51
Bréda plantation, 12

C

Casa de las Americas, 116
Centre d'Art, 173
Censorship, xvi
Chattel slavery, 95, 152
Childbirth, 21, 31, 33, 39, 76, 103,
  126, 131
Civil rights, 91
Code Noir, 10
Créolité, 136
Critical race theory, 23

D

Dechoukaj, 185
Declaration of the Rights of Man,
  132
Democracy, 94, 96, 99, 142
Drowning
  Free men of color, 11
  Soldiers, 11
  Slaves, 12

© The Editor(s) (if applicable) and The Author(s) 2017   237
M.L. Daut, *Baron de Vastey and the Origins of Black Atlantic Humanism*,
The New Urban Atlantic, DOI 10.1057/978-1-137-47067-6

E
Emancipation, 24, 81, 96, 186
Enlightenment, 1, 2, 93, 125
Ensekirite, 198
Exile, 149

F
Federalists, 98
Female Anti-Slavery Society of Salem,
    128
Feminism, 161
French Revolution of 1789, 143

G
Genocide, 126
God, 51, 85
Gothic, 24, 113, 120, 126

H
Haitian Creole (Kreyol), 191
Haitian Declaration of Independence, 104
Haitian exceptionalism, 86
Haitian Revolution, 2, 4, 5, 14, 18,
    25, 46, 65, 86, 87, 93, 95, 97,
    111–113, 118, 130, 136, 140–142,
    144, 145, 147, 149, 151, 152, 154,
    155, 162, 174, 180, 185, 191, 197
Hermeneutics, 15, 22, 90, 108, 125
Hispaniola, 95, 119, 169, 190
Howard University, 146
Humanism
    Black Atlantic (definition of), xviii,
        xx, xxi, xxiii, xxiv, xxviii, xxix,
        xxxii, xxxiv, 2, 18, 22, 26, 32,
        62, 69, 71, 108, 112, 137,
        139, 146, 156, 157, 161, 162,
        170, 175, 196, 198, 199
    Enlightenment, xviii, xix, 4, 93
Hybridity, 90, 160

I
Incest
    miscegenation, 127
    rape, 127
Infanticide, 53, 131
Inheritance, 149

J
Jay's Treaty, 86
Jesus Christ, 177

K
Kidnapping, 144, 173
Kinship, 130

L
Leclerc Expedition
    dogs, 132
    Donatien Rochambeau, 11
    Toussaint Louverture, 12
Literacy
    Enlightenment, 142
    Illiteracy, 84, 160
Liverpool Mercury, 71, 82

M
Marriage, 21, 22, 29
Métissage, 93, 150
Miscegenation
    incest, 127
    Laws-Against, 7
    Rape, 127
    vengeance, 132, 133, 147, 159
Monstrous hybridity, 90, 160
Mulatto/a Vengeance, 132, 159
Mulatto History. *See* Mulatto
    Legend
Mulatto legend, 149

N
Natural history, 71
Négritude, 135, 136, 157
Négrophile, 103
New World (discovery of), xviii, 14,
   16, 87, 94, 100, 136, 140, 181,
   190
Non-Statism, xxxii
Non-Violence
   abolitionism, 118
   independent Haiti, 46, 81, 107,
      136, 148, 185
North American Review, 89, 93

P
Pamphleeter, 74
Parody, 170
Philanthropy, 4, 92, 94, 102
Philosophes, xix, xxxvi
Postcolonial Theory, xxiii
Print culture, 46, 57, 113, 115, 153,
   155
Pseudo-Science
   racism, 23
   travel Writing, 118

R
Racial extermination, 115, 119
Racism, 2, 5, 10, 11, 155, 156, 164
Rape
   culture of, 127
Revolt of Ogé, 11

S
Sentimentality, 24, 70, 119, 128
Silencing, 27, 142

Slave revolts, 148
Social death, 130
Société des Amis des Noirs, 143
Spiralism, 136
Starvation, 70
Statism, xxxii
Stereotypes, 154
Sympathy. *See* Sentimentality

T
Testimonio, 24, 114–116, 118, 120
Théâtre National d'Haïti, 187
"Toussaint's Clause", 98
Trade embargo, 137
Transatlantic slave trade, xxvi
Travel Writing
   Natural history, xviii

U
(U.S.) American Revolution, 4, 6, 87,
   94
U.S. Civil War, xxvii

V
Vanishing Indian narrative, 119
Vodou, 151

W
Wheat, 74–77, 79
Wine, 75, 76

Y
Yale University, 173

Names of Publications (Newspapers, Journals, Magazines)

A
Almanach Royal d'Hayti, 64, 75
Anti-Jacobin Review, 132

B
Beloved, 131
Boston Commerical Gazette, 94
British Review, The, 84, 90

C
Code Henry, 83, 90

D
Déclaration des droits de l'homme, 143
Declaration of the Rights of Man, 132

F
Freedom's Journal, xvi

G
Gardener's Magazine, 74

H
Haitian Constitution of 1805, 96, 142
Haitian Declaration of Independence, 104, 142
Harper's Weekly, 122

J
Julius Caesar, 130

L
L'Abeille haytienne, 52–54
La Décade philosophiques, 37, 39
La Gazette Royale d'Hayti, 20, 167
Lakansiel, 188, 195
La Revue encyclopédique, 101
Les Affiches Américaines, 35
Liverpool Mercury, 73
Literary Gazette, The, 89–91
Liberator, The, 121, 122

M
Monthly Repository, 84

© The Editor(s) (if applicable) and The Author(s) 2017   241
M.L. Daut, *Baron de Vastey and the Origins of Black Atlantic Humanism*,
The New Urban Atlantic, DOI 10.1057/978-1-137-47067-6

N

New Negro, The, 145
New York Times, 178
Niles' Weekly Register, 121
North American Review, 89, 93, 98

P

Pamphleteer, 5, 13

S

Stella, 118

T

Toussaint Louverture's Constitution
    of 1801, xxxiii, 12, 29, 54, 104,
    140, 152, 173

Places

B
Baltimore, 120
Boston, 89, 121

C
Cap-Français, 174
Cap-Haïtien
  Citadel, 156, 162, 176
  Palace at Sans-Souci, 27, 57

D
Dominican Republic, 167, 187,
  190

E
England
  Liverpool, 69, 73
  London, 74, 82, 148

F
French Caribbean, 165

G
Guadeloupe, 188, 191

I
Italy, xvi, 36

J
Jamaica
  Kingston, 63, 64

L
Liberia, xxxv

M
Martinique
  Fort-de-France, 135, 188, 191

N
New York, 35, 178, 187
  American Negro Theater (ANT), 178
  Schomburg Center, 179

© The Editor(s) (if applicable) and The Author(s) 2017   243
M.L. Daut, *Baron de Vastey and the Origins of Black Atlantic Humanism*,
The New Urban Atlantic, DOI 10.1057/978-1-137-47067-6

P
Paris, 28, 32, 38–40, 46, 146
Philadelphia, 67
Port-au-Prince, 19, 40, 51, 52, 56,
    70, 187

S
Saint-Domingue
    revolution, 5, 6, 143, 152
Santo Domingo (Spanish), 116
St. Lucia
    Morne St. Castries, 149, 159

T
Trinidad, 51

Y
Yale, 173

Printed in Great Britain
by Amazon

79987821R00163